Readings in Controversial Issues in Education of the Mentally Retarded

Edited by
Frank Warner
and
Robert Thrapp

MSS Information Corporation
655 Madison Avenue, New York, N.Y. 10021

LC
4601
W38

Library of Congress Cataloging in Publication Data

Warner, Frank, 1931-   comp.
 Readings in controversial issues in education of
the mentally retarded.

 Includes bibliographies.
 1. Mentally handicapped children--Education--
Addresses, essays, lectures. I. Thrapp, Robert,
joint comp. II. Title. [DNLM: 1. Education of
mentally retarded--Collected works. LC 4601 W281r
1972]
LC4601.W38   371.9'28   72-6339
ISBN 0-8422-5007-7

CONTENTS

FOREWORD

Controversy relating to various aspects of the field of mental retardation is not a new subject. Every facet of the subject has been opened to careful scrutiny, no less evaluation. Literally thousands of books and professional journal articles have dissected the subject. Raging arguments continue from even a satisfactory or acceptable definition to the matter of the efficacy or accountability for programs for retarded subjects.

In this volume of current readings, the authors have successfully brought together many controversial issues that should intrigue the professional worker and graduate student in the field of mental retardation. The articles are current, highly readable and technically accurate. The readings should encourage all to seek solutions of the endless controversies.

The editors are men of excellent professional training and have had many years of experience as successful classroom teachers and college instructors. They bring to the field open minds and a total dedication to their work.

Jerome H. Rothstein, Ed. D.
Professor of Special Education
San Francisco State College

5

PREFACE

The purpose of <u>Readings in Controversial Issues</u>
in <u>Education of the Mentally Retarded</u> is to (1) provide
the student with easy access to pertinent readings
covering a broad spectrum of problems in the education
of children who have been diagnosed as mentally retarded,
(2) present information and ideas from a variety of
sources and disciplines and (3) acquaint the student with
some of the current issues and trends in the field of
education for the mentally retarded. It is designed to
serve as a supplementary text to current textbooks in
mental retardation and is appropriate for undergraduate,
graduate and seminar courses in education as well as
related disciplines.

The articles selected for inclusion here
represent an eclectic approach to the problems of
education for the mentally retarded. It is not intended
that they represent a particular philosophy or
school-of-thought. While some of the articles do not
deal with the mentally retarded specifically, their
content is such that the student will recognize their
applicability to the field of special education.

Finally, the editors view education for the
mentally retarded as a life-long experience. For this
reason articles included in this text covers the
entire life-span of the retarded, from pre-school
through adulthood.

F.A.W.
R.W.T.

JOHN R. KERSHNER

Doman-Delacato's Theory of Neurological Organization Applied with Retarded Children

Abstract: To assess the effects of a program of physical activities consistent with the Doman-Delacato theory of neurological organization on the physical and intellectual development of trainable mentally retarded children, pretest and posttest data were collected from a Doman-Delacato experimental group and a nonspecific activity control group. In motor development, no significant pretest, posttest intergroup differences were found. Comparisons on mobility (creeping and crawling) and IQ (PPVT) yielded statistically significant gains in favor of the experimental group. The findings suggest the Doman-Delacato techniques may be beneficial with trainables in public schools.

MENTALLY retarded children, in addition to being below normal in intellectual functioning, are generally found below normal in motor skills (Brace, 1948; Francis and Rarick, 1963; Howe, 1959; Langan, 1965; Malpass, 1960; Thurstone, 1961). However, much of the considerable research seeking to relate physical development to cognitive functioning (Ammons and Ammons, 1960; Giaque, 1935; Ismail, Kephart, and Cowell, 1963; Show and Cordts, 1960; Sprague, 1960) has led to conflicting and inconclusive results. Descriptive studies have been done showing some relationship between such factors as reading deficiencies and cerebral injury (Delacato, 1963; Jensen, 1943), tactile functions and hyperactivity (Ayres, 1964), and intelligence and motor proficiency (Di Stefano, Ellis, and Sloan, 1958; Heath, 1942; Rabin, 1957). But the low reliability and validity of many of the procedures utilized in these studies point up the need for more research to establish and define the precise relationship of physical development to intelligence and academic achievement. Presently, the nature of this relationship remains obscure.

Delacato (1959, 1963, 1966) and Doman, Spitz, Zucman, Delacato, and Doman (1960) make inferences without substantive experimental support connecting motor functions to cognitive competencies. They have explicated a developmental sequence of motor and perceptual experiences that they say is vital for normal child development, and they prescribe these activities in their program of treatment for children with neurological dysfunction, the scope of which, they say, includes the vast majority of children now considered mentally retarded.

While the Doman-Delacato theory of treatment claims a potential for remediating both the physical and intellectual deficits of mentally retarded children through application of a specified program of physical activities, professionals have understandably reacted with skepticism and reservation. Acceptance by the professional community requires more than

Exceptional Children, February, 1968, Vol.34, No.6, pp. 441-450.

9

favorable treatment by popular news media. The present investigation was prompted by the lack of definitive research upon which the conscientious educator could formulate an objective opinion as to the efficacy of the Doman-Delacato physical therapy program.

Problem

As Stein (1963) has reiterated, there is a scarcity of research on physical education for the retarded. To date, few studies have attempted to assess experimentally the effects of a systematic program of physical activities on the development of mentally retarded children. Oliver (1958) advanced the idea that certain intellectual and physical characteristics of educable mentally retarded boys could be enhanced through participation in a planned program of physical education activities. Corder (1966) undertook what was essentially a replication of the Oliver study with the addition of a Hawthorne group, and he found significant differences in favor of the experimental group in both IQ and physical fitness growth. Pangle and Solomon's (Personal communication, 1967) replication of Corder's study does not have identical results: physical fitness performance in educable mentally retarded boys was improved as a result of an eight week structured program of physical education, but IQ was not improved. In a recent doctoral dissertation in reference to the physical fitness gains reported by Oliver and Corder, Lillie (1966) questions whether the training tasks should be used as the criterion variable. In effect, this constitutes teaching for the test.

The limited existing research assessing the effects of systematic physical education programs on mentally retarded children indicates:

1. The effects upon trainable mentally retarded children have not been investigated.
2. The effects upon cognitive functioning are inconclusive.
3. The effects upon unpracticed motor skills have not been determined.
4. The experimental treatments have neither been well defined nor have they been accompanied by stated goals and objectives.

Does one merely have the obligation to outline techniques for perceptual motor training without providing a scientifically based theory underlying these techniques? Is it important to know *why* you are doing something which seems to improve classroom behavior? It is plausible that an urgent need within physical education for programs for the mentally retarded is a well defined rationale for a structured sequence of activities that lends itself to transmission to professionals and modification by them, as new knowledge indicates the need for change.

Background of Neurological Organization

The central concept of the Doman-Delacato approach is neurological organization (Delacato, 1959, 1963, 1966). Neurological organization assumes that ontogeny (the process of individual development) recapitulates phylogeny (the process of species development). This development proceeds in an orderly, anatomical way through the cord and medulla, pons, midbrain, and cortex, and culminates in cortical hemispheric dominance. Neurological organization is defined by Delacato (1963):

> . . . that physiologically optimum condition which exists uniquely and most completely in man and is the result of a total uninterrupted ontogenetic neural development. This orderly development progresses vertically through the spinal cord. . . . This progression is an interdependent continuum hence if a high level of development is unfunctioning or incomplete . . . lower levels become operative and dominant. . . . If a lower level is incomplete, all succeeding higher levels are affected both in relation to their height in the Central Nervous System and in relation to the chronology of their development. . . . If man does not follow this scheme he exhibits problems of mobility or communication [pp. 4-5].

According to this approach, neurological development is directly related to psychomotor development. It follows that mentally retarded children participating in a program of physical activities consistent with this theory should achieve corresponding increases in physical and cognitive proficiency.

Purpose and Hypotheses

The purpose of this investigation was to determine the effects of a structured program of

10

physical activities upon the physical and intellectual development of trainable mentally retarded children.

Null Hypothesis I. No significant difference would develop in creeping and crawling improvement between the experimental and control groups. The instrument used was the Creeping and Crawling Scale, adapted from the Doman-Delacato Developmental Profile (Doman, Delacato, and Doman, 1963). This scale is a 47 point measure of gross perceptual motor and fine perceptual motor performance. Such a measure tested the very basic assumption that creeping and crawling performance improves through participation in a program of neurological organization (that includes creeping and crawling). Delacato (1963) claims, "We can corroborate the progress of neurological organization clinically. The mobility functions of growing and maturing children indicate the level of neurological organization [p. 25]" they have reached..

Null Hypothesis II. No significant difference in motor proficiency improvement would develop between the experimental and control groups. The instrument used was the Kershner-Dusewicz-Kershner (KDK) Adaptation of the Vineland-Oseretsky Motor Development Tests (Kershner, Dusewicz, and Kershner, 1967). The Oseretsky tests examined an explicit contention of the Doman-Delacato theory of treatment, i.e., that recapitulation of early perceptual motor developmental sequences is prerequisite to and improves the performance of more sophisticated perceptual motor skills not practiced. A review of the available tests of motor skill and motor maturity revealed that, among the few similar existing tests, none approached the Oseretsky tests in providing for the assessment of a great variety of skills and levels of performance. The KDK modifications of the Vineland-Oseretsky include the following:

1. For practicality, group administration of tests was done (two examiners with six children), to lessen the children's anxiety and thereby obtain a more valid measure.
2. For facility and less expensive administration, the list of required equipment was altered (including deletions, additions, and revisions).
3. Instructions were clarified to counter ambiguity.
4. Cut off points were empirically chosen for items yielding a numerical score or score in seconds to make the scale sensitive to the ability levels of the children tested.
5. Speed IX, X, XII, XVI, and S.V.M. IX were deleted because double standards for scoring these items require an accumulation of normative data not yet available.

Null Hypothesis III. No significant difference in mean IQ improvement would exist between the experimental and control groups. The instrument used was the Peabody Picture Vocabulary Test (PPVT) (Dunn, 1959). The PPVT was employed to measure the effects the respective programs had on intelligence. Form B was administered for the pretest and Form A for the posttest. The PPVT is designed to provide a well standardized estimate of a subject's verbal intelligence through measuring his hearing vocabulary. If neurological organization is enhanced, and if the child's dysfunction is indeed remediated via the Doman-Delacato neurophysiological model, then improvement in psychomotor functioning should be accompanied by improvement in cognitive functioning.

Procedures

The study was conducted in two schools of the Northern Lehigh School District, Lehigh County, Pennsylvania. Subjects consisted of trainable mentally retarded children: 16 control and 14 experimental subjects enrolled in Lehigh County operated public school special education classes. The criterion for admittance to the trainable class and the meaning of a trainable classification for the purpose of this study was not IQ, but, rather, was the inability on the part of the child to cope with the academic requirements of the educable grouping in the same school. The survey by Connor and Goldberg (1960) confirmed the idea that a multiplicity of factors other than IQ are considerations for placement in trainable public day school classes. In addition, in light of the fact that precise diagnosis remains a technological problem and that the theory under investigation posits no selective assumptions as to etiology, differential reactions to the procedures across diagnostic categories were beyond the scope of this inves-

11

tigation. Treatments were randomly assigned to intact classes in the two schools, and in each case administered by a teacher and teacher aide. The schools are approximately 13 miles apart, and the teachers did not communicate with each other for the duration of the project. CA's ranged from 8 to 18 years in the E group and 8 to 17 years in the C group. The E group consisted of 7 males and 7 females; the C group consisted of 10 males and 6 females. One female was dropped from the E group because of more than 15 absences from the treatment.

The teacher of the E group attended a seven day orientation course offered by the Institutes for the Achievement of Human Potential in Philadelphia. An experimental program of rhythmical balance and coordination activities was designed for the control group. The teacher of the control program participated in two general orientation workshop sessions conducted by the author that were attended by all teachers of trainables in the county, and also participated in three individual training sessions with the author designed to impress upon her the experimental, innovative, and beneficial nature of her program, and to initiate her into its implementation. At no time during the course of the study was the term control group used; all personnel involved were impressed with the experimental nature of both programs.

The experiment was in effect Mondays through Fridays, November 1, 1966, to February 28, 1967. With the interruptions of Thanksgiving and Christmas vacations, the program extended for 74 consecutive teaching days and was administered by the teacher and teacher aides of the respective schools. The principal investigator made weekly visitations to insure adherence to both programs as prescribed.

A pretest, posttest design was employed. Data were obtained by two evaluators from the Department of Public Instruction, Commonwealth of Pennsylvania. The same testers were used in both testing periods. It was emphasized that both programs were by design experimental, and an examiner was not told to which school a particular treatment had been assigned. Inferences drawn by the evaluators from communicating with the staffs of the respective schools and from the testing sessions themselves were not within the author's area of control.

Experimental Treatment

The activities were sequentially structured according to neurological stages of development. These stages have qualitative levels that allow each child to perform at his own functional level. Hence, the activities designed to develop a particular neurological stage were group activities, although an individual program of treatment, based on specific evaluation of competency, was prescribed for each child. Each child was taught, individually, to master his lowest functional level within each stage before going on to the next higher level. The entire school curriculum, five and one-half hours per day, involved activities consistent with the Doman-Delacato theory of neurological organization. The more strenuous activities were conducted for one hour daily in a multipurpose room especially adapted for those activities. The remaining activities took place in the classroom. The E and C group children had no joint activities, nor did they associate in any way during the experimental period. The latter group was ascertained by the author via individual post-experiment parent interviews.

Experimental daily schedule: activities were in accordance with those outlined by Delacato (1963).

Morning

9:00 to 9:15
  Near Point Dominance
9:15 to 9:30
  Far Point Dominance
  Auditory Discrimination
9:30 to 9:40
  (changing to go to multipurpose room)
9:40 to 10:40
  Homolateral Coordination
  Cross Pattern Coordination
  Cross Pattern Crawl
  Cross Pattern Creep
  Tactual Stimulation
  Bilateral Reinforcement
  Kicking with Dominant Foot
  Throwing with Dominant Hand
10:40 to 11:10
  (change clothes, snack, bathroom)
11:10 to 11:50
  Tactual Stimulation and Discrimination
  Auditory Stimulation and Discrimination

Olfactory Stimulation and Discrimination
Gustatory Stimulation and Discrimination
11:50 to 12:00
(prepare for lunch)

Afternoon
12:00 to 12:45
(lunch)
12:45 to 1:30
Unilateral Sleep Pattern Reinforcement
1:30 to 2:30
Bilateral and Unilateral Group Activities
Cross Pattern Walk

Control Treatment

The entire school curriculum, five and one-half hours per day for the control group, involved nonspecific activities designed to achieve better rhythm, balance, coordination, and body image. The games and activities were constructed to give reason for the teacher to direct individual and group praise and encouragement. The children were given attention approximately equal to that received by the experimental group. This was the author's attempt to control for the Hawthorne Effect. For the thirty minutes that the experimental group was visually occluded on the nondominant side, the control group wore the same type of eye occluder in a nonspecific manner on the back of their heads. This was done to compensate for any possible effect that mere ownership of an eyepatch may have had on the children in the experimental group. Also, the more strenuous activities were conducted in a multipurpose room especially adapted for those activities for one hour each day. The remaining activities transpired in the classroom.

Daily schedule for the control group:

Morning
9:00 to 9:15
Table play, i.e., building blocks, etc.
9:15 to 9:30
Show and tell
9:30 to 9:40
(changing to go to multipurpose room)
9:40 to 10:40
Jumping jacks
Jumping rope
Marching in place, swinging arms

Follow the leader to music
Carrying rhythm sticks as flags, etc.
"Freezing" or "squatting" as music stops
Rolling and catching ball
Dodge ball
Hopping, jumping, galloping, skipping
Walking like a duck, elephant, etc.
Flying like a moth, to recorded music
10:40 to 11:10
(change clothes, snack, bathroom)
11:10 to 11:20
Writing numbers and alphabet to music
11:20 to 11:30
(prepare for lunch)
11:30 to 12:30
(lunch)

Afternoon
12:30 to 1:30
Rest period, listening to music
1:30 to 2:30
Movies
Group singing and dancing games, i.e.,
Rig-a-jig-jig, Looby-do, Mexican Hat
Dance, Duke of York, Farmer in the Dell,
Mulberry Bush, London Bridge, Did You
Ever See a Lassie?
Musical chairs
Rhythm band

Pretesting

Pretesting began October 10, 1966, and was terminated October 28, 1966. The testers alternated daily between the two schools. They chose subjects randomly, and generally maintained an equal ratio of tested and untested children between the two groups. PPVT and creeping and crawling evaluations were administered in the morning, 9:30 to 10:30, and motor development test administration was in the afternoon. The PPVT was employed as an index of cognitive abilities as reflected via a measure of vocabulary intelligence. Some investigators (i.e., Rice and Brown, 1967) have questioned the applicability of the PPVT as an individual test of intellectual functioning. Nevertheless, the PPVT's practical value, particularly with nonverbal children, and its high correlations with other tests such as the Wechsler Intelligence Scale for Children (WISC) and the Stanford-Binet Intelligence Scale (Koh and Madow, 1967) indi-

TABLE 1
Pretest and Posttest Scores

Item	Age in Months	Years in Special Education	Absences (Percentages)	PPVT IQ Scores	Creeping and Crawling Raw Scores	Motor Development Raw Scores
Experimental ($N = 13$):						
Pre $\overline{X}$	150.31	4.15	5.15	39.77	51.64	14.51
Post $\overline{X}$				51.77	84.74	25.78
Pre sd	40.62	3.16	5.93	25.36	22.40	10.14
Post sd				21.80	14.37	13.51
Control ($N = 16$):						
Pre $\overline{X}$	151.19	3.31	5.19	61.94	43.53	9.78
Post $\overline{X}$				58.56	44.94	20.26
Pre sd	37.00	1.58	5.36	20.07	13.23	6.07
Post sd				19.16	12.00	9.35

TABLE 2
Analysis of Pretreatment Scores for the Two Groups

Item	Age in Months	Years in Special Education	Absences	PPVT
t ratio	.0603	.8743	.0188	2.57*

Note:—There are 27 df. Differences between groups on pretest IQ scores were statistically significant. None of the other pretest mean scores analyzed by the t ratio were significant.
* Statistically significant at the .05 level.

TABLE 3
Mann-Whitney U
Analysis of Pretreatment Scores for the Two Groups

Item	Creeping and Crawling	Motor Development
Experimental n_1	13	13
Control n_2	16	16
Experimental R_1	232.5	220
Control R_2	202.5	205
U value	66.5	79

Note:—Differences between groups on pretest creeping and crawling and motor development scores are not statistically significant. For a two tailed test a critical U value of ≤ 59 is statistically significant at the .05 level.

cated the appropriateness of using the PPVT in this investigation.

The nonparametric Mann-Whitney U test was chosen to analyze data derived from the Creeping and Crawling Scale and the KDK Revision of the Vineland Oseretsky Test of Motor Development. This was decided upon in view of the variances obtained between groups on these measures, because they are measurements from unstandardized tests which are probably, at most, ordinal scales, and also because the study employs two independent small samples. The remaining data approximated the assumptions of a normal distribution to the satisfaction of the author; therefore, parametric techniques were employed. Comparisons between groups in age, years in special education, absences, and PPVT scores were effected by applying t tests.

The groups were statistically similar in regard to age, time in special education classes, absences for the duration of the project, creeping and crawling score, and motor development score, but they differed statistically in PPVT score.

Posttesting began March 1, 1967, and was terminated March 17, 1967. The procedures followed were identical with pretest procedures.

Results

Each of the three hypotheses was tested in the null form to determine whether differences between groups on each criterion variable could be explained by chance. A relationship was con-

14

TABLE 4

Mann-Whitney U Test
Comparing Creeping and Crawling Gain Scores between Groups

Item	Creeping and Crawling
Experimental n_1	13
Control n_2	16
Experimental R_1	271
Control R_2	164
U value	28*

Note:—Differences between groups on pretest, posttest creeping and crawling gain scores are statistically significant. The direction of the difference favors the experimental group.

* For a two tailed test, a critical U value of ≤ 59 is statistically significant at the .05 level.

TABLE 5

Mann-Whitney U Test Comparing Motor Development Gain Scores between Groups

Item	Motor Development
Experimental n_1	13
Control n_2	16
Experimental R_1	205
Control R_2	230
U value	69

Note:—Differences between groups on pretest, posttest motor development gain scores are not statistically significant. For a two tailed test a critical U value of ≤ 59 is statistically significant at the .05 level.

TABLE 6

Analysis of Covariance Comparing PPVT Improvement between Groups with Pretest PPVT Scores as Covariates

Source of Variation	df	SS	MS	F
Treatments	1	645.79	645.79	6.2137*
Within	26	2,702.10	103.93	
Total	27	3,347.89		

Note:—The F ratio equals 6.2137. There are 1 and 26 df. Correlation coefficients between pretest and posttest PPVT scores for the E and C groups were $r = .81$ and $r = .95$ respectively. This is a statistically significant difference favoring the experimental group.

* Statistically significant at the .05 level.

sidered sufficient to reject the null hypothesis if the obtained level of significance was at least .05.

The statistical tests performed to analyze hypotheses I and III supported the Doman-Delacato theoretical position. Covariance was employed in analysis of PPVT scores to control statistically for preexperimental differences between groups.

The statistical tests performed to analyze hypothesis II yielded differences between groups that were not statistically significant ($p = .05$) (Table 5). Further analysis of intragroup pretest-posttest improvement, however, indicated that both groups improved significantly, with the direction of improvement favoring the control group (Table 7). As the control group participated in a rigorous physical program of nonspecific activities, these data relevant to hypothesis II lent support to both programs and suggested that each may have merit for improving the motor development of mentally retarded children.

TABLE 7

Mann-Whitney U Analysis of Intragroup Pretest-Posttest Gain Scores

Item	E Group Motor Development	C Group Motor Development
Pretest n_1	13	16
Posttest n_2	13	16
Pretest R_1	134.00	181.50
Posttest R_2	217.00	347.50
U value	43*	45.5*

Note:—There is a statistically significant pretest, posttest improvement in motor development for the experimental group and for the control group.

* For the E group, using a two tailed test, a critical U value of ≤ 45 is statistically significant at the .05 level. For the C group, using a two-tailed test, a critical U value of ≤ 75 is statistically significant at the .05 level.

Discussion

Restrictions are imposed upon attempts to apply the findings of this study to contexts differing from the one reported. The author was not concerned with the theory per se but with its practical applicability and its potential utilization in a public school setting. For these reasons the procedures were implemented on a basis of five days a week during normal school hours

15

and without parental aid or supervision. The program purposefully extended throughout the Thanksgiving and Christmas holidays.

Neither a random sampling of the population nor randomized assignment of children to the experimental and control groups was accomplished. The extent to which and to whom the results can be generalized is, therefore, affected to an unknown degree.

The objectives of the study were to determine the effects of a program of physical activities consistent with the Doman-Delacato theoretical position on the physical and intellectual development of trainable mentally retarded children. Two classes of trainable mentally retarded children—an experimental and a control group —were used in the study. Subjects in each of the two groups were administered pre- and posttests to measure their creeping and crawling ability, motor development, and intelligence. Analysis of pretest data indicated the groups were similar in age, time in special education classes, absences, creeping and crawling score, and motor development score, but were different significantly in PPVT score, in favor of the controls.

Since there was one teacher and one teacher aide supervising each group, the extent to which differential teaching effects entered into the findings is unknown.

The statistical test performed led to the following findings:

1. The results from Hypothesis I supported a very basic assumption of the Doman-Delacato position, i.e., that creeping and crawling performance improves through participation in creeping and crawling activities. Delacato utilizes mobility functioning as a clinical index of neurological organization. Neurological organization, however, implies a concomitant change in cognitive functioning, not simply improvement in creeping and crawling.
2. The results from Hypothesis II did not support an explicit contention of the Doman-Delacato position, i.e., that recapitulation of early perceptual motor developmental sequences is prerequisite to the performance of more sophisticated perceptual motor skills that are not practiced. The findings from

Hypothesis II suggest that while ontogenetic phylogenetic recapitulation of experience improves the performance of perceptual motor skills not practiced, these experiences may not be prerequisite for significant improvement to occur. That similar improvement can occur through another type of physical activity program was evidenced by the statistically significant gains of the nonspecific activity group. The results might be interpreted as support for Kephart's (1960, 1964, 1966) position that has been reported (Kershner and Bauer, 1966) as antithetical to ontogenetic phylogenetic sequences of activities, stressing instead the recapitulation of ontogenetic nonspecific movements. It should be noted, however, that the data provided are not conclusive for accepting motor improvement as a singular result of either treatment, as observed gains in both groups on the KDK scores could be attributable to maturation or to the effects of testing.

3. Caution should be exercised in interpreting the results from Hypothesis III that tend to support the Doman-Delacato theoretical position. Analysis of covariance was used to compensate statistically for preexperimental differences on PPVT scores between groups, but this does not alter the indication that both samples represented different populations. Therefore, the significance of the gains exhibited by the E group on the PPVT is affected by (a) the degree that covariance analysis is inferior to randomization, and (b) the unknown extent to which the improvement may have been due to factors associated with initial group differences.

The three hypotheses were chosen to test the Doman-Delacato theory of neurological organization as it applies to trainable mentally retarded children. Some basic assumptions of the theory were supported, and the experimental treatment appeared to have a facilitating effect upon the intellectual development of the children who participated in the experimental group activities. The numerous uncontrolled factors that could have accounted for the PPVT gains necessitate discretion in interpreting these findings. The fact that there was only one teacher in each treatment suggests that factors such as amount of task directed activity, amount of exposure to vocabulary, and teacher enthusiasm may have been operating differentially in the two groups. In addition, the groups were not described in specific terms. Therefore, unaccountable factors associated with initial group differences may have been operating. Within the stated limitations, these findings suggest that the procedures may prove beneficial in application with retarded children in public schools.

On the other hand, the lack of significant difference between groups in motor development and the motor improvement exhibited by the control group question the validity of the Doman-Delacato contentions that ontogenetic development consists of an invariant sequence of stages, and that proficient motor functioning at higher levels is dependent upon successful completion of lower levels. The findings that the E group improved in cognitive abilities may possibly have implications for the present enigmatic relationship of physical to intellectual development. It may be that studies further scrutinizing the Doman-Delacato concept of neurological organization applied with retarded children will provide information useful to the understanding of this problem.

The principal investigator was unable to find any similar experimental investigations in the literature. The small sample and the limitations in research design necessitate caution in deriving valid inferences from these findings. Rather than definitive conclusions, the implications of this initial effort point up the need for more rigorous and larger scale investigations along similar lines.

References

Ammons, R. B., and Ammons, C. H. Skills. In C. W. Harris (Editor), *Encyclopedia of Educational Research.* (Third Edition) New York: Macmillan, 1960.

Ayres, J. A. Tactile functions—their relation to hyperactivity and perceptual motor behavior. *American Journal of Occupational Therapy*, 1964, 18, 6-11.

Brace, D. K. Motor learning of feeble-minded girls. *Research Quarterly*, American Association for Health, Physical Education, and Recreation, 1948, 19, 269-275.

Connor, Frances P., and Goldberg, I. I. Opinion of some teachers regarding their work with trainable children: implications for teacher education. *American Journal of Mental Deficiency*, 1960, 64, 658-670.

Corder, O. Effects of physical education on the intellectual, physical, and social development of educable mentally retarded boys. *Exceptional Children*, 1966, 32, 357-364.

Delacato, C. H. *The treatment and prevention of reading problems.* Springfield, Illinois: Charles C Thomas, 1959.

Delacato, C. H. (Editor), *Neurological organization and reading problems.* Springfield, Illinois: Charles C Thomas, 1966.

Delacato, C. H. *The diagnosis and treatment of speech and reading problems.* Springfield, Illinois: Charles C Thomas, 1963.

Di Stefano, M. K., Jr., Ellis, N., and Sloan, W. Motor proficiency in mental defectives. *Perceptual-Motor Skills*, 1958, 8, 231-234.

Doman, G., Delacato, C., and Doman, R. *The Doman-Delacato Development Profile.* Philadelphia: The Institutes for the Achievement of Human Potential, 1963.

Doman, R. J., Spitz, E. B., Zucman, E., Delacato, C. H., and Doman, G. Children with severe brain injuries. *The Journal of the American Medical Association*, 1960, 174, 257-262.

Dunn, L. M. *Manual for the Peabody Picture Vocabulary Test.* Minneapolis, Minnesota: American Guidance Service, 1959.

Francis, R. J., and Rarick, G. L. *Motor characteristics of the mentally retarded.* No. 1. Washington: U.S. Government Printing Office, 1963.

Giaque, C. Inquiry into the correlation between physical fitness and scholastic standing. *Research Quarterly Supplement*, 1935, 6, 275.

Heath, S. R., Jr. Railwalking performance as related to mental age and etiological types. *American Journal of Psychology*, 1942, 55, 240-247.

Howe, C. E. A comparison of motor skills of mentally retarded and normal children. *Exceptional Children*, 1959, 25, 352-354.

Ismail, H. H., Kephart, N., and Cowell, C. *Utilization of motor aptitude tests in predicting academic achievement.* Technical Report No. 1. Bloomington, Indiana: Indiana State Board of Health, 1963.

Jensen, M. B. Reading deficiencies as related to cerebral injury and neurotic behavior. *Journal of Applied Psychology*, 1943, 27, 535-545.

Kephart, N. C. Perceptual-motor aspects of learning disabilities. *Exceptional Children*, 1964, 31, 201-206.

Kephart, N. C. The needs of teachers for specialized information or perception. In W. M. Cruickshank (Editor), *The teacher of brain injured children.* Syracuse, New York: Syracuse University Press, 1966. Pp. 171-180.

Kephart, N. C. *The slow learner in the classroom.* Columbus, Ohio: Charles E. Merrill, 1960.

Kershner, J. R., and Bauer, D. H. Neuropsychological and perceptual-motor theories of treatment for children with educational inadequacies. Harrisburg, Pennsylvania: Bureau of Research, Department of Public Instruction, 1966.

Kershner, K., Dusewizc, R., and Kershner, J. The KDK adaptation of the Vineland Oseretsky Motor Development Tests. In J. Kershner, *An investigation of the Doman-Delacato theory of neuropsychology as it applies to trainable mentally retarded children in public schools.* Unpublished master's thesis, Bucknell University, 1967. Appendix B.

Koh, T., and Madow, A. A. Relationship between PPVT and Stanford-Binet performance in institutionalized retardates. *American Journal of Mental Deficiency*, 1967, 72, 108-113.

Langan, J. G. A comparison of motor proficiency in middle and lower class educable mentally retarded children. Unpublished doctoral dissertation, Indiana University, 1965.

Lillie, D. L. The effects of motor development lessons in the motor proficiency of preschool culturally deprived children. Unpublished doctoral dissertation, Indiana University, 1966.

Malpass, L. F. Motor proficiency in institutionalized and noninstitutionalized retarded children and normal children. *American Journal of Mental Deficiency*, 1960, 64, 1012-1015.

Oliver, J. The effects of physical conditioning exercises and activities on the mental characteristics of educationally sub-normal boys. *British Journal of Educational Psychology*, 49, 1958, 155-165.

Rabin, H. M. The relationship of age, intelligence, and sex to motor proficiency in mental defectives. *American Journal of Mental Deficiency*, 1957, 62, 507-516.

Rice, J. A., and Brown, L. F. Validity of the Peabody Picture Vocabulary Test in a sample of low IQ children. *American Journal of Mental Deficiency*, 1967, 71, 602-603.

Show, J. H., and Cordt, H. J. Athletic participation and academic performance. In W. R. Johnson (Editor), *Science and medicine of exercise and sports.* New York: Harpers, 1960.

Sprague, A. The relationship between selected measures of expressive language and motor skill in eight-year-old boys. Unpublished doctoral dissertation, State University of Iowa, 1960.

Stein, J. U. Motor function and physical fitness of the mentally retarded. *Rehabilitation Literature*, 1963, 24, 230-242.

Thurstone, T. G. *An evaluation of educating mentally handicapped children in special classes and in regular classes.* US Office of Education Cooperative Research Project Report No. OE-SAE-6452. Washington: US Government Printing Office, 1961.

JOHN R. KERSHNER *is a Doctoral Candidate, Ontario Institute for Studies in Education, Department of Applied Psychology, Toronto, Ontario, Canada. The research reported herein is based on a dissertation by the author in partial fulfillment of the requirements for a master's degree at Bucknell University. The research was conducted under the joint auspices of the Bureau of Research Administration and Coordination of the Pennsylvania Department of Public Instruction and Bucknell University, cosponsors of a two year program designed to train educational research personnel.*

18

BASIC CONSIDERATIONS IN EVALUATING ABILITY OF DRUGS TO STIMULATE COGNITIVE DEVELOPMENT IN RETARDATES [1]

WOLF WOLFENSBERGER

Nebraska Psychiatric Institute

AND

FRANK MENOLASCINO

The University of Nebraska College of Medicine

ABSTRACT

A great deal of effort has been expended in search of pharmacological agents that will improve intelligence or intellectual development of mentally retarded individuals. Regardless of the merit of agents that have been purported to have such an effect, few studies, whether positive or negative in outcome, have constituted an adequate test of drug efficacy. A number of theoretical and methodological issues which underlie adequate design of studies of purportedly intelligence-enhancing drugs are discussed.

MENTAL retardation is widely conceptualized as a disease. The handbook on mental retardation recently issued by the American Medical Association (1965, p. 47; 98) refers to retardation as "illness" and "disease." Retardates are frequently labelled as "patients" in the literature, and many institutions for the retarded have the term "hospital" in their official name.

Many diseases can be cured, and some diseases considered incurable at one time eventually become curable as new treatments are discovered. It is therefore not surprising that many laymen and professionals alike should look forward to the discovery of "cures" of mental retardation. This hope often takes the form of a search for a drug. People who conceptualize mental retardation as a disease usually also conceptualize a potential drug cure to be very similar to, say, the cure of an acute episode of bacterial tonsillitis by means of antibiotics. The treater administers the drug to the sick and passive patient who soon improves and eventually "takes up his bed and walks." As far as mental retar-

dation is concerned, an analogous treatment expectation would be to see an eight-year-old severely retarded non-verbal, non-ambulatory child suddenly bursting forth into talking, walking, and doing the things one would expect an average eight-year-old to do. Not only laymen and parents, but even professional workers may, even if only semiconsciously, hold to such a conceptualization of a potential drug cure of mental retardation which Yannet (1957) has labelled the "magic bullet" theory. Evidence that the "magic bullet" analogy is neither farfetched nor specific to retardation is provided by a recent article (Anonymous, 1966) which advocates greater use of rifles and pistols that fire tranquilizing darts.

While an investigator may not articulate the magic bullet theory explicity, he may adopt an experimental design which clearly implies it. Thus, a number of glutamic acid studies reviewed by Vogel, Broverman, Draguns, and Klaiber (1966) had placed retarded subjects on the experimental drug for such short periods of time (e.g., 1 to 2 months) that effects upon global intelligence would have had to be very dramatic to be statistically significant. The relevant question here

[1] This study was supported by U.S.P.H.S. Grant No. HD 00370 from the National Institute of Child Health and Human Development.

American Journal of Mental Deficiency, November, 1968, Vol. 73, No. 3, pp. 414-423.

19

is not so much whether such effects were then actually reported, but why investigators choose to adopt designs that would only assess quick and dramatic, but not gradual and developmentally equally important, effects. Use of adult subjects rather than of children also carries with it the flavor of magic bullet expectations. Children generally are believed to be much more plastic than adults, and one can easily conceptualize a significant increase in their developmental rate. In adults, on the other hand, a drug effect is difficult to conceptualize except in terms of either performance enhancement or "cure."

The field of mental retardation has witnessed many attempts to improve cognitive functioning by means of drugs, and a number of models of drug action can be discerned. According to one model, drugs are to be used to treat conditions which interfere with the full use, or further development, of intelligence. Examples are the allaying of anxiety by means of tranquilizers, the control of seizures with anticonvulsants, etc. Within this model, terms such as "unblocking" may be encountered. A second model concerns the use of stimulants and energizers such as amphetamines, strychnine, and celastrus paniculata (Louttit, 1965) in an effort to improve performance and maximize a subject's use of his currently existing resources. A third model is concerned with improvement of "real intelligence," rather than secondary behavior or performance. Within this model, drugs may be hypothesized as improving learning; memory; or consciousness or awareness (e.g., Zimmerman, Burgemeister & Putnam, 1949). The use of glutamic acid (Louttit, 1965; Vogel, Broverman, Draguns, & Klaiber, 1966) falls within this model, as may vitamins (House, Wilson, & Goodfellow, 1964), sicca-cell treatments (Goldstein, 1956), and combination treatments such as Turkel's (1963) "U series" of 49 drugs.

While none of the pharmacological agents mentioned above has been convincingly demonstrated to improve the intelligence or intellectual development of retardates, some of the so-called replacement therapies which aim at the amelioration of specific metabolic syndromes associated with retardation have been effective. For instance, thyroid preparations have been shown to be effective in selected cases of hypothyroidism, and several other syndromes associated with metabolic disorders are treated dietetically and apparently with at least some success, (e.g., Kirman, 1965; Waisman & Gerritsen, 1964). However, a general phenomenon associated with such treatments has been that effectiveness is negatively correlated with the age at which treatment was begun.

It is very important to be aware of certain other conceptualizations and attitudes which can affect drug study designs in subtle and/or detrimental ways. For example a curious phenomenon can be discerned in the way people may view attempts to improve the intelligence of retarded versus non-retarded individuals. A "pill" to enhance the intelligence of a college student would probably be expected to improve his learning, memory, and general performance. A moderate and gradually accumulating effect would be considered quite desirable and acceptable. However, with a retarded person, a drug may be scorned if it produced anything but a complete and perhaps even rapid "cure," i.e., unless it produced "normality." Similarly, other types of (non-pharmacological) treatments of mental retardation also have been given the medical therapy interpretation and have been expected to lead to complete cures. Operations to increase the arterial blood flow to the brain (revascularization), and operations designed to prevent the early closure of the cranial sutures in primary microcephaly are typical examples.

Deep-seated unfavorable or conflicted attitudes toward mental retardation may underlie differential expectations regarding the role of drugs in normals and retardates. At least unconsciously, many people measure the worth of an individual by his intelligence and achievement (e.g., Mead, 1942, p. 89-90; 107; 109; Stone, 1948), and a "subnormal" person may thus be viewed as also "subhuman" or "nonhuman." Although such attitudes usually remain unverbalized, they are occasionally openly formulated as when retardates are referred to as "monsters," "vegetables," or "vegetative." At any rate, there appear to be individuals who perceive a qualitative difference between normality and subnormality, and who view subnormality as a unitary construct. From such a viewpoint, it makes little difference whether a retardate has an IQ of 20, 40, or 60; he is still not normal. Therefore, a treatment (drug or otherwise) that significantly improves a retardate's intelligence may be dismissed as ineffective because it did not "cure" (e.g., see Association for Research in Nervous and Mental Disease, 1962, p. 302; Birch & Belmont, 1961).

Recently, the hope to enhance intelligence chemically has been rekindled by reports that RNA, and drugs believed to facilitate the metabolism of RNA in the brain (e.g., magnesium pemoline, registered as Cylert by Abbott Laboratories), result in improved retention or perhaps even acquisition in animals and humans. Other potentially intelligence or development enhancing drugs on which there has been widespread recent publicity include 5-hydroxytriptophane. Research on such drugs is now moving from animal to human trials, and both popular press and serious scientists are emitting optimistic forecasts with increasing frequency and publicity. Krech (*Wash. Rep.*, 1968, 4, (2)) gave relevant testimony before a congressional committee; Linus Pauling (1968) is foreseeing an era of "orthomolecular psychiatry" where drugs play a large role in behavior maintenance and enhancement; and Arthur Koestler (1967) recently joined the ranks of prominent writers anticipating a drug-based utopia.

Inevitably, the question of the "cure" of mental retardation by chemical agents has arisen. At this point, it may be timely to recall the past so as not to repeat its errors.

What we would like to attempt in this paper is to discuss a series of issues which should be considered before embarking upon research designed to assess the ability of drugs to enhance cognitive functioning or development of retarded individuals. Some of these considerations are of a theoretical nature and bear primarily on the role drugs reasonably can be expected to play in the enhancement of intelligence. Other considerations have specific implications for the design of relevant experiments.

A basic assumption throughout the rest of this paper is that we are discussing studies employing a placebo control group and other features of well-designed drug experiments. While there may be a role for uncontrolled exploratory work, we are committed to the view that no drug should be accepted as possessing development-enhancing properties unless it has undergone the most rigorously controlled tests.

We also wish to emphasize that we are not particularly concerned with those pharmaceutical agents which result in improved performance (e.g., central nervous system stimulants) or alleviation of secondary conditions (e.g., hyperkinesis, seizures, emotional disturbance) that interfere with intellectual efficiency and/or development. The focus in this paper is primarily on drugs purported to improve cognitive functioning or development directly. When speaking of drug effectiveness studies, it is to this type of drug we refer.

GENERAL CONSIDERATIONS

The first goal of a study designed to assess a drug's ability to accelerate development should be to explore whether the drug has *any* developmental effect. To demonstrate such an effect is difficult enough without getting involved in tests of sophisticated and advanced hypotheses, or comparisons of several unproven drugs at the same time.

Since attempts to explore the potential effectiveness of drugs are difficult and de-

21

manding of time, money, and other resources, experiments should be designed to maximize the ascertainability of a potential effect. Above all, a study should be designed so as to constitute a fair test of the drug. Many studies of the past have failed in this regard, and whatever the merit of the drug may have been, such studies were simply irrelevant. The history of the field contains instances in which respected and qualified workers enthusiastically embraced belief in the curative action of a drug which was later generally rejected as ineffective, even though neither the original positive nor later negative studies may have constituted adequate tests of the drug's potential effects. Freeman (1966), in an excellent review of studies of drug effects upon learning in children, has pointed out that after 25 years of work with glutamic acid and its derivatives, and 30 years with amphetamines, we still do not possess adequate empirical evidence regarding the behavioral effects of these drugs. Perhaps the same can be said about the use of thyroid preparations with mongoloids.

Failure to consider certain principles and facts of child development and experimental design account for many erroneous or unpromising research strategies. The rest of this paper will concern itself with such considerations.

FALLACY OF THE MAGIC BULLET THEORY

One consideration of crucial importance is that mental retardation is not a disease, and that the magic bullet model is not appropriate to the drug treatment of mental retardation. Let us recall the example of the severely retarded eight-year-old boy. Even if it were possible to restore him instantaneously to normal learning capacity, he would, in all likelihood, have to pass through the developmental stages every normal child goes through. Turning, crawling, sitting, standing unsupported, walking, and running would probably have to be developed sequentially. There is even reason to believe that some behavior skills (e.g., in

the areas of speech, language and perceptual development) may rarely if ever be mastered unless they are acquired during sensitive, or prior to critical, periods of development. Thus, instead of having a magic bullet effect, a development-enhancing drug is more likely to work gradually, additively, directionally, and selectively.

DEFINITION OF DRUG EFFECT

Once we have emancipated ourselves from the magic bullet model, we can address ourselves more productively to the question as to when a drug (or any treatment) can be considered to have been effective. As mentioned earlier, one orientation encountered in the field is that if a treatment does not cure, or at least result in spectacular effects, it is not worth considering. At this point it is important to recall that even very small changes in behavior, or in rate of development, can have major implications to ultimate functioning and to social and management costs. Thus, a real and permanent change in developmental rate equivalent to only seven IQ points will mean a difference of about one year of developmental maturity in adulthood.[2] Being, or not being, toilet trained can mean a difference of two hours' work per day to a mother, and this, in turn, can mean the difference between remaining in the home or placement in an institution at great cost to child, family, and society. Since relatively small differences even in just one behavior area can have very significant implications to care and management, the effectiveness of a drug should not be assessed by its ability to "cure," but on the basis of its having any effect that would not have been achieved, or achieved as efficiently, without the drug. Any drug treatment which makes a "just noticeable differ-

[2] In discussing intelligence and intelligence tests throughout this paper, we are not proposing to defend the construct of intelligence as an entity, beliefs in constancy of IQs, or discontinuance of mental growth in the mid-teens. Although our language may appear to imply such notions, this is only in an effort to discuss parsimoniously principles and paradigms important to drug effectiveness studies.

ence" (Blackman, 1957) in a positive direction should be considered to be effective.

NATURE OF THE EXPERIMENTAL VARIABLE

A common error in the conceptualization of drug effects, and consequently in the design of relevant experiments, is associated with failure to appreciate the nature of intellectual growth. Some traditional theories of child development held that behavior essentially unfolds automatically, much like a normal embryo grows in predictable sequence of development; so one only had to sit back and wait for certain skills and habits to emerge. These skills and habits were believed to appear at specific, almost predetermined, ages, and usually little advantage was seen in developmental exercises, drills, activities, etc.

Today a different view prevails. While it is granted that there is a genetic upper limit to development, it is generally believed that a child's current developmental stage is a better predictor of the next milestone to be attained than his chronological age. A child who holds up his head, turns, crawls, stands with support, and walks while being held by one hand is generally ready to learn to walk unsupported, no matter whether he is 8 or 28 months old. However, it is also generally believed that a normally endowed child can become retarded if his perceptual, motor, linguistic, and social world is severely restricted. Ordinarily, we would not expect an otherwise normal three-year-old child to walk if he had never been allowed to leave his crib.

Adherence to contemporary theories and facts of child development would thus lead us to postulate that the effectiveness of a drug in accelerating development cannot be demonstrated, or only very poorly so, unless the child is exposed to an environment and to experiences which are stimulating and which are appropriate to his developmental level. This means that drug effect must be tested at the interface of readiness and experience. Indeed, the entire concept that the drug is the experimental variable in drug effect studies

should be abandoned. *The interaction between drug and experience should be considered to be the crucial experimental variable.*[3] An instance where this principle emerged during the dietary treatment of phenylketonuric children was mentioned by Umbarger (1960).

Since any factor which jeopardizes the drug-experience interaction may invalidate a study as a fair test of drug potential, we must clearly recognize what these factors are. These factors may have their locus in the subject, the drug, or the structure which governs the interaction between the medicated subject and the enironment. Each of these potentially limiting factors will be discussed below.

Limiting Factors in the Environment

Lack of appropriate developmental stimulation. A common feature of drug studies such as those which involved glutamic acid was the use of perceptually and socially deprived subjects. Thus, residents of institutions appear to have been the main source of subjects to date for many drug effectiveness studies in mental retardation. A more appropriate subject population would have been retardates living at home in a stimulating environment and engaged in intensive developmental programs.

Environmental effects. If institutional or deprived subjects are used, but are placed in stimulating environments for the purpose of a drug study, a special problem must be kept in mind. We must not only expect an ordinary placebo effect in the control group, but a genuine and substantial acceleration of development due to the non-specific environmental treatment component. Thus, the experimental subjects must not only improve greatly, but must improve significantly more than the control subjects who can be expected to improve significantly themselves.

---

[3] While true with development-accelerating drugs, this may not apply to other drugs such as tranquilizers where drug effects tend to be inversely related to the intensity of other types of therapeutic programs (Klerman, 1966).

The drug-experience interaction principle is not restricted to intelligence-enhancing drugs. For instance, there have been attempts to assess the effects of muscle relaxants on ambulatory development of non-ambulatory cerebral palsied children kept under very deprived conditions in an institution. Such designs may have made no provisions for increased stimulation or opportunities, the apparent assumption being that as long as the potential for ambulation was somehow restored, a child *will* learn to walk if he *can* learn to walk.

Limiting Factors in the Subject

Subject handicaps. There are certain conditions within a person which can constitute limits to the drug-experience interaction. Emotional disturbance, severe seizures, sensory impairment, and orthopedic, esthetic, and health handicaps are of this nature. It therefore follows that an optimal subject group, at least during early phases of research with a drug, should be free of such limiting conditions.

Subject age. The subjects' age must be considered to be a limiting factor in drug studies. The rate of mental development is generally accepted to be a positive decelerating function which becomes asymptotic in the mid-teens. There is strong reason to believe that most of the growth potential that is not realized during childhood is lost and cannot be recaptured even with intensive stimulation in adulthood. It follows that the younger the child, the more effective a drug-experience interaction should be in promoting development. Conversely, this interaction should decline in effectiveness as the child gets older.

There is a further implication. A normal mental growth rate consists of one year's mental age gain in one chronological year. Even if we could, overnight, restore a retarded child to a normal mental growth rate, he would still be subaverage at the usual age of maturity. We could expect a negative correlation between his level of adult functioning and the age at which the normal growth rate was instituted. Complete normality could only be attained if the treatment-induced growth rate during childhood exceeded that of average individuals, or if growth after about age 15 continued longer in retardates than it does in the general population. While neither alternative is inconceivable, either is unlikely. Growth rates above average have been observed in retarded children under intensive treatment, but usually such rates have only been sustained for brief periods. Continued growth in adults has been reported for retardates but is also expected to some degree in normals. Be this as it may, one would think that it would be most satisfying to see a person wtih a previously markedly subnormal growth rate attain an average rate of growth, and that expectancy for sustained supranormal growth approaches the unreasonable.

The above considerations imply that a drug effectiveness study is more efficient to the degree that it utilizes younger subjects. If it takes six months to raise the IQ of a five-year-old child by 10 points from 50 to 60, it will take 12 months to raise the IQ of a 10-year-old child by the same amount if we assume equivalent rates of growth. Drug and treatment studies using children of age 12 and above are thus implying expectancy for a dramatic treatment effect. Even in the presence of a strong drug effect, a study of several years' duration would be required to obtain a difference which is significant, keeping in mind that one has to contend with both error of measurement and likely improvement in the control subjects. No matter how well they may have been designed, the many negative drug studies that have utilized older children can thus be considered to have been inadequate tests of drug effectiveness unless they extended over two to three years.

An insight into the advantages of using younger subjects brings with it a dilemma which is due to limitations in assessment techniques for children of low mental age.

Instruments and techniques designed to assess global development are very inadequate for children below a mental age of about two years. Even between mental ages of 2–5, there are few global tests available, and some of these leave much to be desired. The situation for this mental age range is even more problematic in regard to tests of part or underlying functions of intelligence (e.g., attention, learning, memory, etc.). This means that even with 8–10 year old children, we would have the greatest difficulties if their IQs were below about 40–50. The horns of the dilemma are thus constituted of the need for a group young enough to profit considerably from a drug-experience interaction, and the need for children whose mental age is high enough to permit application of appropriate available assessment techniques. Until more and better techniques applicable to subjects of lower mental age are developed, we propose that the optimal solution to the dilemma is to use mildly retarded (IQ 50–80) children between ages of 5–10.

Limiting Factors in the Drug

An agent may have toxic or other undesirable side effects, or may be difficult to administer. Further, potentially effective drugs may only be effective if they are available to the nervous system during the learning process, in which case drug administration must be planned with drug characteristics in mind. For instance, a potentially effective drug may be rapidly absorbed and metabolized. An experimental design involving drug administration upon rising at 6 a.m., and upon retiring at 9 p.m., may not constitute a fair test of that drug because the child may not be exposed to highly stimulating activities until mid-morning, and to none at all at night. One must thus draw a distinction between the administered and the effective dose, and some drugs may have to be administered in timed release capsules or frequent doses. For this reason, the drug absorption rates should be carefully considered.

Finally it is important that drugs be given in doses high enough to be effective if there is an effect. Particularly with new drugs, information about desirable and tolerable doses may be scanty, and pilot studies to explore upper dosage tolerance may be indicated.

OTHER EXPERIMENTAL DESIGN CONSIDERATIONS

It is desirable that a study design be efficient as well as appropriate. First, let us consider that drug effectiveness studies, by their very nature, must be longitudinal. Experimental and control groups are assessed, a treatment is administered, and then both are reassessed. A statistical design typical for such a study is variously referred to as "repeated measurements of several independent groups" (Edwards, 1950, p. 288 ff.), or a "mixed factorial Type I" (Lindquist, 1953, p. 267 ff.) design. In such a design, the crucial statistical test of the drug-experience effect is not of the difference between groups after treatment, but of the interaction effect between groups and time, i.e., the differential rate of change.

Secondly, the efficiency of an experiment is inversely related to its duration. Given a potential effect, the design which permits the most rapid demonstration of this effect is, other things being equal, the most efficient one. The adequacy, appropriateness, and efficiency of a drug experiment can be affected by sample size, criterion score distribution, and the rigor of control.

One may speculate that the common failure to employ controls, or adequate controls, in treatment studies in retardation may, in part, have been due to investigators' conceptualization of retardation and its treatment. If one views retardation as a static, hitherto "incurable," condition that will only yield to a magic bullet therapy, then controls may appear to be unnecessary because no improvement would be expected unless the magic bullet had, indeed, been found, in which case the improvement would be expected to be a drastic and self-evident one. For instance,

Zimmerman, Burgemeister and Putnam (1949) omitted a placebo control group in their glutamic acid study on the assumption that their retarded subjects were not capable of responding to placebo effects.

The better controlled the control variables are, and the more sources of error variance are eliminated, the more efficient a design becomes. For this reason, matching of subject pairs, though more difficult, appears to be preferable to equation of subject groups. When groups are merely equated (often erroneously referred to as matched), the means of the equated vairables are essentially identical, but there may not be a 1:1 correspondence or relevant characteristics between pairs of subjects, and error variance is likely to be higher.

If the design discussed above is employed, care should be taken that the matching does not violate the assumptions that underlie the design. More complex cross-over or Latin Square experiments are frequently employed in drug research, but requiring double the length of time of the above design, they appear more suitable for drugs where fast and strong rather than slow and cumulative effects are anticipated. Particularly where age and treatment effect are expected to interact, a long-term cross-over experiment has an additional shortcoming: the placebo subjects who cross over into the drug condition will be older than the original drug subjects were when they were first placed on the drug. Thus, the two groups will no longer be comparable in age, and if an age-treatment interaction exists, the group that went on the drug later will show a smaller effect, or none at all.

The above considerations underline the desirability for homogeneity of certain variables. However, some investigators have committed an error in strategy by pursuing homogeneity of variables that should not be homogeneous. For instance, researchers characteristically aspire to constitute subject groups with the same clinical diagnoses (e.g., mongolism). Thus, in their review of glutamic acid studies

with retardates, Astin and Ross (1962, p. 432) expressed preference for diagnostic (mostly etiological) homogeneity. Such diagnostic homogeneity is appropriate when there is reason to believe that the drug treatment is of greater benefit in one syndrome than in others. If there is no reason for making such an assumption, diagnostic homogeneity is at best irrelevant and wasteful; at worst it may be destructive to the experiment, for at least two reasons. In some syndromes where biochemical function is disturbed, the drug may be metabolized in atypical fashion and thus may not act as it ordinarily would. For example, Rogers and Pelton (1957) have raised the question whether certain types of retardates are capable of metabolizing glutamic acid in the usual manner. In other syndromes, the structure of the brain may be characteristically atypical, and those areas in or upon which the drug may ordinarily act may be impaired. In either instance, there is an increased likelihood that a general effect that might have been observed in a diagnostically heterogeneous group may not take place or may not become measurable. Thus, the experiment would not constitute a fair test for the drug, and might lead to its premature rejection.

A common but questionable feature of drug and other treatment studies has been reliance on assessment of global or very complex behavior. The use of intelligence tests such as the Binet, Wechsler, etc., is of this nature. This may have been a poor strategy. Global intelligence reflects years of learning and experience and is modified relatively slowly. Lengthy experiments are likely to be necessary to demonstrate changes adequately. A more promising strategy appears to be the assessment of behavior processes which underlie global intelligence, such as arousal, perception (e.g., attention), learning, and retention. For instance, it is conceivable that within a few days or weeks a drug could have measurable effects on vigilance, conditioning speed, or short-term memory, while it might take months and years before such effects are translated into statistically significant improvements on global IQ tests.

If underlying processes do not show any change, no change is likely to occur on the global level. On the other hand, once underlying processes have shown improvement, then it is timely to design "second generation" experiments that may involve more global measures.

One problem in the design of drug and other treatment studies is rarely mentioned. It has to do with the fact that the before-and-after measurements are often made by technicians or other personnel who do not have a high degree of competence with the assessment technique, or who have not developed a consistent assessment style. For instance, a junior psychologist may be hired to give intelligence tests to subjects before and after administration of the treatment. The examiner may only have had experience in testing a small number of individuals with the particular test involved. Thus, he may improve in competence during the "before" assessments, and may obtain systematically higher or lower scores on the "after" assessments on the basis of his increased skills alone. "Improvement" then may be ascribed erroneously to the treatment, and "loss" to detrimental drug effects or to subject characteristics. While such a potential source of error can be handled statistically by having a control group, it is important even then that the order in which experimental and control subjects are tested is random or counterbalanced so that the examiner's learning process is not confounded with a particular type of treatment or subject. Even if this problem is handled statistically, it is still likely that lack of competence, experience, or consistency in assessment will introduce variability which detracts from the efficiency of the design. Much better than statistical handling of the problem would be to ascertain that the assessors have reached a high and stable level of performance. This might be accomplished either by using individuals of high skill, or by training less experienced and skillful personnel on a pilot basis to such a (asymptotic) level of performance.

CONCLUSION

In concluding, we would like to return to the distinction made earlier between direct and indirect effects of pharmacological agents. In the light of the foregoing discussion, it is conceivable to us that this distinction may have limited utility. The difference between such potential agents may lie not so much in their effects as in their mode of action—at least as long as children are used as subjects, and as long as they are exposed to intensive environmental enrichment while on the drugs. Also, we emphasize that we have taken no stand in this paper in regard to two issues relevant to drug research in retardation: (1) What is the theoretical likelihood that intelligence in retardates generally can be significantly improved by a pharmacological agent? (2) What emphasis should be given to research of this nature within a global research strategy in mental retardation and/or pharmacology? The stand we *have* taken is that if studies of the intelligence-enhancing effects of pharmacological agents are to be conducted, they should be so designed as to constitute an adequate, fair, and efficient test of such an effect.

SUMMARY

A great deal of effort has been expended in search of pharmacological agents that will improve intelligence or intellectual development of mentally retarded individuals. Regardless of the merit of agents that have been purported to have such an effect, few studies, whether positive or negative in outcome, have constituted an adequate test of drug efficacy. A number of theoretical and methodological issues which underlie adequate design of studies of purportedly development-enhancing drugs are discussed. It was concluded that if the effect of drugs on cognitive growth of retarded individuals is to be studied, the opimal target group should consist of mildly retarded children with mental ages above 2–3 and chronological ages near or below 6 who are heterogeneous in regard to etiological categories, free of secondary handicaps, and exposed to intensive environmental stimulation during the course of the study. It was proposed that the experimental variable in the study of purportedly intelligence-enhancing drugs is not the drug itself, but the interaction between drug and experiential stimulation. These conclusions call for experimental designs substantially different from those that typically have been employed in the past.

W. W.
Nebraska Psychiatric Institute
602 South 44th Avenue
Omaha, Nebraska 68105

REFERENCES

American Medical Association. *Mental retardation: a handbook for the primary physician.* Chicago: Author, 1965.

Anonymous. *Frontiers Hosp. Psychiat.,* 1966, 3(23), 3.

Association for Research in Nervous and Mental Disease. *Mental retardation: proceedings of the association, December 11 and 12, New York, N.Y.* Baltimore: Williams & Wilkins, 1962.

Astin, A. W., & Ross, S. Glutamic acid and human intelligence. *Psycholog. Bull.,* 1962, 57, 429–434.

Birch, H. G., & Belmont, L. The problem of comparing home rearing versus foster-home rearing in defective children. *Pediat.,* 1961, 28, 956–961.

Blackman, L. S. Toward the concept of a "just noticeable difference" in IQ remediation. *Amer. J. ment. Defic.,* 1957, 62, 322–325.

Edwards, A. E. *Experimental design in psychological research.* New York: Rinehart, 1950.

Freeman, R. D. Drug effects on learning in children: A selective review of the past thirty years. *J. spec. Educ.,* 1966, 1, 17–44.

Goldstein, H. Sicca-cell therapy in children. *Arch. Pediat.,* 1956, 73, 234–249.

House, M., Wilson, H. D., & Goodfellow, H. D. L. Treatment of mental deficiency with alpha tocopherol. *Amer. J. ment. Defic.,* 1964, 69, 328–329.

Kirman, B. H. Metabolic syndromes. In L. T. Hilliard & B. H. Kirman, *Mental deficiency.* (2nd ed.). Boston: Little, Brown, 1965. Pp. 486–526.

Klerman, G. L. The social milieu and drug response in psychiatric patients. Paper presented at the annual convention of the American Sociological Society, Miami Beach, Florida, 1966.

Koestler, A. *The ghost in the machine.* New York: Macmillan, 1967.

Lindquist, E. F. *Design and analysis of experiments in psychology and education.* Cambridge, Mass.: Riverside Press, 1953.

Louttit, R. T. Chemical facilitation of intelligence among the mentally retarded. *Amer. J. ment. Defic.,* 1965, 69, 495–501.

Mead, M. *And keep your powder dry.* New York: Morrow, 1942.

Pauling, L. Orthomolecular psychiatry. *Science,* 1968, 160, 265–271.

Rogers, L. L., & Pelton, R. B. Effects of glutamine on IQ scores of mentally deficient children. *Texas Repts. Biol. & Med.,* 1957, 15, 84–90.

Stone, M. M. Parental attitudes to retardation. *Amer. J. ment. Defic.,* 1948, 53, 363–372.

Turkel, H. Medical treatment of mongolism. In O. Stur (ed.), *Proc. sec. Internat. Congr. ment. Retard.,* August 14–19, 1961. Basel, Switzerland: S. Karger, 1963. Pp. 409–416.

Umbarger, B. Phenylketonuria—treating the disease and feeding the child. *Amer. J. dis. Childr.,* 1960, 100, 908–913.

Vogel, W., Broverman, D. M., Draguns, J. G., & Klaiber, E. L. The role of glutamic acid in cognitive behaviors. *Psychol. Bull.,* 1966, 65, 367–382.

Waisman, H. A., & Gerritsen, T. Biochemical and clinical correlations. In H. A. Stevens & R. Heber (eds.), *Mental retardation: a review of research.* Chicago: University of Chicago Press, 1964. Pp. 307–347.

Yannet, H. Research in the field of mental retardation. *J. Pediat.,* 1957, 50(2), 236–239.

Zimmerman, F. T., Burgemeister, B., & Putnam, T. J. The effect of glutamic acid upon the mental and physical growth of mongols. *Amer. J. Psychiat.,* 1949, 105, 661–668.

BEHAVIOR MODIFICATION RESEARCH IN MENTAL RETARDATION: SEARCH FOR AN ADEQUATE PARADIGM [1]

JAMES M. GARDNER

Columbus State School [2]

ABSTRACT

The methodology and results of research on the application of operant conditioning techniques to the modification of the behavior of mental retardates were examined. It was concluded that, to some extent, all the studies have violated one or more of the following requirements of good experimental design: (1) exact specification of all relevant independent variables, (2) proper sampling techniques, (3) use of adequate controls, and (4) proper assessment of the dependent variable. Suggestions for future research were offered.

THE application of operant conditioning techniques to the modification of the behavior of the mentally retarded can be dated from a study by Fuller in 1949. Since that time, and particularly during the present decade, research in this area has received increasing attention (Gardner, 1968a). In general, the majority of studies have been concerned with training the severely and profoundly retarded. Recent reviews (Hollis & Gorton, 1967; Watson, 1967) indicate that this population has been taught various self-help skills (e.g., dressing) as well as social skills (e.g., language, play). Despite the large number of studies in the area, Watson (1967) concluded:

Although they (the studies) indicate that severely and profoundly retarded children can develop such skills when fairly systematic training procedures are used, in general it is not clear what variables are responsible for the success of these programs and what variables contribute little or nothing or perhaps even interfere with the development of behavior (p. 14).

The reason for the current lack of knowledge concerning the major contingencies can be found in both the confounding of innumerable variables in research designs, and in the lack of comparability among various studies due to insufficient clarification of the significant variables. What is required, therefore, is the specification of the major therapeutic contingencies, the manipulation of the independent variables using multivariate techniques to isolate and evaluate the various factors, the exact specification and measurement of the dependent variable and adequate controls to assess the efficacy of the treatment procedures.

THE INDEPENDENT VARIABLES

Specification

There are four major classes of independent variables in behavior modification research. These have been summarized in Table I.

The most elementary requirements of research demand specification of the independent variables. To evaluate the results of a given study it is essential to know something about the patient's age, sex, duration of institutionalization, physical condition (e.g., ambulation) or diagnostic syndrome (e.g., Cretinism), and pertinent test scores. Reasonable attention must also be given to technique variables, notably the nature, type, and schedule of reinforcement, the physical

[1] Research for this paper was supported by USPHS Traineeship in Mental Retardation and Clinical Psychology (MR 345 01 67T) and NIMH Hospital Improvement Program Grant No. 1 R20 MR 02119-1. The author expresses his appreciation to Gordon Kulberg, Ph.D. for useful suggestions in the early stages of the paper.

[2] Also at Ohio State University.

American Journal of Mental Deficiency, May, 1969, Vol.73, No.6, pp. 844-851.

29

TABLE I
Independent Variables in Behavior Modification Research

1. Patient
   a. Vital statistics
   b. Physical and diagnostic characteristics
   c. Test scores
2. Experimenter
   a. Vital statistics
   b. Training in operant conditioning
   c. Attitude
3. Technique
   a. Nature and type of reinforcement
   b. Training session location
   c. Schedule of reinforcement
   d. Equipment and supplies
4. Situational
   a. Ward conditions and population
   b. Other programs

location of training, and the equipment involved. An area of neglect has been the specification of experimenter variables. Such factors as the age, sex, training, attitude, experience, and social position of the experimenter should be stated. Consider, for example, the finding of Stevenson (1961) that the effect of social reinforcement is dependent on sex correspondence between E and S, or that of Bensberg and Barnett (1966) who found that attendants with more favorable attitudes toward the mentally retarded are likely to be the more effective workers. Without the specification of the independent variables, in toto, comparative examination of studies is impossible, and knowledge of the relationship between or among variables is, at best, tenuous.

There is a direct relationship between the range of the independent variables sampled and the breadth of the generalizations which can be formulated. As the scope of these variables is delimited, the applicability of the findings is simultaneously limited (nonetheless, careful limiting and defining the range of the independent variables provides a more homogeneous population, thus reducing error variance). Verbal praise, for example, may be a generally effective reinforcer; however, it may be of limited usefulness with profoundly retarded patients or with younger, less impaired persons. Failure

to differentiate subjects in terms of age and adaptive functioning in this case would lead to erroneous generalizations. Ideally, research should be designed to manipulate all significant values of the independent variables. The more specific are the populations on which the procedures are standardized, the more valid the generalizations to be drawn, and the more accurate the predictions that can be made.

Related to behavior modification research in mental retardation, for example, the relative efficiency of behavior modification techniques with varying age levels and diagnostic classifications is an area of functional significance. The differential effects of experimenter variables is significant for planning for training programs. In addition, proper teaching methods, ideal locations for training and transfer of training problems, optimal reinforcement schedules, effects of positive and negative reinforcement, etc. are all potentially significant independent variables whose influences need to be determined.

Sampling Techniques

There are a number of sampling methods appropriate to control the effects of the independent variables and thus reduce the possibilities of error. One method is matching (Kimbrell, Luckey, Barbuto, & Love, 1967). Patients (and experimenters) can be matched for related variables so as to form homogeneous groups from which subjects can then be randomly assigned to various treatments. This requires consideration of all potentially significant variables, or the danger exists of confounding one or more effects. A second method commonly used in behavior modification research is randomization (Hundziak, Maurer, & Watson, 1965). Here patients (and experimenters) can be randomly assigned to various groups *theoretically* controlling for all possible sources of error. A third method is to control for the variable by manipulating it within the research design (Hollis, 1965a, b). Thus, one may compare the results of treatment procedures with subjects matched on all significant variables except one (e.g., sex). The decision as to the sampling technique employed depends largely on various factors, including the size of the population, the nature of the dependent variable, the theoretical and/or empirical importance of the independent variables to the dependent variable, and to some extent the personal preferences of the experimenter.

From the viewpoint of proper sampling techniques it is surprising to note the large number of studies employing the "worst" patients in their designs (Bensberg, Colwell, & Cassel, 1965; Dayan, 1964; Edwards & Lilly, 1966; Henriksen & Doughty, 1967; Mazik & MacNamara, 1967; Minge & Ball, 1967; Rogenmuser, 1967). Such a procedure biases the results in the direction of the experimental hypothesis since the possibilities of gains in adaptive behavior are far greater than any possibilities of regression.

THE DEPENDENT VARIABLE

Specification

The principal objective of behavior modification is the development of adaptive behavior. Adaptive behavior is a relatively recent concept. Heber (1961) states:

Adaptive behavior refers primarily to the effectiveness of the individual in adapting to the natural and social demands of his environment. Impaired adaptive behavior may be reflected in: (1) maturation, (2) learning, and/or (3) social adjustment (p. 3).

The American Association on Mental Deficiency states that impairment in adaptive behavior is a necessary condition for the diagnosis of retardation (Heber, 1961).

Most, if not all, adaptive behaviors are learned. It should be noted, however, particularly in regard to the behavior of the severely and profoundly retarded, that maladaptive behavior can result from failure to learn. Thus, the absence of toilet training skills may not be the result of learning the maladaptive response of eliminating at any time in any place, but rather the result of having failed to learn to eliminate in the toilet area. In many instances the retarded function at a maladaptive level because their responses reflect a more primitive (earlier) stage of development. It is easy to see that the concept of adaptive behavior is defined in terms of role expectations, which in turn are determined by such factors as age, sex, culture, etc.

While the general objective of behavior modification research is adaptive behavior change, the dependent variable in any study should be specific. To allow for comparisons between studies and to be able to evaluate the success of a given treatment procedure it is first necessary to know the full range of the dependent variable. Toilet training, for example, is a complex chain of responses that involves urination and defecation in addition to location and temporal factors. The individual must be trained to recognize bowel and bladder cues, inhibit elimination, walk to the toilet area, remove the necessary clothing, eliminate, clean himself and then redress. It is not enough to say that a toilet training program was effective; rather, it is necessary to specify changes in frequencies of urination and/or defecation in and out of the toilet area.

Measurement

The researcher in behavior modification is interested primarily in assessing behavior change (in the direction of adaptive behavior). This is accomplished through direct and indirect methods. Direct measures of behavior change consist of observations and recordings of patient behavior(s) using event or time-sampling techniques (Giles & Wolf, 1966; Hamilton & Allen, 1967). Less time-consuming is the use of behavior rating scales (Nihira & Foster, 1967) periodically completed by

31

ward personnel. A related form of behavior rating scale is the "simulated critical incident technique" (Steiner & Cochran, 1966) which can be translated into situational tests (Minge & Ball, 1967). A somewhat less precise direct method is the use of anecdotal records (Whitney & Barnard, 1966).

Indirect assessment of behavior change involves the measurement of behavior-related events rather than the behavior itself. If behavior X leads to event Y, by measuring the occurrence of event Y an index of behavior X is obtained. For example, an indirect measure of the effectiveness of a toilet training program would be the amount of soiled laundry (Dayan, 1964; Kimbrell et al., 1967). Other examples of behavior-related events would include the amount of tranquilizing drugs used, the number of dresses torn, the extent of first aid required, etc.

The careful researcher should concern himself with direct and indirect measures of behavior change. While the primary objective of behavior modification is to effect adaptive behavior change, secondary gains are prominent in the elimination of nonproductive activities by ward personnel. Thus, effective toilet training programs eliminate wasteful and undesirable activities by attendants, freeing them for more habilitative responsibilities.

In addition to direct and indirect measurement, behavior change can be evaluated in terms of specific and general changes. Here the concern is with the range of behaviors sampled. For example, in eliminating self-destructive behaviors (Peterson & Peterson, 1968), the specific behavior of interest might be headbanging. Nonetheless significant changes are likely to occur in other behaviors, such as eye-contact, paying attention to the experimenter, and social relationships in general.

While both assessment procedures (direct and indirect) can be applied to specific or general changes, certain methods are more appropriate to one or the other. For example, behavior recording and the simulated critical incident technique are better suited to behavior-specific changes, while behavior rating scales lend themselves easily to assessing general changes. For indirect measures the nature of the event selected determines its suitability for evaluating the type of change: specific changes can be assessed through specific events (e.g., number of dresses torn) and general changes through general events (e.g., noise level).

The majority of studies in behavior modification research in mental retardation have been confined to modifying specific maladaptive behaviors and in developing specific adaptive behaviors. Patients have been taught to feed themselves (Spradlin, 1964; Whitney & Barnard, 1966), dress themselves (Ball, 1966; Karen & Maxwell, 1967), or they were toilet trained (Baumeister & Klosowski, 1965; Hundziak, Maurer, & Watson, 1965; Kimbrell et al., 1967), or certain undesirable behaviors were eliminated (Hamilton, Stephens, & Allen, 1967; Wiesen & Watson, 1967). With few exceptions (Bensberg, Colwell, & Cassel, 1965; Minge & Ball, 1967) research has centered on the above behaviors, each specifically modified in one particular population. In those instances where a more nearly global assessment has been attempted, the instrument of choice has been the Vineland Social Maturity Scale (Mazik & MacNamara, 1967; Stuckey, 1967) or a modified version of the Vineland (Bensberg, Colwell, & Cassel, 1965; Kimbrell et al., 1967). Unfortunately, little use has been made of other behavior rating scales (Bensberg, 1965; Dayan & McLean, 1963; Spivack & Spotts, 1966), the most promising of which would appear to be the adaptive behavior check list currently under investigations at Parsons State Hospital and Training Center (Nihira & Foster, 1966).

This use of specific populations for study in modifying single, specific behaviors has been and continues to be an unfortunate practice among researchers in mental retardation. Such procedures provide no information concerning the learning limitations (if any) of the populations sampled. While it has been found that certain very specific populations can be taught certain very specific skills, it has not been demonstrated that any single population can learn a variety of such skills (Gardner, 1968b). Such a demonstration would involve taking the same group of patients and modifying their behaviors in a large number of self-care as well as social skills. Behavioral researchers in the area of mental retardation are forever asked the question: "Isn't there a limit to the retardate's ability to learn?" Unfortunately, to date, no answer has been provided!

In addition, the measurement of specific behavior fails to take account of the total functioning of the individual. Any given individual has differential strengths and weaknesses, all of which determine his relative level of adaptive functioning. It is entirely possible that increasing the level of functioning in one area can lead to a simultaneous decrease in other areas, thus lowering the overall level. This is particularly important in the case of negative reinforcement, under which the application of aversive stimuli may facilitate the learning of a specific skill but depress general activity level, disrupt social relationships, as well as many other undesirable side-effects (Azrin & Holz, 1966). Behavior rating scales are of great importance here since they allow for the concurrent assessment of general as well as specific changes. Certainly the careful researcher should make provisions for assessing behavior changes in both these areas.

Behavior change can be assessed for the individual (Karen & Maxwell, 1967; Rice & McDaniel, 1966; Whitney & Barnard, 1966) or for the group (Edwards & Lilly, 1966; Hamilton & Allen, 1967). In cases where idiographic (or individual) methods are employed the researcher must be guarded in his generalizations from the data. In large part this depends on whether or not he is attempting to demonstrate the effects of a particular technique, describe the general shape of the function, or establish general laws of behavior. While idiographic studies are valuable in demonstrating the efficacy of a particular technique, they have little practical value since the amount of time, the patient-experimenter ratio, and other related factors make the procedure impractical for most purposes (idiographic studies are also valuable in providing negative examples of the ever popular belief that "some people can never be helped"). Having established the phenomenon using the single case, one can proceed to develop group methods. In analyzing the results, however, both individual and group findings should be presented. For example, the fact that a mean score for a group of patients does not change over time could indicate that there was no improvement for the individuals in the group, or, that half the patients improved while the other half regressed, etc. While most studies simply assess the mean improvement of their subjects on various measures, it would be equally (if not more) valuable to describe the results of the treatments for the individuals as well.

In this regard it is important to note that the effective use of behavior modification techniques requires the determination of reinforcement hierarchies (positive and negative) for the individual, and the application of specific incentives as reinforcers. While most studies have employed food as the primary reinforcement, significant differences between as well as within patients have been reported (Watson, Orser, & Sanders, 1968), and Haywood and Weaver (1967) found that the value of an incentive was dependent on the orientation (intrinsic or extrinsic) of the subject. An excellent example of determining reinforcement hierarchies and programming specifically for the individual is provided by Giles and Wolf (1966) who designed specific aversive consequences for five subjects in a toilet training program. Of course, the use of secondary (e.g., praise) or generalized (e.g., tokens, money) reinforcers allows training programs to operate more efficiently.

However, since secondary or generalized reinforcers are established by being paired with primary reinforcers, the need for determining individual preferences is not obviated.

Purpose

The problem of adequate controls is central to good experimental design. Underwood (1957) pointed out the danger of not using controls:

In research, where no control group is used, and where there is esentially only one treatment, the data may demonstrate a significant change in behavior from pretest to posttest. The ambiguity lies in the fact that it is impossible to tell whether the change resulted from the conditions inserted by the investigator or from some factor or factors which occurred between the two testings (p. 136).

The purpose of establishing control groups, then, is to eliminate any possible influences of extraneous variables on the dependent variable. If control procedures are adequate, one is left with only one conclusion, i.e., that the change in the dependent variable is the direct result of the *E*'s manipulation of a particular independent variable. To insure the adequacy of control procedures it is necessary to determine the nature of the extraneous variables which could possibly introduce an unintended influence.

Varieties of Control Procedures

The most obvious control group is the "no treatment" group (Bensberg, Colwell, & Cassel, 1965). This procedure involves assigning subjects at random to either a treatment or a no treatment group, and after some specified interval, pre- and post-interval scores for both groups are compared. If the changes in the treatment groups are significantly greater than the corresponding changes in the no treatment group, the experimenter can conclude that the treatment was effective. The question of sampling technique is important here. If proper methods are not employed in assigning subjects to the various groups, the results will be open to question. For example, employing the "worst" patients in the treatment group, and using the rest of the ward as the control group, is a blatant violation of good design procedures.

A second type of control group which is useful is a "conventional treatment" group (Kimbrell et al., 1967). The inclusion of this group with the no treatment group indicates whether the treatment procedures have produced a significantly greater change than would otherwise be expected. If behavior modification techniques are no more effective than conventional treatment methods for producing adaptive behavior change, then their adoption is a matter of personal preference rather than a logical outgrowth of research.

A third method is to use the subject as his own control (Giles & Wolf, 1966). At some time prior to the start of a training program the dependent variable can be assessed and then reassessed immediately before treatment. This interval provides a baseline period. For the treatment to be considered effective any changes which occurred following training would have to be significantly greater than the changes following the baseline period. Such a procedure does not require a simultaneous no treatment group; however, its inclusion with such a group adds precision to the methodology. Ideally, the length of the baseline interval should be equal to the length of the training period in order to control the possible effects of different time intervals (although such a method still does not control the effects of non-simultaneity).

Somewhat related to this is the "reversal" technique (Baer, Wolf, & Risley, 1968). In this case, after a baseline period has been established, the experimental variable is introduced. If the application of the experimental variable produces a change from the baseline data, the variable is discontinued. Given that the variable was responsible for the change, its removal should result in the behavior returning to the baseline frequency (or nearly so). Following this, the variable is re-introduced to see if the change in behavior recurs. Concerning this technique, Baer et al. (1968) state:

In using the reversal technique, the experimenter is attempting to show that an analysis of the behavior is at hand: that whenever he applied a certain variable, the behavior is produced, and whenever he removes this variable, the behavior is lost (p. 94).

LONG TERM GAINS

One of the questions behavioral researchers are forever being asked is: "Is this form of learning permanent?" It is quite surprising to note that not one single study to date in the area of behavior modification of the mentally retarded has examined the long term gains of training. This is even more alarming in view of the fact that a number of these studies date back several years (Baumeister & Klosowski, 1965; Dayan, 1964; Hundziak, Maurer, & Watson, 1965). Prerequisite to all research in this area, some provision should be made for follow up evaluations at periodic intervals.

SUMMING UP

A review of the literature in the area of behavior modification of the mentally retarded reveals that, to some extent, all the studies have violated one or more of the following requirements of good experimental design: (1) the exact specification of *all* relevant independent variables, (2) proper sampling techniques, (3) use of adequate control procedures, (4) proper assessment of the dependent variable, and (5) evaluation of long term gains. It is disheartening to learn that even the *finest* studies in this area (Giles & Wolf, 1966; Hundziak, Maurer, & Watson, 1965; Kimbrell et al., 1967) have been deficient in at least one of these aspects.

What is needed at this point is the application of more sophisticated methodology to evaluate the advancing technology. The diligent researcher, therefore, should make provision for the following in planning studies: (1) direct and indirect measures of both specific and general changes in behavior, (2) individual as well as group presentation of results, (3) pre- and posttreatment evaluations, including periodic assessment to measure long term gains, and (4) multivariate manipulation of the independent variables, particularly techniques. The adoption of these procedures would introduce the methodological precision which is currently lacking in the field.

REFERENCES

Azrin, N. H., & Holz, W. C. Punishment. In Honig, W. K. (ed.) *Operant behavior: areas of research and application.* New York: Appleton, 1966.

Baer, D. M., Wolf, M. M., & Risley, T. R. Some current dimensions of applied behavior analysis. *J. appl. behav. Analysis,* 1968, 1, 91–97.

Ball, T. S. Behavior shaping of self-help skills in the severely retarded child. In Fisher, J. & Harris, R. (Chmn.) *Reinforcement theory in psychological treatment: A symposium.* Sacramento, California: California Dept. of Mental Health, 1966. Pp. 15–24.

Baumeister, A. A., & Klosowski, R. An attempt to group toilet train severely retarded patients. *Ment. Retard.,* 1965, 3, 24–26.

Bensberg, G. J. *Teaching the mentally retarded: A positive approach.* Atlanta: Southern Regional Education Board, 1965.

Bensberg, G. J., & Barnett, C. D. *Attendant training in southern residential facilities for the mentally retarded.* Atlanta: Southern Regional Education Board, 1966.

Bensberg, G. J., Colwell, C. N., & Cassel, R. H. Teaching the profoundly retarded self-help activities by behavior shaping techniques. *Amer. J. ment. Defic.,* 1965, 69, 674–679.

Dayan, M. Toilet training retarded children in a state residential institution. *Ment. Retard.,* 1964, 2, 116–117.

Dayan, M., & McLean, J. The Gardner behavior chart as a measure of adaptive behavior of the mentally retarded. *Amer. J. ment. Defic.,* 1963, 67, 887–892.

Edwards, M., & Lilly, R. T. Operant conditioning: An application to behavioral problems in groups. *Ment. Retard.,* 1966, 4, 18–21.

Fuller, P. R. Operant conditioning of a vegetative human organism. *Amer. J. Psychol.,* 1949, 62, 587–599.

Gardner, J. M. History of the concept of cure in mental retardation. Paper presented at the 92nd annual meeting of the American Association on Mental Deficiency, Boston, 1968. (a)

Gardner, J. M. The behavior modification model. *Ment. Retard.,* 1968, 6, 54–55. (b)

Giles, D. K., & Wolf, M. M. Toilet training institutionalized, severe retardates: An application of operant behavior modification techniques. *Amer. J. ment. Defic.,* 1966, 70, 766–780.

Hamilton, J., & Allen, P. Ward programming for severely retarded institutionalized retardates. *Ment. Retard.,* 1967, 5, 22–24.

Hamilton, J., Stephens, L. & Allen, P. Controlling aggressive and destructive behavior in severely retarded institutionalized residents. *Amer. J. ment. Defic.*, 1967, 71, 852–856.

Haywood, H. C., & Weaver, S. J. Differential effects of motivational orientation and incentive condition on motor performance on institutionalized retardates. *Amer. J. ment. Defic.*, 1967, 72, 459–467.

Heber, R. F. A manual on terminology and classification in mental retardation. *Amer. J. ment. Defic., Monogr., Supple.*, 2nd Ed., 1961.

Henriksen, K., & Doughty, R. Decelerating undesired mealtime behavior in a group of profoundly retarded boys. *Amer. J. ment. Defic.*, 1967, 72, 40–44.

Hollis, J. H. The effects of social and nonsocial stimuli on the behavior of profoundly retarded children. Part 1. *Amer. J. ment. Defic.*, 1965, 69, 755–771. (a)

Hollis, J. H. The effects of social and nonsocial stimuli on the behavior of profoundly retarded children. Part 2. *Amer. J. ment. Defic.*, 1965, 69, 772–789. (b)

Hollis, J. H., & Gordon, C. E. Training severely and profoundly developmentally retarded children. *Ment. Retard.*, 1967, 5, 20–24.

Hundziak, M., Maurer, R. A., & Watson, L. S. Operant conditioning in toilet training of severely mentally retarded boys. *Amer. J. ment. Defic.*, 1965, 70, 120–124.

Karen, R. L., & Maxwell, S. J. Strengthening self-help behavior in the retarded. *Amer. J. ment. Defic.*, 1967, 71, 546–550.

Kimbrell, D. L., Luckey, R. E., Barbuto, P. F., & Love, J. G. Operation dry pants: An intensive habit-training program for severely and profoundly retarded. *Ment. Retard.*, 1967, 5, 32–36.

Mazik, K., & McNamara, R. Operant conditioning at the training school. *Trng. Schl. Bull.*, 1967, 63, 153–158.

Minge, M. R., & Ball, T. S. Teaching of self-help skills to profoundly retarded patients. *Amer. J. ment. Defic.*, 1967, 71, 864–868.

Nihira, K., & Foster, R. Measurement aspects of adaptive behavior project. In Leland, H. (chmn.) *Conference on measurement of adaptive behavior. II.*

Parsons, Kansas: Parsons State Hospital and Training Center, 1966. Pp. 13–36.

Peterson, R. F., & Peterson, L. R. The use of positive reinforcement in the control of self-destructive behavior in a retarded boy. *J. exper. child Psychol.*, 1968, 6, 351–360.

Rice, H. K., & McDaniel, M. W. Operant behavior in vegetative patients. *Psychol. Rec.*, 1966, 16, 279–281.

Rogenmuser, C L. Training the untrainable. *SK & F Psychiatric Reporter*, 1967, 31, 18–20.

Spivack, G., & Spotts, J. *The Devereux child behavior rating scale. Manual.* Devon, Pennsylvania: The Devereux Foundation, 1966.

Spradlin, J. E. The Premack hypothesis and self-feeding by profoundly retarded children: A case report. Working paper #49. Parsons, Kansas: Parsons State Hospital and Training Center, 1964.

Steiner, K. E., & Cochran, I. L. The simulated critical incident technique as an evaluation and teaching device. *Amer. J. ment. Defic.*, 1966, 70, 835–839.

Stevenson, H. Social reinforcement in children as a function of CA, sex of E, and sex of S. *J. abnorm. soc. Psychol.*, 1961, 70, 147–154.

Stuckey, C. Reward training and behavior shaping: A progress report. Pineville, Louisiana: Pinecrest State School, 1967.

Underwood, B. J. *Psychological research.* New York: Appleton, 1957.

Watson, L. S. Application of operant conditioning techniques to institutionalized severely and profoundly retarded children. *Ment. Retard. Abstr.*, 1967, 4, 1–18.

Watson, L. S., Orser, R., & Sanders, C. Reinforcement preferences of severely mentally retarded children in a generalized reinforcement context. *Amer. J. ment. Defic.*, 1968, 72, 748–756.

Whitney, L. R., & Barnard, K. Implications of operant learning theory for nursing care of the retarded child. *Ment. Retard.*, 1966, 4, 26–29.

Wiesen, A. E., & Watson, E. Elimination of attention seeking behavior in a retarded child. *Amer. J. ment. Defic.*, 1967, 72, 50–52

RETARDED CHILDREN

by
Dr. Burton Blatt
with
Charles Mangel

You see the children first. An anonymous boy,
about six, squeezes his hand through the opening at the
bottom of a locked door and begs, "Touch me. Play with
me." A 13-year-old boy lies naked, on his own wastes,
in a corner of a solitary-confinement cell. Children,
one and two years old, lie silent in cribs all day, without contact with any adult, without playthings, without
any apparent stimulation. The cribs are placed side by
side and head to head to fill every available bit of
space in the room.
        I have recently seen these children in the back
wards of four Eastern state-supported institutions for
the mentally retarded. Although I had visited these
"homes" before--and scores of others like them during
my 18 years as a member of long-forgotten advisory pan-
els--I had paid little attention to their back areas.
(Several colleagues arranged my tour through the places
few but selected staff personnel ever see. With me was
photographer Fred Kaplan, who would take pictures with
a concealed camera.)
        Now I know what people mean when they say there
is a hell on earth.
        The institutions I visited, located in three
different states, are huge repositories for human beings. The largest contains some 6,000 adults and children. The smallest, about 1,000 of all ages. It is the
sight of the children that tears at you.
        Each of the dormitories for the severely retard-
ed had what some like to call a recreation, or day-
room. Groups of young children occupied them, lying on
the floor, rocking, sitting, sleeping--alone. An attendant, silently watching, was the only adult in many
of these rooms. Some had no adults at all.
        The six-year-old who begged, "Touch me," was one
of 40 or more unkempt children of various ages crawling
around a bare floor in a bare room. Their dormitory
held about 100 children. It was connected to nine other
dormitories containing 900 more.
        In one dayroom, two male attendants stood by as
half a dozen fights flared in different corners of the
room. Three teen-agers were silently punching each
other near a barred window. One young child, about
five, was biting a second boy. Another resident, about

LOOK, October 31, 1967, pp. 97-103.

20, had backed a boy of about 10 into a far corner and was kicking him viciously, every now and then looking back at us. There were about 50 persons in the room. Their ages ranged from about 5 to 80.

Some dormitories had solitary-confinement cells. Attendants called them "therapeutic isolation." They were solitary confinement in the most punitive and inhumane form.

These cells were generally tiny rooms, approximately 7' X 7', shielded by locked, heavy doors. A small opening, covered by bars or a closely-meshed screen, allowed observation.

Some cells had mattresses, some blankets, some nothing but the bare floor. None that I saw, and I examined these cells in every institution I visited, had either a bed, a washstand or a toilet.

I found the naked, 13-year-old boy in one of these cells. He had been in confinement for several days because he had cursed an attendant. A younger child, at another institution, had been put into solitary confinement for five days because he had broken several windows.

I asked the attendant in charge of one dormitory what he needed most to supervise residents better and to provide them with a more adequate program. His answer: The addition of two more cells.

(These solitary cells are usually on an upper floor, away from the scrutiny of official visitors. A commissioner of mental health in a Western state, who had heard I was preparing this story for LOOK, called to ask if these conditions existed in his state's institutions. He is the chief mental-health official in his state.)

Children are tied down. I saw many whose hands or legs were bound or waists secured. (One boy, tied on the floor to a bench leg, was trying to roll away from a pool of urine. He could not.) The terribly undermanned staffs used binds as their ultimate resort. The attendant who asked for two new solitary-confinement cells was, with one assistant, responsible for an entire multilevel dormitory housing 100 severly retarded residents.

Almost in desperation, he asked me, "What can we do with those patients who do not conform? We must lock them up or restrain them or sedate them or put fear into them."

I felt at that moment much the same as men of conscience felt, I imagine, upon reading Dr. Johann Christian Reil's description of institutional problems. "We lock these unfortunate creatures in lunatic cells, as if they were criminals," that physician said. "We keep them in chains in forlorn jails...where no sympathetic human being can ever bestow on them a friendly glance, and we let them rot in their own filth." This, in 1803.

Every room in the living quarters of young children--and the moderately and severely retarded of any age--had a stout door and locks. Attendants routinely passed from room to room with a key chain in hand, locking and unlocking as they went.

Some of the children's dormitories offered "nursery programs." These were few and primitive. Several children in one of the "nursery" rooms had severe lacerations from banging their heads against walls and floors. When confronted with young, severely retarded children, many professionals believe head-banging inevitable. This is arrogant nonsense. Head-banging can be drastically reduced in an environment where children are not ignored.

Adults in these institutions fared no better than the children. Many of their dayrooms had a series of bleacherlike benches. Residents sat on them all day, often naked, jammed together, without purposeful activity or any kind of communication with each other. Countless human beings on rows and rows of benches in silent rooms, waiting for--what? One or two attendants stood in each room. Their main function was to hose down the floor periodically to drive wastes into a sewer drain.

Although men and women were kept in separate dayrooms, the scenes in each were the same. The odor was overpowering. Excrement was seemingly everywhere, on walls, ceilings. The smell was permanent and ghastly. I could not endure more than a few minutes in each room.

The physical facilities contributed to the visual horror. All of the quarters were gloomy, barren. Even the television sets in several of the day-rooms appeared to be co-conspirators in gloom: they were broken. (The residents, however, continued to sit on their benches, in neat rows, looking at the blank tubes.)

I heard a good deal of laughter, but there was little cheer. Adult residents played ring-around-a-rosy. Other adults, in the vocational-training center, were playing jacks. Although they were not always the severely retarded, this was the only way they were allowed to behave.

I was told, during one visit, about the development of a new research center. The assistant superintendent said "materials" would come from the institution, and the center would need about 30 or 40 "items."

I didn't know what he meant. After some mumbling, I finally understood. At that institution, and apparently at others in that state, patients are called "materials"; and personnel, "items."

It was so difficult not to believe that this man was joking that, during later visits to other dormitories in that insitution, I asked the attending physicians, "How many 'items' have you in this building? How much 'material' do you have?" Each man knew exactly what I was asking.

Each of the institutions was incredibly overcrowded. The one housing 6,000 had been built for 4,000. Beds were jammed so tightly together that it was impossible in some dormitories to cross parts of the rooms without walking on the beds. The beds were often without pillows. I saw mattresses so sagged by years and the weight of countless bodies that they scraped the floor.

Signs of gross neglect pockmarked many of the older buildings. I saw gaping holes in the ceilings of such vital areas as a main kitchen; in toilets, urinals were ripped out, sinks broken, bowls backed up.

I will not reveal the names of these four institutions. First, it would lead to the inevitable dismissal of the men who arranged our visit and photography. They want conditions altered as badly as we do. Second, I don't want anyone to think that we are discussing just these four "homes." They are the symbol of a national disgrace. These four institutions represent the current conditions in portions of the majority of state-supported institutions for the retarded in this country. This story arose in the hope that attention directed to the desperate needs of these institutions would help open the way to improving them.

Tax-supported institutions for retarded children and adults do not have to be like this. We know better. We can do better--if we want to. A pleasant, estate-like home and school, the Seaside Regional Center in Waterford, Conn., has shown us how.

Seaside resembles a private, and expensive, school. It explodes with noise, the healthful noise of activity, and with color--walls, draperies, decorations, wherever children are. It also explodes with the pride a person takes in doing an important job better than most.

Tim was one of Seaside's youngest admissions. Uncontrollable at home, he had been placed in another institution two years earlier. He was four when he reached Seaside, and helpless. He lay in bed all day. He could not walk or talk. He was totally unaware of anything occurring about him. His label from the earlier institution: severely retarded.

He began to get individual attention. He was taught to dress, to eat, to go to the bathroom. Slowly, words came and then steps. He was put into a preschool class at Seaside. Six months later, he joined a preschool class with children of average intelligence in Waterford. Last fall, he entered kindergarten, and 11 months ago, went home. He is now in first grade in his home community. His IQ, which leaped dramatically before he left Seaside, may yet move into the average range.

40

Chester, 12 when he came to Seaside, had already spent four years in another institution. He could barely talk. He trembled when anyone approached him. In 12 months, he was discharged. His IQ had risen almost one-third. He is now in public school for the first time.

A mother writes a note to Seaside superintendent Fred Finn: "... [after] a year...it almost seems like [our son's] rebirth." Another parent adds, "Betsy entered Seaside a year ago.... There had been much newspaper publicity about the terrible conditions in some state institutions for the...retarded. Seaside is the living proof that it doesn't have to be this way. My husband and I drove up to look the school over for the first time with a considerable amount of apprehension.... To our amazement, instead of shock and sadness, the strongest emotion in our hearts on our drive back was a feeling of joy. ...This was...a big, loving home. [... Betsy would not be] a number, but a very special person.... If I were to talk to parents who have just learned that they have a retarded child, I would tell them two things. First, don't be afraid to love and to get to know your child, no matter who advises you to the contrary. Second, don't be afraid to investigate your state institutions. You may be pleasantly surprised as we were. If you aren't, join those who are trying to do something about it. It can be done."

Each of these children came to Seaside from other state institutions, diagnosed as custodial cases. Each could have been groveling in the back wards of the four institutions we visited, had they been there.

Seaside is a clear break with the past. Opened six years ago as an experiment, it is a small, state-supported regional center designed to be a clearinghouse for all problems involving retardation within a two-county area. It was the nation's first. It has been so successful that Connecticut has already approved 11 more like it.

Two hundred and forty men, women and children of all ability levels live at Seaside, a 36-acre complex of grassy-areas, buildings and woods on the shore of Long Island Sound. Everyone works at something, every day.

One hundred and sixty children attend school, half in the Waterford system and the rest in classes of five or six at Seaside. Forty, the most severely retarded, have daily activity and self-help programs. Forty young adults are getting job training. Some will move into the community and become self-supporting with little or no supervision. Others will stay at Seaside as paid, part-time employees.

Seaside reaches out. The panic that can crush a family unable to cope alone with a retarded child is relieved by the safety-valve role Seaside plays. Half of its programs are in the community. The center helps 850 nonresident retarded children or adults and their families. It operates recreation programs in seven communities, day-care centers in five (for children able to live at home, but not eligible for school), two sheltered workshops and two day camps. There is no waiting list. No one is ignored.

Seaside, for the first time in this nation's history, has given parents alternatives to keeping an unmanageable child at home without anyone to turn to (more than half the nation's school districts have no classes for the retarded), or putting him into the usual institution, often for life.

Relatively few children must be placed in an institution. Most parents, in these cases, want to stay close to their children and to take them home as soon as possible. Too many institutions have built-in systems to separate a child from his family. Some, organized for the convenience of the staff, operate like prisons. When parents visit, for example, their child is brought to, and taken from, a common visiting room.

At Seaside, parents are virtually everywhere. They have no special hours or off-limit areas. They can come when they like, make special trips to feed a youngster if they want. Seaside will take in a child for a month to give her harrassed mother a chance to rest, or for a week if parents want to take a vacation trip.

This takes money. Seaside costs more than the typical institution. Nationally, the average cost in institutions for the retarded is less than $5 per day for each patient. Six states spend less than $2.50. Only seven spend more than $5.50.

The Federal prison system spends $7.67 daily to maintain each inmate. Our better zoos average $7 a day for the care and feeding of some of their larger animals.

Seaside spends $12 a day for each resident. In terms of human suffering and the potential for human growth, places like Seaside are among the few really economical, government-sponsored institutions I know.

Our nation's "homes" for the retarded contain thousands of Timmys and Chesters. Almost 200,000 persons are now in them. About 50 percent are under 20.

Conservatively, at least half of these young people could live and work in their communities if they were properly taught and if supervision were available. We spend about $200,000 to support one person for his lifetime in a state institution for the retarded.

Seaside discharged 40 percent of its residents last year, about eight times the national average. Children went home and into public school, able to live within--not destroy--their families. Adults got jobs.

Seaside is proving that retardation is not unalterable. The capacity of a retarded person can be changed, up or down, within limits, depending upon the

way he is treated. Most retarded youngsters can be
taught to support themselves. Intelligence is influenced by practice and training, just as it is enhanced, or limited, by inheritance, injury or environment.

Seaside wages a strong fight against inertia.
Its staff has scant patience for tomorrow, for in a few
short tomorrows, children become adults, and residents
potentially able to develop can be transformed into
stagnant inmates.

"We have no magic," says Superintendent Fred Finn.
"We just do not believe that because a child hasn't,
means that he can't. The children who have made remarkable progress...at Seaside after years of institutionalization [elsewhere] obviously had this potential,
but...it was not developed. Each of these children is
entitled to the best and the most my child gets. If
one of them can do nothing more than creep, then he
will learn to creep."

Teaching a retarded child with an IQ of perhaps
30, and a severe emotional problem, is like teaching
no other youngster. You have to want to teach him.
Then you have to fight with him for each micro-inch of
progress. When you win a little, you glow. I had
lunch one day recently in Seaside's dining hall with
two teachers who were gloating because one seven-year-
old charge had just, that morning, uttered his first
comprehensible, one-syllable word.

A special love exists at Seaside, a love capable
of belief in the fulfillment of another human being.
I am exasperated with institutional staffs that have
offered me excuses, rationalizations and explanations
for their behavior. Although I am not unsympathetic
about their inadequate budgets, over-crowded dormitor-
ies--leading to the concessions they make and the programs they conduct--their actions speak primarily of
their character.

Mental retardation can bring out the best in
healthy people as well as the worst. The retarded
will not get the care and education they deserve until
institutions cause those who minister to their needs
to become more rather than less sensitive.

Some human beings have been taught to conceive
of others as they think of animals. It isn't that some
attendants are cruel--although, too often, they are--
but that they have come to believe that those in their
charge are not really human.

When one views a group of human beings as "material," an increased budget for resident care and
additional staff alone could never cause the radical
changes necessary in institutional treatment. The
use of such terms demonstrates the basic problem that
has to be solved before state institutions for the retarded will alter substantially: We must become more
optimistic concerning human behavior and its ability

to change.

William James wrote, "The greatest discovery of my generation is that human beings can alter their lives by altering their attitudes of mind." The belief that intelligence is educable refers both to children and those who must deal professionally with them. For Helen Keller to have changed as she did, Anne Sullivan also had to. For children in back wards to change, their attendants must, too. To the extent we can influence the latter's concept of human potential, we shall influence the former's educability.

Every institution, including those discussed earlier in this article, has superb, dedicated attendants and professional staffs. Yet for so many of their residents, they could not possibly do any less than they now do. It is irrelevant how well the rest of an institution's program is being handled if these back wards exist. We have got to instill a fundamental belief among all who work with the retarded that each of them is equally human, not equally intellectually able, not equally physically appealing, but sharing a common humanity.

What can we do? We must at least double per capita expenditures in state institutions and reduce the size of these institutions. In addition:

1. In each state, a board of impartial institutional visitors should be appointed by the governor. This board would report directly to the highest state officials. Appointments should be without regard to political affiliation. They should be based on both knowledge of human welfare and demonstrated public service.

2. Within each state institution for the retarded, the staff of each department (e.g., medical, educational) should have its own board of advisers. This board, through regular visits, would know the institution's problems. Its members could become involved without endangering employees who trust them, because the board would not be responsible for ratings, raises or promotions. Problems now hidden could be given the exposure necessary for solutions.

3. In each state, one university should be given responsibility and resources to provide adequate refresher training and counsel to all institutional employees, from chief administrative officers to rawest attendant recruits.

4. In each state, at least one institution for the retarded should become a center for compulsory, periodic retraining of everyone employed by the state to work with the retarded. Each new employee should have to spend a specified period in the training center.

Few institutions for the retarded in this country are completely free of dirt, odors, naked patients, children in locked cells, horribly crowded dormitories and understaffed and wrongly-staffed facilities. Countless people are suffering needlessly at this moment. The families of these victims of our irresponsibility are in anguish, for they know, or suspect, the truth. Unwittingly, or unwillingly, they have been forced to institutionalize their loved ones into lives of degradation and horror.

I hold responsible each superintendent, each commissioner of mental health, each governor--ultimately, each thoughtful citizen--for the care and treatment of individuals committed to institutions in their state. I challenge every institution in the U.S. to look at itself--to justify its programs, admission policies, personnel, budgets, philosophy.

I challenge every family of a resident in a state institution for the retarded, if it is dissatisfied with conditions at that institution, to protest immediately and repetitively to the governor and to join with other families to force legislative action.

The President's Committee on Mental Retardation reported in August: "Three-quarters of the nation's ...institutionalized mentally retarded live in buildings 50 years old or more." It demanded the virtual doubling of the full-time staff in these institutions "to reach minimum adequacy." Among its conclusions: "Many [facilities and programs] are...a disgrace to the nation and to the states that operate them."

We must have a national examination that will inspect the deepest recess of the most obscure back ward in the least progressive state. A national, qualified commission with authority should review state budgets for the care and treatment of the retarded. Sincere state officials will leap to cooperate.

I will be surprised if this article will change the nature of state institutions for the retarded. My current depression will not permit such grand thoughts. But, as Albert Camus wrote: "Perhaps we can't stop the world from being one in which children are tortured, but we can reduce the number of tortured children."

POVERTY, INTELLIGENCE AND LIFE IN THE INNER CITY

Whitney M. Young, Jr.
Executive Director, National Urban League

*T*HERE IS NOW ample documentary evidence to show that poverty—and the physical, intellectual, and emotional deprivations that go with it—can be a direct cause of mental retardation.

The poor of all races are affected and—in *absolute* numbers—there are more whites than Negroes who suffer from it. I am, however, particularly interested in this subject because the Negro poor are victimized by this alarming situation more than others, since, in *relative* numbers, there are far more poor Negroes than poor whites. Too many children, and all too frequently, Negro children, thus pay a heavy price for the injustices of our society.

We know today that only a few among all those who are mentally retarded suffer from an obvious organic defect with genetic cause. Genetic defects affect all levels of society in the same way, whether those afflicted are rich or poor, white or Negro. But it is quite different when damage to the brain is due *not* to a genetic cause but to disease before or after birth, or else to accident, infection, or poisoning. The *poor*, whether they are white or Negro, are more often its victims. And the mentally retarded who do *not* show any organic brain damage —those who are only *functionally* retarded—come predominantly from the poorer sections of our society. Functional retardation is very rare among those with high incomes and among well educated segments of the community. But it is very common—it can be detected in as many as 15 percent of all children—in deprived rural areas and in the chaos of the inner cities. This is now so well accepted that we have given the name of "socio-environmental retardation" to this kind of functional retardation prevalent among the deprived. More than half of all mentally retarded people fall into this last category.

What in fact are the environmental factors in the life of the poor that stunt their intellectual development?

To begin with, we are now convinced that intelligence itself is largely controlled by the kind of diet a child receives. Evidence was presented at a recent International conference that malnutrition in the first three years of life may permanently impair intelligence and it has been estimated that more than half of the 90 million babies born each year may run a risk of permanent retardation resulting from malnutrition. Moreover, experiments with several kinds of laboratory animals suggest that malnutrition at certain critical times during development of the brain—for the human species this would be about the time of birth— can cause long-term damage to brain structure and to the bodily functions it controls.

So, malnutrition among pregnant women as well as newborn children can be an important cause of mental retardation and is its *major* cause, on a worldwide basis.

In our own country, the Department of Agriculture found that in two Mississippi Delta counties 60 percent of children receive less than two thirds of the minimum dietary allowance recommended by the National Research Council. Among the underprivileged children of our so-

Mental Retardation, April, 1969, Vol.7, No.2, pp. 24-29.

ciety in general, still other factors are at work, probably more often than simple malnutrition. There is a whole catalog of them—ranging from all those circumstances that threaten physical development to insidious but powerful psychological factors.

The children of poverty—those who inherit the circumstances rather than the genes that predispose to mental retardation—have to fight against heavy odds from the very moment they are conceived.

Their mothers—often undernourished themselves—are still victims of toxemia of pregnancy, as well as of infections and physical hardships that the more affluent do not encounter. Thirty percent of the women who live in poverty, either in rural areas or else in towns of over 100,000 people, never get medical supervision during their pregnancies. Among the 500,000 indigent women giving birth each year, 100,000 need special medical help for complications. Most of them never get it. For one thing they give birth to premature children three times more often than middle class mothers, and it is well known that three quarters of all premature children, weighing less than three pounds at birth, develop physical and mental defects.

Knowledge of family planning, as well as realization of the importance of medical attention during pregnancy, is still widely lacking among the poor. Moreover, they don't know how to use, or else, for many reasons, cannot avail themselves of the resources that provide such knowledge and services. So illegitimate births, as well as families which are too large, not only for the parents' income, but also for their emotional and physical resources, occur all too frequently.

Brain damage resulting from continuous low-level exposure to lead, to which the children of the poor are commonly exposed because of the cheap, lead-containing paints frequently used in the slums, occurs almost exclusively among the deprived. One study showed that as many as 5 per cent of the children in slum areas had dangerous levels of lead in their bloodstreams.

In addition, infectious diseases are far more common among the poor: tuberculosis, for example, is 3 to 5 times more prevalent among them than among middle income or affluent groups. Crowded living conditions increase the incidence of several chronic and latent infections that have been suspected as a direct cause of mental defects in unborn babies when their mothers are exposed to such conditions during pregnancy. Childhood infections, some of which —such as measles—can cause brain damage, are more widely spread because too many children remain unvaccinated.

It has been reported, for example, that in New York, in 1961, 21 per cent of children from families whose incomes were three thousand dollars or less, have not received smallpox vaccinations; only 4 percent of children from families with incomes of nine thousand dollars and over remained unvaccinated. The corresponding figures for diptheria-tetanus vaccination are 19 per cent and 2 per cent. "The situation is even worse in the small, minor income groups. In one of these groups (the second-lowest income) 31 percent of all students did not receive smallpox vaccinations, and 2.8 per cent had no diptheria-tetanus shots."

So there are still children who have suffered brain damage, after catching whooping cough, although vaccination has been available for this disease for several decades!

Even accidents are more likely to happen to poor children, usually because they are inadequately supervised: in this country, one million children each year suffer head injuries—about 8 out of each 1000 children between the ages of 4 to 18 every year. Such injuries alone account for 10 percent of the institutionalized population.

All these physical and environmental causes of mental retardation —most of them *preventable*—account for more cases of brain damage in the total population than all the genetic causes lumped together.

And I have mentioned so far only grossly obvious, physically injurious factors.

Let us now consider some others, social and psychological factors that are themselves by-products of the misery of the few and the prejudice of the many.

In poor households, many children are badly cared for and so are deprived of intellectual, sensorial and emotional stimulation.

There are many "unavailable mothers"—not only working mothers, but also those who are unable to supply the needs of their children because of difficulties of their own: they are *emotionally* unavailable. Among them are those who cannot arouse themselves sufficiently from their passivity or lethargy to show affection for their children. Others are deeply depressed or mentally ill and reject their children for any of a multitude of reasons.

As a result of this there is often no proper family structure, the home becomes disrupted and damaging to the child's character. Parents do not seek help and very often distrust the social institutions that can provide it.

Under such conditions, every individual has to use all his meager energies just to keep body and soul together. He has to fight all the time just to survive. Parents have neither the means nor the ability to provide their children with stimulating conversation, with books, music, travel, or the other intellectual and cultural advantages bestowed almost automatically on most children of the middle and upper income groups.

When a lack of motivation and opportunity for learning in early years are added to other adverse conditions such as poor diet, bad health habits and inadequate sanitation, lack of pre-natal and post-natal care, emotional disorders, and crowded living conditions—it should come as no surprise that the result is often stunted intellectual development.

Children from families like these come to school for the first time without either the experience or the skills necessary for learning. They are backward in language and have no ability for the abstract thought necessary for reading, writing, and arithmetic. Their failure to learn becomes complicated by emotional disorders like frustration and anxiety.

And then, too just being poor is a frightful stigma in this country—where accomplishment is largely measured by economic success.

Anyone who has watched poor children and their families in countries where poverty is the usual condition of humanity—in Africa, South America and Asia—is aware that poverty by itself does not necessarily preclude warmth and communication within the family. But in countries where poverty is found side by side with affluence, a new condition exists. It has been aptly described by Oscar Lewis as the "culture of poverty," that appears in all large, poor communities isolated in the midst of general prosperity. It involves an attitude of lethargy and indifference, or sometimes strange forms of escapism and rebellion, that represent both a reaction to the stigma imposed by the affluent world and a defense against the poor opinion the underprivileged have of themselves. In Lewis' words, "the individual who grows up in this slum culture has a strong feeling of fatalism, helplessness, dependence and inferiority."

In the competitive and puritanical white society that prevails in this country, social and economic success have often become equated with goodness and, as a result, the unsuccessful and the economically weak have been regarded as inferior and bad. This belief was frankly and brutally expressed by a New Jersey farmer, who referred to the migrant workers on his land as "nothing . . . they never were nothing, they never will be nothing and you and me and God almighty ain't going to change them."

The tragedy is that the American dream, the myth of equal opportunity for all in this country, is so

48

deeply ingrained, that even the unsuccessful often believe in it, and have therefore a painfully poor opinion of themselves.

So the world of the "culture of poverty" is a world that rejects our targets of success and social status, ethics, and social values not for intellectual reasons, but out of despair. Nevertheless, it is a world with its own rules, taboos, pride, and scale of values. This is a world we have to learn to understand with intelligence and compassion, with which we have to learn to communicate, and which we must convince, despite its skepticism and its suspicion, that our goals are worthwhile. We have to prevent its spread, because it breaks the human spirit and so becomes the breeding ground of retardation.

We, the Negroes, have suffered discrimination, abuse and neglect for generations and we still live, by and large, a life isolated from the mainstream of society. Crowded into urban slums, pressured from all sides, poorly educated, and poorly equipped to compete, we are further demoralized by the indifference of the affluent society around us. So the poorer among us acquire the psychological characteristics of the slum culture. A chronically impoverished and humiliated population cannot respond to opportunity—the better opportunity recently offered by new legislation—as if poverty was a temporary accidental setback. The harm already done is too deep. It has long ago penetrated to the very souls of its victims.

By the time they reach school, poor Negro children already often possess built-in physical and psychological handicaps and in school, they are likely to face new obstacles which, although less obvious, may be just as harmful. What these obstacles are is best illustrated by an experiment of fundamental importance, recently carried out in California by Robert Rosenthal and Lenore Jacobson. To study the effect of teachers' attitudes on the performance of their pupils they chose a school with mixed Caucasian and Mexican children, picked out 20 percent of the children at random, and then told the teachers casually that these children were expected as a result of psychological tests to be "spurters"—that is, to make considerable progress during the next school year. Although these particular children did not receive special tutorial attention, and the curriculum of the school remained unchanged, their IQ—when tested a year later—had gone up remarkably. Those children whose IQ was the lowest to start with, made relatively the most progress. The children not designated originally as "spurters," on the other hand, showed much less progress. This was observed for many teachers, over several grades, as well as in classes designed specially for bright, average, and slow learners. Even more interesting, when the teachers were asked to evaluate their pupils' progress, they described the progress of "bright" children in very positive terms, like "outgoing, curious, sociable, interested, etc." But **when they described progress made by an undesignated child, particu**larly one originally labelled "slow-learner," their evaluation had negative connotations.

What are the implications of this? Mainly that when a child is expected by his teacher to be slow, he conforms to expectations. When the teacher expects the child to be bright—even when he never tells him so and does not change his method of teaching—the child feels it and blooms. The California teachers were busily and, quite unconsciously engaged in fulfilling their own prophecies, communicating to the children, in quite subtle and unintended ways, expectations which, in fact, did influence the child's performance. Moreover, their evaluations expressed resentment towards pupils who made unexpected progress.

It cannot be doubted that similar insidious—even unconscious—prejudice is widespread. In a society where the poor are generally considered inferior beings, where the Negro's potential for intellectual development

49

is still largely doubted, what expectations a middle-class teacher may have for her deprived Negro pupils can be easily guessed and—maybe—their effect can be measured by the thousands of drop-outs, misfits and little rebels that our present school systems produce every year.

Considering all the injurious factors that oppress the poor and particularly poor Negroes, I submit that when we come across a disproportionate number of poor Negro children dropping out of school or sitting in classes for slow-learners or the retarded, there is no need to look for anything *intrinsically* wrong with the Negro people or "the Negro family."

The Negro has been studied, inspected, analyzed and dissected ad infinitum. Thank you for so much attention. I am not against approaching the problem scientifically, nor do I want to discourage a substantial number of white scholars from an interesting academic exercise. But, in view of the conclusions reached by the President's Commission on Civil Disorders on the amount of white racism in this country, may I suggest that instead of more studies of the riots of black people, the anatomy of Watts, or the pathology of the Negro family, we should maybe start investigating the anatomy of Cicero, a city that can welcome Al Capone and reject Ralph Bunche; or the pathology of a Congress that widely applauds the President for saving the redwood trees, but sits on its hands when he talks of saving the lives of black people. Such new subjects of research could also provide some employment for Negroes, for who is better qualified than a former domestic to study white folks? I have always been told by white ladies how much they liked their Negro maids and how much they confide in them. Also who would know better the character of Congress than a former bell-hop?

That much maligned Negro family has shown remarkable endurance. After being systematically broken during centuries of slavery, the mere number of Negroes in this country after 300 years of oppression, deprivation and discrimination, testifies to a remarkable talent for survival.

As one further instance of strength within the Negro family, let me point out that Negro families tend to react far more sympathetically to the presence of a retarded child than do white families. A Michigan State University study shows that "in middle class white families the consequences of having a child labeled retarded usually results in social isolation for the child, whereas, lower class Negro families seem to treat retarded children very much as they do other youngsters."

May I also point out that the higher rates of illegitimate births occurring among deprived Negroes is not evidence of the higher virtues of the white middle class woman. It is due to the high cost of illegal, and the unavailability of, legal abortion; a 12 year study of therapeutic abortion in New York City from 1951 to 1962, reported that only 79 Puerto Ricans and 263 non-whites had obtained legal hospital abortions. By comparison, legal, therapeutic abortions were performed on 4,361 white women. On the other hand, it has been estimated that of all the maternal deaths caused by abortions performed by quacks and criminal abortionists in New York County, 50 percent were Negroes, 44 percent Puerto Ricans, and only 6 percent women from other groups. When Negro women find themselves bearing an unwanted child, not only are **they more likely to carry their pregnancy to term, but they are also much more likely to keep their baby.** They know that adoption for Negro babies is almost impossible, and abandoning the child would mean, for him, childhood in an institution or an orphanage. We need go no further than this to understand the greater proportion of unmarried mothers among Negro women.

Despite the realities of existence in the slums of our cities and in the dilapidated shacks of rural poor, many a "deprived" child is remarkably healthy and well equipped to cope with life. It may not be a reality we would wish on him, but it is *his reality*, and in relation to it, he often functions with an intelligence and a ready exercise of native wit that would leave the child of the white middle class, temporarily put in similar circumstances, hopelessly outclassed.

Insofar as the slum child is adapted to cope with a brutal world and has learned to survive in it, he is well adapted socially and is capable of intelligent behavior.

It is revealing that most of the deprived people who are labeled as retarded at some time in their lives, are usually recognized as such in the school situation. They are not "retarded" either before or after their school years, since they do not then fit the definition of retardation, which includes *both* a low intelligence quotient *and* a failure to adapt to social environment. *School* is the social environment they fail to adapt to. We are at last beginning to recognize that this is so because the attitudes and behavior required by the school, as well as the methods used for measuring what we call intelligence, are charged with cultural concepts foreign to the world of the deprived. Conventional aptitude and achievement tests, largely based on middle class standards, concepts and experience, can be expected to, and we now know *do*, fail to measure accurately the potential aptitudes of slum children.

In simple terms, it is stupid to give a question on cable cars to a New York child (who will fail to understand it) and to one from San Francisco (who obviously knows the answer), and then conclude that the child from San Francisco is more intelligent. One researcher working with the children of the Negro poor found they usually gave an incorrect answer to the question "what is wrong?" when shown a picture of a house with broken windows. In the experience of these children broken windows are normal and it would have been unintelligent of them to

have answered otherwise. In the course of testing a group of Negro children at the University of Pittsburgh, researchers asked them to color a picture of a banana. Every one of them colored it brown. None of them had ever seen a fresh banana, but they all knew the color of the bananas they had seen.

Testing materials based on a white middle class environment complete with trees, flowers, pets, parks, toys, and comfortable surroundings, are simply incomprehensible to deprived youngsters; yet the same children may be able to operate anything that moves and fix anything that breaks. That which a child has not touched, tasted, seen, heard, learned, or experienced, he simply does not know, whatever his intellectual potential.

It is important to bear in mind that the elusive quality *we* call intelligence is intimately related to the amount and quality of verbal ability and schooling. The slum child has little preschool exposure to informed talk, and the schooling he gets has little relevance to his world.

Extensive informal channels of learning, however, exist within the slums, and new tests could be devised that would reveal the truth about the intelligence and aptitudes of the slum child.

I wish you could have, as I often do, the experience of visiting a barber's shop in Harlem on a Saturday afternoon. There the barber shop is a real social institution; few people are interested only in having a hair cut. In one corner a group debates philosophical questions, in another international affairs, a few play checkers; when I come in they all start telling me how to solve the race problem. One feels proud of the great natural wit and the intelligence of these men, and at the same time saddened and depressed by all this human potential that society has obviously failed to utilize. Because if you read the thoughts and the intentions behind the rustic vocabulary and the faulty grammar, you recognize the richness of the substance in their minds and of the feelings in their hearts. As an acquaintance of mine said about the importance of speaking correctly, "It is better to say 'I's rich' than 'I am poor!' "

The alarming thought that a large number of Negro children might be labeled as mentally retarded because of inappropriate intelligence testing methods is supported by a finding of a Michigan State University study; it showed that employability among Negro mentally retarded youngsters was much higher than among white mentally retarded youths. More than 70 percent of the Negroes were in the top employability group as compared to only 36 percent of white youngsters. It was calmly pointed out that the difference might be due to standardized intelligence tests which were acknowledged to be less accurate for Negro children than they were for middle class white children. "Due to such inaccuracy" the study reported, "some of the Negroes in the study should not have been classified as mentally retarded."

I suppose one could take refuge in the position that "our mentally retarded are better than your mentally retarded" but, there being little merit in this kind of comfort, I would rather say that poor Negro children have enough handicaps already without being falsely labeled as retarded. Employability, and the fact that such individuals disappear into society—into *their* society—after they leave the school system, is the real proof, that they were—even if deficient in the school system—functionally adaptable to the society they came from and to which they returned as adults.

Let us now consider the condition of Negroes who are so retarded that their deficiencies require special care beyond the slow-learner classes.

Among the severely retarded, Negroes are underrepresented in institutions because all institutions have long waiting lists, and getting to the top of the list requires a spokesman, —which the Negro seldom has. On the other hand, among the mildly retarded, who may be institutionalized because of mild delinquent behavior, the Negro is overrepresented.

A white middle class child, equally retarded and having committed the same offense, often remains with his family; while the Negro child, not having the same social protections, is apt to end up in an institution. Again the system works against him.

And does the proportion of Negroes in relation to whites in such community programs as day-care centers, sheltered workshops, etc., reflect the proportion of Negroes in need of them in the community? Possibly it does in some places, but in most places it does not. Negroes remain largely unreached by those offering the services they most urgently need. And those needs are desperate because the Negro's ability cope economically with a retarded child at home is usually less than that of his white counterpart.

That Negroes are isolated from the services they need is not only—as often thought—due to their lack of awareness, or to their timidity and reluctance in asking for such services. A survey conducted by the President's Committee on Mental Retardation revealed that—essentially because local communities are required to provide matching funds in order to receive federal funds—95 percent of all institutions for the mentally retarded are built in middle or high income areas, often a long way from the inner cities that need them most. This geographic separation of services from the people who need them is of course basic to the problem of retardation among all the rural poor.

What can be done to prevent a tragic and costly waste of human potential?

In the order of their efficacy per cost, I will mention a number of preventive programs, either already in existence or else in the planning stage, that should be greatly expanded or established promptly so as to reach all of the poor:

1. Easily accessible community-centered *birth control clinics* whose staffs should not only be highly trained in the technicalities of birth

control but who should have respect for human dignity, privacy and freedom of conscience, are an important —maybe the most important—element in the prevention of mental retardation.

2. There is a crying need for *maternal and infant care centers* in the heart of areas inhabited by "high risk mothers." President Johnson's proposed Child Health Act of 1968 would assure medical supervision during pregnancy and delivery for indigent mothers and pediatric care for their children during their first year of life. Such centers could prevent most of the complications of pregnancy and delivery, and make it easier to treat those abnormalities that can be diagnosed early. Such centers would also improve the child rearing practices of indigent or ignorant mothers.

3. A *Head Start-type program* is needed to be combined with a comprehensive health care program, begun at an earlier age than at present, and sustained throughout the elementary school years; this would compensate for cultural deprivation in the home. It would also prevent the unjust classing of thousands of deprived youngsters as mentally retarded. Remedial education and health care, geared specifically to the needs of deprived children, is the only real way to break the vicious cycle of the culture of poverty.

Whether IQ tests measure intelligence or not, it remains true that they do measure the capacity to operate within the present culture of most people in this country, where a certain capacity for abstract thought, communication through verbal expression with a certain accent, and writing using a certain vocabulary, are necessary. It is therefore imperative for all children to learn such skills equally well and early in life, to make sure that they will be able first to cope with the demands of school and later to compete in the search for employment.

These three programs are measures that can save the next generation.

Since so much retardation is due to preventable disease or accident, health care for all must also have a high priority, in any program for the prevention of retardation.

Although the Negroes' bad health is largely due to poverty, increasing the number of Negro doctors, psychiatrists and health workers is probably the best way to correct its many deficiencies.

This is so because in most cities, the amount of health care available for Negroes is directly related to the number of Negro physicians. Every white doctor has 779 potential patients. In the Negro community, there is only 1 doctor for each 3745. At the time of the Watts riot in 1965, there were an overwhelming 4,200 persons for every physician in the Watts area. In Boston, the new Columbia Point Housing Project area, serving over 5,000 people, was not able, to start with, to attract a single doctor or dentist, Negro or white.

Largely owing to the lack of physicians in Negro communities, one third of all non-whites visits to physicians were to hospital-clinics rather than to private doctors. Clinics in low income areas operate under overcrowded conditions and therefore on very impersonal terms. Many Negroes are suspicious of "charity medicine," which they feel quite correctly, as being operated less to serve the poor than the academic interest of medical practitioners. The result is that a disproportionate number of Negroes are suffering, even dying, from diseases the rest of the country conquered as long ago as the 1940's. By comparative standards, the relative health of the Negro continues to deteriorate all the time. Non-white maternal mortality, for example, was twice the white rate before World War II. Since then, it has grown to over four times the white rate, the latter having decreased in the interval.

Negro technicians, nurses, but above all physicians of all specialties, are needed. They will be the most effective, speedy and willing messengers of modern medical service, to the Negro population. The American

Association on Mental Deficiei , concerned as it must be with the alarming and shocking existence in this country of retardation due to socio-economic factors, should act on the pressing necessity of increasing the participation of Negroes in all phases and aspects of its activities for the retarded.

But don't forget that we can never eliminate the threat of retardation due to environmental deprivation unless the whole fabric that produces the "culture of poverty" is destroyed. Woven into it are overt and insidious discrimination, inferior education, poor nutrition and health care, substandard housing, unemployment, and underemployment. You are in a position to know how these can break the spirit of millions of human beings and make them feel faceless and nameless. Your responsibility therefore is also to work at changing that destructive environment.

Since the death of Martin Luther King, I have received thousands of telegrams, letters and calls from white people expressing their sympathy, grief, embarrassment and sorrow. Unless this grief and sympathy can be changed into tangible action, Martin Luther King will have died in vain. But you can do something tangible now, and need not miss your chance to show your humanity. This meeting will have been worthwhile only if it ends with strong resolutions followed by action on the part of each of you and of your organization. Your agencies and institutions should be looked at in

terms of the composition of their board membership, their staffs and their services. The best teaching is by example, not by exhortation alone. Moreover, for too long, your profession, like mine, has been more interested in methodology and technique than in its social impact. If the poor and the families of the mentally deficient are really going to believe the sincerity of our concern for them, we shall have to see that organizations like this one are on their side. The leaders in the movement to eradicate chronic injustice and poverty in this country, should be those people who have benefited the most from the American system. White Americans should stop riding on the moral coattails of the Negro; no longer should the burden of purifying America fall upon the victim; no longer should the patient be expected to be his own surgeon. I therefore insist that the most urgent need of America, in the striving for civil and economic justice for all, is for a tangible, visible commitment on the part of decent, responsible, white people. The responsibility of taking an outspoken, visible leadership in such a movement rests with the "elite" of our citizenry and of our institutions. Only this can justify their claim to high moral standing.

A Greek philosopher was once asked: "When shall we achieve justice in Athens?" To which he replied: "We shall achieve justice in Athens when those who are not wronged are more indignant than those who are." And so it must be in America.

Abstract: Expectations held by the special education teacher can be transmitted unconsciously to, and accurately interpreted by, the pupils. These expectations can serve as cues for modifying the behavior of the child whose achievement will accelerate or decelerate accordingly. Teacher expectancies can be inferred from their manner of interacting with their pupils. If more achievement were expected of special class pupils, more achievement might possibly occur.

When You Wish upon a Star: The Self Fulfilling Prophecy and Special Education

SR. M. SHEILA

No more remarkable tale of credulity founded on unconscious deceit was ever told, and were it offered as fiction, it would take high rank as a work of imagination Being in reality a record of sober fact, it verges on the miraculous [Angell, 1911, p. v].

So stated Professor James R. Angell, University of Chicago, writing in 1911. The subject of this observation was Clever Hans, the trained horse of a German mathematics teacher, Mr. von Osten. Hans could correctly reply by tapping his foot to questions requiring him to add, subtract, multiply and divide fractions; to read; to spell; and to solve problems of musical harmony. His master did not profit from the horse's talent but was firmly convinced of the animal's intellectual prowess. Mr. von Osten freely allowed others to interrogate the horse, even in his absence. There seemed little reason to suspect fraud.

Only the most careful of investigations, by two psychologists, Stumpf and Pfungst, finally yielded the solution to the puzzling riddle of the horse's source of knowledge (Pfungst, 1911). They found that Hans was responding to certain unconsciously given cues of posture, facial expression, and movement. The mere lift of an eyebrow was sufficient to cue Hans that he had tapped enough times and had reached the desired response.

In brief, Hans had mastered the art of interpreting the responses expected of him and of carrying them out with a high degree of accuracy. Further, the investigators found that the animal never responded appropriately unless the questioner himself firmly believed in the possibility of his succeeding in doing so.

Carrying the study a step further, Pfungst himself assumed the role of

Education and Training of the Mentally Retarded,
December, 1968, Vol.3, No.4, pp. 189-193.

Hans, tapping out with his hand answers to questions, similar to those asked of the horse, given by 25 persons of various ages and both sexes. None of the questioners knew the purpose of the experiment, and all but two made the same involuntary movements which provided sufficient cues for a correct response. The true solution of the investigation lay, then, not in the horse, but in the persons who subtly transmitted their expectancies to the horse.

Self Fulfilling Prophecy

This phenomenon has been termed the self fulfilling prophecy, defined by Merton (Rosenthal, 1964) in this manner: "One prophesies an event and the expectation of it then changes the prophet's behavior in such a way as to make the predicted event more likely [p. 112]."

No less fascinating than the story of Clever Hans is the report of the series of experiments conducted under the leadership of Robert Rosenthal, Harvard University (Rosenthal, 1964). One of the more intriguing studies was conducted with six pairs of college students acting as experimenters. One member of each pair was assigned to teach maze running to five supposedly bright rats, and the other member of the pair worked with five presumably dull rats. Actually, there was no known difference in the rats' intelligence—they were from a homogeneous colony and were matched for age and sex.

At the close of the study, those experimenters who believed their rats were maze bright obtained from them performances significantly superior to the performances obtained from rats whose experimenters believed them to be dull. A subsequent experiment upheld these differences in performance.

Generalizing from infrahuman to human behavior frequently follows such experimentation, but Rosenthal carried his work into the realm of human research. He selected two groups of experimenters (psychology majors) who asked their respective subjects (undergraduate students) to rate the degree of success or failure expressed on the faces in 10 photographs. A previous group of students had already designated these photos as being neutral in expression.

Half the experimenters were told they could expect a mean rating of $+5$ on a -10 to $+10$ scale, while the remaining experimenters were led to expect a mean -5 rating. They were further informed that if their results came out properly, that is, as expected, they would be paid double the usual rate.

Results of the experiment indicated a mean rating of $+.40$ for those expecting positive results, and a mean of $-.08$ for those expecting negative results. A second similar experiment confirmed these findings.

The widely cited recent study by Rosenthal and Jacobson (1968) demonstrates the existence of the self fulfilling prophecy in the classroom. Teachers were told that certain pupils held exceptional promise and would "bloom" within that school year; they had, in fact, been randomly selected. At the conclusion of the study, these children whom teachers had expected to show great progress had indeed "bloomed"; they had made intellectual and academic gains significantly superior to progress shown by the control pupils whose teachers had not expected great things of them.

Failure Relates to Expectancy

On the flip side of the record, the theme remains the same but the melody is in a minor key. Lack of school success has also been related to teacher expectancy. Clark (1965), in discussing school failure, commented:

The evidence of the pilot projects in "deprived" schools—odd though it may appear to many—seem to indicate that a child who is expected by the school to learn does so; the child of whom little is expected produces little. Stimulation and teaching based upon positive expectation seem to play an even more important role in a child's performance in school than does the community environment from which he comes [p. 132].

Research findings increasingly support the position that the slower pupil's lack of success functions as a self fulfilling prophecy. Riessman (1962) stated that teachers underestimate the intelligence and intellectual curiosity of these children and therefore formulate too low expectations of them. Teachers themselves confirmed this assumption in an opinion survey of their agreement or disagreement with statements in Riessman's book (Groff, 1964).

Riessman (1966) cited personal experience in the classroom to substantiate his position.

I find in examining my own classroom teaching that I easily fall into the habit of rewarding pupils whose faces light up when I talk, who are quick to respond to me and I respond to them . . . I don't pick up and select the slower pupil and I don't respond to him. He has to make it on his own [p. 53].

The amount of impact the teacher has on pupil achievement has not as yet been adequately assessed. A study by DeGroat and Thompson (1952) indicates that those children who show evidence of having acquired more subject matter knowledge receive a higher proportion of teacher approval, which in turn reinforces further efforts to acquire more knowledge.

From interviews with children Riessman documented that:

. . . from classroom to the PTA they discover that the school does not like them,

does not respond to them, does not appreciate their culture and *does not think they can learn* [Riessman, 1966, p. 55].

These pupils reported that they knew the minute they entered the room that the teacher did not like them and did not think they were going to learn very much.

From such observations two points seem evident: (a) expectations held by one person regarding another can be transmitted unconsciously and interpreted accurately, can provide cues to monitor behavior, and the very fact the expectation is held enhances the likelihood of its fulfillment; and (b) teachers do hold expectancies for their pupils and, in communicating these expectations, serve either to accelerate or decelerate their pupils' achievement.

Low Expectancies Conditioned

While the typical special education teacher probably does not dislike his pupils, there is a high probability that he has been conditioned to expect little achievement from these children. Instructors in teacher training courses tend to expound at length on the disabilities that characterize the mentally retarded child. They prophesy, albeit indirectly, that great effort will be necessary to prepare these children for even marginal adjustment as adults, and that much of this effort will be in vain. The IQ score is frequently invoked as an index of what a child *cannot* do or become, rather than as a useful guideline of what he *can* do or become.

Even a most superficial review of the research conducted within the past half century on the relative efficacy of the special education class versus regular class placement for the educable mentally retarded child reveals that in terms of academic achievement, retarded youngsters make greater progress when they remain in the regular classroom.

In his paper, "To Be or Not to Be: Special Classes for the Educable Mentally Retarded," Dunn (1962) reflected the sobering thought:

At this point we can find little information from studies to justify to school administrators and taxpayers special class programs *in their present form* ... the time appears to be ripe for us to make a number of changes if we are to warrant our continued existence [p. 1].

That educable mentally retarded children do not learn at the level and rate of their mental age expectancy in the special class is now fairly well established. Why this state of affairs is so, however, remains a highly controversial issue. Could it be, perhaps, that failure to achieve in the special education class is but yet another demonstration of the self fulfilling prophecy?

Enthusiasm Is Rare

It is rare indeed in the field today to find the counterpart for the enthusiastic doggedness of an Itard who aspired to life in society for Victor, the wild boy of Aveyron, or a Montessori who sought to liberate the imprisoned spirit of man by the education of the senses. While the enemies of special education gloomily point to the prisons and the welfare rolls to exemplify its failure, how many of its supporters ever think to remind these critics that special education classes have contributed to the success of famous athletes, musicians, and even saints and scholars? Could it be, perhaps, that today's special educators no longer "wish upon a star," no longer believe that given the proper training and materials, they can teach the retarded child, that he can learn and can achieve at grade expectancy?

Could lowered level of teacher expectancy be a factor in lower level of pupil achievement? Could the key to Pfungst's solution regarding the nature of Clever Hans' talents—to look for in the questioners what had previously been sought in the horse—also unlock the door to meaningful research in special education, as investigators look for in the teacher what had previously been sought in the child?

This may seem at first a frightening thought and a threat to the special educator. It could well constitute an acid test of the sincerity of his interest in the best possible education for the mentally retarded. Just as the persons involved in the research of Pfungst could be made aware of the cues they were transmitting, so it might be hypothesized that the special education teacher might also be given some insight into the level of expectancy he is communicating to his pupils, and into the manner in which he is communicating.

Expectancy Can Be Quantified

Rotter (1954) has stated that expectations can be quantified. He does not, however, specify the manner in which this can be done. It would seem that the teacher's expectancies could be measured in terms of the amount of achievement he anticipates for his pupils, the demands he places upon them for independent work assignments, the types of explanations given and responses demanded during instructional periods, and types of scheduling he prescribes for his pupils.

To date scant exploration of the self fulfilling prophecy has been carried on in the special education classroom—a regrettable lack which will hopefully soon be corrected. Haskett (1968) in a pilot study found that the expectancies of special education teachers for their pupils' academic achievement were significantly related to the actual achievement of their pupils. Further investigation of this relationship is needed. Meanwhile, educators themselves might well benefit from an introspective probe of how much they expect their pupils to accomplish, and how these expectancies are being translated into classroom practices and procedures.

They might find that by expecting more achievement and making more demands, their pupils will indeed become more productive. By setting goals based on teacher aspiration rather than on pupil limitation, they may come to find that, as Jiminy Cricket advised, "When you wish upon a star, your dreams come true."

References

Angell, J. R. In O. Pfungst, *Clever Hans*. New York: Henry Holt, 1911.

Clark, K. B. *Dark ghetto*. New York: Harper and Row, 1965.

DeGroat, A. E., & Thompson, G. G. Teachers' responses to different children. In R. G. Kuhlen & G. G. Thompson (Eds.), *Psychological studies of human development*. New York: Appleton-Crofts, 1952. Pp. 429-437.

Dunn, L. M. To be or not to be: special classes for the educable mentally retarded. Unpublished paper, 1962.

Groff P. J. Culturally deprived children: Opinions of teachers on the views of Riessman. *Exceptional Children*, 1964, 31, 61-65.

Haskett, Sr. M. S. *An investigation of the relationship between teacher expectancy and pupil achievement in the special education class*. Unpublished doctoral dissertation, University of Wisconsin, 1968.

Merton, R. K. The self-fulfilling prophecy. *Antioch Review*, 1948, 8, 193-210.

Pfungst, O. *Clever Hans*. New York: Henry Holt, 1911.

Riessman, F. *The culturally deprived child*. New York: Harper, 1962.

Riessman, F. The overlooked positives in disadvantaged groups. In J. L. Frost & G. R. Hawkes (Eds.), *The disadvantaged child, issues and innovations*. Boston: Houghton Mifflin, 1966. Pp. 51-57.

Rosenthal, R. The effect of the experimenter on the results of psychological research. In B. A. Maher (Ed.), *Progress in experimental personality research*. Vol. 1, New York: Academic Press, 1964. Pp. 79-114.

Rosenthal, R., & Jacobson, L. *Pygmalion in the classroom: Teacher expectation and pupils' intellectual development*. New York: Holt, Rinehart and Winston, 1968.

Rotter, J. B. *Social learning and clinical psychology*. Englewood Cliffs, N.J.: Prentice-Hall, 1954.

SR. M. SHEILA *is Personnel Coordinator, St. Coletta School, Jefferson, Wisconsin.*

RAPHAEL F. SIMCHES

The Inside Outsiders

". . . the inside outsiders in the field of education are still handicapped children, teachers of the handicapped, and programs for the handicapped."

In the past ten years the field of special education has produced some very interesting highlights, some significant breakthroughs, and some areas which will not win any Emmy awards for performance. One of the significant accomplishments has been Federal intervention in programs for the handicapped. This intervention took place on two levels: One funneled funds to local educational agencies and state operated programs to strengthen, enhance, and expand programs (Title VI-A of the Elementary and Secondary Education Act and PL 89-313). In addition to the allocation of funds, the Federal government has also undertaken the development of new approaches, new organizations, and new services at the Federal level. These programs include: (a) Regional resource centers to provide testing and evaluation for handicapped children so that appropriate educational programs might be designed; (b) Centers and services for young deaf blind children; (c) A preschool and early education program for handicapped children; (d) Research, training, and dissemination activities in connection with centers and services; (e) A grant program for training students at institutions of higher learning; (f) A research and demonstration program which covers all related areas including recreation for the handicapped; (g) A program of instructional media which incorporates captioned films and other educational media including the establishment of a National Center on Educational Media and Materials for the Handicapped; and (h) The support of special programs and the development of model centers for research on children with specific learning disabilities.

". . . special education has produced some very interesting highlights, some significant breakthroughs, and some activity which will not win any Emmy awards for performance."

These broad programs have tremendous implications for the handicapped children in this country. Unfortunately, the present allocations are far less than the Congressional authorization and in most cases, represent less

Exceptional Children, September, 1970, Vol.37, No.1, pp. 5-15.

than 50 percent of the authorization. The Federal legislation does exist to provide effective change. It is no longer a problem of legislation; it is a problem of money and implementation.

A second significant development during this period of time has been dissemination of information. This development is shown in the rapid expansion of special education instructional materials centers. The effective use of these media has had an impact on teaching methods. Dissemination has brought into sharp focus the need for concern about the problems in research, product development, product distribution, product utilization, and the dissemination and retrieval of information. There are many good things happening in classrooms throughout the country: They need to be disseminated. There are many good teaching methods which can be duplicated. There is much knowledge and educational technology that should be utilized.

A third significant accomplishment is the regionalization of programs for children with low incidence handicaps. Deaf blind centers are an example in this direction and states are continuing to regionalize and centralize programs particularly in rural areas, to meet the needs of severely multiply handicapped children. Regionalization has been accomplished through development of specialized schools, vocational high schools, and regional resource centers.

Behavior management has experienced changes in the past few years. Operant conditioning is becoming a major factor in special education programs. With operant conditioning techniques many teachers have found a method of management control which can accomplish behavioral change in students.

During this period we have also seen the significant growth of parent operated programs for the handicapped. Many states provide funds to private schools for handicapped children who cannot be educated in regular public schools. Many of these private schools are operated by parent organizations. In New York State the funds have been increased from $12,000 in 1957 to approximately $12 million in 1970. This development is positive because it emphasizes concern for the education of all handicapped children whether private or public. However, a question can be raised about the effectiveness of this type of pluralism without the existence of standards, fiscal accountability, and educational responsibility. In addition a serious question is raised in those situations where the development of the private facilities comes about because the local public school district fails to meet the educa-

Spreading the Word: Dissemination and Regionalization

"There are many good things happening . . ."

New Dimensions in Education

"$12,000 in 1957 . . . $12 million in 1970"

tional mandates under which it operates. Is this development of both private and public resources adding, expanding, and strengthening educational options or in fact, is it a substitute of one system for another without any real addition to the broad range of needed educational programs?

An exciting development in the field of programing has been the new emphasis on individualized instruction. One approach, the development of educational materials based on behavioral objectives and related to the individual child, has added a new dimension to our programs. It highlights individual differences and helps guard against curriculum approaches based on the assumption that all handicapped children are alike. The approach highlights the variance that exists between individuals in any group, handicapped or not.

Also there has been a striking increase in the use of new educational technologies. Our dial access programs, computer assisted instruction, compressed speech, sophisticated multimedia hardware, and perceptual and auditory discrimination teaching programs are highly suggestive of additional good things that are yet to come. However, there is the danger that we may rely too heavily on the material or media and forget that the most important instrument in our system is the teacher. In the areas of values, self concepts, and psychosocial adjustment skills, the teacher will be the greatest resource. Let us not forget that the teacher is still the primary tool in good teaching. Care and concern are very important reinforcers. As important as materials and media are in the transmission of knowledge, care and concern transmit love, the very vital ingredient for life.

On the Minus Side

The areas which have not contributed as much as they might have are those concerned with research utiliation; teacher training; implementation of legislation; maximizing options for programs; and labeling in the identification of children. With respect to teacher training, perhaps in the years to come we will see some major changes in this area. Dr. Donald Davies, Associate Commissioner, Bureau of Educational Personnel Development, US Office of Education, with respect to the problem of teacher training, has indicated teacher education has been plagued with "good rhetoric and poor follow-through" and "when you get right down to it, has a pretty low place on the education refill totem pole." Also there is evidence to suggest that the new priorities of the Bureau of Educational Personnel Development consider the college as only one trainer and the summer institute as only one site for teacher training. School systems, state departments of

. . . teacher education has been plagued with good rhetoric and poor follow through . . ."

62

education, and the community will become partners in the education of teachers.

Dr. William Tolley, former Chancellor of Syracuse University, also expresses his concern. He asks, "How many programs should we duplicate over and over with no one concerned with cost, quality, need or waste?" He has said, "the degree of waste in higher education staggers both the conscience and the imagination . . . and is second only to the waste in military expenditures."

I know a high priority has been placed on the right of children to read. However, I wonder if it would not be fruitful to assign a priority to the right of children and college students to be assured good teacher trainers, relevant teacher training programs, and universities which are committed to placing high value on teaching and the relationship between teacher and student.

Yes, there has been more money for research and demonstration, but what has been the nature of the research and demonstration project? Has it been relevant to the problem of educating the handicapped child? Of the millions of dollars spent on research projects, can we find ten which have had an impact on the education of the handicapped, have led to change in programs for the handicapped, or have contributed a body of knowledge which uses education to maximize opportunities for children?

"Of the millions of dollars spent on research projects, can we find ten which have had an impact on the education of the handicapped . . .?"

Probably the most controversial area in recent years has been labeling children for purposes of identification, school placement, and legislation. In some situations, such as legislation and categorical aid, labeling has become important. We have learned through experience that general aid formulas do not benefit handicapped children. The case has been proved many times. When initially passed, Title III of the Elementary and Secondary Education Act was to benefit all children, handicapped and nonhandicapped, but after a short time that law had to be amended to require that 15 percent of the funds be used for programs for the handicapped. The same happened with the Vocational Education Law (1963) which requires that 10 percent of funds be used for the handicapped.

The use of labels to identify handicapped children for purposes of legislation has been positive. Since the handicapped child had not been protected by compulsory education laws, there was the need to back up compulsory education laws with specific laws mandating programs for handicapped children: It has been necessary to identify in law the various handicapped groups entitled to educational programs. However the use of labels for this purpose has not been effective in educational program planning, evaluation, placement, or counseling.

Special Miseducation

In "Special Miseducation" (1970) there is a discussion of the politics of special education. It is directly related to the problems of labels and particularly the problem of placing children in special class programs on the basis of questionable standards. "Assignment to special classes is apt to be both irrational and unrelated to the special needs of a particular child. Indeed in some sections of the city, administrators regard the classes as convenient places for dumping children who prove bothersome in the regular classrooms. Teachers, frustrated by their inability to control particular students and understandably worried about the effect of one disruptive child on the whole class, often seek placement as a way of ridding themselves of a difficult behavioral problem. In many of those cases there is no pre or posttesting, no notice to parents, no record, and no attention to the state regulations which require them all."

The article outlines the importance of legal counsel in special education to guard against the abuse of misclassification. Of particular interest are two recent decisions cases in New York and California. The New York case, *MacMillan v. Board of Education,* involved a game of "brain-injured musical chairs *ad infinitum.*" The issue dealt with the availability of a special class program for a brain injured child. To meet the problem children are reclassified and suddenly programs can be found.

In the California case, the particular children involved were Mexican-American and the question was classification standards. The result of this suit was that the California Board of Education accepted responsibility of drafting formal state regulations which would protect Mexican-American children. The new regulations stipulate that so called mentally retarded students would receive retests in their primary language. Where misplacements were discovered, the state board of education would begin and continue to monitor special supplemental programs designed to reintegrate the misclassified student into the regular curriculum.

Wolfgang Goethe, the German poet, said: "If you treat an individual as he is, he will stay as he is, but if you treat him as if he were what he ought to be and could be, he will become what he ought to be and could be." A recent publication of the President's Committee on Mental Retardation, *The Six-Hour Retarded Child,* described the child who may be "retarded from 9 to 3, five days a week, solely on the basis of an I.Q. score, without regard to his adaptive behavior, which may be exceptionally adaptive to

> "If you treat an individual as he is, he will stay as he is, but if you treat him as if he were what he ought to be and could be, he will become what he ought to be and could be."

64

the situation and community in which he lives."

We have not done well with the problem of labels; we must find new ways to refer to children, new methods to help us understand children, and a greater awareness about the assets and skills of children. We must develop identification systems which provide an understanding of the child so that programs can be built around the child's skills. We cannot continue to use taxonomy of labels that have a tendency to homogenize children into meaningless diagnostic label categories based primarily on psychometrics, medical findings, or psychiatric examinations. Labels are not what is needed if the labels exclude children from programs, constrict objectives, or predetermine aspirations.

A Crisis in Space   Several months ago the world stood still as the Apollo 13 astronauts, with the guidance, direction, and support of the technical wizards in this age of electronics, computers, and scientific sophistication, struggled to come back to earth after a crisis in one of their life support systems. They were brought back hundreds of thousands of miles and all concerned had a right to be proud of this achievement. The cost involved must have been millions of dollars for the entire effort. The cooperation and coordination between personnel must have been superlative.

And One on Earth   Yet within the same period of time, how many school children died from overdoses of narcotics? How many children whose psychological life support systems were being shattered were *we* able to bring home? Perhaps we did not have the options to select, modify, and substitute as the astronauts did. There are very limited educational support systems in our schools and communities for handicapped children. If one system fails, the child is usually lost. He becomes a dropout or a pushout. This failure to maximize the options for choosing educational programs for handicapped children has decreased our chances for success.

In very broad terms, some of the goals we seek are increased mobility in our society, increased degrees of freedom in choosing life styles, and increased range of ability in making decisions. These very valid goals of increasing degrees of options we, as teachers, have failed to obtain in meeting the needs of handicapped children. For the most part we are restricted to special classes, isolated institutions, or home instruction. Within a few disability areas, such as the blind and speech handicapped, success has been made in the employment of an itinerant teacher assisting and providing a support system so that the child can be educated within the regular classroom. There has been isolated use of the crisis teacher and the resource room, but what has been done about strengthening the teaching methods, content and substance of the curriculum, increasing opportunities for post high school handicapped children, and training at the community college level? What has been done to further the interaction of the handicapped and nonhandicapped child in educational programs so that they can develop a feeling of caring and concern? If special education is a discipline, it is a discipline that respects the integrity of the handicapped child regardless of the handicap and speaks of the need to respect, develop, and realize the worth that is part of all human life.

The final area of poor performance during these past years has been the implementation of legislation. This failure has been on several accounts—lack of space, lack of funds, lack of manpower—but unfortunately not because of a lack of children, lack of interest, or lack of need. The failures correspond to the value systems and the priorities that people outside of the field have had in the primary powers for decisionmaking. Until the teachers can affect such decisionmakers, we can expect more of the same. In New York state, legislation was enacted mandating certain programs for mentally ill children in psychiatric institutions. The Citizens Committee for Children directs itself to the problems of implementing this legislation. The failure to implement legislation unfortunately is not restricted to handicapped children. It has been highlighted in problems of civil rights and other social issues affecting minority groups. Perhaps more attention must be paid to the enactors of legislation since the developers of legislation seem to have done their job.

". . . lack of space, lack of funds, lack of manpower . . . but not a lack of children, lack of interest, or lack of need."

The Educational Dollar— Dollars and Sense

What is the sum total of this review of the past ten years? In my system of addition and subtraction it adds up to the conclusion that the *inside* outsiders in the field of education are still handicapped children, teachers of the handicapped, and programs for the handicapped. The outsiders are still you, the special teacher, and your charge, the handicapped child. Yes, we are a concern to the boards of education but we are outside the consideration and determination of priorities for the educational dollar. There are many more special classes for the handicapped, but are they in regular school buildings or are they in outside facilities, isolated and segregated, in rented stores or churches? Yes, there are more children carrying the label of handicapped, but for what purposes? To integrate them? Is it to get them inside the heart and guts of regular education or is it to keep them outside, outside the concern of the regular class teacher, the gym teacher, the art teacher, the music teacher, the industrial arts teacher, and the building principal? Why do we find in certain communities a disproportionate number of Black and Puerto Rican children of low income groups in classes for mentally retarded children or the emotionally disturbed and children from other socioeconomic levels in classes for children with learning disabilities? Is this another technique to keep children outside or is it a way of providing an opportunity for them to become part of the educational fabric? More money has been spent on traineeships and fellowships, but has the quality of teacher education improved? Has the special teacher been provided the opportunity to come inside and participate in the development of training courses? Or are they outsiders with respect to policymaking decisions that affect the quality of teacher training programs? Yes, more states have mandatory provisions for handicapped children and have declared the right for handicapped children to be educated, but what has been the nature of the programs? Are they within the commitment of the state's educational programs or are they being developed outside and apart, isolated and insulated, from the full commitment of the state's effort?

The Teacher: Reactor or Catalyst

I think the paramount problem of the 1970's will be the role, function, and involvement of the special education teacher, both as a member of the educational fraternity and as a concerned citizen actively involved in those areas of society that affect the lives of children. If we are desirous of change, then the teacher must begin to realize the important role he can play as a catalyst. Too often one has the feeling that the special education teacher, like most teachers, is identified not as the producer of new knowledge or the disseminator of knowledge, but only as a utilizer of knowledge; not as an active person instrumental in bringing about change, but mainly as a reactor to change. They have not been considered decisionmakers; they are not considered planners and they are not considered evaluators. I do not know whether this image must remain or must be challenged. Special educators have long been accused of looking for a "cop out" from regular education. Teachers use the excuse of a hard day's work as a cop out for not becoming involved in the sociopolitical arena. This arena is an important place in a country which stresses democracy and peaceful change through legislative process. What can the special class teacher do within the framework of special education?

The special teacher has too often been grateful to a principal for being left alone to accept the awesome re-

67

sponsibility of educating the handicapped child. This is a serious mistake. It is time that principals, administrators, and others identified with regular education have it placed squarely before them that the education of handicapped children is their responsibility and concern. The principal must realize that he is as responsible for the safety of the handicapped child as he is for the nonhandicapped. The special class teacher should be made part of all screening, evaluating, or identifying committees. Too often the diagnosis, labeling, and placement involve people far removed from special class programs and instruction. Only through the teacher can we expect to implement the knowledge obtained from experience in the classroom.

Special education has isolated itself through the continuation of self perpetuating interests and the protective attitudes of special educators. We must emphasize to general educators, legislators, colleges and universities, and administrators the contribution that special education has made to the nonhandicapped child and general education, not permit special education to be considered an isolated approach for handicapped children. Some of the contributions are in testing and programs in early childhood education. There are many other examples in the works of Binet, Montessori, and others.

Special education is an instructional program and not a pupil personnel services program. The success of a special educational program relies on the instructional skills as well as the effective use of instructional materials. The contribution of pupil personnel services is important because effective educational evaluations can enable the teacher to increase his understanding and insight. Such services are vital in crisis periods but, in the end, effective remediation is accomplished through interaction of child, material, and teacher. Teachers must learn to respect their own competencies, skills, and unique knowledge of children. Who else spends as much time with the child during the day as the teacher, particularly at the elementary school level? Teachers must refuse their role as a minority group in decisionmaking with respect to the educational planning and programing of children. There is a reality in classroom teaching that cannot be found in textbooks, the research environment, or the redefining discussions, the college seminar.

How about the role of the special teacher in the sociopolitical arena? Since it has been proved that one cannot change a part of the system without changing the entire system, the special teacher must become involved. Changing the system demands involvement, energy, persistence, and other characteristics difficult to muster after 5 hours of teaching. Change requires sustained effort. Apathy is the ally of those who want to maintain the status quo. If we are really concerned about strengthening educational programs and getting support for these changes, then we must begin to pursue involvement with a principal change agent—the legislator.

Contrary to some popular opinions, I do not believe that teachers and schools victimize children and parents. There may be teachers who should not be in classrooms and school administrators who should not be in charge of buildings, but this is true in every profession. There are doctors who should not be practicing medicine, lawyers who should not be in the field of law, plumbers and carpenters who should not be engaged in their professions. Instead I believe teachers and schools have become victims of the broad social issues that affect children, parents, and educational programs. These issues include poverty, the neglect of inner cities, the decisionmakers who are concerned with educational accountability and cost/benefits but not educational needs, and the importance of providing safe, good schools for teachers, children, and parents.

What About the Future?

Sometimes when I am asked to project the need for future special education programs, a question is raised about medical advances such as the rubella vaccine and the possibility of lowering the number of handicapped children, I point out that many unsolicited contributors to this population are yet to come. Our drug companies have made their contribution through thalidomide and I wonder if other drugs will not also contribute. Certainly our munitions and defense manufacturers, through the use of their products in the battlefields throughout the world, are contributing to a reservoir of handicapped adults to say nothing of the contribution that poverty and malnutrition make. The past ten years have not been good years for consumers, but they certainly seem to have been good years for producers. I am sure they have been excellent years for those who are in the business of manufacturing, marketing, producing, and distributing drugs such as heroin, LSD, opium, and the tangible aids and accessories that go with them. However, it certainly has been far from satisfactory for the consumers of these products. It has been a good ten years for products and a bad ten years for children throughout the world.

"The past ten years have not been good years for consumers, but they certainly seem to have been good years for producers."

Therefore, teachers must become active in social issues. The schools have been the victims, not the victimizers. The schools did not create ghettos, poverty, zoning laws that lead to segregated communities, or the high priorities for spending of federal dollars. If the schools are to be held accountable for both the educational program and the educational dollar then why not ask the same of other segments of our society? What has been the cost/benefit and the accountability of the hundreds of millions of dollars allocated for the war effort? Or the subsidies that are part of our industrial organizations and the discrepancies in our system of taxation? Why is it that, according to the New York City Department of Consumer Affairs, the poor are cheated most frequently? Why is there a tendency for low income groups to pay two to three times the fair market price of items? These are social issues that require our concern. The teacher of the handicapped is not seeking a greater population. Our goal is not to create more special classes in the school system. It is to stress the need to individualize programs, express care and concern for the individual child, and develop the curriculum, methods, and materials compatible with the assets of the child. We are not deficit trainers; we are asset seekers.

"We are not deficit trainers; we are asset seekers."

To be effective in strengthening educational programs, we must be involved in the support of changes within and without the schools. It may mean greater involvement, or involvement with other people who are effective change agents, such as lawyers, legislators, administrators, members of school boards, and the boards of regents. It must be realized that educational reform as well as social reform is achieved through legislative action with the responsibility for implementation at many levels of government. The legislator is our agent for action, particularly within the framework of our democratic society. More attention must be paid to this very important person.

Our salvation lies not in technology, but in wisdom; not in computers, but in people; not in withdrawal, but in involvement with others. We need the employment of people who will create the environments for children to live in and become caring of others and not the employment of methods, labels, and curriculum objectives that create alienation and dissatisfaction.

"What happens to a dream deferred?
Does it dry up?
Does it stink like rotten meat?
Like a raisin in the sun?
Or fester like a sore—
And then run?
Or crust and sugar over—
Like a syrupy sweet?
Maybe it just sags
Like a heavy load.
Or, does it explode?"

"A Dream Deferred"
—Langston Hughes

Change requires that we not defer our dreams for the handicapped child. Perhaps jointly we will prevent our dreams from drying up.

RAPHAEL F. SIMCHES *is Chief, Bureau for Physically Handicapped Children, State Education Department, Albany, New York.*

70

HOW MUCH CAN WE BOOST IQ AND SCHOLASTIC ACHIEVEMENT

Arthur R. Jensen

Arthur R. Jensen is Professor of Educational
Psychology and Research Psychologist in the
Institute of Human Learning of the University
of California, Berkeley. He received his
B. A. Degree from the University of California,
Berkeley, and his Doctorate from Columbia
University.

To answer this question, which I can blame no one but myself for posing
is a big order indeed. I doubt if it can be answered in any precise way at
present. What I wish to attempt, however, is a preliminary analysis of the
question which would indicate the nature of the answers that we might find
and the kinds of research that might lead to improving the intelligence and
educability of children.

First, let me make it clear that I am using the term IQ here as more or
less synonymous with intelligence; it is merely a way of abbreviating the
title of my paper. Also let us assume that we are dealing with intelligence
as measured on an absolute scale. The usual IQ scale is, of course, an
invariant one; its mean is always 100 and its standard deviation is 15.
Systematic changes in the average level of mental ability in the population
cannot show up in test scores that are standardized in such a way that the
mean and standard deviation remain constant regardless of the absolute level
of performance.

Why Boost Mental Ability?

Why should we think about boosting mental ability? Would there by any
advantage, for example, in shifting the entire normal distribution up one
standard deviation (i.e. 15 IQ points) or even in decreasing the spread of
ability by pulling up those in the lower quartile by 10 or 15 IQ points?
Some people have argued that, even if we boosted the average level of intelligence, we would still have a wide spread of individual differences; there
would still be relatively bright and dull children and the material rewards
in our society would still be correlated with differences in ability. Another
question often raised is how important is a difference of, say, 10 IQ points,
more or less, to the individual? Would any of us be much better or worse off

*Proceedings of the Annual State Conference on Educational
Research*, November, 1967, Vol.35, pp. 35-49.

if 10 points were added to or subtracted from our IQ? Ten IQ points, I might add, is about the upper limit of average improvement when intensive systematic efforts have been applied.

One arrives at different answers to these questions depending on whether he thinks only in terms of the individual or in terms of populations. The real significance of an average of 15 points boost in IQ is seen most dramatically in the effect it has in the tails of the normal bell-shaped distribution. Even an average change of a few points can have drastic implications when we look at the part of the distribution that falls more than two standard deviations above or below the mean. For example, the minimum level of ability now required for passing grades in a good college corresponds to an IQ of about 115. Only 16 percent of our population falls above this point. A 15 point boost in IQ would mean that 50 percent of the population would be capable of this level of education. IQs over 130 would be increased from about 2 percent of the population to 16 percent. The advantages of such a boost in the proportion of more able persons, along with the corresponding reduction of persons in the lower tail of the distribution, is a matter for speculation.

The consequences of an equivalent _lowering_ of the mean IQ of the population, on the other hand, seem far less uncertain. A lowering by as much as one standard deviation would probably make civilization impossible.

Given the methods of instruction now at hand, it is clear that the acquisition of certain skills required on an increasing scale in our technological society depend upon certain levels of mental ability, and it makes no difference what the ratio of supply and demand is in this case. For a particular job, given a certain instructional economy in terms of time, teacher-pupil ratio, and particular method of teaching, there is a minimal level of required ability. If this were not true, the Armed Forces would not have to use mental ability tests and would not have to reject anyone from service on the basis of insufficient mental ability.

A proper analysis of the importance and consequences of raising the average level of ability must take into consideration three major factors: (a) the ability requirements of the society, (b) the distribution of the relevant abilities in the population, and (c) the efficiency of the instructional process currently available.

Just a few words about each of these points:

(a) The increasing technological trend of our society suggests that the ability requirements must also be increasing. It probably takes more knowledge and cleverness to operate, maintain, or repair a tractor than to till a field by hand, and it takes more know-how to write computer programs than to operate an adding machine, and so on. What we must look out for, however, is our tendency merely to assume certain ability requirements for a job without establishing these requirements as a fact. How often do employment examinations, Civil Service examinations, high school diploma requirements, and the like, constitute hurdles that are actually irrelevant to performance on the jobs for which they are intended as screening devices? Before we go overboard in deploring the fact that our disadvantaged minority groups fail to clear many of the hurdles we set up for many jobs, including service in the Armed Forces, we should determine whether the educational and mental test hurdles that stand at the entrance of many of these jobs are actually relevant. Wittingly or unwittingly, they may be only instruments of social or racial discrimination. If the hurdle is actually relevant, but only in the correlational sense that it predicts success on the job, we should also know whether the test actually measures the ability required in the job or only measures characteristics that happen to be correlated with some third factor that enters into success on the job. For example, it may be that a certain style of appearance and manners is essential for certain kinds of jobs that involve dealing with the public; and it may be that this combination of appearance and manners is correlated with the narrow range of abstract mental abilities measured by IQ tests, or with having had an academic major and a B average in high school, and so you can use these indirect criteria in select ing persons for the job, even though differences in abstract mental ability and high school record above some very minimal level may be quite unrelated to success on the job. The tests are then an artificial hurdle; they focus attention on what in many cases may be the irrelevant aspects of social and occupational attainment. Changing people in terms of the essential criteria for the job may be much more feasible than trying to boost their abstract intelligence and performance in academic subjects.

(b) What about the distribution of the relevant basic abilities in the population? Do we have a large enough ability pool for the jobs that have to be filled? If we measure ability by IQ tests or by school achievement in academic subjects, I think the picture is a gloomy one for society as a whole and especially for some of our minorities, especially our largest minority, the Negroes. Anyone who has read the Coleman Report, or who examines the results of ability and achievement testing in the schools of our largest cities, or who looks at the Armed Forces rejection rates of Negroes as compared with Whites based on the Armed Forces Qualification Tests (68 percent versus 19 percent), can readily see that the situation is critical and dismal -- if all we look at is whatever abilities are measured by our usual IQ tests. A few years ago I would have said that the IQ tests are not very good, that they are so culturally biased in favor of the white middle-class population and so biased against the disadvantaged minority groups in our population that the tests are practically worthless as ability measures outside the white middle-class population. I now seriously doubt that this is true, and I can honestly find little comfort in the popular cliché that there is gross cultural bias in our IQ tests. We have over-emphasized the cultural bias in tests as a means of rationalizing social class and ethnic group differences. Cultural bias in tests actually is not hard to identify; what is hard -- and I find it increasingly difficult as I examine more and more of the research evidence -- is to make out a strong case that the group differences we observe in our population are mainly attributable to cultural bias in the tests. Most of the IQ tests now in use in the schools, and I still put the Stanford-Binet at the top of the list in order of merit, measure mainly a certain kind of abstract intelligence. I am unable to find any compelling evidence that the individual and group differences that show up on these measures are due in the main to cultural or social environmental differences within our society. The fact that social and cultural differences do in fact exist among different races and social strata in our population is not in itself evidence that these cultural factors are important determinants of IQ differences. The evidence indicates that they are not. The tests are very good for what they measure. Their validity is about the same in all segments of thepopulation, if we limit our concept of their validity to that of measuring the kinds of abstract intelligence that correlate highly with academic achievement under the present methods of instruction. The reason I am not as alarmed by this conclusion and some people might be, is that I see the IQ as representing only a _portion_ of the total spectrum of human abilities.

The same sort of thing may be said concerning measures of school achievement. There are large group differences found in these also. But there is no evidence that these large group differences among segments of our population are due to inequalities of educational treatment, to inferior schools, inadequately trained and underpaid teachers, or otherwise poor educational facilities. I have seen schools in disadvantaged neighborhoods that on all counts are at least as good as, if not superior to, the best schools that exist anywhere in the United States today, and the average achievement level in these schools is far below the average of national norms. In view of the evidence, blaming society or the educational system for inequalities in scholastic achievement is to block the paths that might lead to solutions.

Inequalities in educational facilities still exist in many places and must be removed. But it now seems clear that the removal of all such inequalities barely sets the stage for the kinds of changes and improvements we will need to make in our educational system if the large segment of our population called disadvantaged is to benefit markedly. To aim merely at equality of educational opportunity and to stop there will fall far short of solving the educational problem.

(c) This brings me to the third point: the efficiency of instruction. When we say that IQ tests predict school achievement, we should remember that we are referring to the achievement that results from a particular instructional program. Like most other institutions that have been around for a very long time, our educational practices have evolved. They have not taken their particular form just by chance or decree. They were originally shaped, and have since evolved, in an Anglo-European culture and population, particularly in the upper-class part of this population. For this population and culture, the prevailing educational practices have seemed appropriate. They have not been unsuccessful by any reasonable criteria. The educational appropriateness of this approach for a segment of our U. S. population today, however, seems doubtful to me. Its obvious lack of success is attested by its failure to provide the many children we now called disadvantaged with the minimal essentials for economic self-sufficiency in our present urbanized society. Just as the IQ tests tap too narrow a band of the abilities spectrum, the educational system, through its particular evolutionary history, has developed in such a way as to capitalize on only a rather small range of abilities and patterns of ability. If a child is not in the modal group in these abilities, he falls more or less by the wayside and is never fully a beneficiary of our educational system. In fact, many children are probably worse off for their school experience than if they had never been exposed to school at all. Children for whom the system does not work become "turned off" at an early stage of their schooling, so that at later grades little of the child's actual potential for learning is available to the teacher's efforts.

The Determinants of Mental Ability

As educators, our chief concern is with improving the scholastic achievement of pupils rather than with boosting IQ per se. Probably the reason we are inclined to think of the boosting of IQ as the main means of improving school performance is that IQ is undoubtedly the single highest correlate of school performance. No other single fact we can know about a child can tell us as much about his probable success in school as the IQ tells us. All the other variables we can take into account combined will not predict as much as the IQ. Naturally, if the IQ, or the mental abilities it reflects, is so important for school work, we are led to think in terms of raising the IQ itself as the chief means of improving school success. Indeed, the success or lack of success of various programs of compensatory education are often reported in terms of an increase or a lack of increase in IQ measures. Pre and post testing with the Peabody Picture Vocabulary Test or the Stanford-Binet are a standard part of the official procedures for assessing the effects of Head Start. Various research efforts are now being made to boost the IQs of disadvantaged children, mainly by enriching the early environment through preschool programs. Some slight degree of success was to be expected and indeed has been found. Boosts of 5 to 10 IQ points are often produced within a period of a few weeks. The size of the gain is usually in direct proportion to the degree of cultural bias in the tests and to the degree of cultural deprivation of the testees. To a large degree, "test wiseness," familiarity with interpreting and answering questions, working puzzles, and conforming to the requirements of a timed task, account for this boost. Middle-class children acquire some advantage along these lines at home. Disadvantaged children acquire some of this knowledge and skill in the process of taking tests, in their early encounters with Head Start, or in nursery school or kindergarten. An initial boost after brief exposure to certain educational advantages is easy to demonstrate and it is found repeatedly. What is harder to find is any appreciable gain after one or two years. The initial IQ boost seems to wash out. By this limited criterion, Head Start and other large-scale experiments in early compensatory education must be assessed as failures.

What we are really interested in, of course, are the educational correlates of IQ, not just the IQ itself. If the usual correlates of IQ do not show a boost along with the boost in IQ, practically nothing has been gained. Educators and psychologists who have aimed at boosting IQ directly have not reported significant gains in the educational or social correlates of IQ.

What little gains in IQ have occurred are often fleeting. They are attributable mostly to the culturally biased aspects of the tests - to those very features of IQ tests that many educators point to as a weakness of the tests, since these cultural aspects do not really get to the person's intelligence but only reflect his particular cultural background. It is this aspect of the test score that is easiest to change. But tests differ in their cultural loading, and tests with small cultural loadings are remarkably resistant to the effects of cultural enrichment or even to direct coaching on similar items. The Educational Testing Service in Princeton has been experimenting with teaching children strategies for solving the test items of the Raven Progressive Matrices, for example. The training is intensive and specifically deals with kinds of problems that constitute the Progressive Matrices. The resistance of the Matrices to this type of coaching is rather astonishing. On the other hand, performance on the Peabody Picture Vocabulary Test, which correlates with the Matrices under normal conditions, is much more susceptible to coaching and cultural enrichment. The Stanford-Binet stands somewhere between these two extremes.

It is interesting that children we call disadvantaged actually make a better showing on the more culturally loaded items of tests; for example, they do better on the verbal subtests of the Wechsler or Stanford-Binet than on the performance tests.

Sources of Variance in IQ

In order to understand what is involved in boosting intelligence of the type assessed by tests like the Stanford-Binet, we must look analytically at the main sources of variability in IQ. The main sources of variance in IQs are shown in Table 1. The proportions of the total variance attributable to each of the sources are based on the average of the values of all the major studies in the literature concerned with this issue. (I have presented elsewhere a detailed discussion of the methodology of this research and summary tables of the results of all the major studies /Jensen, 1967/).

Table 1

Variance Components of IQ and Scholastic Achievement

V_{Total}	Between Families		Within Families	
	V_{G_b} +	V_{E_b}	V_{G_w} +	V_{E_w}
I.Q.	.45 +	.12	.35 +	.08
Sch. Ach.	.22 +	.54	.18 +	.06

It should be emphasized that the values shown in Table 1 are not constants or absolutes. These values will differ, within limits, according to the particular measures of IQ or scholastic achievement on which they are based and on the particular populations sampled. The figures in Table 1, however, are highly typical of results obtained with the Stanford-Binet in a cross section of the white school population in the United States and England. Since there have been no adequate studies of this type based on the Negro or other minority populations, we cannot be sure that the results would be the same in these groups. We are now obtaining relevant data in the Negro population, however, and so far there is no indication that the results of this type of analysis will be appreciably different for the Negro than for the white population.

Just what does Table 1 show? First of all, it divides the sources of variance into those that account for the average differences between families and those that account for individual differences among siblings within the same family. In these two categories of between families and within families, the variance is analyzed into a genetic component and an environmental component. This is a most interesting and revealing form of analysis, derived from the methods of quantitative genetics (e.g. Falconer, 1960). As shown in Table 1, something like 80 percent of the variance in IQ has a genetic basis; a little more than half of this genetic variance accounts for genetic differences between families, and a little less than half accounts for genetic differences between siblings within the same family. Only about 20 percent of the variance in IQ is abbributable to non-genetic or environmental factors. (About 5 percent of the variance in IQ is due to error of measurement or unreliability of the test, but I have left this out for the sake of simplicity; thus we are dealing in Table 1 with an analysis of only the "true score" variance.) We see that for IQ some 12 percent of the environmental variance is between families and only 8 percent within families.

This picture can be presented in still another way which may convey the message more directly to those who are not accustomed to thinking in terms of the analysis of variance. We can express the results in terms of the average difference in IQ between persons paired at random from the population. Given an intelligence test like the Stanford-Binet, with a standard deviation of 16 IQ points in the white population of the United States, the average difference among persons paired at random would be 18 IQ points. If everyone had inherited exactly the same genes for intelligence, but all nongenetic environmental variance remained as is, people would differ, on the average, by only 18 IQ points. On the other hand, if hereditary variance remained as is, but there were no environmental differences between families, the average difference among people would be 17 IQ points. If all environmental sources of differences were eliminated, the average intellectual difference among people would be 16 IQ points. In short, the effect of making heredity uniform in the population would result in an average difference among people of 8 IQ points instead of 18, while the effect of making the environment uniform would still leave an average difference of 16 points. If heredity and environment were both uniform, everyone in the population would be even more alike than identical twins -- a condition that could possibly provide the basis for a science-fiction horror story.

The results outlined above definitely belie some of the clichés we often hear in discussions of intelligence testing, such as the statement that IQ tests measure "only performance" or reflect only the child's cultural or socioeconomic background or only what he has learned at home or at school. All these statements are true; but they are also trivial and misleading. The important fact is that currently used IQ tests do indeed reflect innate, genetically determined aspects of intellectual ability in persons from the population on which the tests were standardized and validated. There is no way of getting around this fact, nor is there any good reason to wish to do so. The particular use we make of the fact is another issue, of course. Intelligence test results can be used stupidly or wisely. Let's hope we use them wisely, without having to belittle them with the false notion that they do not measure anything of educational or social importance. We should be able to face the fact that a major portion of individual differences variance in IQ has a biological basis.

My main reservations about standard IQ tests are essentially two: (a) They are excellent as far as they go, but they do not assess certain abilities which may be educationally relevant, particularly for the disadvantaged; and (b) the IQ or the total score they yield is too much an undifferentiated conglomerate of various abilities for the single overall score to be very useful in analytic research or in educational counseling.

Returning to Table 1, we note an interesting and important difference between IQ and scholastic achievement. The scholastic achievement data have been subjected to exactly the same analysis as the intelligence test data. What we find is that genetic factors account for only about half as much of the variance in scholastic achievement as in IQ. Over half the variance is accounted for by environmental factors and by far the most of this is due to environmental differences between families. The fact that school achievement is considerably less heritable than is intelligence means, for one thing, that many other traits, habits, attitudes and values enter into a child's performance in school besides just his intelligence, and these non-intellectual factors are environmentally determined, mainly through the influence of the child's family. Siblings in the same family are much more alike in school performance than in intelligence. This means there is potentially much more we can do to change school performance through environmental means than we can to change intelligence. If compensatory education programs such as Head Start are to have any beneficial effect on later school achievement, it will most likely be through their influence on motivation, values, and other environmentally determined habits that play an important part in school performance, rather than through any direct influence on intelligence per se. The proper evaluation of such programs should therefore be sought in their effects on school performance, not on how much they raise the child's IQ.

Ways of Boosting Intelligence

There are two main ways of boosting intelligence. One way is to improve the use people make of their neural equipment for intelligent behavior. The other way is to improve the basic equipment itself. The first can be accomplished only through environmental means; the second can be accomplished through both genetic and environmental means. The first is presently much more feasible, though much more limited in what it can potentially accomplish, than the second.

Genetic Improvement of Intelligence

As we saw in Table 1, the largest source of variance in intelligence is contributed by genetic factors. There is little doubt that in the long run the surest way of changing the biological basis of intelligence is through genetic selection. It is a fact that many different behavioral traits, including those we would identify as intelligence, can be changed through selective breeding in lower animals. There is no reason to believe this does not also hold true for the human species. But I doubt that we will see any move in this direction of systematic eugenics in the foreseeable future, for several reasons. For one thing, popular attitudes have generally been opposed to eugenic proposals, on the ground that this may be an infringement on the rights of individuals. And who is to say what the most desirable characteristics are that should be emphasized in eugenic selection? By emphasizing one set of characteristics, would we risk diminishing other traits that may be necessary for survival in the future? The reasonable answer, I believe, is to think at present only in terms of negative eugenics rather than in terms of positive eugenics. That is to say, there are probably traits which have no conceivable survival value and which all humane persons would agree are human misfortunes which should be prevented if at all possible. No parents, for example, would willingly choose to have a mentally retarded child. Yet it has been estimated by Elizabeth and Sheldon Reed, in their monumental study of mental retardation, that some five million of the estimated six million mentally retarded persons in the United States have a retarded parent or a normal parent who has a retarded sibling (Reed & Reed, 1965). The Reeds state: "One inescapable conclusion is that the transmission of mental retardation from parent to child is by far the most important single factor in the persistence of this social misfortune" (p. 48). "The transmission of mental retardation from one generation to the next, should, therefore, receive much more critical attention than it has in the past. It seems fair to state that this problem has been largely ignored on the assumption that if our social agencies function better, that if everyone's environment were improved sufficiently, then mental retardation would cease to be a major problem. Unfortunately, mental retardation will never disappear, but it can be reduced by manipulating the genetic and environmental factors involved... When voluntary sterilization of the retarded becomes a part of the culture of the United States, we should expect a decrease of about 50 percent per generation in the number of retarded persons, as a result of all methods combined to reduce retardation" (p. 77).

Another question which is relevant to the genetic basis of mental ability is whether or not dysgenic factors are exerting an influence on the distribution of abilities in our population or in certain segments of it. We know there is a negative correlation between family size and measured intelligence; and we know that a disproportionate number of the unemployed come from large families. No one to my knowledge is pursuing research that would elucidate the implications of these facts for the future.

One set of facts may be viewed as having potentially serious implications for the welfare of Negro Americans as well as of society in general. It appears that forces are at work which may create and widen the genetic aspect of the average difference in ability between the Negro and white populations, with the possible consequence that no amount of equality of opportunity or improvement of educational facilities will result in equality of achievement or in any improvement of the chances for the Negro population to compete on equal terms.

The factual basis of this concern can be found in a recent article by Moynihan (1966). The differential birth rate, as a function of socioeconomic status (SES), is greater in the Negro than in the white population of the United States. Negro middle- and upper-class families have fewer children than their white counterparts, while Negro lower-class families have more. In 1960, Negro women of ages 35 to 44 who were married to unskilled laborers had 4.7 children as compared with 3.8 for non-Negro women in the same situation. Negro women married to professional or technical workers had only 1.9 children, as against 2.4 for white women in the same circumstances. Negro women below the so-called poverty line, with incomes below $2000, averaged 5.3 children. Three out of four Negroes failing the Armed Forces Qualification Test come from families of four or more children. The poverty rate for families with five or six children is 3-1/2 times as high as that for families with one or two children (Hill & Jaffe, 1966). I would like to see more thought and research given to the possible educational and social implications of these trends for the future. Is there a risk that present welfare policies may lead to the genetic enslavement of a substantial segment of our population? Our failure seriously to investigate these matters may well be viewed by future generations as our society's greatest injustice to Negro Americans.

Non-genetic Influences on Intelligence

Let us now turn to the nongenetic determinants, which in our population at present account for about one-fourth of the variance in measured intelligence. I refer to nongenetic variance rather than environmental variance, because the term environmental is usually identified only with the social-cultural environment and not with the physical environment. Yet there is considerable evidence to indicate that prenatal, perinatal, and postnatal physical factors contribute a substantial, probably a major, portion of the nongenetic variance. If this is true, advances in medicine, nutrition, and obstetrics may contribute as much or more to improving the intelligence of the population than will manipulation of the social environment.

Consider the following facts.

Children born prematurely are, on the average, slightly lower in IQ than full-term children; and we know that premature births have a higher rate of occurrence in the low socioeconomic group and particularly in the low SES Negro population. Lowering the prematurity rates in the disadvantaged population should be possible to the extent that the higher rates are due to maternal nutrition and health; and from improvements in nutrition and hygiene we should expect a slight overall upward shift in the distribution of IQs in the disadvantaged segment of the population. Complications of pregnancy and delivery also are associated with slight depression of the IQ. It is known that these complications have a much higher incidence among the disadvantaged.

Since all aspects of mental ability are not developed in the first two or three years of life and cannot be adequately assessed or predicted by means of our current psychological tests, the less severe forms of brain damage, nutritional deficiencies, and the like, may not show up until after the child is four or five years of age, when the specific abilities we recognize as the kinds of intelligence most necessary for school achievement reach a stage of development that permits their reliable measurement.

80

Nutrition during pregnancy affects the child's later IQ. Low socio-economic status women given vitamin supplements during pregnancy had children whose IQs were 8 points higher at four years of age than the children of mothers given a placebo over the same period (Harrell, Woodyard, & Gates, 1955). Vitamin supplements, of course, are beneficial in this respect only when they serve to remedy an existing deficiency.

Other prenatal effects on the later intelligence of the child are known to exist, but their mechanisms are still obscure. There is apparently a degree of variability in the uterine environment that contributes to the variability in children's intelligence. We know, for example, that twins are, on the average, about 7 points lower in IQ than the population of singletons, and this is true in every social class level. Furthermore, identical twins are slightly though significantly lower than fraternal twins. The reason presumably is that twins have a more crowded prenatal environment; having to share the intrauterine environment apparently results in some degree of pre-natal disadvantage. This finding of twin-singleton IQ differences is a striking demonstration of the potency of prenatal effects.

The season of the year in which the child is born also affects intellig-ence, the summer months being the most advantageous time and winter the least. The reason for this seasonal variation in IQ is still unknown, but a likely hypothesis is that there are variations in dietary habits at various seasons which would affect maternal nutrition. Discovery of the precise mechanisms through which season of birth affects intellectual development is an important subject for future research.

A British psychologist, Dennis Stott (1966), has discovered impressive evidence that various forms of prenatal stress, such as an abnormal degree of physical and emotional stress on the mother during the later stages of pregnancy, can have a variety of adverse effects on the psychological develop-ment of the child. It was found, for example, that a much higher percentage of children who are problems in school were born to mothers whose pregnancies were stressful in one way or another. According to Stott, one of the common-est consequences of the subtle congenital impairment due to prenatal stress is juvenile delinquency in all its various forms. Stott believes there are genetically determined individual differences in susceptibility to brain damage through prenatal stress. The stress itself does not cause the damage in any direct way but triggers genetically determined mechanisms which bring about subtle impairments of the fetus, particularly in the brain. For reasons that cannot be elaborated upon here, this genetic triggering mechanism is a result of natural selection and evolution and at one stage of our remote past it had survival value for the species. The existence of a genetic mechanism of this type has been established in many animal species. In the past, congenital impairment of the type described by Stott resulted in much higher rates of infant mortality than we have today. Medical advances have increased the chances of survival probably much more than they have decreased congenital impairment. Slightly more than a century ago a male child born in America had four chances in ten of dying before age 20; today the chances are only four in 100. What are the implications of this? Stott points out: "The paradoxical result is that, so long as the crucial importance of the prenatal phase for the future development of the child remains unrecognized, we shall have to reconcile ourselves to having an increasing number of disturbed children and also of potential delinquents."

Abdominal Decompression

The most important question, of course, is whether we can do much of anything about the quality of the prenatal environment beyond assuring good nutrition and hygiene during pregnancy. There is now evidence that the prenatal environment can be manipulated in ways that have important favorable consequences for the child's mental development. The technique, known as abdominal decompression, was invented by a professor of obstetrics (Heyns, 1963), originally for the purpose of making women more comfortable in the last months of their pregnancy and to facilitate labor and delivery. For about an hour a day during the last months of pregnancy the woman is placed in a device which creates a partial vacuum around her abdomen. This device greatly reduces the intrauterine pressure. The device is also used during labor up to the moment of delivery. Although invented for only obstetrical purposes, this practice was found to affect the child's development, and this may well become its most important use. Heyns has now used the procedure on over 400 women. Their children, when compared with appropriate control groups who have not received the treatment, show more rapid development in the first years of life and manifest overall superiority in tests of perceptual -motor development -- tests of the kind that measure infant "intelligence." The children sit up earlier, walk earlier, talk earlier, and seem generally more precocious than their siblings or other control children whose mothers have not been so treated. We do not yet know if this general superiority persists into later childhood or adulthood, but there is good reason to believe that some substantial overall gain should persist. At two years of age the children in Heyns's experiment had developmental quotients some 30 points higher than the control children (with a mean of 100 and standard deviation of 15). The explanation for the effects of abdominal decompression on early development, according to Heyns, is that the reduction of intrauterine pressure results in a more optimal blood supply to the fetal brain and also lessens the chances of brain damage during labor. The pressure on the infant's head is reduced from about 22 pounds to about 8 pounds. The obvious potential importance of this work warrants much further research on the postnatal psychological effects of abdominal decompression.

Postnatal Environmental Influences

The postnatal environmental influences on intellectual development may not be as easy to manipulate as one might expect, mainly because the total individual differences variance attributable to this source is a result of a multitude of small but significant effects. As we saw in Table 1, about 40 percent of the environmental variance in IQ is due to influences within the family. No one knows how such influences could be systematically controlled. For example, birth order is one of the sources of this variance; first-born children on the average have slightly higher IQs than later born children. The spacing of children is another source of variance; children spaced two or more years apart have an advantage over those spaced less than two years apart. Family size is another source of variance, larger families producing lower IQs. The presence or absence of the father in the home, which is often

given as an explanation for the lower IQs of disadvantaged children, has not
been upheld by large scale research directed at answering this question.
The father's presence may have other desirable influences, but the independent effect of his presence or absence on his children's IQs is nil (Wilson,
1966).

It can be estimated that the total effect of all these home influences
working in the same direction amounts to about 8 to 10 points of IQ. It is
interesting to note in this connection that the average difference between
identical twins reared apart is about 6 IQ points, and the largest difference ever reported between a pair of identical twins reared apart, out of a
total of over 150 such cases reported in the literature, is 24 IQ points
(Newman, Freeman, & Holzinger, 1937).

What about children reared in extremely deprived environments, in which
there is extremely little stimulation of any kind during the first few years
of life? We know that such conditions can result in very low IQs, but the
deprivation apparently necessary to cause decrements of as much as 20 or 30
IQ points must be more extreme than can be found among almost any children
who are free to interact with other children or to run about out-of-doors.
Also, fortunately, there is good evidence that even the most severe forms
of deprivation in the first years of life do not preclude the later attainment of an average level of IQ, scholastic attainment, and social competence
(Skeels, 1966; Davis, 1947). Children reared for the first 18 months to two
years in cribs with sheeting on the sides to allow no view and fed with
propped bottles and with almost no human contacts, when placed in ordinary
middle-class homes, have shown a boost of about 30 IQ points within the first
year of placement, with no further appreciable gain in IQ. But the final
distribution of IQs in this group and their later adult behavior is indis-
tinguishable from that of the general population (Skeels, 1966). A girl
reared for the first six years of her life in an attic, without exposure even
to human speech, had an IQ of about 25 when discovered by the authorities.
After two years in a good environment she was of average mental ability for
her age and at age 8 her scholastic performance was on a par with that of her
classmates of the same age (Davis, 1947).

These findings are consistent with the research of Harlow (1967) on the
effects of extreme restriction of environmental stimulation in the first
year of life in monkeys. These isolated monkeys take somewhat longer than
normally reared monkeys to overcome their fear of the apparatus used for
testing their mental abilities, but once they overcome their fear, they are
as intellectually able as are monkeys of the same age reared in open cages.

In short, psychologists have not yet found any postnatal environmental
effects short of extreme environmental isolation which have any marked
systematic influence on the IQ. The quality of the mother-child interaction
is believed to affect the child's mental development, but the extent of this
influence is not yet clear since the results of most studies (e.g. Hess &
Shipman, 1965) have not separated the effects of the mother's intelligence
from the quality of her interaction with her children. We do know, however,
that the IQs of adopted children correlate not at all with the IQs of their
foster mothers but correlate with their true mothers' IQs to about the

same degree as children who are reared by their true mothers (Honzik, 1957).

The Improvement of Scholastic Performance

At the present time I would conclude from the above facts that educators should not concern themselves with attempting to raise IQs as such. The best evidence indicates that the means for changing intelligence per se lie in the province of biology rather than in psychology or education. I would act according to this conclusion until evidence to the contrary comes forth.

A more realistic aim is to boost school performance directly. As we saw in Table 1, much of the variance in school achievement is due to family influences which are manifest in the child's behavior as interests, values, motivation, and the like. The middle-class child, unlike the disadvantaged child, gets more help with school work at home. Middle-class children, in effect, have a private tutor in the parent. This is extremely important in getting the child over the "humps" in his school work. Disadvantaged children who fail to receive individual parental help with school work and who do not have the experience of interacting with the parent in ways that promote an interest in learning, reading, and the other kinds of things children have to do in school, should be provided with such help and interaction. High school and college students are probably the best recruits for this kind of work.

Intelligence and Learning Ability

My current research at Berkeley is aimed at analyzing by means of the laboratory techniques of experimental psychology the ways in which disadvantaged children differ from middle-class children in their learning abilities when they begin school. In addition to measuring children's IQs and school achievement, we are measuring their ability to learn in the laboratory. This research has been described in detail elsewhere (Jensen, 1968).

One of our findings, I believe, is of major significance. It has been confirmed in several different studies, so that I can report it with considerable confidence in its validity and generality.

The finding is this: Children called disadvantaged who are in the IQ range below 90 are very different in their learning abilities from middle-class children in this same IQ range. Lower-class children in the low IQ range have markedly greater capacity for associative learning than do middle-class children of below-average IQ. It is a serious mistake to judge low-IQ and low-achieving disadvantaged children in terms of what we know about the overall abilities of their middle-class counterparts in IQ and school performance. The disadvantaged children have abilities for learning which make them actually much more advantaged than middle-class children of the same IQ. The same thing is not true, however, in the average and above average IQ range. Children from disadvantaged backgrounds whose IQs are in the average range or above appear to be no different in learning ability from middle-class children. I believe that one of the worst mistakes of educators and of our programs of compensatory education is that they tend to deal with disadvantaged children as if they were essentially like middle-class children with low IQs. But we are finding that they are very different indeed. The difference, I believe, is not due to cultural deprivation or to low socioeconomic status or to cultural bias in IQ tests. The difference is in their pattern of abilities. They have learning abilities that our IQ tests do not measure and which are not being put to use by our present methods of instruction. Literal equality of educational opportunity -- if interpreted to mean that we treat all children exactly alike -- makes as much sense as a doctor giving all his patients exactly the same prescription. Even giving every patient different amounts of the same medicine would be disastrous. The parallel in education is to be avoided, also.

We know from laboratory research on learning and from training methods now being developed in the Armed Forces that there is no single instructional procedure that is optimal for all individuals. Optimal educational results are produced by designing instruction in accord with individual differences, and this means something much more radical than merely having slow and fast tracks in school or simply allowing some students to take more time than others to learn the same amount of subject matter, taught to all students in the same way. The educational plight of the disadvantaged, I am convinced, is the result of our not having taken individual differences seriously enough. We have acted as though human abilities were distributed along only one dimension: that everyone learns in the same way, but that some are merely slower than others. The whole methodology of teaching the so-called slow learner has grown up around teaching middle-class slow learners, and the one thing our research now makes us most sure of is that middle-class slow learners have a different pattern of abilities -- a basically less advantageous pattern from the standpoint of occupational attainment -- from lower-class children who also achieve poorly in school under the present conditions of instruction. The blocks to learning exist primarily in the school, and the educability of the disadvantaged will have to be improved largely in the school itself, rather than by prevailing upon the parents of disadvantaged children to do a better job of child rearing or by trying to get to the child earlier and earlier in his life in order to make him over into something more like the middle-class child who responds relatively favorably to the school environment as it is now constituted.

Schools should by all means be as good as we know how to make them. But when equality of educational opportunity becomes interpreted as uniformity of facilities, instructional methods, and educational aims, I think we now know enough to say that we are on the wrong track. Diversity, rather than uniformity, of approaches and aims is the key to improving education for the disadvantaged.

The vast Federal funds appropriated for experimental educational programs under the 1965 Education Act testify to the public's willingness to support programs for educational improvement. About 80 percent of these funds were authorized for improving the education of the disadvantaged. But a billion dollars a year and the employment of nearly 400,000 persons in Head Start and other compensatory education programs have not shown signs of producing the promised results or, indeed, of any positive results at all with respect to scholastic achievement. The massive Coleman report of the U. S. Office of

Education, furthermore, reports that, contrary to a widespread belief, the schools attended by disadvantaged children do not differ in material terms -- qualifications and salaries of teachers, adequacy and age of buildings, etc. -- from those attended by other children. In fact, it was found that the correlation between these school factors and educational achievement was negligible (Coleman, et al., 1966). We can only conclude that what is required is not just _more_ of the same, but something different, _radically_ different.

If asked to prognosticate the future trends that will improve education for all segments of our population, I would say they will take two main forms: (_a_) increased diversity of instructional procedures, aided by the technology of programmed and computerized instruction and based upon full recognition of differences in patterns of individual differences in the structure of learning abilities, and (_b_) a re-evaluation of the criteria of appropriate educational attainment for full participation in the responsibilities and benefits of our society. When we come really to _respect_ individual differences, rather than trying to minimize their importance in the educational enterprise, we will have made the first great stride toward improving education for _all_ children.

References

Coleman, J. S., et al. Equality of educational opportunity. U. S. Dept. of Health, Education, and Welfare, 1966.

Davis, K. Final note on a case of extreme isolation. Amer. J. Sociol., 1947, 57, 432-457.

Falconer, D. S. An introduction to quantitative genetics. New York: Ronald Press, 1960.

Harlow, H., & Harlow, M. The young monkeys. Psychol. Today, 1967, 1, 4047.

Harrell, R. F., Woodyard, E., & Gates, A. I. The effects of mothers' diets on the intelligence of offspring. New York: Bureau of Publications, Teachers College, 1955.

Hess, R. D. & Shipman, V. Early experience and the socialization of cognitive modes in children. Child Developm., 1965, 36, 869-886.

Heyns, O. S. Abdominal decompression. Johannesburg: Witwatersrand Univer. Press, 1963.

Hill, A. C., & Jaffee, F. S. Negro fertility and family size preferences. In Parsons, T., & Clark, K. B. (Eds.) The Negro American. Cambridge: Houghton-Mifflin, 1966, Pp. 134-159.

Honzik, M. P. Developmental studies of parent-child resemblance in intelligence. Child Developm., 1957, 28, 215-228.

Jensen, A. R. Estimation of the limits of heritability of traits by comparison of monozygotic and dizygotic twins. Proceedings of the National Academy of Sciences, 1967, 58, 149-157.

Jensen, A. R. Learning ability, intelligence, and educability. In V. Allen (Ed.) Psychological aspects of poverty. Glencoe, Illinois: Free Press, 1968.

Moynihan, D. P. Employment, income, and the ordeal of the Negro family. In Parsons, T., & Clark, K. B. (Eds.) The Negro American. Cambridge: Houghton-Mifflin, 1966. Pp. 134-159.

Newman, H. H., Freeman, F. N., & Holzinger, K. J. Twins: A study of heredity and environment. Chicago: Univ. of Chicago Press, 1937.

Reed, E. W., & Reed, S. C. Mental retardation: A family study. Philadelphia: W. B. Saunders Co., 1965.

Skeels, H. M. Adult status of children with contrasting early life experiences: a follow-up study. Child Develpm. Monogr., 1966, 31, No. 3, Serial No. 105.

Stott, D. H. Studies of troublesome children. New York: Humanities Press, 1966.

Wilson, A. B. Educational consequences of segregation in a California community. Univ. of California, Berkeley: Survey Research Center, Dec., 1966.

HOW CHILDREN
DEVELOP INTELLECTUALLY

J. McVICKER HUNT

Professor of Psychology, University of Illinois

THE TASK of maximizing the intellectual potential of our children has acquired new urgency. Two of the top challenges of our day lie behind this urgency. First, the rapidly expanding role of technology, now taking the form of automation, decreases opportunity for persons of limited competence and skills while it increases opportunity for those competent in the use of written language, in mathematics, and in problem solving. Second, the challenge of eliminating racial discrimination requires not only equality of employment opportunity and social recognition for persons of equal competence, but also an equalization of the opportunity to develop that intellectual capacity and skill upon which competence is based.

During most of the past century anyone who entertained the idea of increasing the intellectual capacity of human beings was regarded as an unrealistic "do-gooder." Individuals, classes, and races were considered to be what they were because either God or their inheritance had made them that way; any attempt to raise the intelligence quotient (IQ) through experience met with contempt. Man's nature has not changed since World War II, but

some of our conceptions of his nature have been changing rapidly. These changes make sensible the hope that, with improved understanding of early experience, we might counteract some of the worst effects of cultural deprivation and raise substantially the average level of intellectual capacity. This paper will attempt to show how and why these conceptions are changing, and will indicate the implications of these changes for experiments designed to provide corrective early experiences to children and to feed back information on ways of counteracting cultural deprivation.

Changing Beliefs

Fixed Intelligence. The notion of fixed intelligence has roots in Darwin's theory that evolution takes place through the variations in strains and species which enable them to survive to reproduce themselves. Finding in this the implicit assumption that adult characteristics are determined by heredity, Francis Galton, Darwin's younger cousin, reasoned that the improvement of man lies not in education, or euthenics, but in the selection of superior parents for the next generation—in other words, through eugenics. To this end, he founded an anthropometric laboratory to give simple sensory and motor tests (which failed, incidentally, to correlate with the qualities in which he was interested), established

The work on which this article is based has been supported by the Russell Sage Foundation, the Carnegie Foundation, and the Commonwealth Fund; and its writing by a grant (MH K6–18567) from the U.S. Public Health Service.

eugenics society, and imparted his beliefs to his student, J. McKeen Cattell, who brought the tests to America.

About the same time G. Stanley Hall, an American who without knowing Darwin became an ardent evolutionist, imparted a similar faith in fixed intelligence to his students, among them such future leaders of the intelligence testing movement as H. H. Goddárd, F. Kuhlmann, and Lewis Terman.[1] This faith included a belief in the constant intelligence quotient. The IQ, originally conceived by the German psychologist Wilhelm Stern, assumes that the rate of intellectual development can be specified by dividing the average age value of the tests passed (mental age) by the chronological age of the child.

The considerable debate over the constancy of the IQ might have been avoided if the work of the Danish geneticist Johannsen had been as well known in America as that of Gregor Mendel, who discovered the laws of hereditary transmission. Johannsen distinguished the genotype, which can be known only from the ancestry or progeny of an individual, from the phenotype, which can be directly observed and measured. Although the IQ was commonly treated as if it were a genotype (innate capacity), it is in fact a phenotype and, like all phenotypes (height, weight, language spoken), is a product of the genotype and the circumstances with which it has interacted.[1]

Johannsen's distinction makes possible the understanding of evidence dissonant with the notion of

An infant undertaking a test for brightness and coordination at the National Institutes of Health. Infant tests, according to current theory, have meaning in relation to a child's present development but little predictive value.

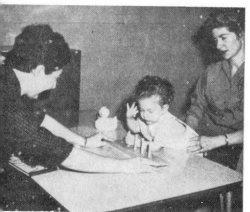

fixed intelligence. For instance, identical twins (with the same genotype) have been found to show differences in IQ of as much as 24 points when reared apart, and the degree of difference appears to be related to the degree of dissimilarity of the circumstances in which they were reared. Also, several investigators have reported finding substantial improvement in IQ after enrichment of experience, but their critics have attributed this to defects in experimental control.

When results of various longitudinal studies available after World War II showed very low correlation between the preschool IQ and IQ at age 18, the critics responded by questioning the validity of the infant tests, even though Nancy Bayley [2] had actually found high correlations among tests given close together in time. Blaming the tests tended to hide the distinction that should have been made between cross-sectional validity and predictive validity: What a child does in the testing situation correlates substantially with what he will do in other situations, but attempting to predict what an IQ will be at age 18 from tests given at ages from birth to 4 years, before the schools have provided at least some standardization of circumstances, is like trying to predict how fast a feather will fall in a hurricane.

Predetermined Development. Three views of embryological and psychological development have held sway in the history of thought: preformationism, predeterminism, and interactionism.[1] As men gave up preformationism, the view that the organs and features of adulthood are preformed in the seed, they turned to predeterminism, the view that the organs and features of adulthood are hereditarily determined. G. Stanley Hall in emphasizing the concept of recapitulation—that the development of the individual summarizes the evolution of his species—drew the predeterministic moral that each behavior pattern manifest in a child is a natural stage with which no one should interfere. The lifework of Arnold Gesell exemplifies the resulting concern with the typical or average that has shaped child psychology during the past half century.

The theory of predetermined development got support from Coghill's finding that frogs and salamanders develop behaviorally as they mature anatomically, from head-end tailward and from inside out, and from Carmichael's finding that the swimming patterns of frogs and salamanders develop equally well whether inhibited by chloretone in the water or stimulated by vibration. Such findings appeared to generalize to children: The acquisition of such skills as walking, stair climbing, and buttoning cannot be speeded by training or exercise; Hopi children reared on cradleboards learn to walk at the same age as Hopi children reared with arms and legs free.[3]

Again, however, there was dissonant evidence. Although Cruze found that chicks kept in the dark decreased their pecking errors during the first 5 days after hatching—a result consonant with predeterminism—he also found that chicks kept in the dark for 20 days failed to improve their pecking. Moreover, studies of rats and dogs, based on the theorizing of Donald Hebb, suggest that the importance of infantile experience increases up the phylogenetic scale.[4]

Evidence that such findings may apply to human beings comes from studies by Goldfarb[5] which indicate that institutional rearing (where the environment is relatively restricted and unresponsive) results in lower intelligence, less ability to sustain a task, and more problems in interpersonal relations than foster-home rearing (where the environment provides more varied experiences and responsiveness). Wayne Dennis[6] has found that in a Teheran orphanage, where changes in ongoing stimulation were minimal, 60 percent of the 2-year-olds could not sit alone and 85 percent of the 4-year-olds could not walk alone. Such a finding dramatizes the great effect preverbal experience can have on even the rate of locomotor development. Presumably the effect on intellectual functions would be even greater.

Static Brain Function. In 1900, when C. Lloyd Morgan and E. L. Thorndike were attempting to explain learning in terms of stimulus-response bonds, they used the newly invented telephone as a mechanical model of the brain's operation. Thus they envisioned the brain as a static switchboard through which each stimulus could be connected with a variety of responses, which in turn could become the stimuli for still other responses.

Soon objective stimulus-response methodology produced evidence dissonant with this switchboard model theory, implying some kind of active processes going on between the ears. But it took the programing of electronic computers to clarify the general nature of the requirements for solving logical problems. Newell, Shaw, and Simon[7] describe three major components of these requirements: (1) memories, or information, coded and stored; (2) operations of a logical sort which can act upon the memories; and (3) hierarchically arranged programs of these operations for various purposes.

Pribram[8] found a likely place for the brain's equivalents of such components within the intrinsic portions of the cerebrum which have no direct connections with either incoming fibers from the receptors of experience or outgoing fibers to the muscles and glands.

So, the electronic computer supplies a more nearly adequate mechanical model for brain functioning. Thus, experience may be regarded as programing the intrinsic portions of the cerebrum for learning and problem solving, and intellectual capacity at any given time may be conceived as a function of the nature and quality of this programing.[1, 9]

As Hebb[4] has pointed out, the portion of the brain directly connected with neither incoming nor outgoing fibers is very small in animals such as frogs and salamanders, whence came most of the evidence supporting the belief in predetermined development. The increasing proportion of the intrinsic portion of the brain in higher animals suggests an anatomic basis for the increasing role of infantile experience in development, as evidenced by the greater effect of rearing on problem solving ability in dogs than in rats.[9] Frogs and salamanders have a relatively higher capacity for regeneration than do mammals. This suggests that the chemical factors in the genes may have more complete control in these lower forms than they have further up the phylogenic scale.

Motivation by Need, Pain, and Sex. Our conception of motivation is also undergoing change. Although it has long been said that man does not live by bread alone, most behavioral scientists and physiologists have based their theorizing on the assumption that he does. Freud popularized the statement that "all behavior is motivated." He meant motivated by painful stimulation, homeostatic need, and sexual appetite or by acquired motives based on these; and this concept has generally been shared by physiologists and academic behavioral theorists.

Undoubtedly, painful stimulation and homeostatic need motivate all organisms, as sex motivates all mammalian organisms, but the assertion that all behavior is so motivated implies that organisms become quiescent in the absence of painful stimulation, homeostatic need, and sexual stimulation. Observation stubbornly indicates that they do not: Young animals and children are most likely to play in the absence of such motivation; young rats, cats, dogs monkeys, chimpanzees, and humans work for nothing more substantial than the opportunity to perceive, manipulate, or explore novel circumstances his evidence implies that there must be some additional basis for motivation.

Reflex *vs.* Feedback. A change in our conception of the functional unit of the nervous system from the reflex arc to the feedback loop helps to suggest the nature of this other motivating mechanism. The conception of the reflex arc has its anatomical foundations in the Bell-Magendie law, based on Bell's discovery of separate ventral and dorsal roots of the spinal nerves and on Magendie's discovery that the dorsal roots have sensory or "input" functions while the ventral roots have motor or "output" functions. But the Bell-Magendie law was an overgeneralization, for motor fibers have been discovered within the presumably sensory dorsal roots, and sensory fibers have been discovered within the presumably motor ventral roots.

The most important argument against the reflex as the functional unit of the nervous system comes from the direct evidence of feedback in both sensory input and motor output. The neural activity that results when cats are exposed to a tone is markedly reduced when they are exposed to the sight of mice or the smell of fish, thus dramatizing feedback in sensory input. Feedback in motor output is dramatized by evidence that sensory input from the muscle spindles modulates the rate of motor firing to the muscles, thereby controlling the strength of contraction.[9]

Incongruity as Motivation. The feedback loop which constitutes a new conceptual unit of neural function supplies the basis for a new mechanism of motivation. Miller, Galanter, and Pribram [10] have called the feedback loop the Test-Operate-Test-Exit (TOTE) unit. Such a TOTE unit is, in principle, not unlike the room thermostat. The temperature at which the thermostat is set supplies a standard against which the temperature of the room is continually being tested. If the room temperature falls below this standard, the test yields an *incongruity* which starts the furnace to "operate," and it continues to operate until the room temperature has reached this standard. When the test yields *congruity*, the furnace stops operating and the system makes its exit. Similarly, a living organism is free to be otherwise motivated once such a system has made its exit.

Several classes of similarly operating standards can be identified for human beings. One might be described as the "comfort standard" in which incongruity is equivalent to pain. Another consists of those homeostatic standards for hunger (a low of glycogen in the bloodstream) and for thirst (a high level of hydrogen ion concentration within the blood and interstitial fluids). A third class, which stretches the concept of incongruity somewhat, is related to sex.

Other standards derive from the organism's informational interaction with the environment. Thus, a fourth class appears to consist of ongoing inputs, and, just as "one never hears the clock until it has stopped," any change in these ongoing inputs brings attention and excitement. Repeated encounters with such changes of input lead to expectations, which constitute a fifth class of standards. A sixth class consists of plans quite independent of painful stimulation, homeostatic need, or sex. Ideals constitute a seventh class.

There is evidence that incongruity with such standards will instigate action and produce excitement.[9] There is also evidence that an optimum of such incongruity exists. Too little produces boredom as it did among McGill students who would remain lying quietly in a room no more than 3 days, although they were paid $20 a day to do so.[9] Too much produces fearful emotional stress, as when a baby chimpanzee sees his keeper in a Halloween mask,[11] a human infant encounters strangers, or primitive men see an eclipse.

While this optimum of incongruity is still not well understood, it seems to involve the matching of incoming information with standards based on information already coded and stored within the cerebrum.[9] Probably only the individual himself can choose a source of input which provides him with an optimum of incongruity. His search for this optimum, however, explains that "growth motivation" which Froebel, the founder of the kindergarten movement, postulated and which John Dewey borrowed; and it may be the basic motivation underlying intellectual growth and the search for knowledge. Such motivation may be characterized as "intrinsic" because it inheres in the organism's informational interaction with the environment.

Emotional *vs.* Cognitive Experience. Another fundamental change is in the importance attributed to early—and especially very early—preverbal experience. Traditionally, very little significance had been attached to preverbal experience. When consciousness was believed to control conduct, infantile experience, typically not remembered, was regarded as having hardly any effect on adult behavior. Moreover, when development was conceived to be pre-determined, infantile experience could have little importance. While Freud [12] believed that preverbal experiences were important, he argued that their importance derived from the instinctive impulses arising from painful stimulation, homeostatic need, and especially pleasure striving, which he saw as sexual in nature.

Freud's work spread the belief that early emotional experiences are important while early cognitive experiences are not. It now appears that the opposite may possibly be more nearly true. Objective studies furnish little evidence that the factors important according to Freud's theory of psychosexual development are significant.[13, 14] Even the belief that infants are sensitive organisms readily traumatized by painful stimulation or intense homeostatic need have been questioned as the result of studies involving the shocking of nursling rats.

Rats shocked before weaning are found to be less likely than rats left unmolested in the maternal nest to urinate and defecate in, or to hesitate entering, unfamiliar territory, and more likely to be active there. Moreover, as adults, rats shocked before weaning often require stronger shocks to instigate escape activity than do rats left unmolested; they also show less fixative effect from being shocked at the choice-point in a T-maze.[15] Evidence that children from low socioeconomic and educational classes, who have frequently known painful stimulation, are less likely to be fearful than middle class children, who have seldom known painful stimulation, suggests that the findings of these rat studies may apply to human beings.[16]

While such observations have contradicted the common conception of the importance of early emotional experience, the experiments stemming from Hebb's theorizing [4] have repeatedly demonstrated the importance of early perceptual and cognitive experience. At earlier phases of development, the variety of circumstances encountered appears to be most important; somewhat later, the responsiveness of the environment to the infant's activities appears to be central; and at a still later phase, the opportunity to understand the causation of mechanical and social relationships seems most significant.

In this connection, a study by Baldwin, Kalhorn, and Breese [17] found that the IQ's of 4- to 7-year-old children tend to increase with time if parental discipline consists of responsive and realistic explanations, but tend to fall if parental discipline consists of nonchalant unresponsiveness or of demands for obedience for its own sake, with painful stimulati as the alternative.

Motor Response and Receptor Input. One more i portant traditional belief about psychological c velopment which may have to be changed concer the relative importance of motor response and ceptor input for the development of the autonomo central processes which mediate intellectual capacit A century ago, the "apperceptive mass" conceived Herbart, a German educational psychologist, w regarded as the product of previous perceptual i put; and Froebel and Montessori both stressed se sory training. However, after World War I, t focus of laboratory learning-studies on respons coupled with the notion of brain function as a stat switchboard, gradually shifted the emphasis fro the perceptual input to the response output. It hard to make the great importance attributed to t response side jibe with the following findings:

1. Hopi infants reared on cradleboards, where t movements of arms and legs are inhibited durin waking hours, learn to walk at the same age as Ho infants reared with arms and legs free.[3]

2. Eighty-five percent of the 4-year-olds in a T heran orphanage, where variations in auditory ar visual input were extremely limited, did not wa alone.[6]

Such observations and those of Piaget [18, 19] sugge that the repeated correction of expectations derivin from perceptual impressions and from cognitive a commodations gradually create the central process mediating the logical operations of thought. Woh will [20] and Flavel [21] have assembled evidence whi relates the inferential processes of thought to e perience and have given this evidence some form theoretical organization.

Counteracting Cultural Deprivation

The intellectual inferiority apparent among many children of parents of low educational ar socioeconomic status, regardless of race, is alrea evident by the time they begin kindergarten or fir grade at age 5 or 6.[22] Such children are apt to ha various linguistic liabilities: limited vocabularie poor articulation, and syntactical deficiencies that a revealed in the tendency to rely on unusually sho sentences with faulty grammar.[23] They also sho perceptual deficiencies in the sense that they reco nize fewer objects and situations than do most mi dle-class children. And perhaps more importar they usually have fewer interests than do the middl ass children who are the pace setters in the schools. Moreover, the objects recognized by and the interests of children typical of the lower class differ from those of children of the middle class. These deficiencies give such children the poor start which so commonly handicaps them ever after in scholastic competition.

So long as it was assumed that intelligence is fixed and development is predetermined, the intellectual inferiority of children from families of low educational and socioeconomic status had to be considered an unalterable consequence of their genes. With the changes in our conception of man's intellectual development, outlined in the foregoing pages, there emerges a hope of combating such inferiority by altering, for part of their waking hours, the conditions under which such children develop. The question is "how?"

Clues From Intrinsic Motivation. A tentative answer, worthy at least of investigative demonstration, is suggested by the existence of a change during the preschool years in the nature of what I have called "intrinsic motivation." An approximation of the character of this change has been supplied by the observations which Piaget made on the development of his three children.[18, 19, 24] At least three stages in the development of intrinsic motivation appear. These may be characteristic of an organism's progressive relationship with any new set of circumstances and seem to be stages in infant development only because the child is encountering so many new sets of circumstances during his first 2 or 3 years.

In the first stage the infant is essentially responsive. He is motivated, of course, by painful stimulation, homeostatic need, and, in Freud's sense, by sex. Russian investigators have shown that the orienting response is ready-made at birth in all mammals, including human beings.[25] Thus, any changes in the ongoing perceptual input will attract attention and excite the infant. During this phase each of the ready-made sensorimotor organizations—sucking, looking, listening, vocalizing, grasping, and wiggling—changes, by something like Pavlov's conditioning process, to become coordinated with others. Thus, something heard becomes something to look at, something to look at becomes something to grasp, and something to grasp becomes something to suck. This phase ends with a "landmark of transition" in which the infant, having repeatedly encountered certain patterns of stimulus change, tries actively to retain or regain them.[24]

During the second stage the infant manifests interest in, and efforts to retain, something newly recognized as familiar—a repeatedly encountered pattern of change in perceptual input. The infant's intentional effort is familiar to anyone who has jounced a child on his knee and then stopped his jouncing only to find the child making a comparable motion, as if to invite the jouncing adult to continue. Regaining the newly recognized activity commonly brings forth such signs of delight as the smile and the laugh, and continued loss brings signs of distress. The effort to retain the newly recognized may well account for the long hours of hand watching and babbling commonly observed during the child's third, fourth, and fifth months. This second stage ends when, with these repeated encounters, the child becomes bored with the familiar and turns his interest to whatever is novel in familiar situations.[24]

The third stage begins with this interest in the novel within a familiar context, which typically becomes noticeable during the last few months of the first year of life. Piaget[18] describes its beginnings with the appearance of throwing, but it probably can be found earlier. While he throws the child intentionally shifts his attention from the act of throwing to the trajectory of the object that he has thrown.

Interest in the novel is also revealed in the infant's increasing development of new plans through an active, creative process of groping, characterized by C. Lloyd Morgan as "trial-and-error." It also shows in the child's increasing attempts to imitate new vocal patterns and gestures.[19, 24]

Interest in the new is the infant's basis for "growth motivation." It has also been found in animals, particularly in an experiment in which rats in a figure-eight maze regularly changed their preference to the more complex loop.

Thus Piaget's[18] aphorism, "the more a child has seen and heard, the more he wants to see and hear," may be explained. The more different visual and auditory changes the child encounters during the first stage, the more of these will he recognize with interest during the second stage. The more he recognizes during the second stage, the more of these will provide novel features to attract him during the third stage.

Effects of Social Environment. Such development prepares the child to go on developing. But continuing development appears to demand a relationship with adults who enable the infant to pursue his locomotor and manipulative intentions and who answer his endless questions of "what's that?", "is it a 'this' or a 'that'?", and "why is it a 'this' or a 'that'?". Without these supports during the second, third, and fourth years of life, a child cannot continue to profit no matter how favorable his circumstances during his first year.

Although we still know far too little about intellectual development to say anything with great confidence, it is unlikely that most infants in families of low socioeconomic status suffer great deprivation during their first year. Since one distinguishing feature of poverty is crowding, it is conceivable that an infant may actually encounter a wider variety of visual and auditory inputs in conditions of poverty than in most middle- or upper-class homes. This should facilitate the intellectual development of the infant during his first year.

During the second year, however, crowded living conditions would probably hamper development. As an infant begins to move under his own power, to manipulate things, and to throw things, he is likely to get in the way of adults who are apt already to be ill-tempered from their own discomforts and frustrations. Such situations are dramatized in Lewis's "The Children of Sanchez," an anthropological study of life in poverty.[26] In such an atmosphere, a child's opportunity to carry out the activities required for his locomotor and manipulative development must almost inevitably be sharply curbed.

Moreover, late in his second or early in his third year, after he has developed a number of pseudo-words and achieved the "learning set" that "things have names," the child in a crowded, poverty-stricken family probably meets another obstacle: His questions too seldom bring suitable answers, and too often bring punishment that inhibits further questioning. Moreover, the conditions that originally provided a rich variety of input for the very young infant now supply a paucity of suitable playthings and models for imitation.

The effects of a lower-class environment on a child's development may become even more serious during his fourth and fifth years. Furthermore, the longer these conditions continue, the more likely the effects are to be lasting. Evidence from animal studies supports this: Tadpoles immobilized with chloretone for 8 days are not greatly hampered in the development of their swimming patterns, but immobilization for 13 days leaves their swimming patterns permanently impaired; chicks kept in darkness for as

Something new has attracted the attention of this child a day-care center where a variety of toys and manip latable objects stimulates the child's creative imaginati

many as 5 days show no apparent defects in th pecking responses, but keeping them in darkness 8 or more days results in chicks which never learn peck at all.[1]

Possible Counteracting Measures. Such observ tions suggest that if nursery schools or day-care ce ters were arranged for culturally deprived childr from age 4—or preferably from age 3—until time school at 5 or 6 some of the worst effects of th rearing might be substantially reduced.

Counteracting cultural deprivation at this sta of development might best be accomplished by givi the child the opportunity to encounter a wide varie of objects, pictures, and appropriate behavio models, and by giving him social approval for a propriate behavior. The setting should encoura him to indulge his inclinations to scrutinize and m nipulate the new objects as long as he is interest and should provide him with appropriate answe to his questions. Such varied experiences wou foster the development of representative image which could then be the referents for spoken wor and later for written language.

Children aged 3 and 4 should have the opportuni to hear people speak who provide syntactical mode of standard grammar. The behavioral models wou

A research-oriented nursery school in an old industrial neighborhood of Pittsburgh provides this little girl with an opportunity to play house, and a pediatric psychiatrist a chance to observe aspects of children's behavior.

lead gradually to interest in pictures, written words, and books. The objects provided and appropriate answers to the "why" questions would lead to interest in understanding the workings of things and the consequences of social conduct. Thus, the child might gradually overcome most of the typical handicaps of his lower-class rearing by the time he enters grade school.

There is a danger, however, in attempting to prescribe a remedy for cultural deprivation at this stage of knowledge. Any specific prescription of objects, pictures, behavioral models, and forms of social reinforcement may fail to provide that attractive degree of incongruity with the impressions which the toddler of the lower class has already coded and stored in the course of his experience. Moreover, what seem to be appropriate behavioral models may merely produce conflict. Therefore, it may be wise to reexamine the educational contributions of Maria Montessori.[27, 28] These have been largely forgotten in America, perhaps because they were until recently too dissonant with the dominant notions of motivation and the importance attributed to motor responses in development.

Montessori's contributions are especially interesting, despite some of the rigid orthodoxy that has crept into present-day Montessori practice, because she based her teaching methods on children's spontaneous interest in learning, that is, on "intrinsic motivation." Moreover, she stressed the importance

of teachers' observing children to discover what things would most interest them and most foster their growth. Further, she stressed the need to train the perceptual processes, or what we would today call the information processes. The coded information stored in culturally deprived children from lower-class backgrounds differs from that stored in children with middle-class backgrounds. This difference makes it dangerous for middle-class teachers to prescribe intuitively on the basis of their own experiences or of their experiences in teaching middle-class youngsters.

Montessori also broke the lockstep in the education of young children. She made no effort to keep them doing the same thing at the same time. Rather, each child was free to examine and work with whatever happened to interest him, for as long as he liked. It is commonly believed that the activity of preschoolers must be changed every 10 or 15 minutes or the children become bored. But Dorothy Canfield Fisher,[29] the novelist, who spent the winter of 1910–11 at Montessori's Casa de Bambini in Rome, observed that 3-year-olds there commonly remained engrossed in such mundane activities as buttoning and unbuttoning for 2 hours or more at a time. In such a setting the child has an opportunity to find those particular circumstances which match his own particular phase of development and which provide the proper degree of incongruity for intrinsic motivation. This may well have the corollary advantage of making learning fun and the school setting interesting and attractive.

Montessori also included children from 3 to 6 years old in the same group. In view of the changes that occur in intellectual development, this has the advantage of providing younger children with a variety of novel models for imitation while supplying older children with an opportunity to teach, an activity which provides many of its own rewards.

Conclusions. At this stage of history and knowledge, no one can blueprint a program of preschool enrichment that will with certainty be an effective antidote for the cultural deprivation of children. On the other hand, the revolutionary changes taking place in the traditional beliefs about the development of human capacity and motivation make it sensible to hope that a program of preschool enrichment may ultimately be made effective. The task calls for creative innovations and careful evaluative studies of their effectiveness.

Discoveries of effective innovations will contribute

also to the general theory of intellectual development and become significant for the rearing and education of all children. Effective innovations will also help to minimize those racial differences in school achievement which derive from cultural deprivation and so help to remove one stubborn obstacle in the way of racial integration.

Although it is likely that no society has ever made the most of the intellectual potential of its members, the increasing role of technology in our culture demands that we do better than others ever have. To do so we must become more concerned with intellectual development during the preschool years and especially with the effects of cultural deprivation.

[1] Hunt, J. McV.: Intelligence and experience. Ronald Press Co., New York. 1961.
[2] Bayley, Nancy: Mental growth in young children. *In* Thirty-ninth yearbook of the National Society for the Study of Education, part II. Public School Publishing Co., Bloomington, Ill. 1940.
[3] Dennis, W.; Dennis, Marsena G.: The effect of cradling practice upon the onset of walking in Hopi children. *Journal of Genetic Psychology,* vol. 56, 1940.
[4] Hebb, D. O.: The organization of behavior. John Wiley & Sons, New York. 1949.
[5] Goldfarb, W.: The effects of early institutional care on adolescent personality. *Journal of Experimental Education,* vol. 12, 1953.
[6] Dennis, W.: Causes of retardation among institutional children: Iran. *Journal of Genetic Psychology,* vol. 96, 1960.
[7] Newell A.; Shaw, J. C.; Simon, H. A.; Elements of a theory of human problem-solving. *Psychological Review,* vol. 65, 1958.
[8] Pribram, K. H.: A review of theory in physiological psychology. *Annual Review of Psychology,* vol. 11, 1960.
[9] Hunt, J. McV.: Motivation inherent in information processing and action. *In* Motivation and social interaction: cognitive determinants. (O. J. Harvey, ed.) Ronald Press Co., New York. 1963.
[10] Miller, G. A.; Galanter, E.; Pribram, K. H.: Plans and the structure of behavior. Henry Holt & Co., New York. 1960.
[11] Hebb, D. O.: On the nature of fear. *Psychological Review,* vol. 53, 1946.
[12] Freud, S.: Three contributions to the theory of sex. *In* The basic writings of Sigmund Freud. (A. A. Brill, ed.) Modern Library, New York. 1938.
[13] Hunt, J. McV.: Experimental psychoanalysis. *In* The encyclopedia of psychology. (P. L. Harriman, ed.) Philosophical Library, New York. 1946.
[14] Orlansky, H.: Infant care and personality. *Psychological Bulletin* vol. 46, 1949.
[15] Salama, A. A.; Hunt, J. McV.: "Fixation" in the rat as a function of infantile shocking, handling, and gentling. *Journal of Genetic Psychology,* vol. 100, 1964.
[16] Holmes, F. B.: An experimental study of the fears of young children. *In* Children's fears. (A. T. Jersild; F. B. Holmes.) Child Development Monographs, No. 20., Teachers College, Columbia University, New York. 1935.
[17] Baldwin, A. L.; Kalhorn, J.; Breese, F. H.: Patterns of parent behavior. *Psychological Monographs,* vol. 58, 1945.
[18] Piaget, J.: The origins of intelligence in children (1936). (Translated by Margaret Cook.) International Universities Press, New York. 1952.
[19] ——: Play, dreams, and imitation in childhood (1945). (Translation of *La formation du symbole chez l'enfant* by C. Gattegno and F. M. Hodgson.) W. W. Norton & Co., New York. 1951.
[20] Wohlwill, J. F.: Developmental studies of perception. *Psychological Bulletin,* vol. 57, 1960.
[21] Flavel, J. H.: The developmental psychology of Jean Piaget. D. Van Nostrand Co., New York. 1963.
[22] Kennedy, W. A., et al.: A normative sample of intelligence and achievement of Negro elementary school children in the Southeastern United States. *Monographs of the Society for Research in Child Development,* Serial No. 90, vol. 28, 1963.
[23] John, Vera P.: The intellectual development of slum children. *Merrill-Palmer Quarterly,* vol. 10, 1964.
[24] Hunt, J. McV.: Piaget's observations as a source of hypotheses concerning motivation. *Merrill-Palmer Quarterly,* vol. 9, 1963.
[25] Razran, G.: The observable unconscious and the inferable conscious in current Soviet psychophysiology: interoceptive conditioning, semantic conditioning, and the orienting reflex. *Psychological Review,* vol. 68, 1961.
[26] Lewis, O.: The children of Sanchez. Random House, New York. 1961.
[27] Montessori, Maria: The Montessori method (1907). Frederick A. Stokes, New York. 1912.
[28] Rambusch, Nancy McC.: Learning how to learn: an American approach to Montessori. Helicon Press, Baltimore, Md. 1962.
[29] Fisher, Dorothy Canfield: A Montessori mother. Henry Holt Co., New York. 1912.

IMPLICATIONS OF A LEARNING DISABILITY APPROACH FOR TEACHING EDUCABLE RETARDATES

by BARBARA BATEMAN

*T*HE purpose of this paper is to suggest some possible implications from learning disabilities research for application to the education of educable mentally handicapped (EMH) children. The work from which these suggestions are derived is for the most part currently in progress and therefore some of what follows is only speculative at this point. Our purpose here is not to provide answers, but to suggest paths for further exploration. Some of them may be fruitful avenues; some are undoubtedly dead-end streets.

The distinction between learning disability research and other research relevant to teaching mentally handicapped is very obscure, if in fact it exists at all. Recent surveys of research literature on how the mentally retarded learn reveal that our state of knowledge is really much more primitive than sheer numbers of studies could indicate. We know that retarded do learn, that much learning is related to MA and/or IQ, and that normals learn "better" than retardates do. However, direct evidence of how the classroom teacher of EMH can facilitate initial learning and retention is conspicuous by its absence.

One contribution of the learning disabilities approach has been in the matter of question-asking. When we in learning disabilities are faced with a child of above average intelligence, from a "good" home, who's been in school four years and can't yet read, we have to first ask some questions. If we're to help him, the questions must be the right ones. We don't always ask the right ones immediately, but perhaps we're learning. We might ask, "Is he brain-injured?"

Often the neurologist will tell us, "Perhaps he has minimal, diffuse brain injury," but then perhaps so does his teacher! Or we might be told, "Yes, he definitely shows an abnormal EEG." Have we gained anything? Do we know any more about how to teach him than we did before?

Suppose we asked, "Is there undue sibling rivalry at home?" "Has he properly identified with his father?" And again imagine we get a definite opinion to the effect that the oedipal situation has not been resolved. Do we yet know how to teach him to read?

In short, while the organic condition of his brain and the condition of his libido or psyche or id or ego are undoubtedly very pertinent to some aspects of his functioning, we do not yet know enough to know how they relate to our job of classroom teaching. Now we are learning to ask a new set of questions—questions which have more educational significance. We ask whether he can sound blend? Can he form the necessary association or bond between the visual symbol we call a letter and the vocal response we call its sound? How is his auditory memory? Does he respond better to massed or distributed practice? Does he learn new rules readily but forget them even more readily? Does he comprehend slowly, but retain well? Can he apply a rule once it is learned? The answers to these kinds of questions do begin

This article was adapted from a paper presented at the 43rd Annual Convention of the Council for Exceptional Children in Portland, Oregon, April, 1965.

Mental Retardation, June, 1967, Vol.5, No.3, pp. 23-25.

to provide us with clues about how to teach him.

These types of questions point directly toward a second possible contribution of the learning disability approach to teaching EMH children, i.e., a rejuvenation of interest in actual learning processes and factors which help or hinder classroom learning. Attention is being given to the effects of the teacher's verbal behavior on certain types of thought processes in children (Gallagher, 1963). We have long been aware that the way a question is asked influences the type of answer offered, but this is now being systematically studied in such a way that we can apply this knowledge to the direct teaching of certain kinds of thinking. Similarly, more systematic attention is being focused on the effects of other environmental factors such as the amount and intensity of relevant and irrelevant cues present in the learning situation. Revived interest in and re-evaluation and application of principles of learning such as repetition, simultaneous multi-sensory approaches, retroactive and associative inhibition, distributed and massed practice, incidental learning, readiness, and feedback is also in evidence (Bryant, 1965).

Just one example of this kind of research which has particular implication to teaching EMH is Vergason's (1964) study in which he trained retarded and normal subjects on a paired associates learning task. Some pairs of words were barely learned and others were overlearned. When retention was checked after 30 days, the retarded remembered significantly fewer of the barely learned words, but remembered as many of the overlearned words as did the normal subjects. This study clearly suggests the importance of overlearning if we wish to increase the EMH child's retention of the material to which he has been exposed.

In a further, unpublished study, Vergason compared retardates' ability to learn sight vocabulary words by traditional teaching methods and by an automated teaching machine.

They learned the words equally well by either method, as measured by their recall the next day. But when they were retested at intervals up to four months, the words taught by the machine were clearly remembered better. Why? Perhaps again, it was due to more systematic overlearning.

Cognitive Abilities

An area of learning disability research which may contribute substantially to teaching the retarded is that on patterns of cognitive abilities. The field of learning disabilities is, of necessity, exploring the different ways by which children learn. If a youngster does not readily learn by the usual procedure, as children with learning disabilities do not, then the study of how they can and do learn becomes crucial. For this reason, the concept of individual diagnoses and program planning based on patterns of cognitive functioning is central to the field of learning disabilities. We know that it is not only likely but highly possible that two EMH children can have the same MA and IQ and yet have radically different cognitive strengths and weaknesses as revealed in testing. These kinds of differences in patterns of abilities and disabilities are also clearly revealed by the Illinois Test of Psycholinguistic Abilities (ITPA). A recent study by Jeanne McCarthy (1965) found 24 unique combinations of high-low ITPA subtest combinations among 30 severely retarded children. We must find ways to teach differentially as a necessary consequent of the fact that children learn differently. Not only do they learn new material differently, but they come to us with differing kinds and amounts of stored knowledge.

Many of the differences in the way children learn and have learned can be broadly categorized as being evidence of either an auditory-vocal or visual-motor preference. The ITPA tester speaks of children who are low on the A-V channel or on the V-M channel; the clinical psychologist might speak of the aphasoid or the Strauss-syndrome child; the experimental psychologist might use the terms "audile" or "visile"; the teacher might describe him as a phonics user or a whole-word reader, and the parents would perhaps say, "He doesn't understand what we say to him but he can do it if we show him."

As teachers of EMH children, we must learn from all of this that a label alone—in this case "EMH"—does not insure that there is a way to teach these children. There are many ways and the crucial task is to efficiently match instructional techniques to each child. We would be surprised if a physician had only one antibiotic drug which he administered to all his patients who needed antibiotics, even though some of them were allergic to it. Let us keep more than one reading pill on our shelves and more than one arithmetic pill in the drawer.

Teaching to Strengths or Weaknesses?

A question that has frequently been asked in learning disability circles is, "After patterns of cognitive, language, or intellectual strengths and weaknesses have been identified in a given youngster, should we then use those instructional methods which are geared to his strengths or those geared to his weaknesses?" Preliminary analysis of unpublished data on this topic suggests that once again we've been asking the wrong question. (In the field of mental retardation, we have hopefully just finished a long session of asking another wrong question: "Are special classes better than regular grade placement for EMH children?" Now that the fallacies in this question have been shown, perhaps we can begin to explore a more appropriate question: "For which EMH child is what type of program best under which circumstances?")

In place of the question, "Should we plan remedial teaching to strengthen the child's deficits or to utilize his assets?" it now appears we must ask "For which child, at what age of learning, should we teach to

the strengths and for which child should we teach to the deficits?" Further preliminary data analyses from this study suggested that normal first grade children who preferred the auditory channel did better with instruction geared to their strengths, while those who preferred the visual channel did better when taught to their weakness!

Perhaps the most important single finding for our purposes from learning disability research has been the observation that children who have reading difficulty (and several other types of learning problems) share with the mentally retarded a disproportionate deficiency in the ability to deal with the mechanical, automatic or rote aspects of language. Specifically, retarded children have significant deficits in short-term memory, in incidental verbal conditioning (grammar) and in structured association (analogies).

The general finding that retarded are relatively stronger in dealing with the meaningful (semantic or conceptual) aspects of language than they are with the nonmeaningful (rote, automatic, perceptual) has far ranging implications for educational practice.

If a child has strong legs and weak arms and we plan a therapeutic program to build up his already strong legs we are doing something quite parallel to insisting that in the education of the retarded we must "make all material meaningful to the child." Is it possible that in our eagerness to put all content on the level of the child's understanding, we have failed miserably to extend his ability to deal with new unfamiliar material?

How to Learn

Since today's world is full of so many things that we cannot realistically retain exposure to the "content" of this world as a reasonable educational goal, perhaps we can now focus more cogently on another possible goal of schooling, namely, teaching children how to learn.

If we view language behavior as a three-fold process of receiving or perceiving bits of information from the environment, processing those bits of information (organizing, storing, recalling) and then expressing the results of the processing or expressing the need for more bits of information, we find we have a useful model for curriculum development.

We know from studies of transfer of training that what actually can or does transfer is not specific bits of information, but rather general principles, which in turn are equal to rules or programs for processing information. Thus, what we should be teaching, especially to retarded children who do not learn how to organize, store, and recall what has been received automatically or without direct teaching, is just this model—the understanding of what is seen, heard, felt, smelled, and tested; rules or procedures for generalizing, deducing and relating; and the expression of ideas both vocally and motorically.

If a pesky little observer were to pop into every classroom in the country several times a day and demand of the teacher, "Why is this child doing that exercise right now?" there might be times when the teacher would have to pause. But if each child had posted on the front of his desk a profile view of his present level of development in areas such as understanding what he hears, categorizing ability, visual memory, etc., with the normal development sequence of ability in each area clearly spelled out, she could see at a glance (a) where the child is, (b) what step comes next and (c) types of classroom activities suitable to move him a bit higher up the ladder.

To come full cycle to our starting point, the learning disabilities approach to teaching educable mentally retarded children suggests above all else that we need to ask a new series of questions at every level. We must take a hard look at the very basic question of why are we teaching. What are we trying to do? If we can get away from the global generalities such as "facilitate effective communication," "foster good citizenship," "teach further awareness of the world around us," which permeate our curriculum guides and teacher training courses, we can get down to the real business of teaching children to behave more intelligently by direct training in understanding visual and auditory cues, concept formation, recall, vocal expression of ideas, etc. Then on the level of minute-by-minute classroom teaching we must ask such questions as how can this task, which Johnny did not master, be taught to him? Must I change the task, i.e., present it to his ears instead of his eyes, break it into smaller parts, and decrease the difficulty level, or must I first change Johnny, i.e., increase his visual memory span, or his auditory discrimination?

In summary, the learning disability aproach to teaching EMH redirects our attention to question-asking as the foundation of teaching and curriculum planning, to specific factors affecting and determining learning processes, to individual appraisal of patterns of cognitive abilities, to a re-examination of a philosophy of teaching through strengths or to weaknesses, and to the need for direct teaching of the processes of thinking rather than the products of someone else's thinking.

A paradox now presents itself. One who believes in the learning disabilities approach to teaching quickly finds that it applies to all children everywhere. Thus we have not really been talking about mentally retarded children, but about a scientific pedagogy for all children.

References

Bryant, N. D. Some Principles of Remedial Instruction for Dyslexia. *The Reading Teacher*, 1965, *18*, April, 567–572.

Gallagher, J. J. & Aschner, M. J. A Preliminary Report on Analyses of Classroom Interaction. *Merrill-Palmer Quarterly of Behavior and Development*, 1963, *9*, *3*, 183–194.

McCarthy, J. M. Patterns of Psycholinguistic Development of Mongoloid and Non-Mongoloid Severely Retarded Children. Unpublished doctoral dissertation, University of Illinois, 1965.

Vergason, G. A. Retention in Retarded and Normal Subjects as a Function of Amount of Original Learning. *American Journal of Mental Deficiency*, 1964, *68*, 5, 623–629.

BURTON BLATT
FRANK GARFUNKEL

Educating Intelligence: Determinants of School Behavior of Disadvantaged Children

Abstract: This report discusses the effects of a two year intervention on preschool disadvantaged children, as found in a one year follow up. Research and experimental variables of a more or less controllable nature tend to obscure any clear cut conclusion as to the extent and quality of change in these children. It is certainly questionable whether existing standardized tests are appropriate with regard to either the intervention or the socioeconomic status of the children involved.

ASPECTS of the very broad, complex, and significant problem of the relationship between social class background and intellectual and academic growth were the foci of this study. More specifically, it was concerned with intervention in the preschool and early school lives of lower class children to reduce the likelihood that they would develop intellectual and academic deficits—i.e., mental retardation—so frequently found in children from such backgrounds.

Procedure

The original plan of this research was to locate a group of preschool children drawn from families designated as cultural familial mentally retarded and, during a two year intervention, to provide them with a variety of experiences calculated to engender and reinforce attitudes, motivations, and cognitive skills that are considered prerequisites for normal intellectual and academic growth. It was expected that, in comparison with an appropriate control group, the experimental group would display significantly fewer intellectual and academic deficiencies. The basic premise was that intelligence is educable and that if an appropriate intervention were provided for children "destined" to become mentally retarded, this retardation would be prevented or, at least, mitigated. As the research proceeded, its direction and focus deviated more and more from the original purpose.

A diagnosis of mental retardation for these preschool children was not a criterion for selection. This reflected the position that case finding difficulties of previous investigators were substantive rather than methodological, a position congruent with the authors' previous experiences in a variety of educational and clinical settings. In addition, it seemed reasonable to assume that if one waited until such a diagnosis were possible, it would be more difficult, or perhaps impossible, to reverse the retardation.

The plan was to select from a population of preschool children where there was a strong likelihood of mild mental retardation (without accompanying central nervous system involvement) within the families of these children. For this purpose, it seemed reasonable to assume that if older retarded siblings were selected as a reference group, their younger siblings would be expected to develop in somewhat similar pat-

Exceptional Children, May, 1967, Vol.33, No.9, pp. 601-608.

terns without outside intervention. In order to maximize the likelihood of mental retardation still further, it was also planned to select subjects who had at least one parent who was mentally retarded, as well as an older retarded sibling. In summary, the original criteria were that subjects: (a) come from a lower social class, (b) be of preschool age, (c) have at least one older retarded sibling, and (d) have at least one retarded parent. These criteria are similar to those for cultural familial retardation listed in the American Association on Mental Deficiency's (AAMD) *A Manual on Terminology and Classification in Mental Retardation* (Heber, 1959).

It soon became apparent from evaluations of the pilot sample (N=14) and the main sample (N=60) that this method of selection was unworkable. All the families could be classified as culturally deprived, and there were inordinate amounts of school failure and lack of intellectual stimulation in the homes. Some of the families could be classified as cultural familial mental retardates, using the AAMD criteria, but the occurrence of documented mental retardation in the parent appeared to be relatively unrelated to its occurrence in the child. It was, therefore, not possible to obtain a sample of any size if the AAMD criteria for cultural familial mental retardation were to be met.

Therefore, the final criteria adopted for subject selection did not include having siblings in a special class or having a retarded parent, although, as it turned out, many subjects did meet these criteria. The most important criterion was residence in a deprived area characterized by high delinquency rates, a considerable proportion of school dropouts and school failures, low occupational status of parents, and run down homes. Other criteria were: (a) the family's residence in the area was not temporary, (b) the level of parental education and occupation was usual for that area, (c) neurological examination of the child revealed no central nervous system pathology, and (d) the parents consented to the child's inclusion in the project.

After a thorough search for eligible children, in which a variety of methods were used, 69 subjects were found who met the criteria. Five were ultimately dropped because their mothers never sent them to the program, two experimental children moved out of the area, and two nonexperimental children moved out of the state, thus reducing the sample to 60 children. Including the pilot sample, 74 cases met all criteria and were accepted as part of the project.

The pilot study, organized one year prior to the principal study, provided the project staff with an exploratory group, permitting study of selection, testing, and curricula procedures before the formal project began. This gave the senior staff of the project the time to train teachers for work with children in a specially designed teaching situation: the Responsive Environment (Moore, 1963). In this method, an electric typewriter was used to enable children to learn through their own discoveries.

The division of the principal sample into two experimental groups and a nonexperimental group was done by stratified random assignment, using Stanford-Binet IQ score, chronological age, and sex in the stratification. This stratification assured maximum efficiency and group equivalence.

Beginning in May, 1962—the case finding year—and ending in May, 1965—the first year of public and parochial school followup of the children—the following types of testings were accomplished yearly:

1. Cognitive (Aptitude, Achievement, Language)

   Stanford-Binet, L-M, 1960
   Peabody Picture Vocabulary Test
   Illinois Test of Psycholinguistic Abilities
   Lee Clark Reading Readiness Test
   Gesell-Ilg Norms for Musical Ability
   Typewriter Test (only taken by subjects in Responsive Environment)
   School Achievement of Study Child (rated by teacher)
   Metropolitan Reading Readiness Test

2. Noncognitive (Personality, Social)

   Rorschach Inkblot Test (overall rating of differentiation and form level)
   Vineland Social Maturity Scale
   Test Taking Behavior (as assessed by psychological examiner)
   Sociogram Score (sociogram developed by teachers)
   Anxiety Scales for Children

102

3. Environmental

Warner Index of Status Characteristics
Absences from Preschool or School
Family Evaluation (quantitative assessment
of interview protocols)

Several characteristics of this research differentiate it from prior and current related investigations:

1. The subject population was systematically randomized into experimental and control groups. In view of the probability that control children received special treatment and educational opportunities, they were later designated as a nonexperimental group. On the other hand, a fair number of experimental children were not afforded the fullest opportunities to participate in the experimental program. However, although execution was imperfect, an experimental design was maintained.

2. In the formal evaluations of subjects, "blinds" were rigorously developed and upheld. Tests of "blinds," using examinations of the psychologists who administered the various protocols, disclosed a lack of knowledge on their part as to which children were in the experimental group and which were not.

3. Subject attrition was insignificant. Of the 74 children originally in the project, all completed participation in the formal intervention years. Of the 60 children from the main sample, only one child was lost during the one year followup of children in public school.

4. A high degree of parental cooperation was maintained throughout the course of the study. Two days prior to the completion of the project, 41 parents attended a social gathering with the total project staff. The families of both the nonexperimental and experimental groups were included.

5. Our hypothesis was that in studying cultural deprivation we were also studying factors that give rise to mental retardation. Several recent studies have made distinctions between "true" mental retardation and "pseudoretardation"; i.e., subnormality is indicative of mental retardation only if it is diagnosed as irremedial. It was our contention that all children whose performances show mental retardation are, in fact, mentally retarded. As Binet pointed out long ago, mental retardation is a state of current subnormal intellectual functioning. Although a child may have an intact central nervous system and may be categorized as culturally deprived or cultural familial mentally retarded, if he behaves in an intellectually subnormal manner, he is as mentally retarded as another child with demonstrable brain damage who is functioning at approximately the same intellectual level.

6. In testing the hypothesis that intelligence is educable and that, in some instances, low intelligence is a manifestation of a deprived cultural experience, there are certain design problems. The study of deprivation and its relationship to social and school performance, by its very nature, must be either partially or wholly retrospective. It is not possible to assign children to experimental and control groups, and then systematically deprive the experimental children of certain experiences in order to observe the effects of that deprivation. Legal and moral codes demand that studies be conducted within existing cultural educational situations, which give indirect insights into the effects of deprivation.

Ideally, the proper study of deprivation would examine the null hypothesis that certain kinds of social and intellectual deprivation will not cause differences between children who are exposed and those who are not exposed. Instead, we are forced to study a less satisfactory null hypothesis: that children from a deprived living situation will not benefit from a stimulating school curriculum. This hypothesis puts the burden of proof on the curriculum rather than on the deprivation which is the focus of the study. Deprivation cannot be systematically controlled and, therefore, cannot be considered a true experimental main effect; the main effect is thus the presence or absence of a preschool program with children described as deprived.

The Curriculum

The objective of our preschool curriculum was to provide an optimal nursery school environment. This was attempted in three principal ways: (a) by helping children learn how to function socially in a group instruction situation so as to be maximally receptive to that instruction; (b) by providing a concentration of experiences designed to arouse curiosity and promote inquisitiveness and positive attitudes toward learning; and (c) by attempting to provide training in certain psychological functions generally considered to be fundamental to acquisition of academic skills in the primary grades.

Certain categories of experiences or activities, or areas of concentration, were commonly used by all teachers: language development, visual discrimination, quantitative thinking, auditory discrimination, auditory memory, speech training, motor coordination, visual memory, speech training, motor coordination, visual memory, and creative and imaginative thinking. The program is described best as experimental, emergent, child centered, and adhering to the basic principles of any sound preschool program—but over and above this, focused on the intensified development of preacademic skills. Intervention consisted of an ongoing, changing, complex social psychological setting having personal, interpersonal, educational, and cultural components.

We do not wish to convey the impression that our curriculum was a separate variable, i.e., that it had an existence and effect independent of the social psychological setting and the person employing it. Such independence never exists. On paper it is possible to compare curricula independent of setting and teacher; in practice it is impossible. To attribute consequence to a curriculum, therefore, is to do more than oversimplify. It is to misrepresent the external reality. For this reason, two major concentrations in this research dealt with the curriculum: one centered on the psychological climate of the intervention and the other on the formal curriculum, its contents and goals, materials used, tasks assigned, skills learned, and overall daily objectives.

Moore (1963) pioneered in the development of theoretical as well as technical aspects of the learning of preschool children, and his contribution to the field fits neatly into our efforts at environmental stimulation. Moore described how children aged two to five can learn to type, read, and write. These skills are acquired through an enjoyable experience, derived from what has been labeled a Responsive Environment. An environment is responsive if it satisfies the following conditions: (a) it is attuned to children's exploratory activities; (b) it informs children immediately about the consequences of their own actions; (c) it permits children to make extensive use of their capacities for discovering relations; and (d) it is so arranged that children are likely to make a series of interconnected discoveries about some aspect of the physical, cultural, and social world.

The setting of this project was not one which made description and manipulation of the component variables easy. In planning and organizing this study, we realized that in the event differences emerged between the experimental and nonexperimental children it would be impossible to say which aspects of the intervention were more or less influential. However, we did assume that a setting (the intervention) could be developed for the experimental children which would contain elements obviously not found in the daily lives of the nonexperimental children. Put in another way: we assumed that we could develop and describe an intervention which would clearly indicate that the two groups of children were experiencing such different things that predicted findings, contrary findings, or no findings would be of significance.

Results

The research hypothesis of this study, that a two year intervention with preschool lower class children will enhance their demonstrated educability, was rejected. This hypothesis was tested with a variety of measurements over a three year period and included testing of cognitive, noncognitive, and environmental factors. Analyses of the data led to the unequivocal inference that there was no more difference between the groups at the conclusion of the study than there had been at the beginning.

This conclusion can be viewed as: (a) failure

of the intervention as an effective force in the lives of the experimental children; (b) failure of the measuring instruments to register differential changes in functioning over a three year period; or (c) evidence of our inability to maintain a true experimental design. The implications of these alternative explanations are explored with the explicit goal of setting the stage for future research in this area.

The Measuring Instruments

The measurements used were comprehensive both with respect to substance and technique. Data were obtained in many ways: tests directly administered to children; rating scales where the information was supplied by parent, teacher, or psychologist; measurements which covered specified testing periods and measurements which represented ratings of a child, or a series of direct measurements over an extended period of time; tests of specific abilities and global abilities; measurements concerned with school behavior and behavior in a testing situation; single measurements obtained in any one of the four testing periods and repeated measurements obtained two, three, or four times on each child; and measurements from the domains classified as cognitive, noncognitive, and environmental. Thus, the testing program did not depend upon either one kind of test or one kind of administration of a test.

Given the particular sample of children, the curricula, and the variety of measurements over an extended period of time, our inability to demonstrate significant differences between experimental and nonexperimental groups caused us to view the rejection of the research hypothesis as an internally valid inference. We have no evidence that all curricula would fail to produce changes in all kinds of children from lower class homes or other kinds of environments (problems of external validity), but we do feel confident that the study throws considerable light on generalized problems of external validity.

Although forced to reject the research hypothesis as specifically applied to the sample studied and the curricula used, we do not necessarily reject the generalized hypothesis about the educability of lower class children. The problem of how intelligence manifests itself—

the extent to which it is affected by behavior, on one hand, and the extent to which it unfolds, on the other—is a spectre which continually faces us. However, there is an implicit contradiction between the supposition that children can change in response to specific teaching techniques and the probability that these changes will be reflected by tests such as the Stanford-Binet Intelligence Scale. Such tests are constructed in line with an operational principle of stability. Items that show relative variability over time are rejected in favor of items that are more stable. The result is an apparent stability of global measures which is an indication of test specific stability, but not necessarily an indication that children do not change. When a child's score is based on a comparison with the scores of his age peers, the chances are not very great that he will change with respect to these same age peers over a period of years. Obviously he is changing and, during preschool years, changing very rapidly. An apparent lack of change is not a reflection of his own growth, but rather of his position in a frequency distribution.

The importance of global measures of scholastic aptitude, or of "intelligence" as this is commonly called, has to do with efficiency in predicting future academic performance. More specific measures of ability do not have a comparable level of efficiency, even when the prediction is to be made within the specific area tested. For example, the Stanford-Binet is reputed to be a good predictor of future mathematical or verbal performance; it does not necessarily follow that it measures a more innate quality, although many investigators have thought so. However, the Stanford-Binet was developed to be stable, and this is reflected in high predictive efficiency with respect to other kinds of test or nontest behavior which relate to intellectual functioning. Therefore, it follows that, for an instrument to be highly predictable of future behavior, the instrument must be concerned with behavior that is extremely stable over time. Just the opposite is necessary in tests designed to be sensitive to changes in individuals. The latter tests tend to be relatively unstable over time and have minimal ability to predict future performance. Tests which are measuring nonstable factors are not necessarily unreliable, although this presents problems for the test constructor, who must use psychometric and statistical techniques of measuring reliability which are more or less independent of the time factor.

The problem alluded to is the obvious dilemma of any curriculum which attempts to provide specific developmental and, if necessary, remedial activities for children. These activities attend very carefully to fragments of the reading process, the quantitative process, or whatever intellectual discipline is being taught, as opposed to those procedures which are more global in their design and execution and which treat larger units of behavior. This does not mean that the more global approach to teaching does not involve attention to pieces of learning behavior, but these are not the main focus. Furthermore, although it is important that some pieces be attended to, it does not make too much difference which pieces they are.

Problems of Validity

The question is whether the results obtained in this study (which, at this point, are assumed to be internally valid) have external validity—i.e., whether they have general application in the area of the preschool education of lower class children. To find some resolution to this rather crucial problem, we see four rather distinct areas for discussion. The first three are concerned with problems of curriculum, timing, and sampling of children. The fourth concerns problems in measuring changes in children over a period of time with instruments that have been designed to measure relatively stable factors.

Curricula Intervention. Many questions can be raised about the optimal strategies in a preschool program for lower class children. The evolving curriculum of this study was clearly teacher dominated, although there was extensive collaboration between the investigators and all of the teaching staff.

The Responsive Environment provided a methodology which, by design, was not teacher dominated and which depended upon detailed instructions aimed specifically at minimizing teacher variability. Of course, it is possible that in spite of the care taken to specify the procedures of the Responsive Environment, the teacher may still have dominated the learning situation.

It might be that optimal strategy calls for comprehensive programing throughout the schooling of lower class preschool children so that the curriculum is dominated by theoretical considerations which are independent of variations among teachers or within any one teacher over a period of time. The view of the principal investigators of this project was that the curriculum should not be preordained, but rather that it should be developed by teachers in response to individual children, the interpersonal relationships between teacher and children, and relationships within groups of children. A great deal of attention and energy was given to observing teachers and children and to holding seminars with the teachers on programs they were developing and methods they were using.

Alternatively, other investigators have discussed the use of tightly prescribed curricula dominated by considerations other than the personalized curricular development of particular teachers. For example, the prescription can go in the direction of specific operant techniques applied to particular learning sequences, or it can be concerned with a therapeutic climate in the classroom.

In light of the above discussion we must raise the question of whether our interventions of a preschool program and a Responsive Environment provided a sufficient test of the hypothesis of educability. Perhaps greater attention should be paid to extensive and systematic variations of interventions which either minimize or use teacher variation and which use measurements directly related to curricular procedures. These problems of measurement of the extent of teacher or methodology domination have always been a source of concern. A teacher dominated curriculum does not lend itself readily to direct measurement. The consequent dependence upon global measurement suggests a dilemma in designing studies that attempt to compare variations along the continuum of teacher domination.

A second criticism of the curriculum concerns the focus of the entire program on the preschool environment rather than specifically attending to the education and treatment of the entire community and the families. It was not within the plans of this study to treat families or to deal extensively with evaluations of siblings and other children in the community. The curriculum was concerned with the Responsive Environment and the preschool program, with peripheral attention to families during occasional meetings and home visits by teachers. The failure of this program, as described, may have been due to the failure of the intervention to affect total family behavior. Since we found a relatively high correlation between a measure of family adequacy and the average school performance of all siblings, the inference follows that school failure is family linked and must, therefore, be family treated.

Timing and Duration. It is possible that the failure of the intervention to produce demonstrable results in the experimental children was due to the timing of the program in the lives of the children or to the duration of the program for individual children. Possibly children of different ages respond to different kinds of intervention in diverse ways. In any event, timing has variable effects when considered in conjunction with curricular strategies, sampling variation, and measurement problems.

Sampling of Children. There is some reason to believe that the children selected did not provide the most advantageous sample for testing the hypothesis of educability of lower class children. Some investigators have reported that transiency in some lower class schools is so high that the turnover in classrooms in a single school year sometimes reaches 100 percent.

The families of the children in this study were unusual in that they tended to stay in the same geographic area and, for the most part, in the same houses—59 of the 60 principal subjects remained with the study over the entire three year period. These families, therefore, had the opportunity to receive different kinds of continuing services from private and public agencies, and the schools were able to maintain contact with families and children. Although the neighborhood was clearly lower lower class and the families in this neighborhood were classified as extremely impoverished and largely dependent on welfare assistance, the general nature of the community may have been such as to support the intellectual growth of the children. If this were true, one might expect that an experimental intervention, such as the one provided, would not produce any demonstrable results.

Along the same line of reasoning, and again in spite of the fact that the neighborhood under consideration was rated as a lower lower class neighborhood, an important discrepancy appears with respect to sampling strategy. The area is not adjacent to other lower lower class neighborhoods; rather, it is a pocket within a city, surrounded by a variety of neighborhoods, universities, and business areas. None of the families were geographically distant from social agencies, hospitals, stores, or universities. Over the past 15 years, there had been city planning projects, university programs, religious group involvement, social work, two well established neighborhood house programs, and many other kinds of service activities.

It is difficult to speculate on the effects of such sampling variation, but we feel that, unwittingly, we did not obtain as educationally disadvantaged a sample of homes and children as desired. The more deprived a child is, the more likely that he will respond to an intervention. This reasoning follows directly from the rationale which maintains that negative deviations from normal functioning are likely to be associated with family and educational deprivations. We are not against the generality of the thesis of educability, but we think, for the time being, that this thesis can best be demonstrated with the most severely deprived children.

Measurement Problems. Measurement problems will always plague investigations such as this one. The day to day intervention which involves a variety of teachers and children is a different kind of substance than the very specific and highly reliable tests often used to measure the effects of interventions. When measurements are concerned with abilities that are closely tied to developmental factors, the apparent relationship between interventions and criteria is spuriously high. It is more parsimonious to conclude that the increased ability of individual children over periods of time is due more to their growth than to any intervention, whether it be school or a particular remedial or therapeutic sequence.

This is partially a question of precision as it applies to different kinds of measurements. A child's growth in mental age refers to his increasing ability to respond to items on a test as he grows older. The concept of chronological age, as it is used in psychometrics, refers to the average performance of children at any particular chronological age. The development of most tests of aptitude and ability hinges upon the changes that take place over time either directly or as can be inferred from the performance of a cross sectional sample of children. Our study was focused upon the question of whether the slope of developmental growth can be affected by an intervention. The question raised was whether the developmental acceleration of particular children can be varied by systematically providing specific interventions. It is altogether possible that developmental levels can be changed, but that this change is hidden in the relatively small amount of variance that is left over after chronological age is literally partialed out. As a matter of fact, the residual variance that remains is not grossly different from that which must be attributed to error. Therefore, relatively little is left for the measurement of changes in children, particularly when these children have more or less normal developmental slopes.

Conclusion

Insofar as this study is concerned, we have neither significant nor convincing data to substantiate our research hypothesis that intelligence is educable, i.e., a function of practice and training. However, this study revealed that we still have a great deal to discover concerning the nature/nurture interaction, about the most efficient and sufficient period to begin interventions, and about the possible intervention models that may have the greatest desired effects. The information obtained in this study has encouraged us to continue the quest for processes and methodologies to educate intelligence and, for certain children, to prevent mental retardation.

References

Heber, R. (Ed.) *A manual on terminology and classification in mental retardation: monograph supplement to American Journal of Mental De-ficiency*. Springfield, Ill.: American Association on Mental Deficiency, 1959.

Moore, O. K. Orthographic symbols and the pre-school child—a new approach. In *Proceedings of the Third Minnesota Conference on Gifted Children*. Minneapolis: University of Minnesota Press, 1963.

BURTON BLATT *is Professor and Chairman, Special Education Department, and* FRANK GARFUNKEL *is Associate Professor and Director, Headstart Evaluation and Research Center, School of Education, Boston University, Massachusetts. This paper summarizes the author's monograph, A Field Demonstration of the Effects of Nonautomated Responsive Environments on the Intellectual and Social Competence of Educable Mentally Retarded Children. Washington: US Office of Education, 1965.*

MENTAL RETARDATION, MENTAL AGE, AND LEARNING RATE

ARTHUR R. JENSEN AND WILLIAM D. ROHWER, JR.

University of California, Berkeley

Zigler's hypothesis that mental age (MA) and not IQ determines the rate of learning is examined in the light of empirical evidence comparing the learning rates of normal and retarded children and young adults matched for MA. The results show that learning rate is a function of IQ as well as of MA. In general, children of average IQ learned serial and paired-associate lists significantly faster than retarded young adults with IQs between 50 and 60 but with approximately the same MA as the children. An interaction between IQ, learning rate, and socioeconomic status is also noted.

Zigler has now stated (1967a) and restated (1967b) a central theme of his theoretical position regarding mental retardation that "... it is the MA [mental age] (level) and not the IQ (the relationship of MA to chronological age) that determines the exact nature, including the rate, of learning any task [1967b, p. 579]." Thus, two persons of different chronological age (CA) and different IQ but matched on MA should show similar learning rates.

Weir (1967) has challenged Zigler's statement on essentially the following basis: If MA is a measure of the knowledge an individual has accumulated by a given CA, the *rate* of acquisition of this knowledge is represented by the IQ, which is (MA/CA) × 100. Therefore, contrary to Zigler's position, persons of the same MA but differing in IQ should show different rates of learning, even in short-term learning tasks. There is evidence that Weir's prediction is indeed borne out in the case of laboratory learning tasks.

The obscurities in the argument between Zigler and Weir can be overcome by making a conceptually clear-cut distinction between developmental rate and learning rate. There is much evidence (White, 1965) that mental abilities have a hierarchical structure, the development of which follows a chronological sequence; the milestones of this developmental sequence are marked by the increasing complexity of the cognitive structures (e.g., heuristics, symbolic mediators, strategies, information processing skills) which the individual can bring to bear on solving problems. The ages at which individuals attain these stages

of cognitive development are regarded as indexes of developmental rate. But two individuals who are at the same developmental stage and who have arrived at this stage at either the same or at different rates of development, may still differ in the rates at which they can acquire new information. This is distinguished as learning rate. Thus, individuals can be retarded or normal in developmental rate and retarded or normal in learning rate. Retardation in either realm will spell retardation as assessed by traditional intelligence tests, since these are a mixture of items that measure acquisition (e.g., vocabulary and general information subtests) and cognitive structures (e.g., problems involving logical reasoning). The 2 × 2 combinations indicated by this formulation suggest three possible classifications of familial retardates. Normal developmental rate and normal learning rate are both necessary for the manifestation of normal intelligence, as traditionally defined; neither alone is sufficient.

Our data pertain only to the relationship of MA to learning rate. No inferences are made here concerning the issue of developmental rate.

Jensen (1965) matched 40 institutionalized mentally retarded young adults (mean IQ = 58) with no known organic defects with 40 normal school children (mean IQ = 105) on MA (9 years). In both serial and paired-associate rote learning, the normal children had learning rates some 3 to 4 times faster, on the average, than the adult retardates. Furthermore, although there was no significant differ-

Journal of Educational Psychology, December, 1968, Vol.59, No.6, pp. 402-403.

ence in the standard deviations for MA in the two groups, the retardates showed a significantly greater standard deviation of learning scores than the normals. The greater heterogeneity of learning rates of groups of retardates as compared with normals, when the groups are equally homogeneous in IQ and MA, was further substantiated in a study comparing learning rates in retarded, average, and gifted children (Jensen, 1963). There are evidently more ways of being retarded than of being either average or gifted in mental ability.

Rohwer (1967) compared a group of 48 institutionalized familially retarded adults with groups of normal children in Head Start and kindergarten and in Grades 1, 3, and 6 on paired-associate learning. The children were sampled from populations of low- and middle-socioeconomic status (SES). (The MA is close to the CA for the school children, but is slightly lower in the low-SES groups.) The results, shown in Figure 1, indicate that the average learning score of the retardates is significantly lower than that of any of the other groups as well as being significantly lower than all the other groups combined ($F = 103.22$, $df = 1/396$, $p < .01$). Comparison of the learning performance of the adult retardates and the middle-SES third graders is especially revealing, since the two groups have approximately the same MA (9.7 versus 9.6). Also, there was a larger standard deviation of learning scores in the retarded group than in any of the normal groups.

The relationship between learning rate and MA, at least in the mildly retarded (i.e., IQs of 50 to 75), is further complicated by socioeconomic status. Rapier (1968) closely matched Caucasian middle- and low-SES elementary school children ($N = 20$ in each group) in classes for the retarded on CA (124 months), MA (88 months), and IQ (70). None of the Ss evinced any organic defects. The low-SES children showed consistently and significantly faster rates of paired-associate learning than the middle-SES children.

In view of the present results and consistent with our conceptualization, equivalence of developmental level need not

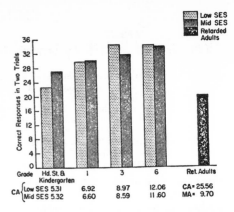

FIG. 1. Comparisons of low- and middle-socioeconomic groups of children at various grades in school with institutionalized retarded adults on paired-associate learning consisting of 24 picture pairs presented two times at a rate of 4 seconds per pair. $N = 48$ in each of the nine groups.

imply equality of performance on intellectual tasks, specifically, learning tasks. When equal-MA comparisons involve normals and familial retardates, differences in learning rate are to be expected, and, indeed, are found.

REFERENCES

JENSEN, A. R. Learning abilities in retarded, average, and gifted children. Merrill-Palmer Quarterly, 1963, 9, 123–140.

JENSEN, A. R. Rote learning in retarded adults and normal children. American Journal of Mental Deficiency, 1965, 69, 828–834.

RAPIER, J. The learning abilities of normal and retarded children as a function of social class. Journal of Educational Psychology, 1968, 59, 102–110.

ROHWER, W. D., JR. On distinguishing the mentally retarded from the culturally disadvantaged. Paper presented at the meeting of the American Association of Mental Deficiency, Denver, May 1967.

WEIR, M. W. Mental retardation, technical comment. Science, 1967, 157, 576.

WHITE, S. H. Evidence for a hierarchical arrangement of learning processes. In L. P. Lipsitt & C. C. Spiker (Eds.), Advances in child development and behavior. Vol. 2. New York: Academic Press, 1965.

ZIGLER, E. F. Familial mental retardation: A continuing dilemma. Science, 1967, 155, 292. (a)

ZIGLER, E. F. Mental retardation, technical comment. Science, 1967, 157, 578. (b)

(Received September 11, 1967)

'Visual and Auditory Learning of the Mentally Retarded'

BY FRANCIS A. WARNER, ED.D.

*Associate Professor of Special
Education,
San Francisco State College*

Excluding the speech handicapped, mentally retarded children comprise the largest group of all exceptional children yet there is considerable disagreement among authorities as to how the educable mentally retarded learn and what teaching techniques are the most effective. In Kirk's opinion, the development of special education is contingent upon the development of clinical teaching procedures (1). Practitioners in the field often claim that special class teachers are trained in instructional skills not normally required of teachers of normal children. Yet, there is little exact knowledge about the way in which mentally retarded learn, and there is a lack of appropriate and special methodology pertaining directly to them. Rothstein has stated:

The intriguing question of how mentally retarded individuals learn has been in the minds of all teachers since the moment that Itard first tried to educate the Wild Boy of Aveyron in 1799. Research in learning theory with mentally retarded children and its educational implications has been long overdue (2).

Principles of learning often seem obvious or merely common sense. One such common-sense statement which appears in numerous survey course texts dealing with the mentally retarded is that learning is reinforced through using a variety of sense modalities — visual, auditory, vocal and kinesthetic. The more senses that are involved the more learning that takes place. However, since it is not always possible to employ all of the sense modalities in the learning situation, it would be benefifical to know which of the two higher senses — visual or auditory — is a more conducive sense modality for learning with the educable mentally retarded. In spite of the increased research on mental retardation, very little is known about the preferred sense modulities of educable mentally retarded children. Krech and Crutchfield have stated:

Individuals differ in their favored mode of imagery. Some people have images that are predominantly visual, others, images that are predominantly auditory. Most people, however, seem to be of the "mixed types" with perhaps some tendency to favor one mode over the other in their imagery (3).

In order to determine whether or not educable mentally retarded children learn best through the auditory, visual or a combination of visual-auditory senses, fifty-nine educable mentally retarded children underwent a paired-associate learning task involving immediate and delayed recall (4). Results indicated that the rate or speed of learning was superior through the visual sense. A combination of

Journal of California Federation C.E.C., March,
1969, Vol.17, No.2, pp. 11-12.

111

sensory stimulation of less value and the auditory sense was inferior to both the others. Retention after seventy-two hours was equally effective through the visual sense as it was through a combination of sensory stimulation. The auditory sense was the least effective sense modality for retention. As age increased, vision became a more effective sense modality for rention. No significant relationship existed between sex and preferred sense modalities.

PEDAGOGICAL IMPLICATIONS:

1. Despite the strong emphasis upon sensory training in the education of the retarded, there is a noticeable lack of concern or interest in the concept of individual sense modality preferences in learning. Since learning materials must be presented to one or more of the sense modalities, the learning process could be facilitated by presenting materials to the preferred sense modality or modalities of the individual student.
2. The results of this study suggest the possibility that the involvement of two sense modalities is an inhibiting factor in the learning processes of some retarded children.
3. Since the auditory sense appeared to be the least effective sense modality for learning, it is recommended that visual presentation of learning materials be more strongly emphasized in learning tasks involving rote-memorization.
4. The amount of verbalization on the part of the classroom teacher should be minimized in order to allow the retarded child to utilize his other sense modalities to the fullest extent during the learning process.
5. The most important finding in this study was not the statistical evidence that showed the superiority of a particular sense modality but rather that retardates do differ within themselves quite markedly in respect to learning through the various sense modalities.

––––

REFERENCES:

(1) Kirk, S., "What is Special About Special Education?" *Exceptional Children*, XIX (1953), 138-42.
(2) Rothstein, J. H., *Mental Retardation —Readings and Resources,* New York: Holt, Rinehart and Winston, Inc., Inc., (1961), 136-37.
(3) Krech, D. and R. Crutchfield, *Elements of Psychology*, New York: Alfred A. Knopf, Inc., (1962), 365-66.
(4) Warner, F., "Preferred Sense Modalities in Paired-Associate Learning of Educable Mentally Retarded Children," unpublished Ed.D. dissertation, Colorado State College, 1966.

Developing

Perceptual-Motor
Skills

OVERBURDENED COGNITIVE PROCESSES

George H. Early *

LEARNING-DISABLED children have a common characteristic: They tend to intellectualize many tasks, activities, and procedures which could be performed more efficiently at an automatic level. In many situations in which a normal child would respond automatically, the learning-disabled child must deal cognitively with the situation before responding.

N. C. Kephart gives a classic example of overburdened cognitive processes in the case of a ten-year-old boy who was asked to write his name on the chalkboard. [1] In response to this simple demand, the boy first placed his wrist on the board and wrote with finger movements, duplicating as nearly as possible the movements involved in writing with pencil and paper. Each stroke of each letter was made as a separate and distinct operation, with a noticeable pause between strokes. Every

teacher and every clinician who deals with learning problems has seen this type of performance at times.

This particular boy, however, gives us a valuable clue to the underlying reasons for this fragmented and agonizing approach to the simple task of writing his name. When he finished, he turned to the examiner and said, "I can write my name. I have memorized the movements." Memorized movements! What he is telling us is that each small portion of each letter requires recall and planning of a specific movement before that small portion can be executed. Moreover, before executing the memorized, fragmented movement associated with any one portion of a letter, he probably must make a mental review of which portions he has already completed, as well as a simultaneous mental forecast of which movement is coming next. Thus, his cognitive processes become overburdened. Too much cognitive attention is required for the movements involved in the act of writing; little, if any, cognitive attention is available for attending to what is being written.

[1] Newell C. Kephart, *The Brain-Injured Child in the Classroom* (Chicago, Ill.: National Easter Seal Society for Crippled Children and Adults, 1963).

* Mr. Early is clinical director of the Achievement Center for Children, Purdue University, West Lafayette, Indiana.

Academic Therapy, Fall, 1969, Vol.V, No.1, pp. 59-62.

Reflect for a moment upon how you write. Do you dredge up from your memory bank a number of highly specific movements for each letter? Must you recall each movement and plan how you will make that movement before you set pen to paper? Surely not. Undoubtedly you have a "wired in" and highly generalized pattern for writing. When you write, you can bring this pattern into action and the specific movements come automatically. Letters, whole words, even entire phrases, can be summoned forth, and the specific movements will take care of themselves. your cognitive processes are free to deal with the ideas about which you are writing. You do not have to clutter the cognitive channels with cognitive garbage such as the movements involved in producing one insignificant part of one little letter. To the extent that you have developed a generalized movement pattern for writing, your cognitive processes are freed of the burden of dealing with specific movements which should come automatically. You can pay attention to what you are writing, rather than to the movements of writing.

One of Kephart's most far-ranging contributions to education is the concept of the generalized movement pattern. The example cited above is only one small aspect of the implications embodied in this concept. The general principle might be summarized as follows: Cognitive processes should be reserved for matters which are properly at the cognitive level. Conversely, cognitive processes should not be wasted on activities which should unfold automatically. The ultimate aim of developing generalized movement patterns is to relegate automatic functions to automatic levels of the central nervous system — freeing, in the process, the cogni-

tive levels for their proper task of dealing with cognitive matters.

When generalized movement patterns have been achieved the child is freed of many blocks to learning. Cognitive attention can focus upon the goal of movement instead of being diverted into wasteful attending to movements *per se*. Movement, and activity in general, is then available for exploration of the environment, for becoming an agent whereby information from the child's surroundings is received, processed, compared with previous experience, and integrated as a meaningful part of his total fund of knowledge. The child who must deal cognitively with the movements incidental to traversing his surroundings inevitably is impoverished by a corresponding loss of meaningful encounter with the world in which he operates.

IF ONE grants the fundamental position just presented, a major educational goal emerges: Many children must be helped to develop generalized movement patterns so that many blocks to learning may be removed. Activities which are preeminently automatic must be removed from the cognitive levels and planted firmly in the automatic levels of functioning. The cognitive processes must be relieved of cumbersome burdens and set free for the exciting task of true learning.

How may generalized movement patterns be developed in children who lack them? Normally, one should first attend to the development of overall and fairly gross motor activity. The child's general motor development should be such that he moves, typically, in a flexible and coordinated fashion. He should be able to make selective and controlled use of each body part through the entire range of movement of which that part is capable. Further, the individual parts should be capable of an equally wide range of flexible and combined movements, where parts work together in solving a variety of motor problems. A child develops such generalized movement patterns at this gross level through numerous experiences in which he employs a great variety of specific movements in performing the same or a similar task. In doing the same task in many different ways, he thus develops a generalized pattern of movement for that task, rather than a narrow set of isolated and specific movements.[2] The that letter. Synchrony of voice, eye, ed body-movement patterns usually should precede attempts to promote development of higher-level generalized movement patterns such as those involved in writing.

In the case of the ten-year-old boy who had "memorized the movements" for writing his name, one would first attend to developing an overall pattern of flexible and coordinated movements, assuming this pattern was not present at the outset. It then would be in order to begin remedial activities aimed at developing a generalized movement pattern for writing.

At the Achievement Center for Children (Purdue University), an approach that is frequently employed is a variation of the Fernald method, the major modifications of which were developed by Rhoda Wharry.[3] Cursive writing

is employed exclusively. If the child does not know the cursive alphabet, it is taught to him, beginning with the letters that are easiest to form and progressing to those that are more difficult. If he already knows the cursive alphabet, the method is used for teaching him spelling words and those words which give him trouble in reading.

At first, large-size cursive writing is used (six to eight inches high) the letters becoming progressively smaller as the child becomes more competent. Thus, the initial stages involve gross arm movements exclusively, and the error of developing fine motor skills ahead of gross motor abilities is avoided.

In teaching a word, the therapist first makes a large cursive copy of the word. The child then traces the word several times, saying the sound (or sometimes the name) of each letter as he traces the letter, and sustaining the sound during the entire period the hand is tracing that letter. Synchrony of voice, eye, and hand is emphasized, and the therapist works for smooth and rhythmical arm movements.

When the child's tracing performance is fairly adequate, he is asked to copy the word several times, referring to the tracing for help as he needs it. When he no longer needs to look back at the tracing, he is asked to write the word from memory. A large flashcard is made for each word learned in this way, with the word written in cursive on one side and in manuscript on the other. The flashcards are used to check for retention, with words that are not retained being treated as new words to be learned.

---

[2] For a full treatment of generalized movement patterns, see Newell C. Kephart, *The Slow Learner in the Classroom* (Columbus, Ohio: Charles E. Merrill, 1960), and *Learning Disability: An Educational Adventure* (West Lafayette, Ind.: Kappa Delta Pi Press, 1968).

[3] Rhoda E. Wharry, "Perceptual-Motor Generalizations and Remedial Reading." Unpublished doctoral dissertation (Lafayette, Ind.: Purdue University, 1969).

Generalized movement patterns for writing are promoted in several ways by the large-cursive-writing program. Writing is done in different body positions: standing at the chalkboard, seated at the table, seated on the floor, on hands and knees on the floor, and in any other position the therapist can devise. Methods of tracing are varied: with the finger, in the air, with chalk, with crayon, with pencil, etc. Writing materials are also varied: chalk with chalkboard, or paper with crayon, felt marker, pencil, etc. The position of the writing surface is changed frequently: vertical, horizontal, and various degrees of slant.

WITH all of these variations, the common task of writing is accomplished. The variations, however, free the child from the necessity of employing a rigid and restricted skill and permit him instead to develop a general and an internalized pattern for writing. Different muscle groups perform the task; different tactual-kinesthetic feedback come from employing a variety of writing materials. Rather than relying on a highly specific set of memorized movements, the child develops a generalized pattern, and when this occurs there is often a corresponding release of cognitive processes for their proper functioning.

PERCEPTUAL HANDICAP: FACT OR ARTIFACT?*

H. Carl Haywood

(Address to the Ontario Association for
Children with Learning Disabilities,
Toronto, May 20, 1966.)

It is assumed that all groups interested in special education have a common goal:
to provide the most appropriate education for each individual child, thus to educate each child to the maximum of his individual capability. The special education
movement has traditionally been less interested in statistical abstractions, i.e.
the average performance in any group, than in individual abilities, deficiencies,
and performances of individual children. Furthermore, one may assume that some degree of brain damage is thought to be present in all children who are diagnosed as
"perceptually handicapped." Brain damage is used to include not only injury, but
also underdevelopment of certain brain areas as well as neurochemical imbalances in
the central nervous system.

It is from these considerations that the questions of the diagnosis of perceptual
handicap and the efficacy of special classes for the perceptually handicapped may
be viewed. Specifically:

1. What are the roots of interest in "perceptual handicap?"
2. How is the condition defined?
   (a) neurologically (slight positive signs, maybe diffuse EEG abnormalities).
   (b) psychologically, i.e. behaviourally (hyperactive, distractible, impulsive,
       near-normal I.Q., highly scattered abilities).
   (c) educationally (jagged achievement, reversals of letters and words).
3. Is the description sufficiently complete and reliable to constitute a clearly
   recognizable condition, so that special-education methods can be devised and
   communicated to teachers-in-training?
4. Do special teaching techniques that can be taught to teachers in training
   now exist, and what is the evidence on the efficacy of such techniques?
5. Are there any dangers in pursuing enthusiastically the early establishment
   of special separate classes for the perceptually handicapped?
6. What is needed in this important area of education?

Historical Perspective
The history of detailed interest in brain-damaged children, particularly in those
whose deficiencies are not associated with acute injury, is somewhat difficult to
trace, but it certainly is not a long history, nor is there a clear pattern of syndrome definition, empirical observation, theoretical integration, and development of
applied procedures for diagnosis and education. Scientific interest in the behaviour
of brain-injured persons had its largest early impetus in the work of Kurt Goldstein,
who studied acutely brain-injured veterans of World War I. In a similar but more
focused effort, Ward Halstead studied the behavioural characteristics of aphasic
soldiers in World War II, applying standardized tests for the first time, and valida-
ting the test results against proved focal brain lesions. Halstead (1947) formed the
concept of "biological intelligence," which concept is being pursued today across the
continent, most prominently in his own laboratory at the University of Chicago and in
Ralph Reitan's (1966) neuropsychology laboratory at the Indiana University Medical
Center.

*Reprinted by IMCSE-USC from Child Study, Vol. 28, No. 4 (Winter 1966-67),
pp. 2-13, permission of H. Carl Haywood and Child Study. 8/67

More clearly behavioural and educational concerns were introduced by Strauss and Lehtinen (1947), Werner, Kephart, and others, who assumed a continuity in Goldstein's observations from adults to children. Even these writers have not been greatly concerned with developmental or growth phenomena.

Educators such as Kirk, Dunn, and Gallagher have focused their attention almost wholly upon the deficiencies in learning exhibited by certain groups of children. Little effort of a collaborative, inter-disciplinary nature has been exerted in an attempt to relate specific learning problems to specific neurological patterns. Such an effort has been most fruitful in work with adults (Reitan, 1966), and should prove useful with children, even though work with the developing brain will be even more tedious and require a longer time than similar work with adults.

Description and Diagnosis of Perceptual Handicap
Dunn has prepared a paper on "Minimal Brain Dysfunction" for a book in preparation Brain Damage in School-age Children. In this paper Dunn cites a typical description of this kind of child:

"Ed is a ten-year-old boy without a motor handicap other than clumsiness. His speech is fairly distinct. Ed's intelligence quotient score is 80. His teacher complains that he talks incessantly and constantly interrupts the class with irrelevant remarks. He has a strong need for attention and thus bothers other children who are working by knocking things off their desk, by hiding pencils, and by hitting them on the head. His learning patterns are very uneven. It is nearly impossible to settle him down to academic work because he cannot concentrate on one thing for any length of time. In fact, he is at the mercy of any idea which occurs to him or any environmental event which reaches him."

Our agreement on the familiarity of that description would seem to indicate that the syndrome can be described and the diagnostic criteria specified with relative ease. It is one thing to agree on the familiarity of a clinical description, and quite another thing to get consistent agreement on the diagnosis of a single case. Dunn points out that clinical teams from several child study centers in the Southern United States were unable to agree on the percentages of patients who fall into the diagnostic categories "emotionally disturbed," "mentally retarded," and "brain-damaged." He concluded that the ". . . diagnostic category selected (in any case) depended on the training, professional make-up, philosophy and pre-disposition of the diagnostic team (and that) . . . three different groups, depending on their biases, could label the same child brain-injured, emotionally disturbed, or mentally retarded." Psychological tests, while individually capable of discriminating groups of retarded, mentally ill, or brain-damaged patients all from a "normal" group, have little success in differentiating these clinical groups from each other, and even less success in diagnosing individual cases. Nor have neurological studies fared significantly better. Various medical specialists report typically that they can find no abnormal signs in these children who are frequently labelled "minimally brain-damaged" or "perceptually handicapped." EEG patterns are often reported to be "within the normal range." Just as in psychological studies, abnormal EEG patterns are more frequent in groups of such children than in groups of children who do not experience these problems, but individual diagnosis is not so fruitful.

Strauss (1947) has suggested four behavioural criteria for the diagnosis of
what has come to be called the "Strauss syndrome." These are: perceptual disorders, perseveration, thinking and conceptual disorders, and behavioural disorders
(hyperactivity and disinhibition). In addition, he has suggested three biological
criteria: slight neurological signs of brain damage, history of neurological impairment, and no history of mental retardation in the family. It should be pointed
out that all four behavioural signs are also prominently associated with severe
emotional disturbance, specifically with schizophrenia, acute brain injury, and
frequently with primary mental retardation. Not all three of the biological
criteria are said by Strauss to be necessary for the definition of the syndrome.

According to Dunn, teachers use four criteria for defining a "Strauss syndrome"
child: hyperactivity, incoordination, lack of inhibition, and distractibility,
and they sometimes add disturbance of perception and disturbance of concept
formation. All six of these criteria are associated with mental retardation, with
severe emotional disturbance, and with acute brain injury. Most are extremely
difficult to measure in any reliable fashion.

Thus it must be concluded that no set of criteria exists for diagnosing the perceptually handicapped child so as to differentiate that condition reliably from
emotional disturbance or from mental retardation.

Education of Perceptually Handicapped Children
Let us look now at some attempts to formulate education and training programmes
for the minimally brain-damaged, or perceptually handicapped child.

Three categories of educational methods have been proposed, and are now being
followed in more-or-less rigidly categorized systems. Each teaching method is
said to derive from the conceptual viewpoint of a particular school, i.e. the
biological or psychological substrata of which the behavioural deficit of the
perceptually handicapped child is the manifestation.

The most prominent and widely-used method of education stresses physical education, motor development, motor training, mobility, and coordination (or psychomotor development). This approach is associated with methods advocated by Doman
and Delacato, Kephart, and Schilder and Bender. Most authorities using these
approaches appear to subscribe to the classical notion that "ontogeny recapitulates phylogeny," i.e. that the developmental sequence of an individual proceeds
according to the evolutionary history of the species. Therefore, training begins
with the most primitive kinds of responses and proceeds stepwise to the most
complex behaviours. A usual assumption is that no steps can be skipped in the
development of behavioural sequences, hence a child must acquire the simpler
responses before he can possibly acquire more complex ones. The extreme of this
point of view is represented in the work of Doman and Delacato in their Institutes
for the Achievement of Human Potential. These workers believe that systematic
training, even passive training, in creeping (especially involving cross-body
creeping) is necessary for the attainment of higher levels of "neurological
organization," which is in turn necessary for the acquisition of complex perceptual learning such as would be involved in learning to read. Both Kephart (1960)
and Doman and Delacato (1960) believe that it is essential that the child develop
laterality i.e., that one side of his brain become clearly the dominant side,
controlling sensation and motor behaviour of the opposite side.

There is little research evidence that can be related directly to these beliefs. The importance of developing laterality is clear, since it is quite frequently reported that "mixed dominance" is greatly more frequent among poor or disabled readers than among adequate readers; however, the effects of laterality training upon reading ability have not been clearly shown. There is even less evidence on the relationship between creeping skills and school achievement, and what evidence there is is not encouraging. A report by Evans (1966) revealed no relationship whatever between creeping skills and reading achievement in first grade children, even though such a relationship is clearly predicted by Doman and Delacato.

The Kephart programme stresses the progression from purely motor training into perceptual training, which may include training in only a single modality such as vision or may involve all modalities. Kephart considers it particularly important that a child learn to integrate perceptual experiences across the sensory modalities, i.e. it is important to integrate visual auditory information with information derived from the tactual sense. This approach is reminiscent of certain principles in the Montessori method, stressing multisensory approaches to learning with deprived and mentally retarded children. At a somewhat more advanced level of development, a California group identified with Marianne Frostig stresses perceptual training using paper and pencil tasks. This group feels that such procedures will be useful in the treatment of specific visual disabilities in which the problem is in the integration of visual information rather than in visual acuity. Again, the volume of research available to be brought to bear on these assumptions is indeed slender! So far, one can read of only one controlled research effort designed to evaluate the Kephart programme, and that one occurred right here in Toronto. Mentally retarded children were trained for one academic year with the Kephart training programme, while matched control children were given only their usual training, with no effort to provide special techniques of perceptual training for the controls. At the end of nine months, there were no differences between the experimental and control groups, even when the test used was the Kephart test, one which is closely related to the training procedures. It can certainly be argued that the training methods employed were not designed for use primarily with mentally retarded children; however, what is important is that an effort was made toward systematic and controlled evaluation, faithfully applying the recommended techniques to an experimental group, and withholding them from a matched control group, then testing both groups both before and after the training period.

Lehtinen in particular has outlined training methods which stress concept formation, a somewhat higher level of skill and learning than we have discussed so far.

1. An undistracting school environment should be provided. Translucent rather than transparent window panes should be used in the classroom. The teacher's dress should be plain and free from ornaments. The classroom should be located on the top floor and made free from distracting stimuli. Cubicles and screens should be used to reduce distractions.
2. Instruction should be individualized. The class groups should be small with 12 children as a maximum. For individual work, pupils should be removed to the periphery of the group, faced toward a wall, or screened off from the rest of the children by the cubicles.

3. An elemental rather than a global approach to teaching should be
emphasized; for example, the teaching of reading should begin with
the learning of individual letters; later these should be assembled into
words, and finally the words should be used in sentences, paragraphs,
and stories.

4. Emphasis should be placed on the use of coloured letters, words, and
numbers as well as other concrete cues to focus the child's attention on
the relevant materials.

5. Motor activity should be involved in academic learning, with emphasis
on concrete manipulative materials.

6. Emphasis should be placed on the basic tool subjects. Instruction in
social studies, geography, and science should be considered incidental.

7. No use should be made of the project or unit method, by which different
subjects are integrated in the study of a broad area.

8. Social activities, group learning, and oral language should be deemphasized.

The Lehtinen programme is obviously a multifaceted one, with many components which
may or may not go together. It is even possible that some of the recommended procedures may work against some of the other procedures; e.g., the recommendation
that stimulation be kept at a minimum would seem to be in conflict with the recommendation that brightly colored letters be used, unless the only purpose is to
make the letters stand out against a drab background. Nevertheless, extensive
work in the animal laboratory and some work with children is already making it
clear that intensive, even though non-specific, stimulation through all sense
modalities may considerably enhance the development of the nervous system, and
result in more efficient learning (Haywood & Tapp, 1966). At any rate, the
recommendations are testable, but have not, to my knowledge, been submitted to
systematic evaluation in the classroom. Rather, systems such as this one have
been adopted with considerable enthusiasm in situations in which the only criteria
of success have been the subjective judgments of the teachers themselves.

Research Related to Perceptual Handicap
In evaluating both the assumption of a separate diagnostic entity having to do
with perceptual handicap, and the efficacy of specific programmes of special
education to deal with such persons, one can make use of the limited supply of
research data available to us. The most commonly mentioned symptom is hyperact-
vity and distractibility. Surveys of different patient and classroom populations
have indicated that hyperactivity is characteristic of the brain-injured, the
emotionally disturbed, and the mentally retarded, although unusually low levels
of activity are also found occasionally in these groups. Therefore, hyperactivity
can hardly be considered a defining characteristic of the perceptually handicapped.
In recommending special educational methods, you will recall that Lehtinen argued
"hyperactivity is heightened even further by a stimulating environment and reduced
by a barren one. Further, it has been argued that the Strauss-type child will
learn better in a barren environment than in one of reasonable stimulation."
There is no support for these assumptions in the research literature. In fact,

the weight of the available research is that many children, particularly the mentally retarded reduce their levels of activity under heightened stimulation, and become more hyperactive when stimulation is held to a minimum (Cromwell, 1963). One investigator (Burnett, 1962) studied the influence of classroom environment on the school learning of retarded subjects with high and low activity levels. He found no differences, indicating that hyperactive children learn as well in a standard classroom situation as they do in a restricted environment.

Another part of the usually assumed syndrome involves the assumption that the minimally brain-damaged child is thought to display particular deficiency in concept formation, usually presenting a jagged profile of abilities and deficits, being high in some areas and quite low in others. Actually, several investigators have found no differences between neurologically impaired subjects and cultural-familial retarded subjects in arithmetic computation, reasoning, achievement, reversals, or understanding of basic arithmetic concepts. Similarly, no differences were found between the two groups either in reading achievement or in patterns of reading errors. (Capobianco, 1956; Capobianco and Miller, 1958). In the great majority of studies, when neurologically impaired children selected for perceptual handicap have been compared with other groups of children who have supposedly different learning disabilities, no differences have been found between the two groups in activity level, in their levels of proficiency at learning different scholastic material, in the kinds of errors made in the learning process, or in the effects of special educational procedures. I can only conclude that the evidence does not exist which would permit us to identify a diagnostic entity as it is defined by Strauss, Lehtinen, Kephart, and others. I would guess that the syndrome is artifactual - that a diagnosis of neurological impairment, perceptual handicap, or minimal brain damage is frequently rendered by exclusion; i.e., the behaviour cluster does not fit readily into any existing diagnostic category, hence it is an artifact of our own ignorance and lack of solid descriptive research.

Administrative Arrangements for Perceptually Handicapped Children
Whether or not a diagnostic entity exists, one may question whether it is wise to establish separate special classes for children who display the kinds of behaviour thought to constitute this syndrome. Several questions arise in this connection: First, one may ask what are the effects of special class techniques on the learning skills of the subjects? Second, which, if any of the programmes of instruction that have been recommended would be most beneficial? Third, how do the recommended techniques differ from sound principles already established for the teaching of other "special" categories of children? Finally, what is likely to be the effect of leaving him in the regular classroom?

Unfortunately, solid research data on the first question are not available. Some proponents of particular techniques and methods for the training of the perceptually handicapped have even held that it is immoral to withhold a treatment if one thinks it could benefit a child, therefore have systematically and categorically refused to compare the performances of children who receive their methods of instruction with the performances of similar children who get no special instruction, or instruction with some other method. This is a familiar argument to psychologists and psychiatrists who have been interested in psychotherapy and its effectiveness in reducing personality disorders. The usual solution is to use the inevitable waiting list as an untreated control group. By so doing, one can

122

offer treatment to the control subjects later, and avoid the moral controversy. I would even wonder whether it is not more immoral to proceed with an unproved treatment procedure, not knowing what the effects will be, than to spend one's time and resources carrying out intensive research comparing treated with untreated subjects.

There is a tiny bit of evidence on which programme may be most beneficial. One investigator (Gallagher, 1960) has studied the effects of highly individualized diagnosis and instruction programmes over three years with neurologically impaired children in a residential school. Each pupil was given one hour a day of individualized tutoring based upon that child's own pattern of strengths and weaknesses. There was a crash programme of perceptual, conceptual, and language development exercises but there was no attempt to follow the Strauss-Lehtinen approach per se. As contrasted with a control group, the experimental subjects improved in intellectual development, increased in attention span, and achieved more in verbal than in non-verbal areas. The experimenters concluded: "It is quite likely that history will also record we have been entirely too pessimistic about the possible training potential of the brain-injured, and that this pessimism has prevented us from giving them the intellectual and educational stimulation that we would wish for all our children" (Gallagher, 1960, p. 168). Dunn interprets this to mean that here "we have evidence that the Strauss-Lehtinen techniques are not necessary to achieve moderately good results with neurologically impaired pupils."

During the last five years, I have made it a practice to visit special classrooms for the educable mentally retarded, the visually limited, the hard-of-hearing, the emotionally disturbed, and recently, the perceptually handicapped. During this time, and for some time before that, I have frequently examined children brought by their parents to a mental health clinic or to the Peabody College Child Study Center because they were having problems in schoolwork or in their social relationships or at home, and I have regularly supervised other psychologists who have worked with such children. Two significant conclusions emerge from this observational experience: the first is that what psychologists recommend in the way of special teaching procedures differs little, whether the diagnosis is high-level mental retardation, emotional disturbance, or perceptual handicap. The second is that there is amazingly little variation in the teaching methods used in these different classrooms.

When one reviews the history of the special education movement in the United States and in Canada, one finds that the most detailed information on teaching methods and on the efficacy of special classes is to be found in the area of the mentally retarded. A large number of studies have been carried out to assess the effect of special class placement on the mentally retarded child, some stressing effects on academic achievement, others stressing effects on social and personal adjustment, and still others investigating both simultaneously. The best of these studies have compared children placed in special classes with quite similar children left in the regular classroom. The most convincing conclusion from this accumulation of studies is that special class placement not only does not enhance the academic achievement of the retarded child, it frequently results in lower levels of achievement than are attained by those children who were left in the regular classes. There is fairly consistent agreement, however, that special class children do develop more adequate social and personal adjustment, although these qualities are much more difficult to measure reliably than is academic achievement. If this experience with the mentally retarded can teach us anything

123

about the perceptually handicapped, it is probably that in looking for alternatives
to special class placement, we should try to find situations in which we can avoid
not only the damaging personal experience of repeated failure in a regular class,
but also the loss of learning in the academic areas that seems to accompany special
class placement. In this connection, a very few studies have been concerned with
the effects of "labelling," i.e. the effect on the child of being officially
designated as "different," "abnormal," "slow," or incapable of learning in the
regular classroom. The consensus is that while special class placement helps to
prevent the development of unrealistic expectations of one's own ability and
achievement, this supposed advantage is usually accompanied by a marked deficiency
in self-concept; i.e. the child sees himself increasingly as "dumb," "a special
case," and incapable generally, even though his deficiency may be quite specific
and he may be capable of learning at a normal rate in some areas of work.

The Future

In the unlikely event that it is not already apparent, let me now summarize what
I believe to be the most justifiable statement one can make about the area of
perceptual handicap, and then propose an educational procedure that I think makes
sense and would be beneficial to children with learning disorders. First of all,
I believe that we do not have sufficient descriptive evidence to support a separate
diagnostic entity labelled "perceptual handicap." It seems to me that some dysfunction of perception is inherent in a number of conditions having quite diverse
etiologies, and that one might well focus not so much on the probable etiology as
on the major symptom itself, which is a disturbance in the efficiency of learning,
especially of school-related material. Second, I believe that commitment to any
specific method of training children identified as perceptually handicapped is
premature, and may have in it the danger of precluding systematic investigation and
experimentation with other methods as they develop. No single instructional or
training method has had adequate controlled evaluation, using untreated control
groups. Until that occurs, and the treatments can be specified and replicated by
other investigators in other places, the special education of this category of
children should remain on an experimental basis, with continuing readiness to shift
to other programmes for trial periods. Third, it has been my observation that
classes for the perceptually handicapped typically include children who are more
properly diagnosed as educable mentally retarded, emotionally disturbed, clearly
brain-damaged, visually limited, or hard of hearing. Hence, there is considerable
work yet to be done in establishing the diagnostic criteria and diagnostic
methods to be used in classifying such children. In a complete and adequate
diagnostic study with a child who is thought to be perceptually handicapped and
with the use of existing instruments and techniques, I would think it imperative
that no diagnosis be rendered unless the following procedures are employed: assessment of intellectual ability using both verbal and non-verbal tests; assessment of
social functioning, using a measure like the Vineland Social Maturity Scale; assessment of neuropsychological functions, using something like the Halstead-Reitan
neuropsychological battery, the Bender Visual-Motor Gestalt Test, the Benton Visual
Retention Test, the Graham-Kendall Memory-for-Designs Test, and other neuropsychological procedures that have clear standardization norms; further assessment of
perceptual functioning, using instruments such as the Kephart tests, the Frostig
tests, and consultation with a neurologist and/or specialist in the particular
area of functioning which is thought to be deficient; educational assessment using
standardized tests of educational achievement, and in particular using such diagnostic reading tests as the Durrell Analysis of Reading Difficulty and the Triggs
Reading Survey; sensory examination to test for deficiencies in vision and hearing;
personality assessment involving the use of clinical interviews and standardized

instruments for personality diagnosis. With such an exhaustive diagnostic survey, particular strengths and weaknesses, both in basic abilities and in learning achievement, can be spotted and a profile of these strengths and weaknesses constructed. I should emphasize particularly the need to chart a child's strong areas as well as his weak ones, since most diagnostic studies concentrate unduly on the latter. The construction of a useful programme of instruction requires knowledge of strong areas of ability as well as weak ones, so that the strong areas can be used to stimulate work in the weak areas.

With diagnostic emphasis on the construction of profiles of particular strengths and weaknesses for every individual child, I should pay no attention whatever to diagnostic labels except in those cases in which very particular sensory or orthopedic handicaps make quite specific educational procedures imperative, such as the blind or deaf child. I should reduce to three or four the fifteen to eighteen different areas of exceptionality now served by the typical city school system. The largest of these areas I should designate simply "major learning disorders." There would be no separate special classes, but there would be special teachers and special classrooms in the regular schools. Children with learning disorders would remain in the regular classes, appropriate for their chronological age level, for those class periods in which they were performing at or near a normal level. For perhaps one or two periods per day they would be taken to the special classroom for remedial instruction in their areas of deficiency, but would always return to the regular classroom for recreational and social events. In the same way, children who are exceptionally competent in particular areas might go to a separate classroom or laboratory or library for periods of extra work and stimulation. Since these children, too, appear to need the social stimulation of their age peers, it would also be quite important that they return to the regular classroom for subjects in which they are not markedly different from the normal expectation, and for social and recreational events.

As part of such a programme, I would urge that parents encourage their children's participation in valid, closely inspected research programmes designed to try out carefully worked-out methods of teaching particular skills and subjects. In fact, I believe that every parent of an exceptional child will want to urge school officials to encourage continuing investigation in teaching methods and curricula. We have as much reason to expect significant change and improvement in this area as in the physical sciences and in technology, and even less reason to wish to cling to traditional curricula and methods in the face of ever-changing demands upon all members of society.

Finally, a personal word to this Association. I have seen, since coming to Canada, what remarkable strides can be made by a volunteer association interested in the development of children. I have become convinced that while science waits for many things, including the development of theory and the development of techniques of measurement, it waits for nothing quite so eagerly as for the enthusiastic prodding that can only be delivered by a dedicated group of persons who are determined to find solutions to pressing social problems. The Canadian and Ontario Associations for the Mentally Retarded have instigated and supported some of the most significant research done in the last ten years in the area of mental retardation. The Crippled Children's Society has done a similar job in insisting that some answers be found in the areas of the causes and treatments of crippling diseases of childhood. I would strongly recommend to you that considerable portions of your energies and resources be devoted at this crucial time in your history to the instigation and support of research in learning disorders, even if some of the energy and resources must be borrowed from your important efforts to provide appropriate educational treatments for today's children today. In spite of the pressing need for appropriate education for every child, your association is concerned with an area in which we simply do not know what the appropriate treatments are. If you vigorously demand well-conceived and well-executed research efforts in this area, tomorrow's children will thank you.

REFERENCES

Burnette, E. Influence of classroom environment on word learning of retarded children with high and low activity levels. Unpublished doctoral dissertation, George Peabody College, 1962.

Capobianco, R.J. Qualitative and quantitative analyses of endogenous and exogenous boys on arithmetic achievement. In L.M. Dunn and R.J. Capobianco, Studies in reading and arithmetic in mentally retarded boys. Child Development Publications, Lafayette, Indiana: Purdue University, 1956. (Monographs of the Society for Research in Child Development, 1956.)

Capobianco, R.J. & Miller, D.Y. Quantitative and qualitative analysis of exogenous and endogenous children in some reading processes. Syracuse, New York: Syracuse University Research Institute, 1958.

Cromwell, R.L., Baumeister, A., and Hawkins, W.F. "Research in activity level." In N.R. Ellis (Editor), Handbook of mental deficiency: psychological theory and research. New York: McGraw-Hill, 1963. Pp. 632-663.

Doman, R.J. & Delacato, C.H., et al. Children with severe brain injuries. Journal of the American Medical Association, 1960, 174, 257-262.

Dunn, L.M. Minimal brain dysfunction: a dilemma for educators. In H.C. Haywood (Editor), Brain damage in school-age children. (In preparation.)

Evans, J.R. Creeping skills and reading achievement of first grade school children. Paper given at American Association on Mental Deficiency, Chicago, May, 1966.

Gallagher, J.J. Tutoring of brain-injured mentally retarded children. Springfield, Illinois: Charles C. Thomas, 1960.

Halstead, W.C. Brain and intelligence. Chicago: University of Chicago Press, 1947.

Haywood, H.C. and Tapp, J.T. Experience and the development of adaptive behavior. In N.R. Ellis (Editor), International review of research in mental retardation. New York: Academic Press, 1966.

Kephart, N.C. The slow learner in the classroom. Columbus, Ohio: Merrill, 1960.

Reitan, R.M. A research program on the psychological effects of brain lesions in human beings. In N.R. Ellis (Editor), International review of research in mental retardation. New York: Academic Press, 1966.

Semmel, M.I. Comparison of teacher ratings of brain-injured and mongoloid severely retarded (trainable) children attending community day-school classes. American Journal of Mental Deficiency, 1960, 64, 963-971.

Strauss & Lehtinen. Psychopathology and education of the brain-injured child. NY,1947.

Creative Thinking in Retarded Children

HOWARD H. SPICKER

Since the publication of Guilford's (1959) theoretical model of the Structure of Intellect, a wave of studies on the intellectual operation he referred to as "divergent" or creative thinking ability has emerged. In the wake of this interest, several investigators have attempted to study the creative thinking abilities of mentally retarded children. These studies have focused on two questions:

1. How do the creative thinking abilities of retarded children compare with those of intellectually normal children?

2. Can the creative thinking abilities of retarded children be increased?

One of the most extensive comparisons of the creative thinking abilities of educable mentally retarded (EMR) children with those of intellectually normal children was made by Smith (1967). Forty-eight EMR children with Kuhlmann-Anderson IQ's below 80, enrolled in regular fifth grades, were matched with 48 intellectually normal (IQ's between 90 and 120) fifth grade children on the basis of sex, race, socioeconomic status, and school setting. The two groups were then compared on 22 creativity factors derived from eight tests of divergent thinking ability developed by Guilford and Torrance. The comparisons indicated that the normal children significantly exceeded the retarded children on 12 of the 14 verbal creativity factors. However, there were no significant differences between the groups on the seven nonverbal creativity factors. Since the selection of the retarded subjects was based on their poor performance on a verbal and pencil group intelligence test, it is possible that the poor verbal creative thinking scores obtained by the retarded children were produced by that selection factor. It is also conceivable that the verbal productive thinking deficits were indices of poor expressive language abilities rather than true deficits in creative thinking abilities.

Several investigators have attempted to determine whether the creative thinking abilities of retarded children can be enhanced. Tisdall (1962), as part of the Goldstein, Moss, and Jordan (1965) special class efficacy study, compared a group of EMR children enrolled in special classes with a group of EMR children and a group of intellectually normal children enrolled in the regular grades on three verbal and three nonverbal tests of creativity developed by Torrance. The special class EMR children had been exposed to a curriculum which had emphasized the discovery approach to learning for approximately two years. The regular class EMR and normal children had been taught by traditional first and second grade proce-

Education and Training of the Mentally Retarded, December, 1967, Vol.2, No.3, pp. 190-192.

127

dures. The comparison indicated that the special class retardates were significantly superior to the regular class retardates on all verbal measures of creativity. In addition, verbal productive thinking abilities of the special class EMR children did not differ significantly from those of the intellectually normal children. However, as in the Smith study (1967), the three groups did not differ significantly from one another on the nonverbal tests of creativity. If, on the basis of random assignment of the EMR children into regular or special classes, one can assume that the verbal creative thinking abilities of the two groups were comparable prior to treatment, then it must be concluded that some aspect of the special class curriculum enhanced verbal productive thinking. Since no direct teaching toward increased divergent thinking was included in the special classes, it is impossible to determine which specific aspect or aspects of the special class curriculum produced the increased verbal creative thinking scores. Tisdall attributes the better performance of the special class subjects to the inductive or "discovery" methods which were employed by the special class teachers. Another possibility is that the extensive prereading language development program (Goldstein, Moss, and Jordan, 1965), to which the special class children had been exposed, produced the gains. This explanation gains credence when one notes the similarity between the language development program and some of the verbal items of the creativity tests.

A more direct attempt at increasing the divergent thinking abilities of EMR children was made by Rouse (1965). Thirty lessons designed to foster creative thinking were presented to 47 EMR special class children between the ages of 7-5 and 16-0 on a daily 30 minute basis for six weeks. The lessons included opportunities for clarifying and developing principles used in making transformations (i.e., size, shape, substitutions). In addition:

> . . . observation was included to make better use of the senses; originality was the goal of some of the lessons; improvisation with materials at hand to solve problems was tried . . . most of the lessons were built around the technique of brainstorming solutions to given problems . . . [Rouse, 1965, pp. 668-669].

Pre- and posttest divergent thinking comparisons between the experimental group and a comparable CA, MA, IQ control group were made, using one verbal and one nonverbal test of creativity developed by Torrance. On both tests, the pre- to posttest gains made by the experimental group were significantly greater than those made by the control group. However, a comparison of the Rouse findings with those of Smith (1967) shows that the creativity scores obtained by the retarded children *after* treatment were merely comparable to those scores obtained by normal children who were two years younger than the retarded children. It remains to be demonstrated whether a longer treatment period would have closed the productive thinking gap between retarded and normal children. Further research is also needed to determine whether the productive thinking gains made during treatment will be retained after the treatment ceases.

Although it appears that retarded children exhibit some degree of divergent thinking ability which can be enhanced by a direct intervention program, the most crucial question concerning the creative thinking abilities of retarded children has not yet been answered by any investigator. How is productive thinking in retarded children manifested? As shown by numerous investigators (Getzels and Jackson, 1962; Torrance, 1962; Wallach and Kogan, 1965), high divergent thinking ability when coupled with an IQ of

115 or better is likely to enhance academic achievement. The fact that the academic performance of the high productive thinking EMR special class children from Tisdall's (1962) study did not exceed that of the EMR regular class children seems to indicate that the creative thinking abilities of retarded children are either inadequate or nonfunctional for enhancing academic achievement. Furthermore, there has been no evidence to indicate that the productive thinking abilities of retarded children are related to superiority in such creative endeavors as inventiveness or artistic and/or musical expression. However, it is possible that the kinds of divergent thinking exercises developed by Rouse may be extremely beneficial for developing the expressive language abilities of retarded children. Should this be the case, the inclusion of divergent thinking lessons in the curriculum for EMR children would be more than justified.

References

Getzels, J. W., and Jackson, P. W. *Creativity and intelligence.* New York: Wiley and Sons, 1962.

Goldstein, H., Moss, J. W., and Jordan, Laura J. *The efficacy of special class training on the development of mentally retarded children.* US Office of Education Cooperative Research Project Report No. 619. Washington: US Government Printing Office, 1965.

Guilford, J. P. Three faces of intellect. *American Psychologist,* 1959, **14**, 469-479.

Rouse, Sue T. Effects of a training program on the productive thinking of educable mental retardates. *American Journal of Mental Deficiency,* 1965, **69**, 666-673.

Smith, R. M. Creative thinking abilities of educable mentally handicapped children in the regular grades. *American Journal of Mental Deficiency,* 1967, **71**, 571-575.

Tisdall, W. J. Productive thinking in retarded children. *Exceptional Children,* 1962, **29**, 36-41.

Torrance, E. P. *Guiding creative talent.* Englewood Cliffs, New Jersey: Prentice-Hall, 1962.

Wallach, M. A., and Kogan, N. *Modes of thinking in young children.* New York: Holt, Rinehart and Winston, 1965.

HOWARD H. SPICKER *is Associate Professor and Chairman, Department of Special Education, Indiana University, Bloomington.*

On Individual Differences in Language Competence and Performance[1]

COURTNEY B. CAZDEN, Ed. D.

Harvard University

In a recent paper (Cazden, 1966) I reviewed research on subcultural differences in child language. While the analyses in that paper are still relevant, there is at least one important omission: no mention is made of the distinction between language *competence* and language *performance* (italicized to signify specialized usage). The purpose of the present paper is to explain that distinction and explore its implications for understanding individual and group differences in command of language. While the phrase "individual differences" will be used hereafter, the discussion applies to group differences as well. They are simply individual differences whose distributions correlate with attributes of group membership such as sex, IQ, social class or degree of physical impairment such as deafness.

The paper is divided into five sections. First, the terms *competence* and *performance* are explained. Next, three specific research areas are discussed. Last, the significance of looking at language in this way is suggested.

COMPETENCE AND *PERFORMANCE*

The term "competence" has two meanings. In the more general and familiar meaning, competence is "the quality or state of being functionally adequate" (Webster's Third International). In his article "Social Structure and the Socialization of Competence," Inkeles defines competence in this sense as "the ability to attain and perform in valued social roles" (1966, p. 280). In Inkeles's scheme, one element of competence consists of skills, "aptitudes which have been trained or developed in accord with some cultural pattern" (Inkeles, 1966, p. 269). One of these skills is "the command of language."

[1] Work on this paper was supported in part by Public Health Service Research Grant MH 7088 from the National Institute of Mental Health to Roger Brown, and in part by Office of Education Contract OE5-10-239 with the Center for Research and Development on Educational Differences, Harvard University.

Journal of Special Education, Winter, 1967, Vol.1, No.2, pp. 135-150.

130

When we turn to recent studies of language, we find the term *competence* in its more restricted and technical meaning. Here *competence* is contrasted with *performance*. This contrast is a special case of the general distinction between learning and performance which has been familiar to psychologists at least since Lashley's 1929 review of the literature on learning: learning is what a person knows while performance is what he does; learning is knowledge, conscious or not, while performance is behavior. In the case of language, *competence* is the speaker-hearer's knowledge of his language—the finite system of rules which enable him to comprehend and produce an infinite number of novel sentences.

A grammar is a description constructed by linguists of such a system of rules. In the range of phenomena they explain, the most powerful grammars available today are those constructed by the group of transformational linguists centering around Noam Chomsky.[2] Grammars, like all scientific descriptions of natural phenomena, are subject to continuous revision and correction.

Current research on language acquisition focuses on the development of *competence*. The aim is to describe and explain the progressively more complex systems of rules with which children comprehend and produce speech or, in other terms, to describe and explain the stages they go through en route to mature *competence* in their native language. For example, what are the stages in the development of the noun phrase? How do children learn noun and verb

inflections? How do they learn to use negatives and ask questions? An excellent overview of the work and the controversies in this area of research is now available in *The Genesis of Language* (Smith & Miller, Eds., 1966).[3]

Performance is the expression or realization of *competence* in behavior. But does it refer to what people *can* comprehend and produce or to what people habitually *do* comprehend and produce or both? I suggest we separate these two meanings. Since both are specialized, let us call them *performance A* and *performance B*. They contrast in the (somewhat oversimplified) ways: (see opposite page).

Note that *performance A* is not the same as *competence*.[4] While any sentence that conforms to a given system of rules is "grammatical," not all grammatical sentences are "acceptable." What a person can accept, or cope with, either in encoding or decoding, is a reduced set of all possible grammatical sentences. For example the following three sentences are all grammatical (a matter of *competence*) but vary in acceptability (a matter of *performance A*) from easy (1) to tolerable (2) to nearly impossible (3).

1. The man the boy pointed out is a friend of mine.
2. The man the boy the student recognized pointed out is a friend of mine.

2 See Chomsky (1965), for a discussion of issues in linguistic theory; see Thomas (1965) for a readable description of a transformational grammar of English.

3 Readers who wish a beautifully written general introduction to language should read the two chapters on "Language: The System and its Acquisition" in Brown, 1965, pp. 246-349.

4 It is important to keep in mind that terminology is a matter of definition and convention. One could subsume what I am calling *competence* and *performance A* under the single term *competence* and then subdivide it into linguistic and psychological components. My colleague, Arthur McCaffrey (unpublished memorandum) and others have suggested just this. What are important are the distinctions among phenomena. The choice of labels matters only to the extent that associations aroused in the user sharpen or blur those distinctions.

Performance A and Performance B Contrasted

	Performance A	Performance B
Definition	Verbal abilities	Verbal habits
	What a person *can* do	What a person *does* do
	The realization of linguistic knowledge in behavior as affected by such intrapersonal factors as attention and memory	The realization of linguistic knowledge in behavior as affected by such interpersonal factors as setting, topic, participants and language function
Investigators	Psycholinguists	Sociolinguists
Setting for research	Experimental situations	Natural speech situations

3. The man the boy the student the dog barked at recognized pointed out is a friend of mine.

One focus of current work in psycholinguistics is the construction of a "model of performance" in the *performance A* sense.

The most we can say concerning a grammatical performance model is that it must incorporate a component that represents the language user's grammatical competence; that it must process speech in a single pass, from left to right, in real time; that it is constrained by the limitations of short-term memory; that it must allow for both the production and the reception of speech; and that it can be generalized to ungrammatical materials. (Miller & McNeill, forthcoming).

Just as *performance A* is the product of interaction between underlying knowledge and non-linguistic psychological factors affecting its expression, so *performance B* is, in turn, the product of interaction between *performance A* and situational factors such as setting and function. In this sense, *competence, performance A* and *performance B* can be placed on a continuum as phenomena of increasing complexity.

We can also look at this continuum in another way—as a progressive narrowing of possibilities for any individual at the point of constructing an utterance. Figure 1 may clarify these relationships.

FIGURE 1

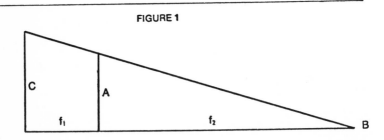

Here, *C*, the vertical line at the extreme left, represents *competence*—the infinite set of sentences which the individual's knowledge makes possible. *A*, the shorter vertical line to the right, represents *performance A*—the subset (still infinite) of grammatical sentences which the particular individual can encode or decode. *B*, the apex of the triangle at the extreme right, represents *performance B*—the utterance actually spoken in a particular situation. The spaces between *C*, *A*, and *B* represent factors affecting the individual: f_1 is the set of intrapersonal constraints which account for the reduction of *C* to *A*; f_2 is the set of interpersonal influences which account for the selection of *B*.

The question about the nature of individual differences can now be formulated more precisely: to what extent can individual differences in competence (functional adequacy) in the command of language be explained by differences in *competence* (linguistic knowledge), differences in *performance A* (psychological constraints on the realization of *competence*) or differences in *performance B* (patterns of use in actual verbal interactions)? The next three sections are devoted to research in these three areas.

INDIVIDUAL DIFFERENCES IN COMPETENCE

Current research on individual differences in *competence* is prompted by the assertion of transformational linguists that such differences do not exist. It is asserted that individual differences in language, other than vocabulary, are a matter of *performance* only, not of underlying linguistic knowledge at all. This assertion usually remains implicit in the writings of transformational grammarians, but often is expressed orally in answers to questions. Occasionally, an explicit written statement is made. For example:

Variation in performance with intelligence (in non-linguistic tasks) contrasts with the performance of speakers with respect to some purely linguistic skill, where no significant individual differences are found (Katz, 1964, p. 415).

This assertion is derived from a theory that the acquisition of language is accomplished by the very young child (approximately 2 to 4 years of age) in a remarkably short time because human beings are so neurologically pre-programmed with a "language acquisition device" that only a minimum of environmental exposure to language is necessary for the realization of innate potentiality. This minimum is almost universally available to the growing child, and a shared competence is the result. See *The Genesis of Language* (Smith & Miller, 1966) for extensive discussion of this theory.

One can separate stronger and weaker versions of the hypothesis of no individual differences. According to the strong version, no individual differences in *competence* exist even during the developmental period. According to the weak version, no such differences are present among mature speakers. That is, *competence* can be the same for all members· of a linguistic community at any given stage of linguistic development; it may be the same for all mature speakers in a linguistic community but differ in the rate at which it is developed or acquired;[5] it may differ even among

5 Again, matters of terminology intrude. I have asked whether members of a linguistic community share a common *competence*. But if the category "linguistic community" is defined in terms of the *competence* or linguistic knowledge of its members, then the question to be asked is whether the category "linguistic community" must be subdivided along such lines as social class.

mature speakers. I doubt if linguists would stand by the strong version if pressed to defend it. It is not necessary to their theory and is directly contradicted by widespread empirical evidence. The status of the weak version is much less clear.

Because of the significance of the theoretical work of the transformational linguists, it is important to spell out why the strong version is not required for theoretical consistency. Three reasons can be suggested. First, the linguists are primarily asserting the importance of common features of the language acquisition process and the *relative* nonsignificance of individual differences. Even Katz qualifies his statement quoted above in this way.

Second, Chomsky (1965) argues against the notion that linguistic or non-linguistic aspects of unique individual experience can in any way determine the *direction* which the acquisition of a given language takes, whatever their effect on rate. About the linguistic aspects of individual experience he says:

> Certain kinds of data and experience may be required in order to set the language acquisition device into operation, although they may not affect the *manner* of its functioning in the least. Thus it has been found that semantic reference may greatly facilitate performance in a syntax-learning experiment, even though it does not, apparently, affect the *manner* in which acquisition of syntax proceeds (Chomsky, 1965, p. 33).

The critical word is *manner*, italicized in the original. I interpret this statement to mean that experience will not affect the course of acquisition but may facilitate or retard it. (Note the similarity to Piagetian ideas on the acquisition of logical operations.) Chomsky also implies that non-linguistic aspects of experience may be facilitating or retarding as well.

> To take one of innumerable examples from studies of animal learning; it has been observed... that depth perception in lambs is considerably facilitated by mother-neonate contact, although again there is no reason to suppose that the nature of the lamb's "Theory of visual space" depends on this contact (Chomsky, 1965, p. 34).

Third, according to transformational linguistic theory, any language includes universal and language-specific elements. For example, it is hypothesized that all languages express basic grammatical relations such as subject-verb, verb-object, and modifier-noun, while languages clearly differ in whether and how number and gender are expressed. (See D. McNeill's chapter "Developmental Psycholinguistics" in *The Genesis of Language*, pp. 15-84 and the ensuing conference discussion.) Variations in individual experience may affect the acquisition of the universal and language-specific components in different ways. Perhaps acquisition of the universal aspects requires less exposure to examples of well-formed speech, shows less variability across children, and is reflected in fewer errors during the period of acquisition by each child. Perhaps, conversely, acquisition of language-specific aspects requires more exposure, shows greater variability among children, and is reflected in more errors by each child. Future research on environmental assistance to the child's acquisition of grammar should recognize this distinction.

In addition to theoretical arguments against the necessity of entertaining the strong version of the hypothesis of no individual differences in linguistic *competence,* there is a large body of empirical data on developmental differences which cannot be interpreted as differences in *performance* only. Lenneberg's chapter "The Natural History of Language" in *The Genesis of Language* (pp. 219-252) includes a discussion of this data with particular reference to "the development of children with various abnormalities." While there is remarkable constancy across children in the age of appearance of what he calls "speech milestones"—the appearance of the first word and the first two-word and later five-word constructions — environmental differences affect the subsequent development of these aptitudes.

Experimental research on *competence* is, in Roger Brown's words (personal communication, 1966) "probing for knowledge rather than letting it display itself." To test the weak hypothesis, we want to know if mature speakers of English control the same grammar or not and we want to know the extent of individual differences in *competence* during the developmental period.

In a recent study, Leila Gleitman and her colleagues probed for linguistic knowledge with adults, specifically to determine whether individual differences in *competence* exist:

Since we must explain people's use of new sentences, we must assume that somehow they have internalized a systematic picture of the web of well-formed sentences. Just how complex that picture must be depends on the variety of the sentential structures and the depth of the network that inter-relates them...How uniform are people in their organization of the language? (Gleitman, Shipley & Smith, 1965, pp. 6, 7).

For their linguistic material, Gleitman *et al.* used the process of forming compound nouns. The full description of the rules for forming nominalizations in English is a long one. Suffice here to give one of the simpler rules and to note its recursiveness:

$$N_1 \begin{bmatrix} \text{that V} \\ \text{for} \end{bmatrix} N_2 \ (+ \text{ plural}) \rightarrow N_2 N_1$$

food for ducks $\rightarrow$ duck food
man that brings duck food $\rightarrow$ duck food man

The task in Gleitman's experiment was to provide a paraphrase for 144 compound nouns. Each stimulus included the words *bird house* plus a third word from a set of 12 familiar ones. Twelve word combinations in six possible orders and two intonation contours gave a set of 144 stimuli for each subject. The subjects were drawn from three educational backgrounds: graduate students (group A), college undergraduates (group B), and people who had not gone beyond high school (group C). The incidence of errors in providing a paraphrase was:

> Group A: 16
> Group B: 64
> Group C: 89

In other terms, group differences account for 28% of the total variance. After extensive discussion of the nature of the stimuli and type of errors within and across groups Gleitman concluded that individual differences in *competence* do exist.

The reactions of a linguist and a psychologist to this study suggest two problems in this kind of research. The linguist said in essence: *"competence* refers only to the possession of the basic set of phrase structure and transformation rules; it does not extend to the use of these rules in various combinations. The latter is properly an aspect of *performance.* Specifically, in the case of nominalization, as long as everybody can cope with a two-word nominalization—e.g. *bird house*—a common or shared *competence* has been demonstrated. Use of the rules recursively to produce or comprehend longer nominalizations is a *performance* matter on which the theory makes no predictions."

The first problem is thus the need for a clear-cut specification by linguists of the boundary between *competence* and *performance*. In order to test the hypothesis that *competence* is the same, we need a clear separation of those kinds of complexity which are subsumed under each category. Otherwise, the argument becomes a circular one: *competence* is shared, and if something is not shared it is simply not a part of *competence*. Such circularity is present in some writings. For instance, here again is the sentence by Katz quoted above and another sentence which appears later in the same paragraph:

> Variation in performance with intelligence [in non-linguistic tasks] contrasts with the performance of speakers with respect to some purely linguistic skill, where no significant individual differences are found...A necessary condition for something to be part of the subject matter of a linguistic theory is that each speaker be able to perform in that regard much as every other does (Katz, 1964, p. 415).

The second problem was raised by a psychologist: "Even if understanding the compound noun may be a matter of *competence*, the experimental task of providing a paraphrase may introduce performance variables, (a point which Gleitman *et al.*, 1965, discuss). Assurance that the knowledge one is probing for is a matter of *competence* is necessary but not sufficient for interpretable research. In addition, the way in which the subjects are asked to demonstrate that knowledge must not introduce performance variables which will mask the results.

In research on children's *competence*, a third problem arises—how to design an experimental situation in which one can successfully probe for children's knowledge. Various techniques have been used in previous research. Children under 3 can be trained to repeat sentences (Menyuk, 1963) but the results are at best an indirect index of knowledge, one which depends on a better understanding than we now have of the relation between imitation, comprehension and production. Berko's (1958) test of English morphology works beautifully, but only for certain morphological rules. Pictures can be used to force a response to single contrasts —e.g. *the sheep is jumping* vs. *the sheep are jumping* (Fraser, Bellugi & Brown, 1963), but only a limited set of contrasts can be pictured. Furthermore, in any test using pictures, differences in linguistic *competence* may be confounded with differences in the ability to interpret pictures. In a classification task, Sigel & McBane found that "lower class children were significantly less consistent in categorization of pictures as compared to three-dimensional objects...The ability to deal with representational material was less developed in these children than in their middle class counterparts, even though there was no difference between the groups in the ability to identify and label the pictures" (1966, p. 3). It is independently important to understand why children respond differently to pictures, but if Sigel's findings are valid we should be wary of using pictures as stimulus materials in experimental situations designed to measure individual differences in linguistic *competence*.

Two other approaches to measuring children's *competence* are being

Ask Mommy what the calendar's for.	What is this for Mom?	+
Ask the man how he can climb out of the water.	How you can climb out of the water with the alligator?	—
Ask him where he can get a boat.	Where can you get a boat?	+
Ask Daddy why he can't make a better bed.	Why you can't make a better bed?	—
Ask him why he can't put in the windows.	Why you can't put in the windows?	—
Ask Daddy what he can make out of that.	What you can make out of that?	—
Ask him why he won't stop tickling.	Why you won't tickle—stop tickling me?	—

Spontaneous Questions

What else we did, Mom?	—
Where does it say my school?	+
What is this gonna be?	+
How come you eat Cereal?	

NB. This alternate colloquial form of why *question eliminates the transposition requirement.*

Sarah: Elicitation of Single and Conjoined Pronouns

The bunny can fall down, or—	He can	+
We can put the glasses on the bunny, or We can put the glasses on—	Her	+
The dollie has glasses on, or—	Him have glasses	—
The bunny rabbit and the big girl are hungry, or the bunny rabbit and—	Her is very hungry.	—
I like the bunny rabbit and the big girl, or I like the bunny rabbit and—	Her.	+
The bunny can hop, or	He can jump.	+
Can the girl and the bunny lie down? or can the girl and—	Him.	—
Can the bunny rabbit jump? or can—	He hop.	+
Can the girl sit? or can—	He sit.	+
Can the bunny and the girl sit? or Can the bunny and—	Her—sit together.	—

tried by Brown and his colleagues at Harvard with Adam, Eve, and Sarah—the three subjects of his longitudinal study (Brown & Bellugi, 1964) who are now 5 and 6 years old. One approach probes for *competence* underlying production. Two examples of Sarah's protocols are shown on the preceding page. In the first example, we elicited questions by an imperative which included the indirect form: *Ask him where he can get a boat.* By selecting *wh*-questions with auxiliaries, we could discover whether Sarah was able to transpose the auxiliary correctly: *Where he can get* to *Where can he get.* The reader may note that some of the questions invoke implausible events in a family kitchen like alligators climbing out of the water. Conversation between puppets is an easy way to remove normal constraints on plausibility and make it easier to condense many experimental situations into a small period of time. One does not have to wait for openings to say, *Ask Daddy* or *Ask Mommy.*

The pluses and minuses in the right-hand column show the pattern of Sarah's responses: she sometimes transposes correctly for positive questions but never for negative ones.

In the second example, we elicited pronouns as a single or conjoined subject to see whether Sarah would use the subject or object form. With dolls and stuffed animals, a simple training procedure was used: The experimenter made the doll jump or sit down, modeled the desired response, and then asked Sarah to provide part of it. *We can say, "The doll can jump," or we can say, "She can jump." We can say, "The doll can sit down," or we can say...."* Here Sarah responded, *She can sit down.* During the training procedure, the object form of the pronoun was also elicited to make sure that in the testing situation both forms (e.g. *he* and *him*) were available to the child. Similarly, when the child was giving many objective forms, we returned to a sentence with a single pronoun in subject position (as in the second and third from the last) to make sure that the child had not simply become conditioned to use the objective form.

The pluses and minuses at the right show the pattern of her responses. Sarah consistently uses the object form for a conjoined subject, and sometimes uses it for a single subject.

The first task has also been used with Eve and Adam. We find both a common developmental progression and individual differences in the age at which this progression is completed. Eve, the same age as Sarah, transformed all auxiliaries correctly. Adam, a year older than the two girls, is in an intermediate developmental position. He consistently transformed those in positive questions and consistently failed to do so in the negative ones. Two of Brown's graduate students, Anita Rui and Donald Finkel, are now using this and other similar procedures (e.g. the elicitation of tag questions: He's going, *isn't he?)* with a group of first grade children from different social class groups. They are also probing for *competence* underlying comprehension by asking the children to manipulate objects: *Show me the boy being chased by the dog. Now show me the dog being chased by the boy.*

Here a fourth problem will arise: how should this data be scored? How does one decide when to credit a child with a particular bit of linguistic knowledge? Psychologists are accustomed to dealing with frequencies

138

and mean scores. But for assessing whether a child knows or doesn't know, such methods seem inappropriate. For linguists, by contrast, one example proves *competence* and all instances to the contrary can be explained by interferences of performance factors such as momentary inattention. This too seems wrong. Take the case of chess, often used to explain the *competence-performance* distinction. A person's knowledge of the rules is his *competence*, while the actual moves constitute his *performance*. Suppose one set up an experimental situation where two people were faced with the same board and then compared in their next moves. Let us say further that both people made the same move. Can one then infer the same knowledge, even in reference only to this part of the total game of chess? May not one person have a more complete understanding of the relation of this move to all other moves? What is the criteria of "understanding?" And how does the problem of criteria relate to the problem of definition?[6]

INDIVIDUAL DIFFERENCES IN PERFORMANCE A

Performance A is a product of the constraints placed on the expression of linguistic *competence* during the encoding or decoding process. There is general agreement in the writings of the transformational linguists that factors such as memory limitation affect all persons in the expression or actualization of linguistic knowledge in verbal behavior. The question at issue is whether additional factors, or different weightings of the common factors, constrain the behavior of some people even further.

Members of the School Language Group at the Harvard Graduate School of Education are engaged in research to answer this question with respect to disadvantaged children. Their research proposal contains a clear statement of the hypothesis that constraints on linguistic *performance* are more important than deficiencies in linguistic *competence:*

Studies of syntax, most of which suggest that culturally deprived students produce a limited percentage of the full range of available syntactic options, remain similarly unexamined. There seem to be three possible interpretations for the findings in these studies. The first is that some children cannot produce the full range of options because they lack the rules governing certain constructions, e.g., the passive voice or the conjunction of elements in a series. The second is that these students have learned a "grammatical dialect" featuring syntactic options different from those of standard English and that they use this different grammar to form their sentences. The third possible interpretation is that the observed deficits in performance do not derive from an incomplete grammar or a different grammar, but result instead from a limited exploitation of the internalized grammar...

Consistent with the general theory of language implicit in Chomsky's transformational grammar, the conclusion in this proposal is that the last explanation given above is the most reasonable. More specifically, it is assumed that all speakers of a language have internalized a grammar

---

6 Again, one is reminded of similarities to theoretical issues in Piaget-type research on the development of such cognitive schema as *conservation*. For example, Bruner finds that conservation develops earlier and is more susceptible to instruction than Smedslund. From an analysis of their procedures, Gruen concludes that the results are related to differences in criteria and these in turn to differences in definition, to "the psychological processes that one assumes underlie conservation" (1966, p. 982). It is further interesting that while Piagetian psychologists and transformational linguists are both philosophically among the new "nativists," they contrast in the rigor of their experimental criteria. The Piagetian psychologists (e.g. Smedslund) demand more rigorous criteria perhaps because they question whether instruction can be effective. The transformational linguists, on the other hand, tend to accept one example as proving *competence*, perhaps because they question whether instruction is necessary.

whose syntax varies only insignificantly from individual to individual, from area to area, from social class to social class, and (once past a critical age) from age level to age level. That is, all speakers share the same linguistic competence, and differ only in their ability to exploit this competence in particular instances of the production or comprehension of language (Plumer, 1966, pp. 3-4).

When we try to spell out what psychological constraints may be hindering the exploitation of linguistic *competence,* we quickly realize how little is known. The design features of Miller & McNeill's (forthcoming) performance model quoted above include limitations on memory. The School Language Group proposal mentions the possible effects of anxiety and impulsivity. In their study of verbal mediation Flavell, Beach & Chinsky hypothesize the influence of such non-verbal skills as "sustained attentional focusing" (1966, p. 297). The best we can do at the moment is combine the speculations of these investigators.

INDIVIDUAL DIFFERENCES IN PERFORMANCE B

Whereas *performance A* refers negatively to constraints, *performance B* refers positively to the child's perception of the function of speech in a given situation as this is affected both by aspects of that situation and by his individual history of being in speech situations, making responses, and receiving reinforcements.[7] If what the child says in a given situation is functionally inadequate, the cause may lie in a conflict between the requirements of the present and the residue of his past. Hymes has issued a strong plea for a sociolinguistic description of performance, here of disadvantaged children, which would

include these relationships:

With regard to disadvantaged children, the goal of an integrated theory of sociolinguistic description would be to guide accounts of the range of settings, function, and means, and their inter-relationships, acquired by the children. Of these the school setting would be one, but not the only one; and the major purpose would be to place the school setting in the context of other settings, so as to delineate the true communicative abilities of the children and to show the extent to which the performance in school settings was not a direct disclosure of their abilities, but a product of interference between the system that they bring and the system that confronts them; or a setting simply irrelevant to the direction their abilities and competence otherwise took. In part the problem is one of conflict of values and of perceived interests (Hymes, 1966, pp. 9-10).

In traditional studies of child language, virtually any stimuli have been used to elicit speech—toys, pictures, or questions. The particular nature of the setting was evidently considered irrelevant, since its effect on the resulting language was rarely discussed. In her 1954 review, McCarthy included a recommendation that varied situations be used to obtain a more stable index of a child's language. But what Hymes recommends is not varied settings from which numbers are averaged to give a more stable mean. Rather the purpose is to yield the multi-dimensional structure of variation across children and across settings, to investigate "the effective abilities of users of a language, as manifest not in inventories of gram-

7 One aspect of the classic *learning-performance* distinction is the notion that reinforcement applies to performance rather than to learning: "Differential effects are, that is, necessary for *selective performance* but they are not necessary or at the most in only a very minor degree, for the mere learning *qua* learning which underlies such performance . . . if there be no such difference in demands there will be no such selection and performance of the one response even though there has been learning (Tolman, 1932, p. 364, emphasis in the original).

mars, but habitual patterns of actual verbal behavior, as these relate to context both within and between groups" (Hymes, 1964, p. 39).

Two particularly promising research projects of this type are now underway. Labov at Columbia University is studying structural and functional features of speech of preadolescent and adolescent boys in Harlem (Labov, Cohen & Robins, 1965). Ervin-Tripp, Slobin, and Gumperz at Berkeley are in the planning stage of a cross-cultural study in linguistic socialization which will include such variables as values and practices affecting how much children talk, the functions of adult and child speech, the range of styles to which adults switch and the development of style-switching in children (Ervin-Tripp, 1966, pp. 43-44).

Last summer Anita Rui and I did a small pilot study in which we collected speech samples of two children in a variety of situations—in contrast to the usual research design with many children in one situation. Both children were in a Boston summer school following a year in the first grade. With the help of the classroom teacher, we selected children at or near the ends of the school achievement continuum. Martin was an avid reader and an articulate participant in class discussions; Rita was virtually a nonreader and much less interested in formal school subjects.

We were limited by administrative arrangements to the confines of the school, and by equipment (without wireless microphones) to sedentary situations.[8] Over the course of four weeks, we collected speech samples in eight situations:

1. Free conversation: largely about out-of-school life.
2. Deutsch telephone interview: six questions used at the Institute for Developmental Studies; administered via telephones connected directly to a tape recorder.
3. Hidden object test: elicitation of description of a candlestick hidden in a bag.
4. School TAT: the child is asked to tell a story about five pictures developed by Mary Engle of the University of Michigan.
5. Free conversation with a male interviewer.
6. Telephone conversation with classmate of the subject's choice on equipment described above.
7. Conversation during an arithmetic game with classmate.
8. Story retelling: the story *Whistle for Willie* was read to each subject, and then the pictures alone shown in sequence (a technique used extensively by Vera John of Yeshiva University).

We also used two vocabulary tests—the Peabody Picture Vocabulary Test (PPVT) and the vocabulary subtest of Lesser's Primary Mental Abilities Test (Lesser, Fifer & Clark, 1965).

So far the samples have been analyzed for length of utterance in each situation separately, and for use of conjunctions in the total output for each child. These data are presented on the page following, with selected sentences spoken by each child.

Length was used as an inadequate index of syntactical complexity in the absence of more linguistically valid measures. We counted what Hunt (1965) calls terminal units—independent clauses and any syntactically related dependent clauses. The first

8 Wireless microphones are becoming more common (though still expensive) items of equipment in language research. Soskin and John (1963) were pioneers here, and their analysis of the conversation of a newly-married couple deserves to be more widely known.

Analysis of Speech Samples of Two Children
for Length of Utterance and Use of Conjunctions

	Rita		Martin	
Length of Terminal Unit				
First interview	7.94 (36)		6.05 (31)	
Deutsch Telephone Interview	7.53 (53)		5.48 (23)	
Hidden object test	5.76 (21)		6.52 (52)	
School TAT	6.12 (59)		6.44 (27)	
Interview—male	6.20 (129)		5.96 (71)	
Arithmetic game with peer	4.50 (40)		4.78 (77)	
Telephone conversation with peer	5.60 (92)		3.58 (12)	
Story retelling	6.10 (28)		7.09 (22)	

Incidence of Conjunctions

	Rita		Martin	
and		43		43
because	5		5	
but	4		13	
if	7		14	
(and) so (i.e., therefore)	0		12	
or	0		6	
so (i.e., in order to)	0	16	1	51
where	0		2	
(and) when	58		13	
(and) then	2		1	
(and) then when	2		0	
after	11		0	
until	1	74	2	18
		133		112

Vocabulary Tests

	Rita	Martin
PPVT—mental age	6-3	10-2
Lesser test (raw score)	63	80

Sample sentences

Rita:

She had to stay in to mind the new baby because my mother had to feed her.
When I clean the house up my mother said, "You gonna stay in from outside."
If anybody bothers her I'll get all my sisters and brothers to jump in with it.
I give her a bottle and take her up and put her over my back.

Martin:

You put your finger through it so you can look where you're going in the dark.
When he saw a boy whistle to his dog the dog ran straight to him.
Peter got some chalk out of his pocket and made a line to his house.

number in each row gives the mean length of terminal units in words and the number in parentheses gives the number of terminal units averaged. Four generalizations can be made: (a) Martin and Rita differ in their response to particular situations; Martin's longest utterances are in the structured task situations (story-retelling, hidden object, and School TAT) while Rita's are in the three interviews with or without the telephone. (b) For both children, the shortest utterances were spoken, on the average, to their peers. (c) The situational variation for each child is greater than the over-all difference between the two children. (d) The over-all similarity on this measure of length of utterance is in marked contrast to differences in use of conjunctions and vocabulary test scores.

The use of conjunctions was not analyzed by each setting separately because the numbers became too small to yield any discernible pattern. With pooled data, the pattern is clear. We divided the conjunctions into *and* plus two large groups. Conjunctions in the first group—*but, if,* etc.—express logical relationships which do not inhere in the world of events but in some way are imposed on events by the construing mind. The second group—

where, when, etc.—describe spatial and temporal relationships in the events being discussed. In other words, conjunctions in the first set relate propositions while those in the second set relate events. Rita is much more apt to use the first set, and Martin the second.

On the PPVT, the difference in mental-age equivalents is from 6-2 for Rita to 10-2 for Martin. On the Lesser test, the raw scores can be compared with his means for New York City first graders (Lesser et al., 1965, pp. 48, 50). Rita comes from a lower-class Negro family. Her score of 63 almost exactly matches Lesser's means of 62.90 for lower-class Negro children. Martin comes from a lower-middle-class Irish family, an ethnic group which was not included in the New York study but is included in the Boston replication now underway. His score of 80 is almost up to Lesser's middle-class mean of 82.21 for all ethnic groups combined.

SOME IMPLICATIONS

What is the value of this way of viewing child language? Does the distinction between *competence, performance A* and *performance B* have significance beyond the realm of basic research? Does it generate any suggestions for educational practice? I think it does.

FIGURE 2

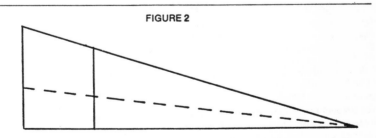

Let's consider again the triangular representation in Figure 1. This time (see Figure 2) we will add within the triangle a second smaller dotted triangle to represent the *competence* and *performance* of a child whose command of language is in some way inadequate, whose actual utterance in a given situation (*performance B*) does not meet the criterion of functional adequacy.

It seems to me that our efforts to remedy this situation have largely been devoted to extending the range at the left. We have largely been concerned wtih creating the kind of stimulating verbal environment which is the best nourishing medium for the development of linguistic *competence* as far as we now know. These efforts have met with considerable success. Witness the data on children with special problems reviewed by Lenneberg (Smith & Miller, 1966, pp. 219-252), the striking results reported by D. B. Fry in the same volume (pp. 187-206) for deaf children who were provided with powerful hearing aids at an early age, and the general reports on the benefits of Head Start programs with disadvantaged children. These are very real accomplishments. But for some of these children, especially the disadvantaged, this may be only a partial solution to their functional command of language, and the easiest part at that. Developmental lags in the acquisition of *competence* may be more easily eliminated than individual and group differences in the cognitive factors influencing *performance A* or the sociolinguistic interference present at *performance B*.

We have done little to design educational environments for the explicit purpose of extending the range at *performance A* by intervening in non-linguistic factors such as attention, though the reported success of the more structured pre-school environments may point to just such a possibility. Examples that come to mind are Montessori-type classrooms (Kohlberg, 1966), Bereiter's training procedures at the University of Illinois and O. K. Moore's automated responsive environment.

We have done even less to totally redesign the situation at the time of *performance B* to create new roles, new functions, and new communication requirements. Consider one concrete example—the beginnings of a movement to have students "learn by teaching." In some ESI programs, high school students learn physics by teaching elementary school pupils. In a Boston settlement house, high school dropouts are tutoring younger retarded readers. In a nearby town, a proposal is being written for a summer program to train high school French students to become substitute teachers in their own schools. These programs were not designed for the purpose of language intervention. But the opportunity to perform in a new and valued social role with its new and demanding communication requirements may have far more impact on the new "teacher's" command of language than traditional classroom routines.

References

Berko, J. The child's learning of English morphology. *Word*, 1958, 14, 150-177.
Brown, R. *Social psychology.* New York: The Free Press, 1965.
Brown, R., & Bellugi, U. Three processes in the child's acquisition of syntax. *Harvard Educational Review*, 1964, 34, 133-151.
Cazden, C. B. Subcultural differences in child language. *Merrill-Palmer Quarterly*, 1966, 12, 185-219.
Chomsky, N. *Aspects of a theory of syntax.* Cambridge: M.I.T. Press, 1965.
Ervin-Tripp, S. Projected activities. *Project literacy reports*, VI. Ithaca: Cornell University Press, 1966. Pp. 41-44.

Flavell, J. H., Beach, D. R., & Chinsky, J. M. Spontaneous verbal rehearsal in a memory task as a function of age. *Child Development*, 1966, 37, 283-299.

Fraser, C., Bellugi, U., & Brown, R. Control of grammar in imitation, comprehension and production. *Journal of Verbal Learning and Verbal Behavior*, 1963, 2, 121-135.

Gleitman, L., Shipley, E. F., & Smith, C. S. An experimental study of the use of compound nouns. Technical Report, III, 1965.

Gruen, G. E. Note on conservation: methodological and definitional considerations. *Child Development*, 1966, 37, 977-983.

Hunt, K. W. Grammatical structures written at three grade levels. Research Report III. Champaign, Ill.: National Council of Teachers of English, 1965.

Hymes, D. Directions in (ethno-) linguistic theory. In A. K. Romney & R. G. D'Andrade (Eds.), Transcultural studies in cognition, No. 3, Part 2. *American Anthropologist*, 1964, 66, 6-56.

Hymes, D. On communicative competence. Paper read at Research Planning Conference on Language Development Among Disadvantaged Children, Yeshiva University, June, 1966.

Inkeles, A. Social structure and the socialization of competence. *Harvard Educational Review*, 1966, 36, 265-283.

Katz, J. Semi-sentences. In J. Katz & J. Fodor (Eds.), *The structure of language.* Englewood Cliffs, N. J.: Prentice-Hall, 1964. Pp. 400-416.

Kohlberg, L. Paper read at the Social Science Research Council Conference on Preschool Education, Chicago, February, 1966.

Labov, W., Cohen, P., & Robins, C. A preliminary study of the structure of English used by Negro and Puerto Rican speakers in New York City. C. R. P. #3091. New York: Columbia University, 1965.

Lashley, K. S. Learning. In C. Murchison (Ed.), *The foundations of experimental psychology.* Worcester, Mass.: Clark University Press, 1929. Pp. 524-563.

Lesser, G. S., Fifer, G., & Clark, D. H. Mental abilities of children in different social and cultural groups. *Monographs of the Society for Research in Child Development*, 1965, 30, No. 4 (Serial No. 102).

McCarthy, D. Language development in children. In L. Carmichael (Ed.), *A manual of child psychology.* (2nd ed.) New York: Wiley, 1954. Pp. 492-630.

Menyuk, P. A preliminary evaluation of grammatical capacity in children. *Journal of Verbal Learning and Verbal Behavior*, 1963, 2, 429-439.

Miller, G. A., & McNeill, D. Psycholinguistics. Draft of chapter for Lindsey & Aronson (Eds.), *Handbook of social psychology.* (2nd ed.) Reading, Mass.: Addison-Wesley, forthcoming.

Plumer, D. A proposal submitted to the Shadow Faculty and the Harvard Research and Development Center for the School Language Group, April, 1966.

Sigel, I. E., & McBane, B. Cognitive competence and level of symbolization among five-year-old children. Paper delivered to the American Psychological Association, New York City, September, 1966.

Smith, F., & Miller, G. A. (Eds.), *The genesis of language.* Cambridge: M. I. T. Press, 1966.

Soskin, W. F., & John, V. The study of spontaneous talk. In R. G. Barker (Ed.), *The stream of behavior,* New York: Appleton-Century-Crofts, 1963. Pp. 228-281.

Thomas, O. C. *Transformational grammar and the teacher of English.* New York: Holt, Rinehart & Winston, 1965.

Tolman, E. C. *Purposive behavior in animals and men.* New York: Century, 1932.

145

Sex Education and the Mentally Retarded

HARRIE M. SELZNICK, *Director of Special Education, Baltimore City Board of Education, Maryland.*

It is the hope that, through a properly organized program of instruction, the educable mentally retarded child will be able to prepare himself for both occupational employment and a personal adjustment to life in society, which will permit him to function with a minimum of outside direction and supervision. For many of these young mentally retarded persons, it is expected that marriage and family life will be a long range possibility. It is our observation that many young people who have been recently enrolled in the special programs of Baltimore have entered marriage at a very early age. Too frequently, marital status is assumed without a necessary program of preparation.

Exceptional Children, May, 1966, Vol.32, No.9, pp. 640-643.

Among the responsibilities confronting the educator charged with the job of providing appropriate learning experiences to the mentally retarded is that of preparing the mentally retarded for all aspects of family life and marital adjustment. Among the understandings which we should try to encourage are those relating to sex education. In organizing a program of sex education, our aim is to bring up young men and women who will have wholesome respect for themselves and others and in whom the ability to found a home that can endure will be developed.

Need for Updating Programs

An educational program concerned with helping individuals achieve a satisfactory sex adjustment must attack the whole problem of emotional maturity, personality development, and social adjustment. Sex is so integrally a part of a total personal adjustment that either over emphasis or exclusion of sex is an error which distorts the whole situation. Educationally, the problem is to so incorporate sex education into the whole program of instruction that proper balance and perspective are attained. Our central concern must be for improved individual and social adjustment.

Changes have taken place in economic and social life, in the family, and in the school population during the past fifty years. New emphases in education and new responsibilities are placed on the schools. A decrease in the solidarity of the family group, changes in the economic status of families, and increased freedom for young people in their social life have brought new and greater responsibilities to young people for their behavior. It has become more important than ever before that young people develop attitudes, ideals, and behavior patterns that will enable them to live wholesomely and effectively as individuals, as members of families, and as citizens of the community.

Three years ago at the request of principals, teachers, social workers, parents, and in some instances pupils, a committee was organized within the Division of Special Education of the Baltimore City Public Schools with the charge to investigate the various current programs of sex education in public school systems of our country. Our contacts with other school systems suggested that, while the majority had located need for instruction in this important area, few had organized their efforts.

New Approaches in Sex Education

Methods for providing sex education to the youth in our schools have progressed from the form of special lectures and the showing of films to an integrated effort where functional courses are offered in many school systems. In these courses, help is given in various matters of personal adjustment and human relations, including sex adjustment and relationships. Through this approach, sex becomes an inseparable part of total adjustment.

During school year 1964-1965, approximately 700 girls who had withdrawn from school because of pregnancy were reinstated. Many others from among the 6,100 girls of the Baltimore City Public Schools may have had similar reasons for dropping out of school, but we did not know about them. The reports on the sexual behavior of many of our adolescent girls suggested the urgent need for the schools to become more active in their instructional efforts in this area. The social and moral patterns of many of our adolescent, mentally retarded girls were not in keeping with the acceptable patterns of society. Our efforts toward improved patterns of social behavior were required.

We started with a clear view of the problem. We decided that we would have to start our instructional programs at the level at which we found our young people. This beginning would have to include acceptance of terminology which is not usually mentioned in so called polite society. Our efforts would not include condemnation of the social patterns of the groups with whom our young people lived and associated, but would, instead, be directed toward an understanding that there are others who live differently.

Our goals included the recognition that change in behavior would be slow, but that these young people could be helped to live in a manner which was more acceptable to society as a whole. In the preparation of our guides for teachers, we tried to keep in mind ways in which mentally retarded pupils learn. We also recognized that not all groups of young people are either ready for this program emphasis, nor do all have similar needs. We also considered the teacher and her readiness for participation in this effort. All prepared materials were provided to all teachers, but the choice as to use remained with the teacher and her principal.

We decided that the program of sex education for mentally retarded children should be an integral part of planned offerings at all levels. The conditioning should begin at an early age. The kinds of learning are based upon the indicated needs and the readiness of the group. We considered that the mentally retarded, like all children, have more than one vocabulary. The listening or understanding vocabulary is usually the most highly developed. The child understands many words which he does not use in his speaking vocabulary. His reading vocabulary is more limited than either his understanding or speaking vocabulary. His writing vocabulary is most limited of all.

In recognition of these varying levels of comprehension and use, and in preparation for future learning experiences of these children, our first sex education efforts were directed toward the learning of the correct names for the parts of the body which the children see and need for elimination. The primary approach to the instructional program was through the spoken word, with reinforcement through the use of pictorial illustrations and audiovisual devices. These teaching approaches are supplemented with other information, depending upon the maturation level of the group. The questions which the boys and girls ask will be indicative of the amount and type of information which they need and are ready to handle.

As the children grow and mature, additional learning experiences should be provided which deal with such matters as bodily changes which accompany maturity. The eleven and twelve year olds should be provided with an understanding of menstruation as part of their study of body function. The young persons should be helped toward an understanding of their role in society and the responsibilities involved.

When the pupils indicate a readiness, the story of human reproduction should be taught as a natural function, but the stress should be placed on the fact that it is part of a larger experience, involving love, marriage, and parenthood. The emphasis should be on high moral principles. The instructional program should go beyond the mere presentation of the biological facts of life. The total program must be designed to give wholesome information about the social and emotional problems which one may encounter during the life process. Ideals should be supplemented with sound social information which will help build emotional stability.

Basic to our efforts is the concept that we would concern ourselves with the development of appropriate learning experiences in sex education for all children, since our goals for the retarded were similar to those we hope to achieve with all children. The means by which one approaches these goals may in many cases require modification through organization and teaching procedures.

Aspects of a Comprehensive Program

Sex education is part of the training we should try to provide to all children in our efforts to build a complete and balanced individual. A comprehensive program of sex education should include:

1. Biological aspects. Assistance toward an understanding of the reproductive processes, sex as a universal biological function, the relation of mental viewpoint to physical urges, the nature of biological sex maturity, inheritance, eugenics, and similar topics.
2. Preparation for marriage, family life, and child care. Emphasis on choosing a mate and preparing for marriage; the responsibilities of various members of the home if a stable, happy, family life is to be achieved; the place of children in the home; and allied topics.
3. Sociological aspects. The family as a social institution, the significance of marriage and divorce, the causes and effects of divorce, the social costs of sexual misconduct, and illegitimacy.
4. Health. Cleanliness and hygiene, and information about venereal diseases.
5. Personal adjustments and attitudes. Premarital standards, boy-girl associations, personal sex habits and practices, and the building of proper attitudes about sex and its manifestations.

6. Interpersonal relations. Emphasis on helping the individual work out his relationships with those immediately associated with him, and on helping him build a sense of social responsibility and a desire to contribute to the good adjustment of others.
7. Establishment of values. Helping the individual to build values by which to live and standards by which he can judge important decisions.

Desirable outcomes of a sex education program are:

1. Knowledge which will help the pupil understand himself and the many day by day situations which he meets and which will help him protect himself and others from harmful physical and mental consequences of misuse of sex.
2. An improved personal adjustment, helping the pupil to be at ease with himself.

Objectives

Ultimate objectives of a sex education program include the following:

1. To provide the pupil with an adequate knowledge of his own physical maturity and physiological development.
2. To develop wholesome objective attitudes toward sex and a desire to achieve a mature, balanced personality.
3. To give the individual insight concerning his relationship with members of both sexes and to help him understand his obligations and responsibilities to others.
4. To give the pupil an appreciation of the positive satisfaction which wholesome human relations can bring, in both individual and family living.
5. To eliminate fears and worries related to individual adjustment.
6. To build an understanding of the reason for moral values.
7. To provide enough knowledge about misuses of sex that the youth may protect himself against exploitation.
8. To help prepare for parenthood.
9. To create an awareness of human interdependence and the social costs of sexual experimentation.

10. To leave the pupil with an appreciation of his role in the chain of human propagation.

To this point, our prepared guides have had limited use. In some ways this is fortunate in that we have had the opportunity for reconsideration and revision of our previous efforts. The challenge for us is, however, even greater than it was at the time we began our studies. The changing pupil populations, the revised social standards, and the new responsibilities assigned to our schools all suggest the importance of this area of instruction. That we can assist the mentally retarded toward behavior patterns which will permit them to live socially acceptable lives is a goal toward which we must continue to strive.

JOHN W. KIDD

Some Unwarranted Assumptions in the Education and Habilitation of Handicapped Children

Abstract: Nine "unwarranted assumptions" are examined. Regarding them, the writer requests the readers to "think through these selected aspects of special education . . . not necessarily to agree . . . ."

Portions of the professions and the public concerned with the mentally retarded and other handicapped children and youth appear to be operating under certain unwarranted assumptions. Perhaps no one clings to all of them, but the following seem to resist critical thinking most persistently. Based on the premise that an educator should habitually reexamine his most cherished beliefs at frequent intervals, the reader is asked to think through these selected aspects of special education with the writer—not necessarily to agree with his conclusions.

Unwarranted Assumption Number 1. Most mental retardation cannot be prevented. The recent book *Mental Retardation—a Handbook for the Primary Physician*, published by the American Medical Association (1965), states that there are over 200 known causes of mental retardation. They base their work on the following definition: "Mental retardation refers to significantly sub-average intellectual functioning which manifests itself during the developmental period and is characterized by inadequacy in adaptive behavior" (Kidd, 1964). The genetic factors, about

which one would expect the AMA to be concerned, account for only a minority of the cases of mental retardation; the majority, particularly of measured IQ 65 and up, are the products of experiential deprivation and are, thus, preventable. By experiential deprivation is meant deprivation of linguistic stimulation (mental); deprivation of "anchoring" (emotional)—usually represented by a secure, reassuring, consistent home-parents situation; and deprivation of conditions necessary to physical health (physical). All, theoretically, can be prevented with present know-how. It is not suggested that we *should*—merely that we *can* if we, as a society, so choose.

Unwarranted Assumption Number 2. The rate at which and the amount which a given retardate can learn is predictable. It is granted that for the vast majority of the mentally retarded, proper administration of usually the Binet or a Wechsler test is quite predictive of learning rate and amount. But this prediction is valid *only under conventional learning situations.* What happens if the retardate is placed in a reassuring, but continually

Education and Training of the Mentally Retarded, April, 1966, Vol.1, No.2, pp. 54-58.

stimulating linguistic environment? What happens if the retardate is instructed, not four or five hours per day, 170 to 180 days per year for a total of 680 to 900 hours per year—but for six to eight hours per day for 225 to 240 days per year for a total of, not 680 to 900, but 1350 to 1920 hours per year? Frankly, we do not know. No one seems to have tried to find out. The writer would like to but has not been able to find the money it would take for an experiment. The setting exists (an air conditioned school); there should be no problem with most of the parents or children. Maybe we prefer not to know?

Unwarranted Assumption Number 3. There is a terminal plateau of learning at about age 16 for retardates. As far as there is tangible evidence, "there ain't no such thing!" It seems that the idea is an artifact of the original standardization of the Binet-Simon Test in the early 1900's. Since they terminated planned differentiation among abilities of learners after about age 15, many people seem to have found solace in the thought that mental retardates cannot learn anything after about that age. As a matter of fact, mental retardates can learn at least to senility. This assumption, coupled with the Vocational Rehabilitation eligibility age of 16, and contaminated by the fact that most of the states terminate compulsory schooling at 16, has provided a rationale for failure entirely too common in our work.

To combat this practice, we in our school system have adopted the following statement:

In general, Special School District shall attempt to find employment for its mentally retarded adolescent pupils during or subsequent to their last (diploma) year in its program. Typically, this will occur during their eighteenth or nineteenth year of age. This position is based on the principle of maximum readiness. Since normal adolescents are not usually moved into the world

of full time work until age 18 or 19 or later, and since mentally retarded adolescents are, by virtue of their handicap, usually less able to hold jobs than are average workers, it would be contrary to logic to expect mentally retarded workers to be in a competitive work position at a younger age than average workers.

Unwarranted Assumption Number 4. Educable mentally retarded children and youth are far better off if placed in a school with normal youngsters. Let's take a really close look at this tradition of integrating retarded pupils in regular schools. We have heard of its value, its uncritical acceptance for about 15 years. Research evidence on the practice is inconsequential. Yet, most educators and special educators, as well as parents of the retarded, assume, it seems, that something magical happens to benefit them when the retarded youngsters pass the regular school kids in the hallways.

Why and how did this notion get started? It is likely that the National Association for Retarded Children, when it organized in 1950, found many of the public school classes for the educable mentally retarded housed in attics and basements, in rooms abandoned by other programs, in annexes and churches, and in rented and donated rooms around the community. It is understandable that these parents insisted that their children have rooms just like other school children. These rooms existed only in "regular schools." Instead of demanding "Place them in nice rooms, or in regular schools," their campaign to get the retardates out of the attics and basements took the form "Integrate them with normal children." Much was made of the possible values of this arrangement, particularly the so-called socialization which would occur.

What actually happens when a class of educable retardates is placed in a regular school? Too often (and once is too often), the building administrator learns of the arrangement from his superintendent. He may not have been consulted—just told. The building principal, in turn, tells certain members of his faculty and staff that they have to work with the retardates—his physical education teacher, his lunchroom and playground supervisors, and his home economics and shop teachers. They may resent it, or be afraid and uncertain. It is the exception, rather than the rule, for the building administrator and his faculty to ask for the special class and to take a role of leadership in seeing that it is accepted by the school and community. It *can* be a beneficial experience but it doesn't just happen because the retarded class is placed in a regular building.

What about having the educable retarded in a separate building? If given a modern building, a good and attractive faculty, special teachers of physical education, shop and home economics, what is it that can be done in an integrated class which cannot be done in a segregated one? About the only answer that can be given has to do again with the theoretical advantages of the physical proximity of normal children—the so called advantages of socialization. Now, if a school system has enough educable retardates (say, two or three hundred) to justify a special building, then it can have special teachers of shop and physical education and home economics working full time with the retarded. Further, it can group the children much more homogeneously than it is likely to be able to do by integrating them. Surely, in such a special school, everything can be done as well or better than by integrating classes except for that one intangible —the possible benefit of the presence of average children.

Two thoughts occur on this theoretical advantage of the so called socialization with the normal. In the first place, the retarded special class in the regular school is often subject to rejection and derogation both individually and collectively. Secondly, children are in school less than 1,000 hours per year; they sleep about 3,000. This leaves nearly 5,000 hours of before and after school hours, weekends, and vacations during which awareness of and association with the normal world is all but inevitable. It suggests that the advantages of the integrated class are, at least partially, a myth. The advantages are not automatic. The critical factor is not whether the class is in a regular school building—"integrated"—or in a special building. The critical factor is the totality of learning experiences provided for the children—the curriculum, teachers, supervisors, and administrators of the program.

Unwarranted Assumption Number 5. America's monetary expenditures on the handicapped are solely attributable to our humane and altruistic value system. While it is true that we, as a society, are making the most heralded effort in history to educate, habilitate, and rehabilitate the handicapped, the hearings in the legislative and congressional committees and halls which produced the flood of dollars, particularly since 1950, were marked by agreement with the "investment argument"—the logic which supports the contention that it is cheaper to educate and habilitate the handicapped than to support them in life long dependency. Let's not overrate our generosity.

Unwarranted Assumption Number 6. A society will support full employment of the handicapped at a time of significant unemployment of the able. I suggest a readiness for the time when our usual three to five percent unemployment rate becomes six, eight, or ten percent, or even more. I suggest the likelihood that such a condition, *if* it comes, will radically alter the present mood of acceptance of employment of the handicapped. Let's hope that it doesn't come, but let's realize the nature of the tight rope we walk. When the chips are down as a choice between personal survival (feeding, housing, and clothing oneself and one's family) or continuing to support maximal employment of the handicapped as an expression of humane values—well, it would be more than surprising if the humane values universally held sway.

Unwarranted Assumption Number 7. All employment can be so classified that workers can be prepared for jobs by categories, i.e., welders, mechanics, cosmetologists, nurses aids, etc. Dr. Thomas Jordan recently told some of us in a conference of his "nesting" theory of job placement of the handicapped. He suggested that the tradition is to get the worker ready for a supposed type of job. However, a more productive approach, particularly for the handicapped, would be first to find the specific job, then get *it* ready for the prospective employee while getting him ready for that particular "nest." It is increasingly recognized that the success of job placement of the handicapped rests on the readiness of the job (the supervisors and fellow workers) for the handicapped worker as well as readiness of the worker for the job.

Unwarranted Assumption Number 8. We are all but infallible in predicting employability. Really, you know, we are not possessed of either the instruments or the judgment—much less the extra-sensory perception or clairvoyance—to warrant any such assumption. And as we work with the handicapped, we are even less certain of our ground.

One of the most significant contributions to the literature on job placement is *A Guide to Jobs for the Mentally Retarded* by Peterson and Jones (1964). This publication was the product of a five year study subsidized by the Vocational Rehabilitation Administration (OVR when the project started). It is and will remain for a decade at least the definitive work in its field. Practically everything one needs to know on the subject is included. It is a difficult book to use. It needs study. It should be read from front to back. It is cross indexed. It indicates the results of job placement of mental retardates by some 40 agencies. It specifies content of work readiness education in the school, the workshop, and on the job. Yet this invaluable work, I find, is all but unknown to special educators and, indeed, to many Vocational Rehabilitation personnel. Its widespread study and use are urged. It has been observed by many that preparation for the world of work should start when the child enters school, not when he becomes an adolescent.

Unwarranted Assumption Number 9. Medical personnel are experts in matters of classifying, treating, and predicting the consequences of handicapping conditions. I quote from *Mental Retardation* (American Medical Association, 1965): "No physician can, of course, predict with absolute accuracy the future development of any single retarded individual" (p. 45).

The very publication of this work and the conference which led to it symbolize the recognition that some medical practitioners need more sophistication in this field. We find parents who have been told, "Don't worry, he'll outgrow it"— and he didn't; and parents who have been told, "He's a hopeless cripple for life" —and he wasn't.

Let's not go beyond our roles; educators can ill afford to render medical judgments, *and vice versa.* Vocational Rehabilitation personnel cannot declare a person really employable; only the employer can determine that! Let's not be surer than we are. Let's not raise false hopes, but do let us encourage it where it is merited. Let's not sugar coat the facts beyond recognition, nor be so cautious as to induce undue pessimism. Let's remember that each individual has a potential for growth, and it is our responsibility to use all our patience, dedication, and ingenuity in stimulating and guiding this growth.

References

American Medical Association. *Mental retardation—a handbook for the primary physician.* Chicago: Author, 1965.

Kidd, J. W. Toward a more precise definition of mental retardation. *Mental Retardation,* 1964, 2, 209-212.

Peterson, R. O., and Jones, Edna M. *A guide to jobs for the mentally retarded.* Pittsburgh: American Institute for Research, 1964.

A STATE-WIDE SCHOOL-WORK PROGRAM
FOR THE MENTALLY RETARDED

by GARY M. CLARK

*T*HE Texas Cooperative Program, or Texas Plan, is a design for the habilitation of the educable mentally retarded through a cooperative working arrangement between two divisions of the Texas Education Agency (Vocational Rehabilitation and Special Education) and the independent school districts throughout the state. The impetus for this plan came from professionals' and parents' recognition that a serious gap existed between the provisions of special education and readiness for competitive employment.

Early concepts of a type of program which would bridge this gap have been study-work programs in which pupils were provided pre-vocational preparation at school, on-the-job training in the community, and supervised employment. Communities such as Lansing, Michigan, Baltimore, Maryland, Cincinnati, Ohio, Jacksonville, Florida, and others have led the way for others to follow. Up until 1962, however, this concept of study and work in the public school setting had been left to individual school districts. The expansion of this approach to a state-wide program has broadened the scope of possibilities and the implication for other states has been made apparent.

To provide continuity in the total educational program for the retarded, a change from the traditional subject-matter orientation to preparation for vocational proficiency and social competence was required. This involved major changes in curriculum and administrative organization. As both the Division of Vocational Rehabilitation and Division of Special Education were already within the authority of the Texas Education Agency, the basic structure for central control and administration of a cooperative program was present. To promote the cooperation which was necessary to make the proposed venture work, the position of Assistant Commissioner of Education for Vocational Rehabilitation and Special Education was established.

The next step was to develop a new curriculum guide to assist each local school district to make its total program for the educable retarded consistent with the programs of other districts and sequential within its own program. This was accomplished through the development of a separate curriculum track including seven developmental levels leading to employment and a high school diploma (Eskridge & Partridge, 1963).

The Texas Plan is now in its sixth year of operation. Approximately 3,300 student-clients were served over the state through the program during the 1965–66 school year. There were 104 school districts participating in the program with 147 vocational adjustment coordinators (persons responsible for the program at the local level) and 30 full-time vocational rehabilitation counselors assigned to these school districts. Thirty-two more rehabilitation counselors had part-time assignment to the program. As of June 1966, Texas Education Agency personnel reported that 4,509 cases had been closed in employment.

The soundness of the philosophy underlying the program appears obvious by the large increases in older retardates being served in the schools and being placed in employment. The Cooperative Program has remained virtually unchanged since its beginning. A follow-up study of its effectiveness over a period of time will be needed to determine future

Mental Retardation, December, 1967, Vol.5, No.6, pp. 7–10.

revisions or developments. At this point, however, there are some considerations which can be shared to help others in planning such a program. No program of this size and nature can develop without problem areas. Some of these will be discussed in order to illuminate aspects of the plan which needed special attention.

Problem Areas

Changing and adjusting to a new curriculum. Many teachers have had no problems in changing and adjusting to a new curriculum. Others have offered some resistance. Teachers who do resist major changes seem to fall into two general categories, although there may be a variety of reasons for resisting. The first category includes those who are generally competent and who spend much time and effort in planning and preparing materials to fit the needs of their particular group. When such a teacher has had very little in the way of curriculum materials and has developed her own, it is understandable that a complete change of emphasis would not be welcome at the outset of a new program. Fortunately, these teachers do overcome their resistance and adapt their methods as required.

The second category includes those teachers who have had little training in adapting or improvising materials and who attempt to teach as if the pupils had the same academic needs as pupils of average intelligence. They cling to available curriculum materials in the school system and adjust the texts or workbooks to the grade level they feel is appropriate. When teachers such as these have to depend upon regular curriculum materials it is again understandable that a radical change would not be well-received.

Understandable as these reactions may be, the success of a new curriculum rests largely upon the teachers who put it into effect. Rigidity or resistance by the teachers are negative forces which can create major problems. Teachers, as a rule, want to develop professionally and desire programs and materials which offer their pupils the best. Therefore, an educational program to stress the importance of curricular changes and teacher cooperation is necessary.

Texas attempted to provide this through the usual means of inservice training, area workshops, section meetings at conferences and conventions, and through the revised curriculum guide. Mere knowledge of what was expected was found to be insufficient. In making the transition, personal guidance and assistance from state consultants as well as the provision of appropriate materials are needed. When teachers have guidance and materials, resistance and negative attitudes are greatly reduced. This leads to the second major problem in implementing a new program at the state level.

Suitable curriculum materials for personal, social, and vocational adjustment. At the outset of the Texas Plan a common problem among secondary teachers was the lack of appropriate materials. This may have been due largely to a lack of knowledge about the availability of such materials, but much of what was found did not seem appropriate for high-school-age youngsters. Some school officials complained that their budget would not allow the relatively high cost of the materials which did seem desirable. Fortunately, more funds are now available and the publishing companies are making more and better materials.

Materials still need to be evaluated carefully in such a program as this. The temptation to grasp at workbook series, film and film strip series, and pamphlets on specific jobs is great. Strickland (1964) found in his survey of the types of employment in which trainees of the Texas Cooperative Program were functioning that approximately 100 different types of jobs were represented. This points up the great need for materials with high interest and low-reading levels which give practical information regarding work habits, attitudes, and social adjustment without being too specific about a particular job. Until a sufficient amount of such materials has been produced, field-tested, evaluated, and placed in the hands of local teachers a serious obstacle to the educational aspects of the program will remain. Hopefully, the new regional materials centers will be of assistance in this.

Parental understanding of the new curriculum. It was anticipated at the outset that an intensive education program for parents would be necessary. Individual contact for a personal explanation was felt to be the best way to begin. This was accomplished by both the vocational adjustment coordinators and the vocational rehabilitation counselors. Joint contacts proved most effective but were not always possible. Other means of initial communication included parent meetings, open-house and visitation days at school, parent handbooks, and press releases. Occasional problems with parents indicated the need for continuous communication. Again, personal conferences for reporting pupil performance, solicitation of assistance and support in problem areas, and providing parents support and encouragement in home problems proved crucial.

Generally, the extent of problems from parent misunderstanding can be directly related to the extent and quality of parent communication by both school and vocational rehabilitation representatives.

Attitudes of employers in the community toward the retarded. Obtaining the cooperation of employers in a training or employment program with a retarded youngster is quite different from selling the concept to a teacher or parent. The employer is in business for profit and not to serve as a rehabilitation agent. The two major aspects to be dealt with are the understanding of the social and humanitarian factors of his participation and the economic and legal aspects of his participation. Previous experiences with handicapped workers or exposure to years of public information programs may have been helpful in creating a favorable attitude toward the problem but the unique aspects of a mentally handicapped employee presents a

need for a real understanding by employers. Some employers recognize the humanitarian and civic responsibilities of the program but cannot reconcile the practical and economic aspects as far as their own participation is concerned.

The vocational rehabilitation counselor or the vocational adjustment coordinator have had to concentrate on the areas of most concern to employers—the financial, practical, and legal considerations of hiring or training a retarded youngster. Here, again, personal contact is a necessary approach in order to establish the type of communication and relationship needed to promote understanding and cooperation. Counselors and coordinators have found certain labels and terminology such as "mentally retarded," "special education" and "mentally deficient" objectionable to some employers and acceptable to others—but actually understood by few. Experience proved that being frank and honest in describing the nature of the youngsters in general, or preferably an individual in particular, and avoiding the use of labels which might have a negative effect were the best procedures to use. In addition to this, certain facts regarding the counseling and supervision needed, the expectations of the employer, the financial expectations of the youngster, and the legal implications of training or employment have to be established prior to the completion of a placement. Problems arising in these areas reflect the effectiveness of the initial and continuing contact with the employers.

Legal implications of a school-work program for the retarded. The legal considerations for which employers show the most concern are minimum-wage laws, employee casualty liability, and unemployment compensation. A few employers will not consider participation in the program if any of these aspects are involved, regardless of legal provisions for handicapped workers or assurances of legal protection. Fortunately, others are willing to participate if all legal problems are solved.

157

The usual approaches to these problems are:

(1) Minimum wage requirements can be met through special arrangements between the Department of Labor and the state vocational rehabilitation office which allows subminimum wages for training and/or employment.

(2) The risk of employee injury is subject to the various state laws concerning employee casualty. Workers in the school-work program have to become familiar with these laws and be able to interpret them accurately to employers. Interpretation of the law is often sufficient, but occasionally an employee feels secure only after consulting his attorney, insurance carrier, or the local representative of the Department of Labor.

(3) Federal laws govern unemployment insurance and employers with small businesses sometimes resist participation in the program because by taking on one additional employee they become subject to a federal unemployment tax. No exceptions to this regulation are possible for a handicapped worker and the counselor or coordinator is obligated to so inform the employer.

Other legal considerations are related to minimum ages, hazardous occupations, and union regulations. Each placement has unique considerations and the counselors and coordinators must be prepared to discuss laws, answer questions, and explain legalities in terms which employers will understand and accept. Inservice orientation and training should be provided to make workers more knowledgeable in this area.

Placement of retardates in training or employment. The problem of placement in training or employment without sufficient pre-vocational training or placement in unsatisfactory situations has lessened as the program has progressed. Initially, however, there was a tendency in many schools to make placements on the basis of age, classroom space, teacher load, length of time in school, or factors other than job readiness. Improvement in this area has come through (a) attainment of experience in evaluating job readiness, (b) better pre-vocational training, (c) better evaluative records and information from teachers at the lower levels, and (d) better coordination at all levels in regard to space and teacher load.

In addition to premature placements or errors in judgment in placement, there are two factors which limit placements. These are (a) the overemphasis on earnings of the pupil by the parents or the pupils, and (b) difficulty with transportation to and from job stations.

In regard to earnings, it has been the policy of most schools to see that the trainee receives compensation in relation to his productivity in order to provide incentive and give practical experience in handling money. The overemphasis may in some cases be the fault of the counselor or coordinator who get some personal satisfaction from being able to quote salaries and wages of student-clients whom they have placed. At any rate, the training which is provided and the goal of high school graduation should be the points of emphasis here, in spite of the limitations on placement.

Transportation is essentially the responsibility of the parents. Hopefully, the student-client is capable of traveling independently or being trained to do so. However, when parents are unable to provide transportation or if public transportation is unavailable or inadequate, limitations on placement are imposed. In cases of severe economic deprivation, vocational rehabilitation funds have provided transportation during training. In some cases, training or employment may have to be limited to areas within walking distance. Use of public conveyances and developing the ability to get about in the community are vital to the curriculum, but practical considerations of scheduling and expense prevent the most desirable or appropriate placements.

Locating and securing placement opportunities have been no great problem in Texas due to economic conditions over the past five years, the decrease in unemployment conditions, and the assistance of agencies such as Goodwill Industries, U. S. Civil Service, Texas Employment Commission, and local opportunity centers.

Inter-disciplinary cooperation. This aspect of any cooperative venture is vital to its success. Workers in special education and vocational rehabilitation have long had common goals for the same group of people. Emphasis in services has been at different age levels, but both were working toward the same end independently. Varying degrees of cooperation and misunderstanding have existed in the past between the workers of these two agencies. A program for a close working relationship at the state-wide level is long overdue. The Texas Plan has and is demonstrating the possibilities of the strength afforded in such a cooperative program.

The degree of success in cooperative effort thus far is due in large part to the fact that (a) both divisions are under the direction and administration of the same person, and (b) most of the vocational rehabilitation counselors were brought into the program without prior experience in the general rehabilitation program or were transferred from the general program voluntarily. The importance of the first factor is obvious because of the central control afforded. With both organizations under one administrator, activities can be better planned and coordinated to insure cooperation.

The second factor's importance may not be as apparent, except to those who have experienced negative attitudes of vocational rehabilitation personnel toward the mentally retarded in the past. These attitudes are somewhat understandable when viewed from the counselor's limitations on time, budget, and pressure for rehabilitation "closures." Bringing in new counselors without preconceptions regarding the feasibility of the retarded and imposing no closure quota for the first year did much to convince the local schools and special education workers that vocational rehabilitation had a new look.

Cooperation at the state level is vital in providing organization, direction, and supervision which are required in an operation at the state level. However, the elements of cooperative relations in the day-to-day problems of the local workers cannot be underestimated. The vocational rehabilitation counselor and vocational adjustment coordinator must be able to work harmoniously together. As a team they must cooperate with building principals and directors of special education, and all must work together to make this part of the total school program a positive feature in the eyes of the parents, employers, and community. Problems in communication and cooperation can be minimized through careful selection of key participants in the program, appropriate supervision by principals and administration staff, regional workshops for cooperative planning and problem-solving, exchange of visits of workers in various communities, and professional meetings at the state level.

State-wide Implications

The implications of a state-wide school-work program are actually not much different from a community program except in magnitude. The major tasks involve curriculum changes and the development of a close working relationship between two state agencies at the local, as well as the state, level of operation. In light of the problem areas discussed above, these major implications which can be drawn:

(1) Curriculum goals must be in harmony with the goals of the school-work phase of training and must effect a transition from functional skills and knowledge to adult behavior and vocational proficiency.

(2) Curriculum materials should be planned and prepared in advance of the initiation of a program at the state level by the Divisions of Special Education and Vocational Rehabilitation and improved during the implementation by the counselors and classroom teachers at the local level.

(3) Education of parents, teachers, and administrators to the roles and levels of participation expected of them should be carefully planned and implemented before the initiation of a cooperative program in a

159

community.

(4) Written agreements and detailed plans should be developed before programs are initiated. This is necessary to provide a clear understanding among all participants of the responsibilities and expectations for all concerned.

(5) Continuous inservice training for counselors and coordinators in evaluation, placement, and legal aspects is essential.

(6) Involvement of school personnel, parents, civic groups, employers, and related community agencies in the planning and operation of the program is highly desirable.

(7) Administrative organization at all levels should be such that the unique services provided by special education, vocational rehabilitation, and the local school district are coordinated from a central point.

It is recognized that much remains to be done in the development and improvement of the Texas Plan. Expansion, reorganization, training of new personnel, development of curriculum materials, and explorations into new occupational areas are continuously in progress over the state. Immediate needs for research and self-evaluation through follow-up studies of graduates and dropouts and the efficacy of current training practices are pressing. The numerical results of the first four years are indicative of the possibilities of a statewide approach. The retarded throughout the nation deserve the opportunity to claim the same types of possibilities in their own states, and their claim should not be denied by those who could make it possible.

References

Eskridge, C. S. & Partridge, D. L. Vocational Rehabilitation for Exceptional Children Through Special Education. *Exceptional Children*, 1963, *29*, 452–458.

Strickland, C. G. Job Training Placement for Retarded Youth. *Exceptional Children*, 1964, *31*, 83–86.

160

CLIFFORD E. HOWE

Is Off Campus Work Placement Necessary for All Educable Mentally Retarded?

Abstract: A comparison was made of the postschool adjustment of two comparable groups of educable retarded persons; one group had off campus work experience and the other had a program limited to the school setting including on campus work experience. The results of the study indicated that those without off campus work experience were achieving as well as those who had been placed in work situations in the community as part of their high school program. The majority of both groups were making an adequate adjustment. It is suggested that on campus work experience may be adequate for the majority of the educable mentally retarded. The multiply handicapped and those who test in the lower IQ range of the educable retarded may be the ones who most need more intensive work experience.

A SERIOUS problem in public education today is how a school system can best prepare educable mentally retarded students to become productive adult citizens of the community. At the secondary level, there is a current upsurge of interest in developing programs combining classroom work and parttime placement in actual work situations. This educational plan is referred to by various names—work study, work experience, or school work programs. Very little research, particularly of a longitudinal nature, has been conducted to evaluate the effects of this approach in educating the high school age mentally retarded. The assumption made is that a graduate whose program combined practical on the job training off campus with related and reinforcing curricula in the classroom will be better prepared to enter the work world and succeed than will one whose program was limited to the school setting. Presumably, the person with such training and experi-

ence will make a better community adjustment as an adult.

A number of followup studies of the community adjustment of the mentally retarded have been conducted. Studies done through the middle 1950's were reported by Tizard (1958). More recently, Charles (1966) summarized longitudinal followup studies of community adjustment. The report of these studies indicated a fairly good adult adjustment for most mentally retarded students throughout their life. The majority were employed, few were institutionalized, and although many were involved in law violations, the offenses tended to be of a less serious variety.

Success in adult employment appears to be tied rather directly to the conditions of the nation's economy. Since the majority of retarded adults hold unskilled and semiskilled jobs, they are often the first to be laid off during a recession period. However, the general tenor of the

Exceptional Children, December, 1968, Vol. 35, No. 3, pp. 323-326.

161

TABLE 1

Summary of Mean Scores and t Values Between Experimental and Contrast Groups for Age, IQ, Months in Class, and Father's Occupation

	Men			Women		
Variable	Experimental $N = 29$	Contrast $N = 22$	t value	Experimental $N = 7$	Contrast $N = 10$	t value
Chronological age (in months)	259.21	252.05	2.22*	260.57	263.30	0.54
IQ	69.07	69.36	0.16	65.29	68.1	1.05
Months in special class	63.28	60.82	0.26	70.14	72.3	0.12
Father's occupation (Warner Scale)	5.72	5.32	1.31	6.14	5.6	1.40

Men: $/t/ \geq 2.02$; $df = 49$
Women: $/t/ \geq 2.13$; $df = 15$

* Significant at .05 level

studies of community adjustment is optimistic. Tizard (1958), in fact, raises questions as to whether or not there is a need for additional longitudinal research of this nature.

The major purpose of this study was to compare the postschool adjustment of students having off campus work experience with a contrast group who did not have school sponsored placement or supervision on jobs in the community. All students in both groups were enrolled in senior high school classes for the educable mentally retarded, and both groups had had on campus work experience in the school cafeterias, building, and grounds, etc. The educable students were enrolled in three comprehensive senior high schools. Each had an enrollment between 3,000 and 3,500 regular students in grades 10 through 12. Both groups had been instructed over a period of 3 years in curricula which emphasized preparation for work at the termination of their high school program of study. The variable differentiating the two programs was that the experimental group participated in off campus work experience and the contrast group did not.

Procedure

Personal interviews were conducted with 68 former students 2 to 4 years after they had terminated their high school careers. Approximately half of the students had been enrolled at Long Beach Polytechnic High School ($N=36$), in a work experience program which included parttime off campus placement and supervision on jobs in the community. The remaining subjects ($N=32$) were enrolled in comparable high schools which had special classes but provided no off campus work experience.

Individual personal interviews were conducted with each of the 68 subjects. The typical interview averaged one and one-half hours in length. After all the interviews were completed, the data were summarized on cards and the subjects were identified only by number. A 5 point rating scale was developed for each of the following factors: (a) weekly wage, (b) continuity of employment, (c) ability to travel independently, (d) degree of self support, (e) ability to conform to laws, (f) material possessions, and (g) overall rating of subject's postschool adjustment.

Five raters, all with experience in teaching the mentally retarded and with training beyond the masters degree level, rated each student for these seven factors. The subjects were randomly assigned for interviews and no evidence on the summary cards indicated whether subjects were from the experimental or contrast groups.

A computer program was developed to calculate scores for each rater on each of the seven factors. Interjudge reliability was high and scores of raters were combined. The major analysis was by chi square in comparing the overall ratings of adjustment between the experimental and the contrast groups.

Before the data were analyzed regarding postschool adjustment, comparisons between

162

the two groups were made of age, intelligence quotient, number of months enrolled in classes for the educable retarded, and socioeconomic status. The results are shown in Table 1.

The men who were in the off campus work experience group were 7 months older on the average than were those in the contrast group. This was the only difference significant at or beyond the 5 percent level. A further inspection of the records indicated that, although the off campus group was older, length of time out of school and length of time in the secondary school program were the same for both groups. Any advantage that would accrue to this older group could be attributed to additional maturity resulting from their having lived 7 months longer.

Both groups were comparable in recorded intelligence test scores. The scores of Stanford-Binet, Wechsler Intelligence Scale for Children, or Wechsler Adult Intelligence Scale were available for each subject, and the scores of several of the above tests had been recorded in the record for the majority of subjects. For each subject, therefore, the most recent test score was used. The intelligence test scores ranged from a low of 45 to a high of 78. Of the 68 subjects, 5 had test scores of 60 or below.

The average length of time enrolled in special classes for the educable retarded was slightly over 5 years. Women, on the average, had been in special classes for about one year longer than boys. Special class attendance ranged from slightly over one year to more than 10 years. As a group, they had been identified and placed and had remained in special classes for a good part of their school careers.

Although it is well known that the majority of the educable retarded typically come from the lower social classes, a comparison based on the father's occupations was made to determine if there were significant differences between the two groups. The classification followed Warner's Index of Status Characteristics (1957). The scale was collapsed at the upper end; ratings of one, two, and three were all assigned to the three category. This was done because few fathers rated higher than four on the scale. The majority of occupations were found to be in the unskilled and semiskilled classifications. Although the differences in the occupations of the

TABLE 2

Summary of Analysis of Overall Adjustment and Chi Square Value for Experimental and Contrast Subjects

Overall rating	Experimental $N = 36$	Contrast $N = 32$	Chi square value
Poor	11	10	
Average	13	8	
Good	12	14	
Chi square value			1.19

Note:—The original 5 point rating scale was collapsed into the three categories—good, average, and poor—so that this analysis would satisfy requirements for the use of chi square.

$$\chi^2_{05} = 5.99; \, df = 2$$

fathers were not significant between the experimental and contrast groups, the trend was that the fathers in the experimental group achieved lower ratings.

Results

The data in Table 2 indicate that there was no significant difference between the two groups in terms of overall adjustment.

Additional analyses of the data were reported in the original manuscript (Howe, 1967) and yielded the following results:

1. The mean weekly wage for men in the experimental group was $80.25, and for the contrast group, $92.25.
2. All subjects who were from minority groups were employed and, as a group, were earning wages slightly higher than their white counterparts.
3. Eighty-four percent of the original groups were located and interviewed 2 to 4 years after they had left school.
4. Eighty-six percent of the experimental and 84 percent of the contrast group were employed in July, 1966.
5. The unemployed as a group were multiply handicapped or tested near the bottom of the IQ range of the group.
6. The jobs held by the members of both the experimental and the contrast groups were distributed through the major occupational groups. Most were employed in the areas of service occupations or structural work. One-third were members of unions.

163

7. Eighteen percent had dropped out of school before graduation.
8. Approximately one-third of each group had married. There had been no divorces; one woman had been deserted by her husband. Only one subject of the 26 who were married had wed another person who was known to be retarded.

The results of this study have implications for the organization of secondary programs for the educable mentally retarded. It should be remembered that this study was done in a metropolitan area of California during a period of high employment. It would appear useful to replicate this study in other areas of the United States, in different size school districts or units, and during times of higher unemployment.

Implications

Findings of this research suggest that not all educable mentally retarded students in high school work study programs may need off campus placement as a part of their program. There is no reason to believe, at this time, that the off campus phase of the program is detrimental to their later adjustment as adults. It would seem that the more crucial question is that of the most efficient allocation of available resources. Perhaps the work study coordinator should spend more of his time in the placement and supervision of students in the on campus phase of the work study program. One advantage of the on campus aspect of a program is that it lends itself more easily to supervision and control of the job setting. It is also less time consuming in that the work stations are concentrated within the physical plant of the senior high school. With the advent of larger and more comprehensive high schools, additional and more varied work stations are available. Senior high schools with enrollments of 2,000 to 4,000 students are good sized communities within themselves and provide numerous work opportunities.

The on campus phase of the work study program may have another advantage. Past research studies have emphasized the relationship between success on the job and behavioral attitudes such as punctuality, ability to conform and accept limits, etc. Many of these skills in the affective domain can be taught in the classroom. Perhaps these skills and attitudes taught in the classroom setting can transfer rather directly into the job setting in the community.

Another aspect of the work study program on which the results of this study may have bearing has to do with the type of student who may most need off campus placement. The typical practice is to provide off campus placement for the students who seem to have the best chance of being successful. This practice usually stems from a combination of motivating and rewarding students to do well in their on campus work experience and classroom work and of developing good public relations in the community. Work coordinators often place the better students first in order to develop confidence in the program by the business leaders in the community. An implication from the results of this study could be that the multiply handicapped and those with lower potential are the ones who most need placement and supervision in order to improve their job holding potential at the termination of their school careers. A point that needs to be restated is that the majority of the students in this sample were higher level functioning retardates. One measure of this was that only 5 of the 68 had individual intelligence test scores below 60.

References

Charles, D. C. Longitudinal follow-up studies of community adjustment. In S. G. DiMichael (Ed.), *New vocational pathways for the mentally retarded*. Washington, D. C.: American Personnel and Guidance Association, 1966. Pp. 37-45.

Howe, C. E. *A comparison of mentally retarded high school students in work study versus traditional programs*. Washington, D. C.: US Department of Health, Education, and Welfare, 1967.

Tizard, J. Longitudinal and follow-up studies. In A. Clarke and A. D. B. Clarke (Eds.), *Mental deficiency*. London: Methuen and Co., 1958. Pp. 422-449.

CLIFFORD E. HOWE *is Professor and Chairman, Division of Special Education, College of Education, The University of Iowa, Iowa City. The research reported was performed pursuant to a grant with the Office of Education, US Department of Health; Education, and Welfare.*

A Report on the Institute for Advanced Study of Preparation of Teachers of the Mentally Retarded

JOHN R. PECK

Introduction

John R. Peck

In August, 1967, an Institute for Advanced Study was provided by the United States Office of Education in cooperation with The University of Texas at Austin. Faculty members of colleges throughout the southern region, whose primary responsibility was the training of teachers and other specialists in the area of mental retardation, were invited. Attending the Institute were representatives from most of the southern colleges who were receiving grants in teacher preparation under Public Law 88-164. The nine states included were Alabama, Arkansas, Florida, Georgia, Louisiana, Mississippi, New Mexico, Oklahoma, and Texas. The overall objective was to bring together faculty people from throughout this nine state region for intensive study of new concepts and developments in the area of teacher preparation. The group was interested in latest trends, methods, and approaches in overall programs for the mentally retarded. Twenty-three of the 25 colleges invited were able to send representives.

Faculty for the Institute included Dr. Louis Fliegler, Chairman of the Department of Special Education, Kent State University, Kent, Ohio; Dr. Thomas Jordan, at that time Chairman, Department of Guidance and Educational Psychology, Southern Illinois University, Carbondale, Illinois; Dr. John W. Kidd, Assistant Superintendent, Department for the Mentally Retarded, Special School District of St. Louis County, St. Louis, Missouri; Dr. Jerome H. Rothstein, Professor of Education, School of Education, San Francisco State College, San Francisco, California; Dr. Godfrey D. Stevens, Professor of Education, Department of Special Education, School of Education, University of Pittsburgh, Pittsburgh, Pennsylvania; and Dr. William G. Wolfe, Chairman of the Department of Special Education, The University of Texas at Austin. Director of the Institute was Dr. John R. Peck, Associate Professor of Special Education and Coordinator of Programs in Mental Retardation at The University of Texas at Austin.

The conference consisted of major lectures by the several visiting faculty followed by general and group discussions throughout the conference. Special fea-

Education and Training of the Mentally Retarded, April, 1968, pp. 97-105.

tures in the Institute included sessions on certification problems, professional standards, and work study programs, and a panel discussion by parents of mentally retarded children.

In the final session, evaluation of the Institute was made by four members selected from the Institute participants: Dr. Alfred Stern of Louisiana State University in New Orleans, who reviewed undergraduate matters; Dr. Andrew Shotick, University of Georgia, who reviewed the area of graduate studies; and Dr. Alfred Moore, University of Houston, who reviewed the area of research. The final speaker was Dr. Jasper Harvey of the University of Alabama, who summarized the conference as Chariman of the "Watchdog Committee."

The following are summaries of the points made by each of the faculty in their lectures covering several areas of interest.

National Trends and Their Implications for Teacher Education

Jerome Rothstein

Dr. Rothstein outlined ten major points which he considered to be the critical trends occuring in teacher education for the mentally retarded:

1. *The establishment of a continuum of services in the schools for the mentally retarded,* starting at preschool level and moving through elementary and junior and senior high school for both the educable and trainable mentally retarded. Teachers should be prepared to handle the education of the retarded at the various levels and various ages to a much greater extent than has been done in the past.

2. *The whole new concept of clinical teaching approach should be taken into consideration.* We are entering a new age where good clinical tools are important and should be more widely used than they have been in the past.

3. *The availability of research and demonstration programs and curriculum materials centers.* For the first time we are starting to see, on an operable basis, the results of research on which the government has expended a great deal of money. This is providing us with equipment and materials that can and should be used in the classroom by the teachers.

4. *The movement toward a five year certification pattern.* This is definitely a trend, going on in many of the leading states, in which the building of a block of courses for undergraduates seems to be requiring more than the four years that traditionally is taken to prepare a teacher for both regular and special education.

5. *The advent of camping, physical education, recreation, and outdoor education programs for the mentally retarded.* This is a rapidly expanding area of interest and is extremely important not only for recruiting teachers and other specialists but also for giving them first hand experiences with the retarded.

6. *With the potential development of new and expanded programs under Title VI of the Elementary Education Act, how are we going to ready ourselves to meet these needs?* Title VI will bring in many more opportunities for the expenditure of funds in special education in all of the states. In what way can teacher's colleges prepare their students to use the improved techniques and equipment to the maximum in the schools?

7. *New trends in institutions for dependent mentally retarded.* Many new opportunities are developing in

166

the institutional settings for the care and improvement and new training and educational approaches for children who are seriously retarded. Internship of students in these locations has done much for these institutions as well as for the students.

8. *The availability of commercially prepared materials.* Too many of our commercially prepared materials are turned out with little opportunity for trial in the classroom, and many people are trying to turn this great demand for materials into a "fast buck." We must be careful to prepare our people to very skillfully evaluate the kinds of commercially prepared materials being turned out.

9. *Special education classes are not enough;* merely adding more classes to satisfy the great demand for services to the retarded is not the answer to improvement of special education in the public schools. If there is going to be a real therapeutic intervention, we cannot have a canned curriculum, but, rather, we must have a curriculum that is developed by small groups of teachers to meet individual needs of those children in that particular school and that particular school district. This places the burden on the teacher education institution for providing an opportunity during training to learn how to work with individual children under specific circumstances for highly personalized and localized curriculum development.

10. *The whole concept of cultural deprivation:* How are we preparing our young people in social and behavioral sciences to cope with the myriad of materials that are coming out and the writings that are conflicting and confusing in the field of cultural deprivation? Are they aware of such fields as cultural and personality factors as they interrelate with the development of the human being?

New Definitions: Learning Disability and Multiple Handicap

William G. Wolfe

I was privileged to attend an institute last week at Northwestern University in Evanston, Illinois, which was called by Dr. Myklebust and which brought together about 15 people from around the nation. The Institute's purpose was to attempt to put together two definitions: (a) a definition of learning disability and (b) a definition of multiple handicap.

Many leaders of the field were present, including Samuel Kirk, Jim Chalfant, Corrine Kass, Bill Heller, Louis Fliegler, Harrie Selznick, and others. We spent three days deliberating on these two definitions.

What is meant by a learning disability? Dr. Myklebust has given me permission to share our deliberations with you at this conference. This is the first time either of these definitions have been shared by a professional group. We would appreciate your reactions. These are the two definitions we came up with:

> *Learning Disability* refers to one or more significant deficits in essential learning processes requiring special educational techniques for remediation. Children with a learning disability generally demonstrate a discrepancy between expected and actual achievement in one or more areas, such as: spoken, read, or written language, mathematics and spatial orientation. The learning disability referred to is not *primarily* the result of sensory, motor, intellectual, or emotional handicaps, or lack of opportunity to learn.

> *Deficits* are defined in terms of accepted diagnostic procedures in education and psychology.

167

Essential learning processes are those currently referred to in behavioral science as involving perception, integration and expression, either verbal or nonverbal.

Special education techniques for remediation refers to educational planning based on diagnostic procedures and results.

Multiple Handicap refers to combinations of handicaps (two or more of the following: emotional disturbance, learning disability, mental retardation, sensory or motor impairment) which interact to impede development and learning in ways which require special education services different from those required for children with a single handicap. Such services are not necessarily the sum of programs and methodologies commonly used with those having single handicaps.

Learning Disability. To pick out certain items within these definitions, we might start here with the word "significant." We found that we could not define this term because it meant different things to different people.

We were trying to take the definition of learning disability out of its medical setting and make it applicable to an educational setting. We were trying to have it pinned down so that we would not have as high as 40 and 50 percent of all children being given this particular label.

It is important to realize that we are in a state of emergency. We are in a way of life that actually demands, at the moment, that we label a certain condition. I am talking here about the necessity of labeling in order to get legislative support for the problems of the child. We are living in a time when the only way to get funds is to label. We felt that these particular children needed help—needed funds—and therefore the way to do it was to identify them as a separate entity.

We should be just as interested, I think, in *not* designating a child as having a learning disability as we are interested in designating him as having a learning disability. We feel that included in such a large group would be children who are cerebral palsied or mentally retarded. People say, "This child is not learning so he has a learning disability"; but it is not necessary to use this term if we apply this particular definition when talking about crippled children or mentally retarded children.

Multiple Handicapped. If a child were blind or deaf (this being his main problem) we should include him in a program for the blind or the deaf. On the other hand, if he has a particular handicap, combined with another handicap, he would be placed in the multiple handicap category. We feel that this definition says that there has to be a specific program for this particular child who is presenting a specific kind of need. He cannot be treated as though he had two separate problems. His combination of handicaps in themselves would be considered one certain problem.

In regard to both of these definitions, it could not be said that these are by any means finalized, but they should be the basis for good discussion in professional meetings. We at least feel this was something which was worth our time. No claim has been made that these definitions are perfect, but we felt that this part of our charge was to define these two types of disabilities. Eventually these two definitions, or modifications of them, would presumably be used by the US Office of Education to define categories.

Implications for Research and Graduate Study in Mental Retardation

Thomas E. Jordan

It is important to discuss the role of scholarship for those who have a commitment to the pursuit of ideas. The first function of scholarship is to stimulate thought. A second function is to put the items of everyday experience into perspective. One function of scholarship is to formally and deliberately try to put the commonplace into perspective. When one does this, one simply distills the day by day experience and occasionally brings out a new idea. Another obligation of the scholar is to take ideas and develop them, in the sense of extending them. This is rather lonely and fruitless work for the most part, but it is one of the things the scholar must do.

An important element for those who work in universities and colleges and who are concerned with mental retardation is the changing of practices in special education classrooms. Human activities are basically practice centered or conceptually centered. Education is traditionally practice centered. We do what we do because we have hammered out, painfully and slowly, ways of producing change in children; but the price we have paid of making practice centered orientation the touchstone of our work is that we have neglected our own private business. It seems that special education is now beginning to enter a period of introspection which has been long overdue, and it falls to each of us here to be either the hammer or the anvil in shaping up the new form of special education.

The college professor, with regard to research, is a practitioner plus. He has to be able to understand what is going on at the practice centered level—to know what we do with children and why we do it— but he has to be something else too. He has to be conceptually oriented so that innovations that are clearly being pressed upon us will be productive.

Research is showing us several fruitful results. Social and vocational efficiency is being studied with some optimistic results as we expand programs for the intervention of children who are intellec-tually limited and culturally impoverished. Operant conditioning is being used rather extensively today in helping to achieve better ways to reach children who are particularly unable to respond to the more traditional methods of teaching. Headstart research and the research on cultural deprivation have brought up some interesting points. It seems, however, that every culturally deprived child is a learning disability case and ought to be in special education; this suggests then that some reformulation is appropriate.

It is time for us to do more research on the effectiveness of special education. We can demonstrate that it works, but the nature of the this evidence is rather gross. It now remains for future researchers to move in with a slightly higher resolution to their intellectual microscopes and focus on more precise considerations.

The work of Piaget and of his student, Enhelder, on preschool children, found that the cognitive processes of selection, storage, and retrieval can be taught, but that the coordination—or (as we would say in psycholinguistic terms) the integration—of these things cannot be taught. Studies done by Lyle have shown that although institutions are generally depriving, it is entirely possible to make institutions superior to the home from the point of view of language enrichment and general intellectual growth. We have the institutions but, unfortunately, we are running them in precisely the opposite way from the way they need to be run. They are not inherently depriving, but they are functionally depriving. This is one observation which has many implications for our work on retarded children.

(In the remainder of his talk, Dr. Jordan discussed the research he is doing with lower, middle, and upper class mothers in the pattern of punitiveness which they display with their handicapped children. These children were selected in accordance with meeting or not meeting a criterion of early developmental adversity.)

What the Consumer Looks for in Teachers Trained in the Colleges and Universities

John Kidd

What are the weaknesses most commonly observed in teachers employed from the teacher training institutions; or, putting it more positively, in what important ways could these teachers be stronger than they typically are?

1. *A thorough understanding of the meaning of mental age and intelligence quotient.* Teachers in general could be better trained in understanding of readiness and of performance levels in relation to mental age. Two references of great importance are *Psychology of Readiness* by Gettman and Kane, together with the manual, and *Readiness for Learning*, by Pierce and McCloud, a second resource for teachers going into the field.

2. *The importance of records.* Records on individual children and on class groups, generally, should be kept, should be more accurate than they ordinarily are, and need to be used as part of the tools of the training. Dramatize the notion that the teacher may not be back tomorrow—and that the children will suffer anytime a change is made and no records are available for a new teacher to use on a particular child. Something is needed to provide the continuity of program and to provide for the welfare of the children.

3. *The teachers need to be aware of the important developments of the student chapters of CEC.* This has to do primarily with a greater pride in our profession. Out of a national convention of 6,000 people at CEC, we find that 2,000 of them are students with full voting power and full representation in adult assembly. This is bound to have a remarkable effect upon our profession.

4. *We hope that the teachers who come to us would have some notion of the meaning of the term phonic and its implications, especially as applied to such things as the initial teaching alphabet.* Phonetics and phonics are very important to the retarded child and need to be taught more effectively than they are.

5. *Concretizing the experience of the retarded is something that has to be constantly kept in mind by the teacher.* Encourage your teachers to become more competent is using concrete experiences with retarded children.

6. *Be sure teachers have a depth of understanding on what percentage of the child's life is spent in school from the time he starts at age six until he finishes at 16 or 18.* Few people are aware that the child spends only 12 to 18 percent of his time with the special teacher in the classroom and that a great deal of his learning occurs outside of these hours. It is important for the teacher to know what this implies for the kind of learning experiences she wants him to have.

7. *The teacher of the mentally retarded needs to be more knowledgeable about the culturally disadvantaged or culturally deprived.* There is so much overlap between the mentally retarded and the culturally deprived that a teacher is not properly prepared for the school unless she understands the cultural implications.

8. *Theories of learning are generally misunderstood or not understood by most teachers in special educa-*

tion. There must be a lack in their training which creates this problem. It is important that they have a little bit of acquaintance with the terminology of such currently used ideas as operant conditioning and perceptual field theory. The laws of learning prevail as much in the special classroom as they do in the regular classroom or in the clinic.

9. *The term, generic special teacher, is one that is developing out of our newer understandings and is a concept that needs to be understood today.* The concept refers to the preparation of the teacher to work with one particular disability. Many of the retarded children with whom our teachers spend their school year are multiply handicapped children who have, in addition to retardation, general learning disability and other specific disabilities. Therefore, a generic approach on the part of the teacher is a great necessity in today's education milieu.

10. *Teachers need to better understand techniques of crisis avoidance.* When they are challenged by a child they need not feel that they must immediately confront the child and continue until the confrontation becomes sharper and sharper, particularly in front of the class. Administrators are anxious to find special teachers who can avoid crises but can handle them in the proper way when they occur in the classroom. By all means the temperament of the teacher has a great deal to do here. Neither the child nor the teacher needs to lose face if the teacher has equilibrium, control, and insight when certain crises develop in the classroom.

11. *Finally, the teacher must have an understanding of her pervasive responsibility for her pupils.* Not enough teachers recognize this. The teacher

has greater responsibility than just to keep them from bell to bell, see that they learn a little something, or teach them good manners. When a child needs some special attention to which the teacher's personal concern could be brought to bear, the teacher needs to move in and do something for the sake of the child. This is particulary true if the child can be helped to overcome a defeat of his ego or certain external abnormalities which might be corrected, such as a poor dentition, not bathing, poor grooming, and other factors that prevent the child from being accepted. The teacher needs to intervene personally and has a real responsibility to persuade this child to change for the better as fast as possible.

Preparation for Teachers of the Mentally Retarded

Louis Fliegler

Basic concepts for preparing teachers for the mentally retarded include: (a) the teacher of the mentally retarded must understand the core of ideas which all teachers must have; (b) this teacher is primarily a special educator and therefore must understand the core of ideas which all special educators must possess; (c) the teacher of the mentally retarded by the nature of her instructional operations requires definitive information about her area of specialization to become proficient.

Perhaps, as part of the core, a course should be introduced called Behavioral Science of Mental Retardation. This would be advisable since the teacher's preparation must be based on a behavioral science of special education rather than elementary and/or secondary education. Rather than special education concepts being built upon elementary or secondary education, it might be more relevant to the task to provide the concepts of special education initially and then plug in those segments of information from elementary or secondary education which are essential for understanding of the educational process.

Although the traditional approaches are adequate in presenting curriculum content through language arts, social studies, arithmetic, arts, and so forth, the main difference is more at the developmental level of the child. Perhaps we can place greater emphasis on instructional processes which stem from the psychology of learning for the retardate. In essence, the teaching strategies of clinical education may be the real substance of special education. However, this area needs greater investigation and exploration. While taking the instructional process (or methods and materials) course, the preservice teacher should be allowed to try out aspects of curriculum and methodology immediately with a group of children, rather than wait for student teaching as the appropriate time. If immediate reenforcement is strategic for learning, it seems wise to apply the theory to practice conjointly.

Practicum experiences are of great value to a teacher in training. One of the glaring weaknesses in our programs is the lack of (a) broad orientation to retarded children in a variety of situations, and (b) interactive relationships with other professional persons. If possible it is important that practicum and theory be applied concurrently. Practicum experiences should begin early in the student's career and continue throughout the entire teacher education program. There could be a 'live in'' basis in some aspects of the teacher's training. For some, but not all, teachers, contact with retarded children on a 24 hour basis would lead to greater understanding of the retardate.

A rather important aspect to teacher education generally is omitted from most of our programing practices. This may be referred to as specificity of function. The term assumes that all good teachers cannot teach any child—that teachers, because of their interests, needs, and personality, prefer certain dimensions of the schooling process more than others. For example, the factors may be delineated as (a) age of child; (b) level of programs (elementary or secondary); (c) geographical area (urban, rural, suburban); (d) socioeconomic level (low or middle class); (e) educational setting (public schools, community hospitals, institutions); and (f) the type of retarded child (educable, trainable, or multiply handicapped).

The teacher in training needs to be made aware of the similarities and differences that exist in children at different school levels. There are many things that can be taught to teachers going into either elementary or secondary school teaching. On the other hand, there are great differences between the approaches in the two areas that need to be understood. The elementary teacher, for example, is not deeply concerned that her children understand the importance of sex life, vocations, material things (such as money and clothing), social welfare, home economics, and vocational counseling (including the work study program). These, however, need to be very thoroughly covered by the teacher who is going to work with the adolescent high school age retardate.

Obviously, at the secondary level we must develop work experience situations that are more realistic. To foster more meaningful school work experiences, we need a team of work study coordinators. We also must drastically alter our orientation for teaching of motor skills. After considering the vast changes occurring in the market place, we must teach for a cluster of job skills rather than for a single job. Also the work potential for the retardate has increased immeasurably through the use of prosthetic adaptations such as the use of power tools, electronically controlled equipment, and other modern developments which bring the retarded much closer to the normal adult in quantity, quality, and production.

The magnitude of preparing teachers of the mentally retarded is in a state of flux. It is presumptuous for any individual to suggest that any single pattern be the appropriate way to educate teachers, but we still have certain critical dimensions that must be considered. The major thrust should be in the direction of developing a behavioral science in mental retardation with implications for instructional processes. If the contention is appropriate that special education is differential education, then it is incumbent upon us to delineate a differential pattern for preparing teachers for the mentally retarded.

Conclusion

The Institute was considered to be very productive and successful by the majority of the participants. There has been demand for the distribution of the proceedings of this Institute, which include the full speeches of all of the visiting faculty plus the summary comments of the four participants at the end of the conference. Copies of these may be obtained from Dr. John R. Peck, Associate Professor, Department of Special Education, The University of Texas, Austin, Texas 78712.

JOHN R. PECK *is Associate Professor, Department of Special Education, University of Texas, Austin.*

173

Charles Meisgeier

The Identification of Successful Teachers of Mentally or Physically Handicapped Children

Abstract: To accomplish the purpose of identifying and quantifying characteristics which contribute to successful student teaching of mentally and physically handicapped children, five dimensions of human behavior were investigated. Three characteristic patterns of successful student teaching experiences emerged from the investigation. The successful student teachers (a) were well adjusted, emotionally stable, and able to encounter difficult special class situations; (b) possessed physical energy, vitality, and enthusiasm necessary to meet special classroom demands; (c) obtained high scores on measures of scholastic achievement and ability.

Although many studies have been made of the characteristics of regular class teachers, there is an overall lack of empirical information concerning the characteristics of effective special education teachers. One dimension recurrently subjected to scrutiny is the early selection of students who, for various reasons, aspire to teach mentally or physically handicapped children. With the exception of one major study conducted over ten years ago (Mackie, Williams, and Dunn, 1954) there is a paucity of information regarding either the characteristics of teachers of mentally or physically handicapped or the prediction of effective teaching of these children.

Purpose of the Study

The purpose of this study was (a) to identify and quantify the characteristics that might contribute to successful student teaching of mentally or physically handicapped children and (b) to establish criteria for the selection of prospective teachers of these children. To accomplish this, five dimensions of human behavior were investigated to determine the relationship, if any, to successful student teaching of handicapped children. The five areas were: (a) scholastic aptitude, (b) scholastic achievement, (c) educational (vocational) interest, (d) personality, and (e) attitudes toward children and toward teaching.

Method

The 41 subjects included in this investigation were student teaching in special classes for either mentally or physically handicapped children. With the exception of one 30 year old subject, the students ranged in age from 20 to 24 years, with a mean age of 21 years. The mean IQ of the group was 122 with a standard deviation of 7.07. The students were undergraduates in their junior or senior years from seven colleges offering training programs for students preparing to become teachers of mentally or physically handicapped children.

Test Battery. The sources of information consisted of (a) academic transcripts, (b) admission records, (c) a battery of seven selected instruments, and (d) the criterion measures—the *Evaluation Record for Teachers of Handicapped Children* (ERTHC). The test battery completed by each student consisted of the following seven instruments: Otis Gamma Test of Mental Ability Form E_M (OGT); Personal

Exceptional Children, December, 1965, Vol.32, No.4, pp. 229-235.

174

Information Blank (PIB); Sixteen Personality Factors Questionnaire, Form C (16 PF Test); Thurstone Temperament Schedule (TTS); Gordon Personal Inventory (GPI); Educational Interest Inventory (EII); Minnesota Teacher Attitude Inventory (MTAI). The OGT was administered to each student either in groups at the colleges by a member of the staff or individually by the cooperating teacher; the remainder of the tests were administered by mail.

The PIB and ERTHC were developed particularly for use in this investigation. The PIB provided information pertaining to the student's reasons for entering special education, the age when the choice was made, and the student's satisfaction with the choice. Items pertaining to the choice of vocation were included in six major areas of influence: personal, educational, professional, occupational, social, and miscellaneous.

The ERTHC, a new criterion measure, was developed to measure the effectiveness of student teachers of mentally or physically handicapped children. A cumulative rating on the ERTHC was made by the cooperating teacher and the college supervisor.

The *Teaching Evaluation Record* by Dwight Beecher (1953) formed the basis for the new evaluation instrument. After critical analysis by a panel of teachers and a panel of professors, 19 inappropriate items of the original 32 Beecher items were deleted, and the remaining 13 items were modified in varying degrees to meet the particular needs of this study. Nine completely new items were added, making a total of 22 items on the experimental form of the new instrument. Several hundred items from six major sources formed the basis for the modification of the Beecher items and for the construction of the new ones.

After examination of the experimental form by the panel of teachers and professors, a competent jury of experts reviewed the instrument and further modifications were made. The final form of the new instrument (ERTHC) contained 20 items. The reliability of the new instrument is .82.

Several techniques, including a factor analytic study of observer ratings, were used to determine the best possible way to administer the criterion measure. The factor analysis and varimax rotation indicated that the loading of the Composite ERTHC (composite rating of college supervisor and cooperating teacher) on the Performance Factor (F3) was significant beyond the .01 level. These results, combined with analysis of the degree of saturation of the criterion variable, indicated that the Composite ERTHC was the most useful criterion variable.

Results and Conclusions

Successful student teaching in special classes is correlated with observable criteria which can be measured objectively. Nineteen predictor variables measuring five dimensions of human behavior were found to be significant at or beyond the .05 level. The five measured dimensions were: (a) scholastic aptitude, (b) scholastic achievement, (c) personality traits, (d) educational (vocational) interests, and (e) teacher attitudes. Thirteen of the correlations were significant at the .05 level and six were significant at the .01 level. The coefficients of correlation of the 19 significant predictor variables with the criterion measure are indicated in Table 1.

Considerable evidence was found to indicate acceptance of the five hypotheses of the investigation, and thus all five were accepted. Conclusions one to six summarize the findings pertaining to the five hypotheses.

1. A positive, significant relationship was found between scholastic aptitude and successful student teaching of mentally or physically handicapped children. The correlation between the OGT and the measure of successful student teaching was positive and significant beyond the .05 level.

2. A positive, significant relationship was found between scholastic achievement and successful student teaching of mentally or physically handicapped children. Four measures of college achievement—the All College Cumulative Grade Point Average (CGPA), CGPA Psychology, CGPA Special Education, and the CGPA General Courses—were significantly correlated with the measure of successful student teaching beyond the .05 level. The correlations of the All College CGPA and General Education CGPA to the criterion measure resulted in positive correlations significant at

175

TABLE I

Coefficients of Correlation of 19 Predictor Variables with the Criterion Measure of Successful Student Teaching (Composite ERTHC)

Predictor Variable	Correlation with Criterion Measure
6 Otis Gamma Test of Mental Ability	.36*
10 Gordon Personal Inventory—Vigor	.43**
15 Thurstone Temperament Schedule—Dominant	.34*
16 Thurstone Temperament Schedule—Stable	.36*
24 16 PF Test F Enthusiastic, Talkative (Surgency)	.32*
26 16 PF Test H Adventurous (Parmia)	.37*
27 16 PF Test I Tough, Realistic (Harria)	—.42**
29 16 PF Test M Conventional, Practical (Praxemia)	—.30*
35 16 PF Test Q_4 Phlegmatic, Composed (Low Ergic Tension)	—.31*
36 Minnesota Teacher Attitude Inventory	.41**
40 Educational Interest Inventory—Elementary Teacher	—.39*
42 Educational Interest Inventory—Elementary Principal	—.36*
47 Educational Interest Inventory—Researcher	.33*
49 Cumulative Grade Point Average, All College	.43**
50 Cumulative Grade Point Average, Psychology	.39*
51 Cumulative Grade Point Average, Special Education	.37*
53 Cumulative Grade Point Average, General College Courses	.49**
56 Number College Courses—General Education	.37*
60 No Student Teaching Experience in Regular Class	.40**

* Correlation significant at the .05 level.
** Correlation significant at the .01 level.

the .01 level. It is interesting to note that only the CGPA in "professional education" courses failed to produce a significant correlation, although it did load highly with the others in the factor analysis.

Indirect measures of achievement such as background or experience were found generally to be unrelated to successful student teaching of handicapped children. Of the ten background experience measures, only two resulted in significant correlations. The correlation of the number of general courses completed, with the criterion measure, was significant beyond the .05 level. Prior student teaching experience in a regular class was not positively related to successful special class teaching. The correlation was significant beyond the .01 level.

3. A significant relationship was found between various measures of personality and successful student teaching of mentally or physically handicapped children. Eight significant measures of personality were found on the three personality instruments used in the study. These measures and significant subscales were: (a) the GPI—Vigor (V); (b) the TTS—Dominant (D), Emotionally Stable (E); and (c) the 16 PF Test, Form C—Enthusiastic (F), Adventurous (H), Realistic (I), Practical (N), Stable (Q_4).

4. A significant relationship was found between three measures of educational (vocational) interest and successful student teaching of mentally or physically handicapped children. These measures were on the EII. The significant subscales were Elementary Teacher, Elementary Principal, and Researcher.

5. A significant relationship was found between certain attitudes toward children and teaching, and successful student teaching of mentally or physically handicapped children. The correlation between the MTAI and the criterion measure was significant beyond the .01 level.

6. By factor analysis, it was determined that the measures of scholastic achievement were the most highly associated with successful student teaching of mentally or physically handicapped children.

7. Three patterns of successful student teachers of mentally or physically handicapped children emerged from this investigation. All three patterns were characteristic of the successful student teacher. They were found (a) to be well adjusted, emotionally stable, able to successively encounter the many trying situations that arise in a special class, (b) to possess the physical energy, the vitality and enthusiasm necessary to meet the demands of special class teaching, and (c) to obtain high scores on measures of scholastic achievement and general ability or intelligence and to possess a favorable

attitude toward teaching and children. These three patterns and subpatterns were: *Pattern 1*—Achievement-Ability-Attitude; *Pattern 2*—Personal Adjustment-General Emotional Stability: (a) Experimenting (b) Sociable (c) Composed (d) Emotionally Stable; *Pattern 3*—Dynamic Energy: (a) Energetic (b) Responsible (c) Realistic.

8. The student teachers of mentally or physically handicapped children differed markedly from other college students and from students preparing to teach in other fields on selected measures of personality, interest, and attitude. Comparisons of the mean scores of the student teachers with published norms on the GPI, 16 PF Test, MTAI, and EII indicated that the student teachers possessed relatively unique characteristics. Thirty of the 40 comparisons resulted in differences significant beyond the .05 level.

On the GPI, the student teachers were compared with a norm group of college students and significant differences were noted on all five of the scales (Cautiousness, Personal Relations, Original Thinking, Vigor, and Total Score). A similar comparison with college students on the 16 PF Test indicated significant differences on ten of the scales (Factors A, B, C, G, H, I, M, Q_1, Q_2, Q_4). On the MTAI, comparisons were made on nine norm groups selected as being most like the study group. Out of the nine comparisons, seven were significantly different at the .01 level. There were no significant differences for beginning education juniors on the "Secondary nonacademic" group or for "Experienced Elementary Teacher." Significant differences were found on eight subscales of the EII. No significant differences were found on either the Elementary Teacher scale or on the Supervisor scale.

9. Personal, educational, and professional experiences or desires comprised the major components influencing the student's decision to enter the field of special education.

The student teachers in the present investigation indicated that they entered the field primarily because of personal reasons. Few indicated they had become interested in special education because of high school counseling programs. The challenge of the field, the desire to help the handicapped, visits to special classes,

schools or hospitals, and the opportunities for jobs caused by teacher shortages were some of the choices most frequently checked by the students as influencing their decision to become teachers of mentally or physically handicapped children. No clear cut patterns were observed, nor was any systematic recruitment procedure discernible. Rather, there seemed to be a haphazard combination of accidental, unrelated experiences responsible for their choice.

10. Two multiple regression equations computed for testing and use in future studies concerned with the problem of predicting successful teaching of mentally or physically handicapped children resulted in multiple R's of .62 and .72 significant beyond the .01 level.

11. The multiple regression with parsimony process was utilized in each case to determine the one regression equation with maximum prediction value and minimum number of independent predictor variables. The first multiple regression analysis included the variables from Factor 3 (the achievement-performance factor), and all 19 of the significant predictor variables were employed in a second analysis regardless of factor loadings. This was done since the significant variables before factor analysis could be considered more complex than the variables only loading in the achievement-performance factor. Thus, it would be expected that a higher multiple R would result from an analysis of the 19 variables than would result from an analysis utilizing only the variables from a common factor such as Factor 3. This expectation was verified by the results. The contribution to the variance of the five variables was significant beyond the .01 level for each equation.

Equation One—computed on Factor 3 variables resulted in a multiple R of .62 and the following equation:

$$Y = .089 \ X_1 - 10.8493 \ X_2 + 2.6571 \ X_3 + 2.5796 \ X_4 + 7.9294 \ X_5 + 55.719$$

where:

Y = Criterion Measure—Composite ERTHC
X_1 = Adjusted MTAI Score
X_2 = CGPA All College
X_3 = CGPA Psychology Courses
X_4 = CGPA Special Education
X_5 = CGPA General Education

Utilization of Equation One would result in a prediction about 22 percent better than what probably would occur by chance.

Equation Two—computed on 19 significant variables plus the remaining Factor 3 variables resulted in a multiple R of .73 with the following equation. The five variables in the equation measured personality, attitude, and scholastic achievement.

$$Y = .4458\ X_1 - .5998\ X_2 + .0679\ X_3 + 2.9799\ X_4 + .6657\ X_5 + 44.223$$

where:

Y = Criterion Measure—Composite ERTHC
X_1 = 16 PF Test—Subscale F (enthusiastic)
X_2 = 16 PF Test—Subscale I (realistic)
X_3 = Adjusted MTAI Score
X_4 = CGPA General Education
X_5 = Number of General Education Courses

The standard error of R is .042 indicating that the obtained R probably will not vary more than .11 from the population value of R. Utilization of Equation Two would result in a prediction about 32 percent better than what probably would occur by chance.

Though results for both equations indicate little room for doubt that a genuine significant multiple correlation exists in the population, caution must be exercised in applying these equations to larger groups since this investigation is the first of its type on the prediction of success of special class teachers, and as such, has many exploratory aspects. However, it is quite likely that the identified factors will appear with some consistency in future studies.

Characteristics and Qualifications of Student Teachers

The results of this investigation have some explicit implications relative to the characteristics and qualifications of student teachers of mentally or physically handicapped children. Throughout the long process of selection, guidance, and training, certain patterns should become apparent if the students are to be effective in the classroom. The findings indicated that student teachers of mentally or physically handicapped children are a relatively unique group of individuals with characteristics different from those of other college students and other education students. However, their inter-

ests and attitudes are most like elementary teachers.

Three significant characteristic-qualification patterns of successful student teachers of mentally or physically handicapped children emerged from this study which are applicable to a selection and recruitment program. By projecting these results it can be concluded that prospective teachers of mentally or physically handicapped children should possess the following characteristics.

Pattern 1. Achievement - Ability - Attitude. Prospective teachers should possess high ability (intelligence), a good attitude toward children and teaching, and should be good students with high grades in college preparatory courses.

Pattern 2. Personal adjustment-General emotional stability (experimenting, sociable, composed, emotionally stable). Prospective teachers of mentally or physically handicapped children should be well adjusted and emotionally stable in order to be able to effectively deal with the adjustment problems of parents and the emotional and social needs of the children. The following personality characteristics are important aspects of this pattern:

- Experimenting. They should be adventurous, experimenting, impulsive, ready to try new things.
- Sociable. They should be responsive, friendly, cheerful, and sociable.
- Composed. They should be composed, unannoyed at leaving a task unfinished. They should possess an even disposition and be able to remain calm in a crisis.
- Emotionally Stable. They should be abundant in emotional response, able to face people and grueling emotional situations without fatigue. They should be emotionally stable and free from various nervous and instability symptoms.

Pattern 3. Dynamic energy (energetic, responsible, realistic). Prospective teachers of mentally or physically handicapped children need to be vigorous and energetic in order to be able to effectively meet the physical, mental, and emotional demands of the special classroom. They should be realistic, practical, and responsible since many times they are left on their own with little help and inadequate supervision, and thus need to have a maximum capacity for self direction. The following characteristics are important aspects of this pattern:

- Energetic. They should be vigorous, energetic, enthusiastic, talkative, expressive, alert, and extroverted.
- Responsible. They should be responsible, independent, leaders, and organizers. They should enjoy promoting new projects and influencing others.
- Realistic. They should be practical, logical, and able to keep a group operating on a practical and realistic basis.

Regular Class Teaching—a Prerequisite?

The results of the investigation also raised the question of the relationship of regular class teaching to special class teaching. "No prior regular class teaching experience" was found to be significantly related to effective special class teaching. The implications of such findings need no elaboration.

The question of whether or not regular classroom experience should be a prerequisite for the special class teacher has been discussed and debated for many years. Tenny (1954) was interested in this problem and expressed a series of objections to the concept that the recruitment of special class teachers should be limited to those who have had teaching experience in the regular classroom. In contrast to Tenny, Lord and Kirk indicated that in general ". . . teachers of exceptional children should first obtain education and experience in teaching normal children. . ." (Lord and Kirk, 1950, pp. 104-105). Lord and Kirk did, however, list a number of practical limitations to this requirement.

As part of the US Office of Education study (Mackie, Williams, and Dunn, 1957), an inquiry form was sent to the participating educators on which they noted the amount of classroom experience they considered as necessary and desirable for teachers of mentally retarded children. The results indicated that the responding groups generally favored some teaching experience in the regular classes. The college instructors generally were satisfied with less regular class teaching than were the other groups. The results would seem to indicate that further study of this problem in detail might cast some interesting light on this question.

Recommendations for Further Research

Several possibilities for further research result from this study. They include the following:

1. A study should be made on a large sample of students preparing to be teachers of mentally or physically handicapped children to test the prediction equations resulting from this investigation.
2. There is a need for further detailed study of the criteria for measuring the effectiveness of teachers and student teachers of mentally or physically handicapped children.
3. A study should be made of (a) the relationship of regular class teaching experience to student teaching in a special class and (b) the relationship of regular class teaching experience to successful teaching of mentally or physically handicapped children in the field.
4. A large scale study of the problem of predicting successful teaching of mentally or physically handicapped children should be made over a long period of time involving hundreds of teachers. Such a study should delineate the differences, if any, between teachers of physically handicapped children and teachers of mentally handicapped children as well as any variation in characteristics resulting from sex differences of the teachers.

References

Beecher, D. E. *The teaching evaluation record.* Buffalo, New York: Educators Publishing Company, 1953.

Berry, J. R. *Professional preparation and effectiveness of beginning teachers.* Coral Gables, Florida: University of Miami, 1960.

Cattell, R. B., Saunders, D. R., and Stice, G. *Handbook for the sixteen personality factor questionnaire—forms A, B,* and *C.*

Cook, W. W., Leeds, C. H., and Callis, R. *Minnesota teacher attitude inventory—manual.* New York: Psychological Corporation, 1952.

Gordon, L. V. *Gordon personal inventory—manual.* Yonkers, New York: World Book Co., 1956.

Lord, F. E. and Kirk, S. A. The education of teach-

179

ers of special classes. In *The Education of Exceptional Children*, Forty-Ninth Yearbook of the National Society for the Study of Education, Part II. Bloomington, Illinois: Public School Publishing Company, 1950. Pp. 103-116.

Mackie, Romaine P., Williams, H. M., and Dunn, L. M. *Teachers of children who are mentally retarded*. Office of Education Bulletin No. 13. Washington, D.C.: US Government Printing Office, 1954.

Otis, A. S. *Otis quick-scoring mental ability tests: new edition gamma test: E_M*. New York: Harcourt Brace and World, Inc., 1954.

Ryans, D. G. *Characteristics of teachers: their description, comparison, and appraisal*. Santa Monica, California: System Development Corporation, 1962.

Symonds, P. M. *A manual of instructions for the educational interest inventory*. New York: Bureau of Publications, Teachers College, Columbia University.

Tenny, J. W. Preparing teachers of mentally handicapped children. *American Journal of Mental Deficiency*, 1954, 566-572.

CHARLES MEISGEIER *is Coordinator, Program for Administrators of Special Education, The University of Texas, and Special Consultant, The Texas Mental Retardation Planning Study, Austin.*

LOUIS SCHWARTZ

An Integrated Teacher Education Program for Special Education—a New Approach

Abstract: Preparation of the clinician educator, capable of providing diagnosis and remediation of the variety of learning difficulties presented by exceptional children, is proposed in an integrated teacher education curriculum for special education. The gap between accumulated knowledge regarding exceptionality and existing teacher education curricula is discussed, along with problems posed by shortages of personnel and increasing concern over the qualitative aspects of special education. Courses in the integrated sequence are described, and limitations noted.

DRAMATIC advances on the local, state, and federal levels in the education and rehabilitation of exceptional children and youth have produced challenging issues for the professional workers in the field. Dynamic changes in population, patterns of service, and the explosion of knowledge in the helping disciplines have posed conflicting problems presented by rapidly changing concepts and current practices. The enormous expansion of health, education, and welfare programs concerned with exceptional children and youth has identified special education and rehabilitation needs more completely, highlighted the need for professional personnel, and focused attention upon the need for a systematic refinement of existing information in order to bridge the gap between the rapidly increasing knowledge about problems in special education and the ensuing implications for the exceptional individual in the classroom.

One of the most crucial issues paralleling this period of growth is the increased concern for the numerical and qualitative aspects of teacher preparation required for the various categories of exceptionality. Although considerable effort has been devoted to increasing our supply of teachers, little attention has been placed upon the nature and extent of their preparation in terms of the changing population, patterns of service, and the growing accumulation of knowledge concerning learning and rehabilitation.

Kirk (1965) summarizes the recent decade of developments in the education of the handicapped and raises several basic issues related to the preparation of professional personnel.

Under the pressure of extreme shortages of professional personnel, a major issue becomes whether to (a) focus on immediate needs in terms of the numbers of special educators without regard to quality; (b) concentrate on quality in the preparation of professional personnel, even though it may mean a decrease in the numbers thus prepared; or (c) find a radically new method of accomplishing both goals at the same time (p. 102).

The teacher education program proposed herein is an attempt to approach the problem posed by Kirk through an integrated sequence (including five traditionally separate fields of

Exceptional Children, February, 1967, Vol.33, No.6, pp. 411-416.

exceptionality) into one unified curriculum for the preparation of teachers of exceptional children.

Background and Approach

Finding a radically new method is not a formidable obstacle; however, translating current trends into a new curriculum structure and attempting to break from the bounds of tradition initially at the college level and eventually in the public school poses serious challenges at both the leadership and managerial levels.

Notwithstanding the many significant barriers blocking the path of change, the essential problem is translating current knowledge about (a) the changing population of exceptional children, (b) existing services in special education and rehabilitation, and (c) evolving conceptualizations about the nature and process of special education into curriculum format.

A brief review of the literature has been selected to highlight the fundamental theme, namely, that every teacher is a diagnostician (Laycock, 1934) capable of providing for the variety of learning and behavior problems presented by exceptional children without regard to separate etiological categories.

The conceptualization of an integrated teacher education curriculum evolving about a core is neither unique nor radical, and finding substantial support from the literature is fruitful. However, moving away from such traditional labels as mental retardation, deaf or hard of hearing, blind or partially seeing, physically limited, or socially and emotionally maladjusted on an implementation level presents almost insurmountable barriers.

On the national level, Davens (1965) traces the changing pattern of health services for the handicapped in our country and highlights the trends brought about by increased interdisciplinary and interagency efforts.

During the next five years, there are likely to be further trends toward broadening the definition of handicapped children and toward the organization of services and facilities to permit an integrated approach to the whole child, regardless of the number, type, or combination of handicaps he presents (p. 53).

New Jersey (Commission on the Education of the Handicapped, 1964) appears to be moving toward the implementation of an integrated approach to the education of the handicapped by recommending the following:

Education needs so identified should be met without any delimitation based upon arbitrary categorization or presumed causation of the manifest educational disability. School laws and regulations which arbitrarily discriminate between children on the basis of a medical classification rather than educational need should be revised or combined and the best features of each made accessible to all (p. 8).

This changing conceptualization of patterns of service for the handicapped has not evolved overnight. Special education has traditionally concerned itself with the individual learning needs of children; however, programs and services organized to meet these needs often have neglected to insure the attainment of this objective.

Sporadic expressions of concern over the apparent paradox between principle and practice in special education have been expressed in the literature, particularly during the period of rapid growth of programs and services of the past decade. Lord (1956) stated:

Rehabilitation does not begin its thinking with disability categories. It begins with individuals and plans in terms of individual needs. It defines needs carefully and established priorities for meeting those needs. . . . We seem to be bogged down in services to categories and with somewhat of an overemphasis on assumed differences between the children we serve. . . . We tend to specialize our services rather than attempt to make them comprehensive and inclusive. We continue to do this in spite of the fact that we are dealing with heterogeneous groups to which we have fixed our little disability labels. We seem to cherish the labels and even safeguard them as our individual private field of operation. Special Education is bigger than mere classifications; bigger than labels, categories, and teachers' credentials. Special Education for the handicapped has one major objective—maximum habilitation or rehabilitation of the individual child. The individual child and his constellation of particular needs is our focus of primary attention (p. 342).

Criticism of the growing number of voluntary agencies springing up in response to the variety of disability categories identified during the past twenty years was perhaps best expressed by Hill (1959), former Chief of the Section on

Exceptional Children and Youth, US Department of Health, Education, and Welfare, when he stated:

In so far as education is concerned, special education has developed illogically and unrealistically, just as have voluntary health agencies and clinical services, around the isolation of supposedly discrete entities of disabilities . . . rather than in terms of learning problems. . . . The conclusions of these observations must be that clinical classifications have little relation to learning disability, and that there is no such thing as a typical example of any type of child. . . . However, the differentiation in programming must be undertaken on the basis of needs and learning characteristics rather than in terms of arbitrary classification (pp. 298-299).

Essentially, the fundamental issue appears to evolve around the changing concept toward learning handicaps presented by children, rather than specific categories of disability, and implementing this idea into programs and services.

Kirk and Bateman (1962) have most recently reawakened interest in this approach to the education of exceptional children in stressing the need for the educator to diagnose the specific learning problems indicated by the behavioral symptoms and then provide subsequent remediation, without regard to etiological factors.

Laycock (1934), thirty years earlier, had urged special educators to seriously consider every teacher a diagnostician.

As education has become increasingly scientific so the business of the teacher has likewise increasingly become that of a diagnostician, and nowhere has this been more evident than in the field of special education. The diagnostic point of view has been both the cause and result of special education. It has been the cause since only a keen appreciation and understanding of the problems of those who deviate from the typical have given rise to special education; and it has been the result since the problems of special education can be solved only by the use of the diagnostic method (p. 47).

Although there have been many similar expressions of interest in the diagnosis and remediation of learning disabilities, moving forward from philosophy and principle to actual program implementation has eluded the practitioner in the field; and for several years the dialogue has continued on the theoretical level. Kaya (1961), Levine (1961), and Reynolds (1962) are among those who have attempted to translate the changing concepts into a program format.

Fermentation of these ideas, despite the continued urging within the profession, has failed to produce some direction or even an outline for the change being advocated. Perhaps the educational lag presents too formidable an obstacle between knowledge and innovation. Programs and services for the handicapped continue to develop by the categories; in fact, additional discrete diagnostic labels have emerged into separate new areas of exceptionality. Naturally, teacher education curricula in special education have reflected the continuous development of separate fields of specialization, i.e., mentally retarded, physically limited, deaf, blind, etc.

Assumptions

A curriculum for preparing the teacher as diagnostician requires a radical departure from traditional categories of exceptionality, with new emphasis on the psychoeducational aspects of special education. Ultimately, the diagnosis and remediation of learning disabilities, regardless of etiological categories, are dependent upon (a) a clinical assessment of the characteristics of the learner; (b) a pedagogical analysis of the task, the material, the techniques, and the teacher; (c) interaction among these factors; and (d) utilization of existing personnel and agencies. All of these factors, planned and organized to maximize individualized instruction for the exceptional child, appear to be the evolving conceptualizations regarding special education in the current and future decades.

The challenge at hand is bridging the gap between knowledge and practice into a planned and meaningful sequence of academic and clinical laboratory experiences within the confines of a college curriculum pattern for special education. The proposed integrated teacher education program for special education represents an initial attempt at innovation.

Proposed Integrated Teacher Education Curriculum

Setting. The translation of current knowledge and trends into a curriculum pattern for the preparation of teachers of exceptional children is proposed within the framework of the exist-

183

ing curricula pattern established by the New Jersey Department of Education for the six state colleges. It should be noted that Trenton State College as early as 1917 conducted a two year program for teachers of the mentally subnormal and deaf. In 1959, part time graduate programs in these two fields were offered to meet the needs of the growing number of teachers of the handicapped in New Jersey. The year 1961 marked the introduction of two undergraduate majors (mental retardation and the deaf) for full time students. A new graduate program for teachers of the socially and emotionally maladjusted was recently approved, stimulated by a US Office of Education program development grant, and initiated in 1966.

The college currently participates in the fellowship program for the preparation of professional personnel in the education of the handicapped under provisions of PL 85-926 as amended in the three separate fields previously mentioned. This year marked the establishment of a child study and demonstration center on the college campus under provisions of Title III of the Elementary and Secondary Education Act of 1965. Designed primarily as a teacher education facility, the center will involve the exceptional child, teachers, and teacher trainees in the diagnostic remediation process common to all children with learning difficulties.

The proposed integrated undergraduate sequence in special education is dependent upon the clinical facilities, demonstration, practicum, and student teaching opportunities in a variety of existing local residential and day schools serving exceptional children and youth. It is anticipated that this revision will replace the current undergraduate majors in mental retardation and the deaf and avoid separate major sequences in the future. Furthermore, articulation between the new program and existing graduate specialization will require continued study and subsequent revision.

Objectives. The fundamental theme of the proposed program is based upon the assumption that the preparation of the teacher of exceptional children as an educational diagnostician and tactician requires the planned integration of a formal course of study with a variety of observational and practicum experiences: (a) normal child growth and development; (b)

deviations in physical, psychological, educational, and social development; (c) clinical child study practices and procedures for the diagnosis and remediation of learning disabilities; (d) remedial programs and services within the clinic, special classes, and regular classroom; (e) special class teacher as an educational diagnostician and tactician; and (f) interdisciplinary team approach.

While disregarding traditional labels, the proposed program retains the basic New Jersey certification requirements for each area and, in addition, focuses on the common core of learning handicaps present in all categories. Specifically, the proposed program offers in separate and integrated courses all the required certification areas with additional emphasis on child study, learning disabilities, and remediation.

Figure 1 illustrates the four year distribution of semester hours, with the specialized professional sequence of 53 semester hours containing the integrated approach.

Limitations. Many significant limitations become readily apparent with any such major departure from well established patterns. Serious consideration has been given to the following issues emerging from the proposal:

1. Feasibility of submerging individual identity of traditionally separate categories of exceptionality, i.e., legislation, fund raising, etc.
2. Difficulty in utilizing existing college personnel in the implementation of the program.
3. Existing practicum and laboratory facilities currently organized by separate disability groups.
4. Problems of teacher placement.
5. Usual barriers to innovation and change within college, state departments of education, and local school districts.
6. Continuous debate over graduate versus undergraduate preparation for special education.
7. Opportunity for demonstration and research of concepts, structure, operation, and results of innovation.

Recognizing the various obstacles to innovation within the academic community and implications of the change for the practitioner in the field should caution any hasty or uncritical acceptance of the proposal. Nevertheless, a re-

FIGURE 1. Semester Hours in Proposed Special Education Curriculum

College Year	General Education	Basic Professional	Specialized Professional	Free Electives	Totals
First[a]	28	0	4	0	32
Second[b]	14	6	11	3	34
Third[c]	4	6	22	0	32
Fourth[d]	2	3	16	9	30
Totals	48	15	53	12	128

[a] Survey of Exceptional Children and Youth I and II (4 semester hours). Integrates the certification areas of introduction to education of the handicapped and psychology of the handicapped. Provides orientation to the educational and psychosocial aspects of exceptional children and youth in terms of philosophy, history, nomenclature, classification, incidence, characteristics, etiology, special educational provisions, and current issues. Study of physical, sensory, mental, emotional, and social deviations.

[b] Child Study of Exceptional Children (5 semester hours). Integrates the certification areas of orientation in psychological tests, audiometry and hearing aids, and counseling, vocational guidance, and rehabilitation services for the handicapped. Provides orientation to the roles and processes of assessing individual differences of exceptional children and youth, with emphasis on the utilization of existing interdisciplinary and interagency resources and current evaluative techniques. Includes visits to campus, local community clinics, and centers.

Orientation to Learning Disabilities (6 semester hours). Understanding the nature and needs of exceptional children in terms of the variety of learning impairments (a) developmental: health, motor, sensory; (b) communication: language, speech, hearing (covers anatomy and physiology of the ear and speech mechanisms); (c) behavioral: social, emotional; (d) intellectual: perceptual and cognitive; and (e) adaptive: later life.

[c] Teaching Exceptional Children in the Elementary School (6 semester hours). Adapting the general principles and practices of teaching reading, arithmetic, language arts, social studies, arts, and crafts for children with learning impairments. Organizing and modifying the curricula from primary through intermediate levels for exceptional children.

Diagnosis and Remediation of Learning Disabilities I and II (10 semester hours). This course integrates the certification areas of reading disabilities, teaching language to the deaf, teaching speech and speech-reading to the deaf, braille, and auditory training. Includes analysis of the concepts and techniques of diagnosis and remediation of learning impairments of exceptional children. Part I will stress evaluation and Part II will develop remedial techniques.

Occupational Laboratory (4 semester hours). Interdepartmental course—special education and industrial education and technology. Exploration of the world of work through actual experiences with the processes, tools, and materials of the various occupational families, i.e., industry, commerce, service, and agriculture.

Audiovisual Education (2 semester hours). Curriculum utilization of audiovisual materials, mastery of many types of audiovisual devices and equipment, principles of operation, possibilities for utilization, techniques for evaluation of materials and equipment, knowledge and skills in the production of simple audiovisual materials.

[d] Special Education Practicum (8 semester hours). This course integrates the certification areas of curriculum, methods, and materials for teaching the mentally retarded, physically limited, deaf or hard of hearing, blind or partially seeing, and socially and emotionally maladjusted. Observation and participation in selected demonstration classes of exceptional children and youth and various maturation levels. Field work during summer session.

Student Teaching (8 semester hours).

newed dialogue over the apparent discrepancy between current practices and curricula design would liberate constructive forces toward the reduction in the gap between knowledge and practice.

Conclusion

The enormous expansion of health, education, and welfare programs dealing with disability has identified rehabilitation needs more completely, highlighted the need for professional personnel, and focused attention upon the need for a closer coordination than ever between rehabilitation and related services. All of these factors pose demands for a volume and level of performance, for a degree of planning, ingenuity, coordination, and understanding that will challenge the conservation and rehabilitation of our human resources as it has never been-challenged before.

Programs and services that have arisen over the past several hundred years may be governmental, private, and voluntary. Patterns of service vary markedly; some are for designated types of disabilities, some for definite age groups, and others for certain types of services. This structure of community services was built largely without blueprints. Organizations and agencies have been created to meet the needs seen at a particular time. Many of our public and private health, welfare, educational, and recreational agencies have been established with little or no regard to those already existing and or in terms of the actual need.

The selection, collation, and synthesis of existing concepts into a new integrated teacher education program for special education is recommended as an approach to the rapidly growing body of knowledge concerning learning disabilities and remediation. "Every teacher a diagnostician," suggested over thirty years ago, is not radical or innovative today; however, bridging the gap between concept and practice appears to present many realistic limitations.

Connor (1964) offers a challenge for change to special educators,

> With teacher educators' focus on liberation through preparation for assumption of responsibility in approaching educational tasks, special education's revolution will be toward restructuring of most teacher education programs and reviewing the patterns of teacher placement, supervision and professional regard generally (p. 395).

References

Commission on the Education of the Handicapped. *The education of handicapped children in New Jersey 1954-1964*. Trenton, New Jersey: New Jersey Department of Education, 1964.

Connor, Frances P. The sword and the spirit. *Exceptional Children*, 1964, 30, 393-401.

Davens, E. View of health services for mothers and children. *Children*, 1965, 12, 47-54.

Hill, A. S. The status of mental retardation today with emphasis on services. *Exceptional Children*, 1959, 25, 298-299.

Kaya, E. A curricular sequence based on psychological processes. *Exceptional Children*, 1961 27, 425-428.

Kirk, S. A. Educating the handicapped. In *White House Conference on Education*. Washington, D.C.: Superintendent of Documents, US Government Printing Office, 1965, 100-107.

Kirk, S. A., and Bateman, Barbara. Diagnosis and remediation of learning disabilities. *Exceptional Children*, 1962, 29, 73-78.

Laycock, S. R. Every teacher a diagnostician. *Exceptional Children Review*, 1934, 2, 47.

Levine, S. A proposed conceptual framework for special education. *Exceptional Children*, 1961, 28, 83-90.

Lord, F. E. A realistic look at special classes—extracts from the president's address. *Exceptional Children*, 1956, 22, 321-325, 342.

Reynolds, M. C. A framework for considering some issues in special education. *Exceptional Children*, 1962, 28, 367-370.

LOUIS SCHWARTZ *is Professor of Special Education, Trenton State College, New Jersey.*

Abstract: This study attempts to delineate through the critical incident technique the task of teachers of educable mentally retarded children. With this selective observational methodology, professional educators observed and recorded incidents of significant teacher behavior in the classroom. These behaviors were analyzed revealing teacher deficiencies in meeting the educational needs of the educable mentally retarded.

Defining the Task of Teachers of the Educable Mentally Retarded

JAY M. ROTBERG

To determine what classroom tasks are essential for teachers of educable mentally retarded (EMR) children, a selective observational methodology called the critical incident technique was used in schools having EMR classes in Pittsburgh and Allegheny County public schools, Pennsylvania. The results of this study not only provided a classification of teacher behaviors which defines their classroom tasks, but also revealed severe deficiencies in meeting the educational needs of the educable mentally retarded.

Using the critical incident technique, four groups of observers made direct observations of teacher behavior; these observers were all professionally associated with the education of the mentally retarded in Pittsburgh or Allegheny County. They included: (a) 132 teachers of educable mentally retarded children,

(b) three supervisors of such teachers, (c) 45 principals of schools with classes for the educable mentally retarded, and (d) 11 student teachers.

After observers were oriented and trained either in group meetings or individually, standard forms were provided for reporting three incidents of both effective and ineffective teacher behavior. Each observer was not only asked to report observed behaviors, but also to evaluate them as to whether they contributed positively or negatively to the stated general aim of the teacher. All observers accepted the content of the general aim and agreed to use it as the contextual limit when reporting teacher behavior in the classroom.

The 191 observers reported 917 usable incidents; 64 incidents were not used because they failed to meet the established criteria. The classification of these behaviors into four major categories was accomplished inductively and then checked independently by three special educators. The percentages of agreement were 84.4, 80.0, and 94.4, respectively. These four categories of behavior defined the basic

Education and Training of the Mentally Retarded,
October, 1968, Vol.3, No.3, pp. 146-149.

classroom tasks of teachers of the educable mentally retarded. Of the usable incidents, 36.8 percent were classified under Category I, Methods for Managing Individual Behavior in the Classroom.

I. *Methods for Managing Individual Behavior in the Classroom*
   A. Uses Punishment
   B. Uses Techniques for Motivating Learner
      1. Provides verbal encouragement
      2. Modifies activity
      3. Promises reward for successful task performance
      4. Provides supplemental activities
      5. Gives extra attention to learner
   C. Reinforces Acceptable Behaviors
      1. Gives verbal reward
      2. Provides real reward
   D. Discusses Learners' Problems
      1. Discusses problems with learner
      2. Discusses behavior problems with the class
      3. Discusses problems with other persons
   E. Ignores Unacceptable Behavior
   F. Assigns Diverting Activity
   G. Tells Learner What to Do
   H. Uses Nonverbal Actions

An analysis of reports of incidents from this category indicates that teachers had difficulty managing individual classroom behavior.

It is interesting to note that of the incidents reported in this category, 53.6 percent involved the use of some kind of punishment—most often physical punishment. This is a matter for particular concern since 77 percent of these incidents were reported to be ineffective. Conversely, behaviors reported to be effective 80 percent of the time were employed in only 10 percent of the cases.

A possible explanation for this excessive reliance on punishment is that immediate suppression of a child's undesirable behavior is rewarding to the teacher.

Another possibility is that teachers employ the same methods used by their parents and former teachers. Teachers appear to be unaware of rapidly changing theories of child rearing and education, and they do not seem to know techniques other than punishment for behavior management.

Category II, Methods for Managing Group Behavior, included 6.8 percent of the incidents.

II. *Methods for Managing Group Behavior*
   A. Uses Punishment
   B. Promises Reward as a Technique of Motivation
   C. Reinforces Desirable Behaviors
      1. Gives verbal praise
      2. Provides real reward
   D. Discusses Group Behavior Problems with the Class
   E. Ignores Inappropriate Behavior
   F. Provides Another Activity
   G. Tells Learners What to Do
   H. Uses Nonverbal Actions

On the basis of the frequencies of ineffective behaviors reported, teachers tend to use means of managing group behavior reported to be ineffective more often than those reported to be effective. The use of punishment was reported on 25 occasions (46.3 percent of the behaviors in Category II), although it was reported to be ineffective 76 percent of the time.

Plans for Learning Activities, Category III, included 10.5 percent of the usable incidents.

III. *Plans for Learning Activities*
   A. Plans to Meet Identified Needs of Learners
      1. Plans to use appropriate materials
      2. Plans learning activities according to appropriate ability level of learners
      3. Plans activities that can be completed efficiently
      4. Assigns learners to other classes when appropriate

B. Uses Community Resources to Enrich Instruction

C. Allows Learners to Assist in Class Planning

From reports in this category, specific teaching plans developed to meet the needs of the learners were considered to be ineffective. One can speculate that either the learner's needs are not being identified or the teacher activity is inappropriate to the learner's needs. If either is true, research should be undertaken to determine methods of identifying the learner's abilities and deficiencies as well as ways to plan for the modification of the learner's behavior based on these capabilities.

Category IV, Techniques for Teaching Subject Matter, included 45.9 percent of the incidents.

IV. *Techniques for Teaching Subject Matter*

A. Methods of Subject Presentation
1. Uses appropriate teaching aids including:
    a. Concrete objects
    b. Graphic representations
    c. Audiovisual aids requiring special equipment
2. Employs variety of methods to present the same subject matter
3. Presents subject matter material by lecturing
4. Uses realistic examples which are meaningful to learner

This category relates to the act of teaching itself, whereas the previous category involved planning for the act of teaching. The incidents reported show that although teachers had effectively used techniques for presenting subject matter, they had difficulty adapting instruction to the abilities and interests of the learners.

In addition to delineating the task of the teacher of the mentally retarded, an analysis of the observations revealed another major finding. Prin-cipals and supervisors differed significantly from teachers in their emphasis on particular aspects of the teaching task. Teachers focused on managing individual classroom behavior and deemphasized planning of learning activities; principals and supervisors placed more emphasis on planning learning activities and less emphasis on methods for handling individual behavior.

This difference may exist partly because supervisory personnel, being removed from day to day classroom problems and stresses, tend to be more analytical and theoretical in their approach to learning. This difference may have important implications for teaching. Adequate planning may help to minimize individual classroom behavior problems. Although a relationship may exist between adequate lesson planning and improved classroom management, not all management problems are attributable to lack of planning for a particular child or children. Optimum instructional programs cannot be offered when supervisory and teaching personnel differ so radically in their approaches.

Conclusion

The results of this study may aid in (a) establishing criteria for evaluating teachers of the educable mentally retarded; (b) formulating a checklist providing criteria for self appraisal by such teachers; (c) orienting candidates in educational and special educational administration; (d) developing course content designed to train principals, supervisors of special education, and teachers of the educable mentally retarded; and (e) evaluating present teacher training courses to ascertain whether prospective principals, supervisors, and teachers of the educable mentally retarded are receiving adequate preparation.

Finally, the results may have significant implications for training all teachers.

As observed in this study, managing the classroom, planning to meet identified needs of learners, and adapting instruction to these needs are fundamental to all teacher training. It behooves teacher training personnel to evaluate training programs to determine whether teachers are being adequately instructed and to conduct followup studies to ascertain whether teachers are using these skills to the best advantage of the learners.

Improved training methods in both teacher training institutions and inservice programs are needed to assist teachers in improvement of their instruction to meet the demanding task of teaching the educable mentally retarded child.

JAY M. ROTBERG *is Assistant Professor of Education, Department of Special Education, and Field Director, New England Materials Instruction Center for Handicapped Children and Youth, Boston University. This article is based on the author's unpublished doctoral dissertation at the University of Pittsburgh.*

STANLEY C. KNOX

Turnover Among Teachers of the Mentally Retarded

Abstract: This study compared a group of teachers who had taught mentally retarded children in Minnesota for 2 years or less with a group who had taught for a more extended period. Those who quit with 2 or less years of experience tended to be younger men, employed in larger school systems, with minimum certification. There was no difference between the groups with regard to number of years of training, differential salary, or laboratory experiences.

THE demand for teachers of the mentally retarded has increased steadily following World War II until today in many localities the shortage of teachers is critical. This study was an attempt to identify some of the variables associated with the turnover of teachers of the mentally retarded.

Some studies have tried to identify variables related to teacher turnover generally. It has been demonstrated that turnover is related to such factors as the size of the school systems (Charters, 1956; National Education Association, 1960), salary (National Education Association, 1960; Minnesota Education Association, 1965), home responsibilities (Browning, 1963; Charters, 1956), and age (National Education Association, 1960; Charters, 1956). However, there is very little literature dealing specifically with teachers of the mentally retarded.

Design

The subjects in this study included all teachers who began teaching the mentally retarded during a 5 year period and were reimbursed by the Minnesota State Department of Education on a fulltime basis. The data necessary for the analysis were collected from the records of the Minnesota Department of Education.

The subjects were divided into two groups. Persisting teachers were those who had taught mentally retarded children for more than 2 years. Nonpersisting teachers were those who had quit teaching mentally retarded children before or at the end of a 2 year period. The 2 year period was selected for two reasons—first, of 196 teachers who quit teaching the mentally retarded during this 5 year period, 108 or 55 percent had taught for 2 years or less; second, it was possible to obtain provisional certification in Minnesota for a 2 year period.

The following comparisons were then made between the two groups:

1. The ages at which teachers began their experience in programs for the mentally retarded were compared for nonpersisting and persisting teachers over the years involved in the study. An analysis of variance was used to test the hypothesis that there were no significant differences in the mean ages of persisting and nonpersisting teachers over the 5 years.

2. The schools which operated programs in which these teachers were employed were divided into five categories. These included the major cities (Minneapolis, St. Paul, and Duluth), suburban districts (those enrolling 5,000 or more students located adjacent to the major cities), large school districts (those enrolling 5,000 or more students lo-

Exceptional Children, November, 1968, Vol.35, No.3, pp. 231-235.

cated outside of the metropolitan area), medium school districts (those enrolling 1,000 to 4,999 students), and small school districts (those enrolling less than 1,000 students). A chi square analysis was used to test the hypothesis that there were no significant differences between the proportions of persisting and nonpersisting teachers when categorized according to the type of school system.

3. Many of the teachers had completed training programs and were fully qualified at the time they began teaching the retarded. Others, while having experience in other educational settings, had partially completed a training program and were therefore eligible only for provisional certification. Still others who did not have enough training to qualify for provisional certification in special education were nevertheless employed as teachers of the mentally retarded. A chi square analysis was used to test the hypothesis that there were no significant differences in the proportions of persisting and nonpersisting teachers when categorized as to whether they held full, provisional, or no certification.

4. The teachers in this study were then classified according to the method by which they obtained their training. Some teachers completed their certification programs while they were on campus undergraduate students and before their initial teaching experience; these teachers were classified as on campus inexperienced. On campus experienced were those teachers who took time off from their teaching responsibilities to return to college on a fulltime basis in order to obtain certification. The majority of the teachers received their training during summers, evenings, and late afternoons while remaining in teaching positions; these were classified as off campus. There were also those who had no training. A chi square analysis was used to test the hypothesis that there were no significant differences in the proportions of persisting and nonpersisting teachers when grouped according to the way in which they received their training.

5. A chi square analysis was used to test the hypothesis that there were no significant dif-ferences in the proportions of persisting and nonpersisting teachers when grouped according to sex.

6. The subjects in this study were then grouped according to the amount of training they had. The three categories used in this instance consisted of those teachers with less than a 4 year degree, those with a 4 year degree, and those with more than a 4 year degree. A chi square analysis was used to test the hypothesis that there were no significant differences in the proportions of persisting and nonpersisting teachers when grouped according to number of years of preparation.

7. Teachers who had a supervised laboratory experience (student teaching, clinical practice, etc.) on their transcripts constituted one group, while those who had no such experience constituted the other. A chi square analysis was used to test the hypothesis that there were no significant differences in the proportions of persisting and nonpersisting teachers when grouped according to whether or not they had a supervised laboratory experience.

8. A chi square analysis was used to test the hypothesis that there were no significant differences in the proportions of persisting and nonpersisting teachers when grouped according to whether or not they taught in a school district which provided extra remuneration for teachers of the retarded.

Results

1. The results of the analysis of variance applied to the ages of the teachers are given in Table 1. There were significant differences between the ages of persisting and

TABLE 1

Analysis of Variance for Ages of Persisting and Nonpersisting Teachers, 1957-1958 Through 1961-1962

Source of variance	df	MS	F	p
Among types	1	2385.38	19.48	<.01
Among years	4	227.32	1.85	ns
Interaction	4	233.35	1.90	ns
Within subclasses	397			
Total	406			

TABLE 2

Relationship of Size of School District to ,Teacher Turnover

Teacher group	Major cities		Suburban		Large		Medium		Small	
	N	Per-cent	N	Per-cent	N	Per-cent	N	Per-cent	N	Per-cent
Persisting teachers	71	69.60	53	65.43	25	75.75	86	78.79	64	78.04
Nonpersisting teachers	31	30.40	28	34.57	8	24.25	23	21.11	18	21.96

$(\chi^2 = 25.15, \text{df} = 4, p < .001)$

nonpersisting teachers, with the persisting teachers being older. The mean age for persisting teachers was 39.2 years as opposed to 34 for nonpersisting teachers. There were no significant differences in age over the years involved in this study.

2. The results of the analysis according to type of school district are presented in Table 2. Significant differences existed in the proportions of persisting and nonpersisting teachers in these school systems. Because of similarities between the major cities and surburban districts, and because of similarities in the remainder of the categories, the data were regrouped according to metropolitan and nonmetropolitan categories. The percentage of nonpersisting teachers was 32.25 for the metropolitan districts as opposed to 21.88 for the nonmetropolitan. This difference was significant at less than the .02 level $(\chi^2 = 5.49)$.

Since this difference could be related to the age of the teacher, an analysis of variance was computed comparing the mean ages of beginning teachers in programs for the mentally retarded in these various school systems. The results are given in Table 3. The mean age of beginning teachers in the suburban districts was 32.37 years and ranged to 42.05 in the small school districts. Therefore, it would appear that the higher proportion of nonpersisting teachers in the metropolitan schools may be related to the ages of the teachers employed in those schools.

3. The results of the analysis relating to type of certification appear in Table 4. The proportion of persisting teachers was much higher for those who had full certification

TABLE 3

Analysis of Variance of Ages of Teachers Employed in School Districts According to Size of School

Source of variance	df	MS	F	p
Among age groups	4	538.83	5.02	<.01
Within age groups	85	107.36		
Total	89			

than for those who had provisional certification. The highest rate of loss occurred in those teachers having no certification. The differences were significant and the null hypothesis was rejected.

4. The data relating to the method of obtaining their training are presented in Table 5. The differences were significant and the null hypothesis was rejected. The teachers with no training had the highest rate of loss. Because this may have contributed heavily to the results, the data were analyzed again omitting those who had no training, and the results are presented in Table 6. Again there were significant differences, with the experienced teachers more likely to remain in the field than inexperienced teachers.

5. Of the 77 men in the study, 36 percent were classified as nonpersisting teachers. Among the 330 women, 24 percent were classified as such. These differences were significant at less than the .05 level $(\chi^2 = 4.68)$. Therefore, the null hypothesis relating to sex differences was rejected. The proportion of persisting teachers was higher among women.

6. Table 7 contains the data relating to amount of training. The analysis did not yield significant results, so the hypothesis of no dif-

193

TABLE 4

Relationship of Type of Certification to Teacher Turnover

Teacher group	Full certification		Provisional certification		No certification	
	N	Percent	N	Percent	N	Percent
Persisting teachers	169	84.50	127	67.91	3	15.00
Nonpersisting teachers	31	15.50	60	32.09	17	85.00

$(\chi^2 = 50.46, df = 2, p < .001)$

TABLE 5

Relationship of Type of Training to Teacher Turnover

Teacher group	On campus inexperienced		On campus experienced		Off campus		None	
	N	Percent	N	Percent	N	Percent	N	Percent
Persisting teachers	20	57.14	10	76.92	266	76.21	3	15.00
Nonpersisting teachers	15	42.86	3	23.08	73	23.79	17	85.00

$(\chi^2 = 7.97, df = 2, p < .05)$

TABLE 6

Relationship of Type of Training to Teacher Turnover (Omitting Those with No Special Training)

Teacher group	On campus inexperienced		On campus experienced		Off campus	
	N	Percent	N	Percent	N	Percent
Persisting teachers	20	57.14	10	76.92	266	76.21
Nonpersisting teachers	15	42.86	3	23.08	73	23.79

$(\chi^2 = 7.97, df = 2, p < .05)$

TABLE 7

Relationship of Number of Years of Training to Teacher Turnover

Teacher group	Less than 4 year degree		4 year degree		More than 4 year degree	
	N	Percent	N	Percent	N	Percent
Persisting teachers	65	71.42	78	68.42	156	77.22
Nonpersisting teachers	26	28.58	36	31.58	46	22.78

$(\chi^2 = 3.09, df = 2, p < .30)$

TABLE 8

Relationship of Supervised Laboratory Experience to Teacher Turnover

Teacher group	Supervised experience		No supervised experience	
	N	Percent	N	Percent
Persisting teachers	38	70.37	261	73.93
Nonpersisting teachers	16	29.63	92	26.07

$(\chi^2 = .28, df = 1, p < .75)$

ference was accepted. It would appear that the amount of training was not a factor related to whether or not teachers continued in programs for the mentally retarded.

7. As shown in Table 8, supervised laboratory experience did not appear to be related to whether or not the teacher continued in the program. The results of the analysis were not significant.

8. Of the 128 teachers who received additional salary for teaching mentally retarded children, 31.25 percent were nonpersisting

teachers. This category also accounted for 24.06 percent of those who did not receive additional salary. These differences were not significant and the hypothesis was accepted. ($x^2 = 2.24, p < .20$)

Discussion

This study indicated that among younger teachers the turnover rate was somewhat higher. It was apparently higher in metropolitan areas than in nonmetropolitan areas, but evidence was presented that this may have been related to an age factor rather than to the size of the school system.

These results raise some questions regarding the desirability of approving programs with uncertified personnel or with provisionally certified personnel since the loss over the first 2 years on these programs was extremely high. In light of the fact that the loss in programs which had fully certified personnel was minimal, policies regarding provisional certification should be reassessed.

Results showing that there were differences in the proportion of teachers remaining in programs according to the type of training they had received may indicate that recruitment efforts should be directed towards experienced teachers as well as towards students, if maintaining stability in the teaching population is a concern. It is quite possible again that the significant variable may be age rather than type of training.

The findings which indicated that women were more likely than men to remain in the field over a period of time deserves further study. In a questionnaire mailed by the investigator to school systems to ascertain the present status of some of the individuals who had left the programs for the mentally retarded, it was noted that many of the men had moved into administrative positions while many of the women had left for homemaking responsibilities. It may well be that the men stay in educational programs but in a different capacity than that of teacher.

It would appear that school districts which

are paying additional salary to teachers of the mentally retarded are not much more successful in retaining teachers than those who do not. If the purpose of this additional salary is to encourage teachers to remain in these programs, such policies should probably be reassessed. However, it may be that this is strictly a recruiting device which school districts use to obtain teachers in these programs.

This study is, of course, subject to some severe limitations. Since it involved only teachers in the state of Minnesota, it is questionable whether these results could be generalized to other states. Whether these findings would be applicable in other special education programs is also open to question.

The most important aspect of any educational program is the quality of instruction. Assumptions have been made that this may be related to certain aspects of training. However, research relating the quality of instruction to such factors as certification standards, length and type of training, laboratory experiences, and experience in other educational programs is needed to determine if such assumptions are warranted. Such research could have a profound effect on our programs of teacher preparation.

References

Browning, R. C. How to tackle the problem of teacher turnover. *School Management*, 1963, 7, 80-82.

Charters, W. W., Jr. What causes teacher turnover. *School Review*, 1956, 64, 294-299.

Minnesota Education Association, Research Service. *Teacher turnover in Minnesota public schools, 1964-65 school year.* (Circular No. 95) St. Paul: The Association, 1965.

National Education Association, Research Division. *Some whys and wherefores of teacher turnover.* (Research Memo 1960-24) Washington, D.C.: 1960.

STANLEY C. KNOX *is Chairman, Department of Special Education, St. Cloud State College, St. Cloud, Minnesota.*

Special Education for the Mildly Retarded— Is Much of It Justifiable?

LLOYD M. DUNN

A Preface *In lieu of an abstract to this article, I would like to preface it by saying this is my swan song for now—as I leave special education and this country for probably the next two years. I have been honored to be a past president of The Council for Exceptional Children. I have loyally supported and promoted special classes for the educable mentally retarded for most of the last 20 years, but with growing disaffection. In my view, much of our past and present practices are morally and educationally wrong. We have been living at the mercy of general educators who have referred their problem children to us. And we have been generally ill prepared and ineffective in educating these children. Let us stop being pressured into continuing and expanding a special education program that we know now to be undesirable for many of the children we are dedicated to serve.*

A better education than special class placement is needed for socioculturally deprived children with mild learning problems who have been labeled educable mentally retarded. Over the years, the status of these pupils who come from poverty, broken and inadequate homes, and low status ethnic groups has been a checkered one. In the early days, these children were simply excluded from school. Then, as Hollingworth (1923) pointed out, with the advent of compulsory attendance laws, the schools and these children "were forced into a reluctant mutual recognition of each other." This resulted in the establishment of self contained special schools and classes as a method of transferring these "misfits" out of the regular grades. This practice continues to this day and, unless counterforces are set in motion now, it will probably become even more prevalent in the immediate future due in large measure to increased racial integration and militant teacher organizations. For example, a local affiliate of the National Education Association demanded of a local school board recently that more special classes be provided for disruptive and slow learning children (Nashville *Tennessean,* December 18, 1967).

The number of special day classes for the retarded has been increasing by leaps and bounds. The most recent 1967-

Exceptional Children, 1968, Vol.35, No.1, pp. 5-21.

1968 statistics compiled by the US Office of Education now indicate that there are approximately 32,000 teachers of the retarded employed by local school systems—over one-third of all special educators in the nation. In my best judgment, about 60 to 80 percent of the pupils taught by these teachers are children from low status backgrounds—including Afro-Americans, American Indians, Mexicans, and Puerto Rican Americans; those from nonstandard English speaking, broken, disorganized, and inadequate homes; and children from other nonmiddle class environments. This expensive proliferation of self contained special schools and classes raises serious educational and civil rights issues which must be squarely faced. It is my thesis that we must stop labeling these deprived children as mentally retarded. Furthermore we must stop segregating them by placing them into our allegedly special programs.

"This expensive proliferation of self contained special schools and classes raises serious educational and civil rights issues which must be squarely faced."

The purpose of this article is twofold: first, to provide reasons for taking the position that a large proportion of this so called special education in its present form is obsolete and unjustifiable from the point of view of the pupils so placed; and second, to outline a blueprint for changing this major segment of education for exceptional children to make it more acceptable. We are not arguing that we do away with our special education programs for the moderately and severely retarded, for other types of more handicapped children, or for the multiply handicapped. The emphasis is on doing something better for slow learning children who live in slum conditions, although much of what is said should also have relevance for those children we are labeling emotionally disturbed, perceptually impaired, brain injured, and learning disordered. Furthermore, the emphasis of the article is on children, in that no attempt is made to suggest an adequate high school environment for adolescents still functioning as slow learners.

Reasons for Change

Regular teachers and administrators have sincerely felt they were doing these pupils a favor by removing them from the pressures of an unrealistic and inappropriate program of studies. Special educators have also fully believed that the children involved would make greater progress in special schools and classes. However, the overwhelming evidence is that our present and past practices have their major justification in removing pressures on regular teachers and pupils, at the expense of the socioculturally deprived slow learning pupils themselves. Some major arguments for this position are outlined below.

Homogeneous Grouping

Homogeneous groupings tend to work to the disadvantage of the slow learners and underprivileged. Apparently such pupils learn much from being in the same class with children from white middle class homes. Also, teachers seem to concentrate on the slower children to bring them up to standard. This principle was dramatically applied in the Judge J. Skelly

Wright decision in the District of Columbia concerning the track system. Judge Wright ordered that tracks be abolished, contending they discriminated against the racially and/or economically disadvantaged and therefore were in violation of the Fifth Amendment of the Constitution of the United States. One may object to the Judge's making educational decisions based on legal considerations. However, Passow (1967), upon the completion of a study of the same school system, reached the same conclusion concerning tracking. The recent national study by Coleman, et al. (1966), provides supporting evidence in finding that academically disadvantaged Negro children in racially segregated schools made less progress than those of comparable ability in integrated schools. Furthermore, racial integration appeared to deter school progress very little for Caucasian and more academically able students.

What are the implications of Judge Wright's rulings for special education? Clearly special schools and classes are a form of homogeneous grouping and tracking. This fact was demonstrated in September, 1967, when the District of Columbia (as a result of the Wright decision) abolished Track 5, into which had been routed the slowest learning pupils in the District of Columbia schools. These pupils and their teachers were returned to the regular classrooms. Complaints followed from the regular teachers that these children were taking an inordinate amount of their time. A few parents observed that their slow learning children were frustrated by the more academic program and were rejected by the other students. Thus, there are efforts afoot to develop a special education program in D.C. which cannot be labeled a track. Self contained special classes will probably not be tolerated under the present court ruling but perhaps itinerant and resource room programs would be. What if the Supreme Court ruled against tracks, and all self contained special classes across the nation which serve primarily ethnically and/or economically disadvantaged children were forced to close down? Make no mistake—this could happen! If I were a Negro from the slums or a disadvantaged parent who had heard of the Judge Wright decision and knew what I know now about special classes for the educable mentally retarded, other things being equal, I would then go to court before allowing the schools to label my child as "mentally retarded" and place him in a "self contained special school or class." Thus there is the real possibility that additional court actions will be forthcoming.*

"What if the Supreme Court ruled against tracks, and all self contained special classes across the nation which serve primarily ethnically and/or economically disadvantaged children were forced to close down?"

---

* Litigation has now occurred. According to an item in a June 8, 1968, issue of the *Los Angeles Times* received after this article was sent to the printer, the attorneys in the national office for the rights of the indigent filed a suit in behalf of the Mexican-American parents of the Santa Ana Unified School District asking for an injunction against the District's classes for the educable mentally retarded because the psychological examinations required prior to placement are unconstitutional since they

198

Efficacy Studies   The findings of studies on the efficacy of special classes for the educable mentally retarded constitute another argument for change. These results are well known (Kirk, 1964) and suggest consistently that retarded pupils make as much or more progress in the regular grades as they do in special education. Recent studies such as those by Hoelke (1966) and Smith and Kennedy (1967) continue to provide similar evidence. Johnson (1962) has summarized the situation well:

> It is indeed paradoxical that mentally handicapped children having teachers especially trained, having more money (per capita) spent on their education, and being designed to provide for their unique needs, should be accomplishing the objectives of their education at the same or at a lower level than similar mentally handicapped children who have not had these advantages and have been forced to remain in the regular grades [p. 66].

Efficacy studies on special day classes for other mildly handicapped children, including the emotionally handicapped, reveal the same results. For example, Rubin, Senison, and Betwee (1966) found that disturbed children did as well in the regular grades as in special classes, concluding that there is little or no evidence that special class programing is generally beneficial to emotionally disturbed children as a specific method of intervention and correction. Evidence such as this is another reason to find better ways of serving children with mild learning disorders than placing them in self contained special schools and classes.

Labeling Processes   Our past and present diagnostic procedures comprise another reason for change. These procedures have probably been doing more harm than good in that they have resulted in disability labels and in that they have grouped children homogeneously in school on the basis of these labels. Generally, these diagnostic practices have been conducted by one of two procedures. In rare cases, the workup has been provided by a multidisciplinary team, usually consisting of physicians, social workers, psychologists, speech and hearing specialists, and occasionally educators. The avowed goal of this approach has been to look at the complete child, but the outcome has been merely to label him mentally retarded, perceptually impaired, emotionally disturbed, minimally brain injured, or some other such term depending on the predispositions, idiosyncracies, and backgrounds of the team members. Too, the team usually has looked for causation, and diagnosis tends to stop when something has been found wrong with the child, when the why has either been found or conjectured, and when some justification has been found for recommending placement in a special education class.

---

have failed to use adequate evaluation techniques for children from different language and cultural backgrounds, and because parents have been denied the right of hearing to refute evidence for placement. Furthermore, the suit seeks to force the district to grant hearings on all children currently in such special classes to allow for the chance to remove the stigma of the label "mentally retaded" from school records of such pupils.

In the second and more common case, the assessment of educational potential has been left to the school psychologist who generally administers—in an hour or so—a psychometric battery, at best consisting of individual tests of intelligence, achievement, and social and personal adjustment. Again the purpose has been to find out what is wrong with the child in order to label him and thus make him eligible for special education services. In large measure this has resulted in digging the educational graves of many racially and/or economically disadvantaged children by using a WISC or Binet IQ score to justify the label "mentally retarded." This term then becomes a destructive, self fulfilling prophecy.

What is the evidence against the continued use of these diagnostic practices and disability labels?

First, we must examine the effects of these disability labels on the attitudes and expectancies of teachers. Here we can extrapolate from studies by Rosenthal and Jacobson (1966) who set out to determine whether or not the expectancies of teachers influenced pupil progress. Working with elementary school teachers across the first six grades, they obtained pretest measures on pupils by using intelligence and achievement tests. A sample of pupils was randomly drawn and labeled "rapid learners" with hidden potential. Teachers were told that these children would show unusual intellectual gains and school progress during the year. All pupils were retested late in the school year. Not all differences were statistically significant, but the gains of the children who had been arbitrarily labeled rapid learners were generally significantly greater than those of the other pupils, with especially dramatic changes in the first and second grades. To extrapolate from this study, we must expect that labeling a child "handicapped" reduces the teacher's expectancy for him to succeed.

Second, we must examine the effects of these disability labels on the pupils themselves. Certainly none of these labels are badges of distinction. Separating a child from other children in his neighborhood—or removing him from the regular classroom for therapy or special class placement—probably has a serious debilitating effect upon his self image. Here again our research is limited but supportive of this contention. Goffman (1961) has described the stripping and mortification process that takes place when an individual is placed in a residential facility. Meyerowitz (1965) demonstrated that a group of educable mentally retarded pupils increased in feelings of self derogation after one year in special classes. More recent results indicate that special class placement, instead of helping such a pupil adjust to his neighborhood peers, actually hinders him (Meyerowitz, 1967). While much more research is needed, we cannot ignore the evidence that removing a handicapped child from the regular grades for special education probably contributes significantly to his feelings of inferiority and problems of acceptance.

Another reason self contained special classes are less justifiable today than in the past is that regular school programs are now better able to deal with individual differences in pupils. No longer is the choice just between a self contained special class and a self contained regular elementary classroom. Although the impact of the American Revolution in Education is just beginning to be felt and is still more an ideal than a reality, special education should begin moving now to fit into a changing general education program and to assist in achieving the program's goals. Because of increased support at the local, state, and federal levels, four powerful forces are at work:

Changes in school organization. In place of self contained regular classrooms, there is increasingly more team teaching, ungraded primary departments, and flexible groupings. Radical departures in school organization are projected—educational parks in place of neighborhood schools, metropolitan school districts cutting across our inner cities and wealthy suburbs, and, perhaps most revolutionary of all, competing public school systems. Furthermore, and of great significance to those of us who have focused our careers on slow learning children, public kindergartens and nurseries are becoming more available for children of the poor.

Curricular changes. Instead of the standard diet of Look and Say readers, many new and exciting options for teaching reading are evolving. Contemporary mathematics programs teach in the primary grades concepts formerly reserved for high school. More programed textbooks and other materials are finding their way into the classroom. Ingenious procedures, such as those by Bereiter and Engelmann (1966), are being developed to teach oral language and reasoning to preschool disadvantaged children.

Changes in professional public school personnel. More ancillary personnel are now employed by the schools—i.e., psychologists, guidance workers, physical educators, remedial educators, teacher aides, and technicians. Furthermore, some teachers are functioning in different ways, serving as teacher coordinators, or cluster teachers who provide released time for other teachers to prepare lessons, etc. Too, regular classroom teachers are increasingly better trained to deal with individual differences—although much still remains to be done.

Hardware changes. Computerized teaching, teaching machines, feedback typewriters, ETV, videotapes, and other materials are making autoinstruction possible, as never before.

We must ask what the implications of this American Revolution in Education are for special educators. Mackie (1967), formerly of the US Office of Education, addressed herself to the question: "Is the modern school changing sufficiently to provide [adequate services in general education] for large numbers of pupils who have functional mental retardation due to environmental factors [p. 5]?" In her view, hundreds—perhaps even thousands—of so called retarded pupils may make satis-

Improvements in General Education

". . . special education should begin moving now to fit into a changing general education program. . . ."

201

factory progress in schools with diversified programs of instruction and thus will never need placement in self contained special classes. With earlier, better, and more flexible regular school programs many of the children should not need to be relegated to the type of special education we have so often provided.

In my view, the above four reasons for change are cogent ones. Much of special education for the mildly retarded is becoming obsolete. Never in our history has there been a greater urgency to take stock and to search out new roles for a large number of today's special educators.

A Blueprint for Change

Two major suggestions which constitute my attempt at a blueprint for change are developed below. First, a fairly radical departure from conventional methods will be proposed in procedures for diagnosing, placing, and teaching children with mild learning difficulties. Second, a proposal for curriculum revision will be sketched out. These are intended as proposals which should be examined, studied, and tested. What is needed are programs based on scientific evidence of worth and not more of those founded on philosophy, tradition, and expediency.

A Thought

There is an important difference between regular educators talking us into trying to remediate or live with the learning difficulties of pupils with which they haven't been able to deal; versus striving to evolve a special education program that is either developmental in nature, wherein we assume responsibility for the total education of more severely handicapped children from an early age, or is supportive in nature, wherein general education would continue to have central responsibility for the vast majority of the children with mild learning disabilities—with us serving as resource teachers in devising effective prescriptions and in tutoring such pupils.

A Clinical Approach

Existing diagnostic procedures should be replaced by expecting special educators, in large measure, to be responsible for their own diagnostic teaching and their clinical teaching. In this regard, it is suggested that we do away with many existing disability labels and the present practice of grouping children homogeneously by these labels into special classes. Instead, we should try keeping slow learning children more in the mainstream of education, with special educators serving as diagnostic, clinical, remedial, resource room, itinerant and/or team teachers, consultants, and developers of instructional materials and prescriptions for effective teaching.

The accomplishment of the above *modus operandi* will require a revolution in much of special education. A moratorium needs to be placed on the proliferation (if not continuance) of self contained special classes which enroll primarily the ethnically and/or economically disadvantaged children we have been labeling educable mentally retarded. Such pupils should be left in (or returned to) the regular elementary

202

grades until we are "tooled up" to do something better for them.

Prescriptive teaching. In diagnosis one needs to know how much a child can learn, under what circumstances, and with what materials. To accomplish this, there are three administrative procedures possible. One would be for each large school system—or two or more small districts—to establish a "Special Education Diagnostic and Prescription Generating Center." Pupils with school learning problems would be enrolled in this center on a day and/or boarding school basis for a period of time—probably up to a month and hopefully until a successful prescription for effective teaching had been evolved. The core of the staff would be a variety of master teachers with different specialties—such as in motor development, perceptual training, language development, social and personality development, remedial education, and so forth. Noneducators such as physicians, psychologists, and social workers would be retained in a consultative role, or pupils would be referred out to such paraeducational professionals, as needed. A second procedure, in lieu of such centers with their cadres of educational specialists, would be for one generalist in diagnostic teaching to perform the diagnostic and prescription devising functions on her own. A third and even less desirable procedure would be for one person to combine the roles of prescriptive and clinical teacher which will be presented next. It is suggested that 15 to 20 percent of the most insightful special educators be prepared for and/or assigned to prescriptive teaching. One clear virtue of the center is that a skilled director could coordinate an inservice training program and the staff could learn through, and be stimulated by, one another. In fact, many special educators could rotate through this program.

Under any of these procedures, educators would be responsible for the administration and interpretation of individual and group psychoeducational tests on cognitive development (such as the WISC and Binet), on language development (such as the ITPA), and on social maturity (such as the Vineland Social Maturity Scale). However, these instruments—with the exception of the ITPA which yields a profile of abilities and disabilities—will be of little use except in providing baseline data on the level at which a child is functioning. In place of these psychometric tests which usually yield only global scores, diagnostic educators would need to rely heavily on a combination of the various tools of behavior shapers and clinical teachers. The first step would be to make a study of the child to find what behaviors he has acquired along the dimension being considered. Next, samples of a sequential program would be designed to move him forward from that point. In presenting the program, the utility of different reinforcers, administered under various conditions, would be investigated. Also, the method by which he can best be taught the material should be determined. Different modalities for reaching the child would also be tried. Thus, since the instructional program itself becomes the diagnostic device, this procedure can be called diagnostic teaching. Failures are program and instructor failures, not pupil failures. In large measure, we would be guided by Bruner's dictum (1967) that almost any child can be taught almost anything if it is programed correctly.*

"Failures are program and instructor failures, not pupil failures."

This diagnostic procedure is viewed as the best available since it enables us to assess continuously the problem points of the instructional program against the assets of the child. After a successful and appropriate prescription has been devised, it would be communicated to the teachers in the pupil's home school and they would continue the procedure as long as it is necessary and brings results. From time to time, the child may need to return to the center for reappraisal and redirection.

Clearly the above approach to special education diagnosis and treatment is highly clinical and intuitive. In fact, it is analogous to the rural doctor of the past who depended on his insights and a few diagnostic and treatment devices carried in his small, black bag. It may remain with us for some time to come. However, it will be improved upon by more standardized procedures. Perhaps the two most outstanding, pioneering efforts in this regard are now being made by Feuerstein (1968) in Israel, and by Kirk (1966) in the United States. Feuerstein has devised a *Learning Potential Assessment Device* for determining the degree of modifiability of the behavior of an individual pupil, the level at which he is functioning, the strategies by which he can best learn, and the areas in which he needs to be taught. Also, he is developing a variety of exercises for teaching children with specific learning difficulties. Kirk and his associates have not only given us the ITPA which yields a profile of abilities and disabilities in the psycholinguistic area, but they have also devised exercises for remediating specific psycholinguistic disabilities reflected by particular types of profiles (Kirk, 1966). Both of these scientists are structuring the assessment and remediation procedures to reduce clinical judgment, although it would be undesirable to formalize to too great a degree. Like the country doctor versus modern medicine, special education in the next fifty years will move from clinical intuition to a more precise science of clinical instruction based on diagnostic instruments which yield a profile of abilities and disabilities about a

---

* By ignoring genetic influences on the behavioral characteristics of children with learning diffiiculties, we place responsibility on an inadequate society, inadequate parents, unmotivated pupils, and/or in this case inadequate teachers. Taking this extreme environmental approach could result in placing too much blame for failure on the teacher and too much pressure on the child. While we could set our level of aspiration too high, this has hardly been the direction of our error to date in special education of the handicapped. Perhaps the sustained push proposed in this paper may not succeed, but we will not know until we try it. Insightful teachers should be able to determine when the pressures on the pupil and system are too great.

specific facet of behavior and which have incorporated within them measures of a child's ability to learn samples or units of materials at each of the points on the profile. If psychoeducational tests had these two characteristics, they would accomplish essentially the same thing as does the diagnostic approach described above—only under more standardized conditions.

Itinerant and resource room teaching. It is proposed that a second echelon of special educators be itinerant or resource teachers. One or more resource teachers might be available to each sizable school, while an itinerant teacher would serve two or more smaller schools. General educators would refer their children with learning difficulties to these teachers. If possible, the clinical teacher would evolve an effective prescription for remediating the problem. If this is not possible, she would refer the child to the Special Education Diagnostic and Prescription Generating Center or to the more specialized prescriptive teacher who would study the child and work out an appropriate regimen of instruction for him. In either event, the key role of the resource room and itinerant clinical educators would be to develop instructional materials and lessons for implementing the prescription found effective for the child, and to consult and work with the other educators who serve the child. Thus, the job of special educators would be to work as members of the schools' instructional teams and to focus on children with mild to moderate school learning problems. Special educators would be available to all children in trouble (except the severely handicapped) regardless of whether they had, in the past, been labeled educable mentally retarded, minimally brain injured, educationally handicapped, or emotionally disturbed. Children would be regrouped continually throughout the school day. For specific help these children who had a learning problem might need to work with the itinerant or resource room special educator. But, for the remainder of the day, the special educator would probably be more effective in developing specific exercises which could be taught by others in consultation with her. Thus, the special educator would begin to function as a part of, and not apart from, general education. Clearly this proposed approach recognizes that all children have assets and deficits, not all of which are permanent. When a child was having trouble in one or more areas of learning, special educators would be available to devise a successful teaching approach for him and to tutor him when necessary. Perhaps as many as 20 to 35 percent of our present special educators are or could be prepared for this vital role.

Two other observations. First, it is recognized that some of today's special educators—especially of the educable mentally retarded—are not prepared to serve the functions discussed. These teachers would need to either withdraw from special education or develop the needed competencies. As-

205

suming an open door policy and playing the role of the expert educational diagnostician and the prescriptive and clinical educator would place us in the limelight. Only the best will succeed. But surely this is a responsibility we will not shirk. Our avowed *raison d'etre* has been to provide special education for children unable to make adequate progress in the regular grades. More would be lost than gained by assigning less than master teachers from self contained classes to the diagnostic and clinical educator roles. Ainsworth (1959) has already compared the relative effectiveness of the special class versus itinerant special educators of the retarded and found that neither group accomplished much in pupil progress. A virtue of these new roles for special education is that they are high status positions which should appeal to the best and therefore enhance the recruitment of master regular teachers who should be outstanding in these positions after having obtained specialized graduate training in behavior shaping, psychoeducational diagnostics, remedial education, and so forth.

Second, if one accepts these procedures for special education, the need for disability labels is reduced. In their stead we may need to substitute labels which describe the educational intervention needed. We would thus talk of pupils who need special instruction in language or cognitive development, in sensory training, in personality development, in vocational training, and other areas. However, some labels may be needed for administrative reasons. If so, we need to find broad generic terms such as "school learning disorders."

New Curricular Approaches

Master teachers are at the heart of an effective school program for children with mild to moderate learning difficulties —master teachers skilled at educational diagnosis and creative in designing and carrying out interventions to remediate the problems that exist. But what should they teach? In my view, there has been too great an emphasis in special classes on practical arts and practical academics, to the exclusion of other ingredients. Let us be honest with ourselves. Our courses of study have tended to be watered down regular curriculum. If we are to move from the clinical stage to a science of instruction, we will need a rich array of validated prescriptive programs of instruction at our disposal. To assemble these programs will take time, talent, and money; teams of specialists including creative teachers, curriculum specialists, programers, and theoreticians will be needed to do the job.

"... our most creative special educators need to be identified, freed from classroom instruction, and placed in a stimulating setting where they can be maximally productive in curriculum development."

What is proposed is a chain of Special Education Curriculum Development Centers across the nation. Perhaps these could best be affiliated with colleges and universities, but could also be attached to state and local school systems. For these centers to be successful, creative educators must be found. Only a few teachers are remarkably able to develop new materials. An analogy is that some people can play music adequately,

206

if not brilliantly, but only a few people can compose it. Therefore, to move special education forward, some 15 to 20 percent of our most creative special educators need to be identified, freed from routine classroom instruction, and placed in a stimulating setting where they can be maximally productive in curriculum development. These creative teachers and their associates would concentrate on developing, field testing, and modifying programs of systematic sequences of exercises for developing specific facets of human endeavor. As never before, funds are now available from the US Office of Education under Titles III and VI of PL 89-10 to embark upon at least one such venture in each state. In fact, Title III was designed to support innovations in education and 15 percent of the funds were earmarked for special education. Furthermore, most of the money is now to be administered through state departments of education which could build these curriculum centers into their state plans.

The first step in establishing specialized programs of study would be to evolve conceptual models upon which to build our treatments. In this regard the creative teachers would need to join with the theoreticians, curriculum specialists, and other behavioral scientists. Even the identification of the broad areas will take time, effort, and thought. Each would require many subdivisions and extensive internal model building. A beginning taxonomy might include the following eight broad areas: (a) environmental modifications, (b) motor development, (c) sensory and perceptual training, (d) cognitive and language development including academic instruction, (e) speech and communication training, (f) connative (or personality) development, (g) social interaction training, and (h) vocational training. (Of course, under cognitive development alone we might evolve a model of intellect with some ninety plus facets such as that of Guilford [1967], and as many training programs.)

In the area of motor development we might, for example, involve creative special and physical educators, occupational and physical therapists, and experts in recreation and physical medicine, while in the area of language development a team of speech and hearing specialists, special educators, psychologists, linguists, and others would need to come together to evolve a conceptual model, to identify the parameters, and to develop the specialized programs of exercises. No attempt is made in this article to do more than provide an overview of the problem and the approach. Conceptualizing the specific working models would be the responsibility of cadres of experts in the various specialties.

Environmental modifications. It would seem futile and rather unrealistic to believe we will be able to remediate the learning difficulties of children from ethnically and/or economically disadvantaged backgrounds when the schools are operating in a vacuum even though top flight special education instructional programs are used. Perhaps, if intensive around the clock and full calendar year instruction were provided beginning at the nursery school level, we might be able to counter appreciably the physiological weaknesses and inadequate home and community conditions of the child. However, the field of education would be enhanced in its chances of success if it became a part of a total ecological approach to improve the environments of these children. Thus special educators need to collaborate with others—social workers, public health officials, and other community specialists. Interventions in this category might include (a) foster home placement, (b) improved community conditions and out of school activities, (c) parent education, (d) public education, and (e) improved cultural exposures. For optimal pupil development, we should see that children are placed in a setting that is both supportive and stimulating. Therefore, we must participate in environmental manipulations and test their efficacy. We have made a slight beginning in measuring the effects of foster home placement and there is evidence that working with parents of the disadvantaged has paid off. The model cities programs would also seem to have promise. But much more human and financial effort must be invested in this area.

Motor development. Initial work has been done with psychomotor training programs by a number of persons including Delacato (1966), Oliver (1958), Cratty (1967), Lillie (1967), and others. But we still need sets of sequential daily activities built around an inclusive model. Under this category, we need to move from the early stages of psychomotor development to the development of fine and large movements required as vocational skills. Programs to develop improved motor skills are important for a variety of children with learning problems. In fact, one could argue that adequate psychomotor skills constitute the first link in the chain of learning.

Sensory and perceptual training. Much of our early efforts in special education consisted of sensory and perceptual training applied to severe handicapping conditions such as blindness, deafness, and mental deficiency. Consequently, we have made a good beginning in outlining programs of instruction in the areas of auditory, visual, and tactual training. Now we must apply our emerging technology to work out the step by step sequence of activities needed for children with mild to moderate learning difficulties. In this regard, visual perceptual training has received growing emphasis, pioneered by Frostig (1964), but auditory perceptual training has been neglected. The latter is more important for school instruction than the visual channel. Much attention needs to be given to this second link in the chain of learning. Children with learning problems need to be systematically taught the perceptual processes: they need to be able to organize and convert bits of input from the various sense modalities into units of awareness which have meaning.

Cognitive and language development including academic instruction. This is the heart of special education for slow learning children. Our business is to facilitate their thinking processes. We should help them not only to acquire and store knowledge, but also to generate and evaluate it. Language development could largely be included under this caption—especially the integrative components—since there is much overlap between the development of oral language and verbal intelligence. However, much of receptive language training might be considered under sensory and perceptual training, while expressive language will be considered in the next topic.

A major fault of our present courses of study is failure to focus on the third link in the chain of learning—that of teaching our children systematically in the areas of cognitive development and concept formation. A major goal of our school program should be to increase the intellectual functioning of children we are now classifying as socioculturally retarded. For such children, perhaps as much as 25 percent of the school day in the early years should be devoted to this topic. Yet the author has not seen one curriculum guide for these children with a major emphasis on cognitive development—which is a sad state of affairs indeed!

Basic psychological research by Guilford (1959) has provided us with a useful model of intellect. However, little is yet known about the trainability of the various cognitive processes. Actually, Thurstone (1948) has contributed the one established set of materials for training primary mental abilities. Thus, much work lies ahead in developing programs of instruction for the training of intellect.

We are seeing more and more sets of programed materials in the academic areas, most of which have been designed for average children. The most exciting examples today are in the computer assisted instruction studies. Our major problem is to determine how these programed exercises need to be modified to be maximally effective for children with specific learning problems. Work will be especially needed in the classical areas of instruction including written language and mathematics. Hopefully, however, regular teachers will handle much of the instruction in science and social studies, while specialists would instruct in such areas as music and the fine arts. This will free special educators to focus on better ways of teaching the basic 3 R's, especially written language.

Speech and communication training. This area has received much attention, particularly from speech correctionists and teachers of the deaf. Corrective techniques for specific speech problems are probably more advanced than for any other area, yet essentially no carefully controlled research has been done on the efficacy of these programs. Speech correctionists have tended to be clinicians, not applied behavioral scientists. They often create the details of their corrective exercises while working with their clients in a one to one relationship. Thus, the programs have often been intuitive. Furthermore, public school speech therapists have been spread very thin, usually working with 75 to 100 children. Many have been convinced that only *they* could be effective in this work. But remarkable changes have recently occurred in the thinking of speech therapists; they are recognizing that total programs of oral language development go far beyond correcting articulation defects. Furthermore, some speech therapists believe they could be more productive in working with only the more severe speech handicaps and devoting much attention to the development and field testing of systematic exercises to stimulate overall language and to improve articulation, pitch, loudness, quality, duration, and other speech disorders of a mild to moderate nature. These exercises need to be programed to the point at which teachers, technicians, and perhaps teacher aides can use them. Goldman (1968) is now developing such a program of exercises to correct articulation defects. This seems to be a pioneering and heartening first step.

Connative (or personality) development. This emerging area requires careful attention. We must accept the position that much of a person's behavior is shaped by his environment. This applies to all aspects of human thought, including attitudes, beliefs, and mores. Research oriented clinical psychologists are providing useful information on motivation and personality development and before long we will see reports of research in shaping insights into self, the effects of others on self, and one's effects on others. It is not too early for teams of clinical psychologists, psychiatric social workers, creative special educators (especially for the so called emotionally disturbed), and others to begin developing programs of instruction in this complex field.

Social interaction training. Again we have an emerging area which overlaps considerably with some of those already presented, particularly connative development. Special educators have long recognized that the ability of a handicapped individual to succeed in society depends, in large measure, on his skill to get along with his fellow man. Yet we have done little to develop his social living skills, a complex area of paramount importance. Training programs should be developed to facilitate development in this area of human behavior.

Vocational training. Closely tied to social interaction training is vocational training. Success on the job for persons that we have labeled educable mentally retarded has depended on good independent work habits, reliability, and social skills, rather than on academic skills. Consequently, early and continuing emphasis on developing these traits is necessary. In fact, it is likely to be even more important in the years ahead with fewer job opportunities and increasing family disintegration providing less shelter and support for the so called retarded. Therefore sophisticated programs of instruction are especially needed in this area. Even with our best efforts in this regard, it is likely that our pupils, upon reaching adolescence, will continue to need a variety of vocational services, including trade and technical schools, work study programs, and vocational training.

Another observation. It seems to me to be a red herring to predict that special educators will use these hundreds of specialized instructional programs indiscriminately as cookbooks. Perhaps a few of the poor teachers will. But, the clinical teachers proposed in this article would be too sophisticated and competent to do this. They would use them as points of departure, modifying the lessons so that each child would make optimal progress. Therefore, it seems to me that this library of curriculum materials is necessary to move us from a clinical and intuitive approach to a more scientific basis for special education.

An Epilogue

The conscience of special educators needs to rub up against morality. In large measure we have been at the mercy of the general education establishment in that we accept problem pupils who have been referred out of the regular grades. In this way, we contribute to the delinquency of the general educations since we remove the pupils that are problems for them and thus reduce their need to deal with individual differences. The *entente* of mutual delusion between general and special education that special class placement will be advantageous to slow learning children of poor parents can no longer be tolerated. We must face the reality—we are asked to take children others cannot teach, and a large percentage of these are from ethnically and/or economically disadvantaged backgrounds. Thus much of special education will continue to be a sham of dreams unless we immerse ourselves into the total environment of our children from inadequate homes and backgrounds and insist on a comprehensive ecological push—with a quality educational program as part of it. This is hardly compatible with our prevalent practice of expediency in which we employ many untrained and less than master teachers to increase the number of special day classes in response to the pressures of waiting lists. Because of these pressures from the school system, we have been guilty of fostering quantity with little regard for quality of special education instruction. Our first responsibility is to have an abiding commitment to the less fortunate children we aim to serve. Our honor, integrity, and honesty should no longer be subverted and rationalized by what we hope and may believe we are doing for these children—hopes and beliefs which have little basis in reality.

"The entente of mutual delusion between general and special education that special class placement will be advantageous to slow learning children of poor parents can no longer be tolerated."

". . . we have been guilty of fostering quantity with little regard for quality of special education instruction."

Embarking on an American Revolution in Special Education will require strength of purpose. It is recognized that the structure of most, if not all, school programs becomes self perpetuating. Teachers and state and local directors and supervisors of special education have much at stake in terms of their jobs, their security, and their programs which they have built up over the years. But can we keep our self respect and continue to increase the numbers of these self contained special classes for the educable mentally retarded which are of questionable value for many of the children they are intended to serve? As Ray Graham said in his last article in 1960: [p. 4.]

We can look at our accomplishments and be proud of the progress we have made; but satisfaction with the past does not assure progress in the future. New developments, ideas, and facts may show us that our past practices have become out-moded. A growing child cannot remain static—he either grows or dies. We cannot become satisfied with a job one-third done. We have a long way to go before we can rest assured that the desires of the parents and the educational needs of handicapped children are being fulfilled [p. 4].

"We have a long way to go. . . ."

References

Ainsworth, S. H. *An exploratory study of educational, social and emotional factors in the education of mentally retarded children in Georgia public schools.* US Office of Education Cooperative Research Project Report No. 171(6470). Athens, Ga.: University of Georgia, 1959.

Bereiter, C., & Engelmann, S. *Teaching disadvantaged children in the preschool.* Englewood Cliffs, N.J.: Prentice-Hall, 1966.

Bruner, J. S., Olver, R. R., & Greenfield, P. M. *Studies in cognitive growth.* New York: Wiley, 1967.

Coleman, J. S., et al. *Equality of educational opportunity.* Washington, D.C.: USGPO, 1966.

Cratty, P. J. *Developmental sequences of perceptual motor tasks.* Freeport, Long Island, N.Y.: Educational Activities, 1967.

Delacato, C. H. (Ed.) *Neurological organization and reading problems.* Springfield, Ill.: Charles C Thomas, 1966.

Feuerstein, R. *The Learning Potential Assessment Device* Jerusalem, Israel: Haddassa Wizo Canada Child Guidance Clinic and Research Unit, 1968.

Frostig, M., & Horne, D. *The Frostig program for the development of visual perception.* Chicago: Follett, 1964.

Graham, R. Special education for the sixties. *Illinois Educational Association Study Unit,* 1960, **23,** 1-4.

Goffman, E. *Asylums: Essays on the social situation of mental patients and other inmates.* Garden City, N.Y.: Anchor, 1961.

Goldman, R. *The phonemic-visual-oral association technique for modifying articulation disorders in young children.* Nashville, Tenn.: Bill Wilkerson Hearing and Speech Center, 1968.

Guilford, J. P. *The nature of human intelligence.* New York: McGraw-Hill, 1967.

Hoelke, G. M. *Effectiveness of special class placement for educable mentally retarded children.* Lincoln, Neb.: University of Nebraska, 1966.

Hollingworth, L. S. *The psychology of subnormal children.* New York: MacMillan, 1923.

Johnson, G. O. Special education for mentally handicapped—a paradox. *Exceptional Children,* 1962, **19,** 62-69.

Kirk, S. A. Research in education. In H. A. Stevens & R. Heber (Eds.), *Mental retardation.* Chicago, Ill.: University of Chicago Press, 1964.

Kirk, S. A. *The diagnosis and remediation of psycholinguistic disabilities.* Urbana, Ill.: University of Illinois Press, 1966.

Lillie, D. L. The development of motor proficiency of educable mentally retarded children. *Education and Training of the Mentally Retarded,* 1967, **2,** 29-32.

212

Mackie, R. P. *Functional handicaps among school children due to cultural or economic deprivation.* Paper presented at the First Congress of the International Association for the Scientific Study of Mental Deficiency, Montpellier, France, September, 1967.

Meyerowitz, J. H. Family background of educable mentally retarded children. In H. Goldstein, J. W. Moss & L. J. Jordan. *The efficacy of special education training on the development of mentally retarded children.* Urbana, Ill.: University of Illinois Institute for Research on Exceptional Children, 1965. Pp. 152-182.

Meyerowitz, J. H. Peer groups and special classes. *Mental Retardation,* 1967, 5, 23-26.

Oliver, J. N. The effects of physical conditioning exercises and activities on the mental characteristics of educationally sub-normal boys. *British Journal of Educational Psychology,* 1958, 28, 155-165.

Passow, A. H. *A summary of findings and recommendations of a study of the Washington, D.C. schools.* New York: Teachers College, Columbia University, 1967.

Rosenthal, R., & Jacobson, L. Teachers' expectancies: Determinants of pupils' IQ gains. *Psychological Reports,* 1966, 19, 115-118.

Rubin, E. Z., Senison, C. B., & Betwee, M. C. *Emotionally handicapped children in the elementary school.* Detroit: Wayne State University Press, 1966.

Smith, H. W., & Kennedy, W. A. Effects of three educational programs on mentally retarded children. *Perceptual and Motor Skills,* 1967, 24, 174.

Thurstone, T. G. *Learning to think series.* Chicago, Ill.: Science Research Associates, 1948.

Wright, Judge J. S. *Hobson vs Hansen: U. S. Court of Appeals decision on the District of Columbia's track system. Civil Action No. 82-66.* Washington, D. C.: US Court of Appeals, 1967.

LLOYD M. DUNN *has been Director, Institute on Mental Retardation and Intellectual Development, George Peabody College for Teachers, Nashville, Tennessee. An early version of this paper was presented as the Ray Graham Memorial Address at the 18th Annual Convention of the Illinois Council for Exceptional Children, Chicago, October, 1967.*

CHAUNCY N. RUCKER
CLIFFORD E. HOWE
BILL SNIDER

The Participation of Retarded Children in Junior High Academic and Nonacademic Regular Classes

Abstract: A sociometric instrument was administered in 30 regular junior high classes to measure various aspects of the acceptance of 23 educable mentally retarded special class students participating in these classes with 1,010 nonretarded students. The retarded were found to be (a) significantly less accepted than the nonretarded, (b) equally low in the social structure of both the academic and nonacademic classes in which they participated, and (c) seemingly unaware of their low social position in regular classes. Their level of acceptance in the special class was positively related to their degree of acceptance in regular classes. A discussion of implications for educational placement and areas in need of further study concludes the article.

RESEARCH on the social acceptance of the educable mentally retarded (EMR) has offered certain implications regarding the educational placement of these children. Several studies have investigated the acceptance of EMR children enrolled in regular classes (Baldwin, 1958; Johnson, 1950; Johnson & Kirk, 1950). These studies have concluded that EMR children in regular classes are generally not accepted, but rather are isolated or actively rejected by their nonretarded classmates.

In view of this rejection the retarded students receive in regular classes, a special class setting would seem preferable. But would it be better for the special class to be segregated or integrated? That is, would it be better for the retarded students to remain in the special class full time, or for them to be placed in regular classes for part of the school day? The studies mentioned previously are not directly applicable to this question since they were concerned only with retarded children enrolled full time in regular classes. In addition, these studies were conducted in elementary schools. Although the policy of integration is practiced at the elementary level, it is much more prevalent at the junior and senior high school levels (Fuchigami, 1965).

Only one study (Lapp, 1957) has investigated the social acceptance of EMR children in a school that practiced integration. Lapp's findings were generally in accord with the previous sociometric studies, except that the retarded were not as actively rejected. Her results are difficult to generalize to other situations due to the selection procedure employed to determine which children were "ready" to participate in regular classes. Again, this was

Exceptional Children, April, 1969, Vol. 35, No. 8, pp. 617-623.

an investigation that was conducted in an elementary school setting.

It is currently popular to advocate integration for educable children, particularly in nonacademic classes at the junior and senior high levels. However, this practice does not seem to have been implemented on the basis of research findings. There are several questions regarding the social acceptance of the mentally retarded relating to the policy of integration that require further investigation.

Purpose

The purpose of this study was to investigate the social acceptance or social position of educable mentally retarded children participating in academic and nonacademic regular classes at the junior high school level. The questions of primary concern in this investigation were:

1. What is the social position of retarded children participating in regular classes at the junior high level?
2. How does the social position of retarded children differ in an academic as compared to a nonacademic regular class?
3. How accurate are retarded children in appraising their social position in a regular class?
4. What is the relationship between the social position of retarded children in a special class and a regular class?

Selection and Description of School

An Iowa city with a population of approximately 90,000 was selected for this study. A particular junior high school was chosen which offered a cross section of the community's socioeconomic status. The total school enrollment was 1,089 in grades seven, eight, and nine.

There were two educable special classes in the building, and since the retarded students participated in regular classes more than half of each school day, one teacher was employed for both classes. The curriculum in the special class centered around English (with an emphasis on spelling), reading, and mathematics. Regular classes in which retarded students participated included physical education, science, civics, geography, music, art, homemaking, and woodworking. The nonacademic class chosen for investigation was physical education and the academic class chosen was science. A strict selection procedure was not employed for the regular class assignments. That is, every retarded student participated in four regular classes each day without special considerations and these classes were not grouped by ability.

Subjects

The subjects consisted of 23 retarded students with a mean IQ score of 71 (range 54 to 80) and mean CA of 14 years 9 months (range 13-5 to 16-3). The 14 boys and 9 girls were divided between the two special classes.

Fourteen of the retarded subjects participated in seventh grade science and 7 were enrolled in eighth grade science. Two retarded students were not enrolled in science but were included in the retarded sample. One was enrolled in a seventh grade geography class and the other in an eighth grade civics class. Twenty-two subjects were enrolled in physical education; one could not be enrolled due to health reasons. The retarded subjects were enrolled in 16 academic classes and 14 nonacademic or physical education classes. The 1,010 regular class students enrolled in these 30 classes made up the group of nonretarded subjects. The median class enrollment for the nonretarded subjects was 30 in academic classes and 39 in the nonacademic classes.

Instrument

The Ohio Social Acceptance Scale (Fordyce, Yauck, & Raths, 1946) was chosen to determine the social position of the subjects in this investigation. The directions for the Ohio Social Acceptance Scale (OSAS) are intended for children of elementary school age and imply that the teacher will discsss the results with each child. These directions were rewritten for children of junior high age and it was made clear that the results would be confidential. The OSAS consists of six descriptive paragraphs ranging from high acceptance to active rejection. The modified directions and the paragraphs are reported in more detail elsewhere (Rucker, 1968).

Each subject in the present study was provided with a set of paragraphs and a class list. The teacher read each paragraph aloud while the students read them silently. After each descriptive paragraph was read, the subjects were asked to select those children in the class who fit that particular description and place a number, corresponding to the paragraph, in front of the children's names they had selected.

The paragraphs were assigned a weight obtained from the OSAS Manual (Fordyce et al., 1946). Each student's social position within the class was computed by summing the weighted choices he received and dividing by the number of subjects who rated him. This process yielded a social position score (SPS) for each subject. These SPS's were employed in evaluating the four questions of this investigation.

Procedure

The OSAS was administered in all of the regular classes in May 1967 to measure the level of acceptance of retarded and nonretarded students in those classes. The OSAS was also administered in the special classes following the same procedure. The results of this latter testing provided a measure of each retarded student's social acceptance as judged by his retarded classmates.

Secondly, the investigator met individually with the retarded students after the regular and special class administrations of the OSAS. After spending time to gain rapport, he gave the students a copy of the class list from their respective academic and physical education classes plus a set of the OSAS descriptive paragraphs. It was explained that they were to estimate the rating given them by each of the participants of their regular classes. The investigator then read the paragraphs aloud, pausing after each to allow the subjects to indicate the choices they thought they had received. For example, after the first paragraph was read, the subjects were asked to write the number "1" in front of every student's name on the class list who they thought had given them a rating of one.

These ratings were later converted into the SPS the retarded students thought they received in their regular academic and nonacademic classes. By comparing their estimated social position to their actual social position, a measure was provided of the retarded subjects' accuracy in judging their social acceptance in regular classes.

Results

SPS's of retarded versus nonretarded. The first question was evaluated by comparing the mean SPS of the retarded subjects to the mean for the nonretarded subjects. This was done separately for academic and nonacademic settings. The number of retarded subjects differed in the two comparisons because one of the subjects was not enrolled in physical education. Due to the disproportionate sample sizes and inequality of variances, a t' statistic was employed (Lindquist, 1953). The results of this analysis are shown in Table 1.

The social position scores of the retarded subjects were significantly below those of the nonretarded subjects in both academic and nonacademic classes. The previous finding that retarded children are less accepted than their nonretarded classmates in elementary classrooms (Baldwin, 1958; Johnson, 1950; Johnson & Kirk, 1950) appears to hold when retarded children participate in junior high classes as well.

Academic versus nonacademic SPS's of retarded. The second question required three separate comparisons. In the first, the social position scores the retarded subjects received in academic classes were compared to their SPS's in physical education. This comparison included 8 boys' physical education classes, 6 girls' physical education classes, and 16 academic classes. A t test for related measures (Blommers & Lindquist, 1960) was employed for this analysis.

This procedure involved comparing the SPS's retarded subjects received in a class composed only of members of their own sex (physical education) to the scores they received from a class in which there were members of both sexes. An analysis of the social position scores of the nonretarded subjects in academic classes, employing a Z test (Blommers & Lindquist, 1960), revealed that they significantly favored their own sex ($p < .01$). In view of this marked sex cleavage, it was felt necessary to conduct two further analyses deal-

TABLE 1

Nonretarded Versus Retarded Social Position Scores:
Academic and Nonacademic Classes

Class	Nonretarded			Retarded			Difference	
	N	$\overline{X}$	s^2	N	$\overline{X}$	s^2		
Academic	474	5.09	2.431	23	2.81	.576	2.28	12.88*
Nonacademic	536	6.14	3.567	22	3.14	1.320	3.00	11.36*

*Significant at .01 level.
$t'_{.01} = 2.48$, $df = 473,22$
$t'_{.01} = 2.50$, $df = 535,21$

TABLE 2

Retarded Subjects' Social Position Scores:
Academic Versus Nonacademic Classes

Subjects	Academic	Nonacademic	$\overline{D}$	s_D	t
	$\overline{X}$ SPS	$\overline{X}$ SPS			
All Retarded Subjects	2.81	3.14	—.33	.963	—1.57
($N = 22$)					
Retarded Boys[a]	4.14	3.19	.95	1.101	2.99
($N = 13$)					
Retarded Girls[b]	3.30	3.05	.25	.930	.76
($N = 9$)					

[a] Academic $\overline{X}$ SPS based on choices received from male classmates.
[b] Academic $\overline{X}$ SPS based on choices received from female classmates.
$t_{.01} = 2.83$, $df = 21$
$t_{.01} = 3.06$, $df = 12$
$t_{.01} = 3.36$, $df = 8$

ing with the second question. One approach compared the SPS's retarded boys received in their physical education classes to the SPS's they received from the nonretarded boys in their academic classes. The final test compared the SPS's retarded girls received in physical education to the SPS's they received from the nonretarded girls in their academic classes. Again, t tests for related measures were employed. The results of the three comparisons are shown in Table 2.

The resulting t values were nonsignificant for each of these comparisons. The retarded subjects were equally low in the social structure of both their academic and nonacademic classes. The common assumption that lower intellectual ability would have a more detrimental effect on the retarded children's per-

formance in an academic subject and thus be reflected in a higher social position in a nonacademic class was not supported.

Retarded children's self appraisal of social position. The third question was tested by comparing the SPS's the retarded subjects estimated they received to the scores they actually received in both academic and nonacademic classes. The results of these two related t tests are shown in Table 3.

The retarded subjects significantly overestimated their level of acceptance in both academic and nonacademic classes. Although they were significantly low in the social structure of both their academic and nonacademic classes, they were either unaware of or denied this lack of acceptance by the nonretarded students. The SPS's the retarded subjects estimated

TABLE 3					
Retarded Subjects' Social Position Scores: Estimated Versus Actual					
Class	Estimated $\overline{X}$ SPS	Actual $\overline{X}$ SPS	$\overline{D}$	^{8}D	t
Academic (N = 22)	5.14	2.79	2.35	2.510	4.29*
Nonacademic (N = 21)	6.22	3.14	3.08	2.800	4.92*

*Significant at .01 level.
$t_{.01} = 2.83$, $df = 21$
$t_{.01} = 2.85$, $df = 20$

TABLE 4				
Retarded Subjects' Social Position Scores: Special Versus Regular Classes				
Special Class $\overline{X}$ SPS	Regular Class $\overline{X}$ SPS	$\overline{D}$	^{8}D	t
7.14	2.81a	4.33	2.210	9.19*
7.02	3.14b	3.88	2.129	8.35*

[a] Academic regular class (N = 23).
[b] Nonacademic regular class (N = 22).
*Significant at .01 level.
$t_{.01} = 2.82$, $df = 22$
$t_{.01} = 2.83$, $df = 21$

they received were also compared to the SPS's actually received by the nonretarded subjects in academic and nonacademic classes. In this case, t tests with a significance level of .01 revealed that there were no significant differences between the scores the retarded thought they received and the scores the nonretarded actually did receive. The retarded overestimated their social position, but, as a group, considered themselves to be of average social acceptance rather than being the "stars" of their regular classes.

SPS's of retarded in special versus regular classes. To evaluate the fourth question, a product moment correlation was computed between the SPS's the retarded subjects received in their special class and in their academic classes, and between the special class SPS's and their SPS's in nonacademic classes. The resulting coefficients of $r = .59$ for the academic comparison and $r = .57$ for the nonacademic comparison were found to be significant at the .01 level (Walker & Lev, 1953). Although the retarded were significantly low in the social structure of their regular classes, those judged most accepted by the retarded tended to be judged more favorably by the nonretarded as well.

A further comparison was made between special and regular class SPS's by means of related t tests. The results, shown in Table 4, indicate that the retarded subjects received significantly higher social position scores from their retarded classmates in the special class than from their nonretarded classmates in regular classes.

Discussion and Implications

The results of this investigation seem to support the following conclusions:

1. Retarded children participating in regular junior high classes are less accepted than their nonretarded classmates.
2. Retarded children are as low in the social structure of nonacademic classes such as physical education as they are in academic classes such as science.
3. Retarded children overestimate their social acceptance in regular classes.
4. The more popular children in a special class tend to be more accepted by the nonretarded.

In considering these conclusions certain limitations are readily apparent. The integration issue cannot be solved by such sociometric findings without the support of related studies. The results of this investigation are based on a relatively small sample in one midwestern city. The conclusions may not be as applicable to a larger metropolitan setting.

Contradiction in interpretation. The present study indicates that retarded children are not accepted by nonretarded children regardless of whether they are participating in an academic or nonacademic setting. This in turn may suggest to some that a special school or a segregated special class would be the most suitable placement for these students. The finding that the retarded were most accepted by the classmates in their own special rooms adds support to this contention. However, since the

218

retarded overestimated their social acceptance or were seemingly unaware of their low social status in regular classes, others may suggest that acceptance need not be considered in placing retarded children. These contradictory interpretations of the results indicate that the best educational placement for the retarded has yet to be resolved. Several components of this issue are in need of further consideration.

Are the retarded truly unaware of their low social status? Miller (1956) found that elementary level retarded children overestimated their social status, but not significantly so. Perhaps junior high age retarded children are actually more sensitive about their lack of acceptance and thus more denying of it. Whether the tendency of the retarded to overestimate their social acceptance represents unawareness or denial of their rejection was not determined. Further study is needed to determine which is the more likely explanation.

Type of rejection. The position held by the retarded in the social structure of elementary and junior high classes appears similar. Although the retarded lack acceptance in either setting, the type or quality of this rejection may be different. It is probable that nonretarded junior high age children are not as overt in their rejection as elementary age children. If this suspicion were confirmed by future research it might help to account for the retarded children's inaccurate assessment of their acceptance in junior high settings.

It would thus be of interest to study overt and covert rejection with a sample representing various age levels of nonretarded children. If overt rejection of the retarded was found to subside as a function of age, what would this change represent? Would it signify a development of empathy for the handicapped, or would it be similar to the attitude change of many white children toward Negroes? Allport (1954) stated that white children pass from a stage of "totalized rejection" to a stage in which verbal rejection is replaced by behavioral rejection but verbal acceptance.

We know that by the third or fourth grade, retarded children are not accepted in regular classes. It is probable that these children occupy a higher social position when they first enroll in preschool or kindergarten. If this is indeed the case, when does their social position begin to decline and is it directly related to the increasing academic emphasis? How is the retarded child's social status in his neighborhood affected during this period of declining acceptance? Further, does placement in a special class have a significant effect upon the social acceptance of the retarded child in his neighborhood?

Integration. What is the justification for a policy of integration for the retarded? Kidd (1966) stated that much has been made of the "socialization" which could occur when retarded children associate with normal children in a school setting. He questioned, however, whether the retarded actually gain anything in such a setting. The present study suggests that if they do gain something, that which is gained could not be termed true socialization. The retarded may need to associate with normal children in order to realistically prepare for adult life, but further research is needed to determine the nature and extent of whatever benefit they derive.

If the practice of placing retarded children in regular classes for part of the school day is to be continued, there is need to study ways of improving their acceptance in such settings. This would require the cooperation of both special and regular class teachers. Special class teachers could attempt to promote the development of attitudes and behaviors that would help the retarded cope with the demands of regular classes. Techniques should be designed for the regular class teachers to use in attempting to improve the social status of the retarded students participating in their classes. The effectiveness of this combined program could be evaluated by means of the modified Ohio Social Acceptance Scale employed in this investigation.

References

Allport, G. W. *The nature of prejudice.* Cambridge, Mass.: Addison-Wesley, 1954.

Baldwin, W. K. The social position of the educable mentally retarded child in the regular grades in the public schools. *Exceptional Children,* 1958, 25, 106-108.

Blommers, P., & Lindquist, E. F. *Elementary statistical methods.* Boston: Houghton Mifflin, 1960.

Fordyce, W. G., Yauck, W. A., & Raths, L. *A manual for the Ohio guidance tests for the elementary grades.* Columbus, Ohio: Ohio State Department of Education, 1946.

Fuchigami, R. Y. *An investigation of the extent of integration and some related factors affecting the social relationships of educable mentally handicapped children in Illinois.* (Doctoral dissertation, University of Illinois) Ann Arbor, Mich.: University Microfilms, 1965. No. 65-3586.

Johnson, G. O. A study of the social position of mentally-handicapped children in regular grades. *American Journal of Mental Deficiency*, 1950, **55**, 60-89.

Johnson, G. O., & Kirk, S. A. Are mentally-handicapped children segregated in the regular grades? *Exceptional Children*, 1950, **17**, 65-68, 87-88.

Kidd, J. W. Some unwarranted assumptions in the education and habilitation of handicapped children. *Education and Training of the Mentally Retarded*, 1966, **1**, 54-58.

Lapp, Esther A. A study of the social adjustment of slow learning children who were assigned part-time to regular classes. *American Journal of Mental Deficiency*, 1957, **62**, 254-262.

Lindquist, E. F. *Design and analysis of experiments in psychology and education.* Boston: Houghton Mifflin, 1953.

Miller, R. V. Social status and socioempathic differences among mentally superior, mentally typical, and mentally retarded. *Exceptional Children*, 1956, **23**, 114-119.

Rucker, C. N. *Acceptance of mentally retarded junior high children in academic and non-academic classes.* (Doctoral dissertation, University of Iowa) Ann Arbor, Mich.: University Microfilms, 1968. No. 68-973.

Walker, H. M., & Lev, J. *Statistical inference.* New York: Holt, Rinehart, & Winston, 1953.

CHAUNCY N. RUCKER *is Assistant Professor of Education, University of Connecticut, Storrs;* CLIFFORD E. HOWE *is Professor and Chairman, Division of Special Education, and* BILL SNIDER *is Assistant Professor, Computer Center, College of Education, University of Iowa, Iowa City.*

JAMES J. GALLAGHER

New Directions in Special Education

Abstract: An attempt is made to examine future prospects in special education, with suggestions of questions to be posed, assumptions to be challenged, and areas to be investigated and developed.

THE winds of change, dramatic and rapid change, are blowing through American education and rapidly modifying the educational system that we grew up with to something very different. Whether special education gets borne aloft by these winds or gets blown down trying to deny their power is not a casual question.

In many cases, special education has moved along with these changing tides and has maintained its leadership position; in many others, it seems to have lagged behind or not been aware of important developments. The public is impatient for new answers to old problems and, for the first time, is willing to pay for these answers.

At the last White House conference, John Gardner, current Secretary of Health, Education and Welfare, enjoined American educators to stop nibbling around the edges of educational problems and take a "barracuda bite" at them. Another way of saying the same thing is to say that we must train ourselves and our students to think unthinkable thoughts. An unthinkable thought is a projection of a present problem to a probable future situation that is so different from what we know now, or so disturbing, that most of us don't even want to think about it. But in a dynamic and changing society, we cannot confront our problems adequately unless we have the courage to peer over the horizon and see them while they are still just a small

dot. Some examples of unthinkable thoughts might be:

America may some day not be the strongest nation in the world.

Maybe special classes for mentally retarded really don't help them very much in preparation for life in modern society.

Perhaps the speech correctionist need not deal with functional articulation cases at all.

Maybe gifted students do need gifted teachers, even if they are taught most of their work via television.

All available systems for teaching language to deaf children are, to one degree or another, failures.

Everyone can make up his own list of unthinkable thoughts, a useful, if sobering, exercise. As my belief of what part of the face of the future looks like, I would like to share with you some unthinkable thoughts that cut across all areas of special education and deal with training, curriculum development, and research.

Conventional Goals of Special Education

Let us start with the best of conventional wisdom. What kind of a program would we be satisfied with in special education today? The adequate program of special education would have a large number of special class programs. There would certainly be a special class program for the mentally retarded ranging from preschool through secondary and a sheltered

Exceptional Children, 1967, Vol.33, No.7, pp. 441-447.

workshop program for the older trainable. If the community were large enough to have a good population base, there would be special classes for the hard of hearing and the deaf child, and perhaps even for the partially seeing child. We would have a number of speech correctionists in the schools working mainly with children with articulation problems but dealing, in some degree, with the more serious problems of children who have cleft palate or cerebral palsy or who stutter. The gifted would have a special staff to help develop a program more in line with their abilities.

There would be a program for the emotionally disturbed perhaps through the use of social workers or through another type of special class program. A really alert program would have some provisions for the children with severe learning disorders or neurologically handicapped which would include individual educational diagnosis or remediation. There would be an active psychological services branch that would not only involve itself with the usual testing but be active in remediation programs and research, perhaps exploring the uses of creativity tests or tinkering with special diagnostic tools such as the Illinois Test of Psycholinguistic Abilities. Over all of this operation would be a director of special education who would administrate the program, see to it that competent and well trained teachers are chosen, and keep lines of communication open between the local school district and the state office of special education.

At the university level, there would be a department of special education employing several persons to train teachers in the special areas of exceptional children, teach about special characteristics of various kinds of exceptional children, and supervise student teaching. A well developed department would also add one or two persons at the graduate level to supervise research and give courses for persons going into advanced graduate training. To skim briefly over this broad operation is not to downgrade it. It would look like paradise to the special educator of twenty years ago, but where do we go from here?

You will notice that the major description has had to do with administrative structure but not content, the heart of the program.

What is the special program? This brings me to my first unthinkable question.

Unthinkable Thought Number 1.
Curriculum Development

Is curriculum development for exceptional children too important to be left to the classroom teacher or, for that matter, to the special educator? A little playlet may serve to illustrate the general problem. Miss Bravada, fresh from one of the university's teacher training programs in special education, appears for her first job and asks about the special curriculum that will be applied to her exceptional children.

The administrator, a model of democratic correctness, says that he is determined not to impose his ideas on her, no siree. She is going to have that freedom that all professionals yearn for, the freedom to work out her own program. Two weeks later, Miss Bravada is back in the supervisor's office begging, nay pleading, for him to take away her freedom, to dictatorially tell her what to do, to give her some program, some materials with which to operate. Ever sympathetic, the administrator proposes that a committee be formed to develop a curriculum for their system for, if the truth be known, other special education teachers have been asking for the same thing. So, after much hard work and hours of labor, they paste together an amalgamation of their own experience and knowledge. Meanwhile, in school systems all over the country, this little play is reproduced with variations, and innumerable little curriculum programs and pamphlets get mimeographed.

The huge curriculum reform movement that struck the United States in the late fifties and early sixties, sponsored mainly by the National Science Foundation, was devoted to the proposition that local school systems simply did not have the expertise to write about mathematics or chemistry or history or biology. Furthermore, if biology is going to be a part of the curriculum program, their position was that maybe a biologist ought to have a hand in its development. Talk about your unthinkable thoughts!

Do we in special education have nothing to learn from these teams of curriculum developers who have operated in practically every content field and who have drawn from a wide background of knowledge and skills at the highest possible level to produce a consistent set of materials that was cognitively sound (the psychologist's job), content sound (the content specialist's job), and pedagogically sound (the teachers' and educators' job)?

Are we destroying Miss Bravada's freedom? No, her freedom, like so much of freedom in education, was an illusion. We might as well go down to the corner garage and announce to them that they have the freedom to build a DC 8 jet. What we are giving her is the freedom to fail, and fail she will, when she is given a task beyond her capabilities and resources.

Miss Bravada does have a role in total curriculum development. She has to take the proposed curriculum and field test it for her own class. She and her fellow teachers may have to make an intelligent choice between competing curricula. She certainly can provide important feedback to the curriculum developers on what works and what doesn't in that all important crucible—the classroom. But it is one thing to learn how to play a sonata and quite a different one to compose one. Our teacher training programs are in the business of training performers not composers.

Henry Morgan once commented on what it took to start a modern newspaper. He said that it demanded intelligence, integrity, raw courage, and ten million dollars. That well may be the precise price tag for some viable curriculum programs for the emotionally disturbed child. We should not expect Miss Bravada, or a committee of Miss Bravadas, to come up with it.

One of the most encouraging recent developments in special education has been the establishment of the series of instructional materials centers through the US Office of Education. In their early stages of operation, they have concentrated on the collation and collection of materials. Very soon now they will realize that what is really needed is not the collection of existing materials but rather the systematic production of new materials,

sound in theory and exciting and interesting in practice.

When that time comes, let us be wise enough to not pass the job of curriculum innovation around only within our little group of special educators, but also seek out the active cooperation of anthropologists, sociologists, psychologists, and all others who can, with our pedagogical help, bring content validity to our curriculum. It is a huge problem and demands a heroic response. If we can listen to the anguished cries of teachers around us, we should know that nothing we could do could so aid our general special education program as a major effort of this sort.

Unthinkable Thought Number 2. Research

Is it possible that all of the millions of dollars that we placed into evaluation of special programs for various kinds of exceptional children were wasted and that, in fact, the wrong approach to the problem was used? As well you know, one of the most popular research designs is to take a group of exceptional children—it doesn't matter whether we choose mentally retarded children, emotionally disturbed children, children who have severe hearing impairment, or children with articulation problems—and compare their performance with a control group of children who have similar problems but who are not in the special program. We should seriously consider whether or not we should pursue any more of that kind of research. The reason for abandoning this design is not that we are getting discouraging results, which we are, but rather because we cannot really evaluate the results at all. Is the program for the EMH in Crossroads Junction the same as the program in Big Town? Is the one in Big Town the same as the one in Main Street? Indeed, is there such an animal as a special class program or curriculum?

The author's own research at the Institute for Research on Exceptional Children has tried to concentrate, over the last seven or eight years, on the development of a system of classroom observation and analysis that possessed some sound theoretical footing in cognitive theory. As part of this operation, a project financed by the US Office of Education and the Biological Sciences Curriculum Study was completed recently that has direct relevance to the question of variations in special classes. The research question was the degree to which there was teacher variation even when there appeared to be a common curriculum. Through the cooperation and support of the BSCS program, we were able to identify six classrooms in the state of Illinois, all of which had substantial similarities.

1. In each classroom, the students were high ability honors groups at the junior high school level.
2. Each teacher was a man.
3. Each had received some type of additional training in BSCS material.
4. Each was using the BSCS Blue version with accompanying materials.
5. At the time we recorded their classrooms, each was teaching the same concept—that of *photosynthesis*.

Thus, any difference in the performance and presentation of materials was due not to the ability level of the students, the available materials or the concept that was being taught, but instead, related directly to different and individual teacher styles. We found significant variation in how the material was presented to the students, a difference in teacher emphasis on student mastery of research skills as opposed to biological content, and on the actual level of conceptualization in the class discussions. In our classification system, only one dimension remained relatively constant across all classes—all teachers placed a major emphasis on description and explanation as opposed to evaluation and extension. This seemed to be, in part, a function of the subject matter itself.

A closer examination of the actual presentation of the photosynthesis concept revealed that one teacher spent as many as thirty-six topics or units of discussion on the introduction and background of "evolution in a changing world"; whereas, another teacher spent as few as seven topics on the same area. Two teachers spent nine and ten topics on the "nature of light," while two other teachers spent only one or none on the same subject. On "factors that affect photosyn-

thesis," one teacher felt it necessary to use ten topics; two other teachers did not touch on the subject at all.

In terms of drawing in outside material, one teacher used twenty-eight topics that were outside the chapter on photosynthesis but were being covered in other chapters or involved supplementary material. Another teacher used no outside topics at all. Another area of teacher style rests in the amount of student talk allowed. In this case, it ranged from five percent of the total discussion in one class to thirty-four percent in another class.

One of our conclusions was that there really is no such thing as a BSCS curriculum presentation. There is, rather, the Uriah interpretation of the BSCS curriculum, or the Virgil interpretation of that curriculum, or the Zorba interpretation, etc. But if we can get substantial differences between teachers who had so much in common, just think of what the differences might be if we analyzed different classrooms of educably retarded children in which the curriculum was not the same. How can we then bunch all of these classes together and run an ability grouping study or test the effectiveness of special classes? The answers are clear. We cannot.

Our program evaluation research, to some extent, reminds me of my youth when we played a game on Christmas Eve. We were not allowed to open our packages until the next morning, but they were all laid out under the tree so we played a guessing game on the basis of the shape and size of the packages. In many respects, this is what we still do in the area of curriculum evaluation. We have various sized and shaped packages, and we try and guess what might have been inside them.

But, of course, the answers to our questions cannot really be precise until we actually open them up and look inside, and this will happen to a greater and greater degree in the field of research in special education. We'll actually open the classroom package and look inside, and this means more and more attention will be paid to actual classroom operation, teacher-student interaction, and sequencing of ideas and materials. However, such a change will bring a need for different research techniques and approaches, a painful change for those used to the kind of research that required only a period of testing prior to the special program and again when the program was completed.

Unthinkable Thought Number 3. Training

Do our training programs for specialists to work with exceptional children have to be conducted exclusively within the halls of the college or university? Let us consider what the best of current wisdom has created. The student attends college for three years taking a liberal arts background for the first two years, more technical courses the third year, and finally enters into his practicum year where he learns what teaching is all about as a senior. During this crucial year, his supervision is often handled by a faculty member who risks ptomaine and exhaustion or worse racing from student to student, and often from town to town, spending a few brief hours with each, never really knowing what the student is doing.

After graduation, the former student is considered a professional and is on his own. If he returns to the university for further training, it is often in the summer where he sits in classrooms and learns more theory that he finds very hard to apply to his situation. He may also attend inservice training programs, of which the most distinctive feature is likely to be a scalding cup of instant coffee which threatens at any moment to break through the fragile paper cup and cause grievous bodily injury. Here he may listen to a lecture from a visiting celebrity talking about his research or special program. Is this the best that we have to offer? How can we break out of a system that we know is less than our best?

One approach is to substitute for this dim and overdrawn portrait a concept of continuous training, where the university plays a distinctive, but not a total training role. In this view, the university can provide preservice training and special advanced training, but practicum courses and supervision take place within the clinical setting or the school situation itself. The concept of a clinical professor which describes a person extremely knowledgeable in the skills of his trade, who is on the university staff but stationed in the school system, and whose job is to supervise and conduct inservice training programs, has just begun to be appreciated. To my knowledge, it has hardly received any notice in special education.

This is one potential way to extend our training program beyond an unavoidable university bottleneck. If the university can be convinced that it should spend its slender resources of staff on training personnel to conduct summer programs or an inservice training program that uses the most modern knowledge and techniques for modifying and improving teacher behavior, then we are using our resources with some imagination and wisdom. We also are a little closer to that time when the school system or the institution accepts as one of its natural and important functions that of training, and staffs itself to provide these services.

Where such training should be done is one issue, and how it is to be done is another. The key to the preparation of teachers lies in the need to show the teacher how to interact meaningfully with the learner. It is not enough that a set of general principles of how children learn or the nature of the curriculum should be mastered. If that were all there was to it, a quiet room and some clearly written textbooks would suffice. But teaching is like other skills that require a complex set of interactions with a changing environment such as cooking, acting, flying an airplane, or playing golf. These skills cannot be learned solely through the written word but must be mastered through observation, practice, and provisions for sufficient feedback about their own performances to allow the teachers or performers to analyze systematically their own behavior and modify it accordingly. It is this area which is the much misunderstood province of the educator and which, when fully realized, will provide the basis for greatly improved professional preparation in all fields of education.

Since the interaction with the environment, in the case of special education, means dealing with children with a wide variety of special learning problems, it is doubly important that the embryonic teacher be given the best in training opportunities. The blind child, who needs to develop a perceptual field to replace the space leaping visual sense, the deaf child whose limited reception of language leads to limited production of language and eventually limited conceptualization, the neurologically impaired child who has trouble coordinating his receptive and expressive skills—all need persons who have had the best in teacher preparation to deal with such special learning problems.

One trend now in its infancy but which promises much improvement and change in specialist preparation in education relies on a particular marriage of technology and educational theory. Feedback information about one's own performance as a teacher has not been easy to obtain. Ideally, one would like to have the means to study at leisure one's own performance and then to apply theories of instruction that would make such analysis maximally profitable.

The football coach, whose vulnerable status has perhaps made him more appreciative of the need for excellence in instruction, has been using such techniques for years. By replaying the game film in an atmosphere of quiet contemplation, it is possible to do extensive analysis of how the various interactions necessary to success were executed, what precise problems existed, and how such execution can be improved.

The beginning steps have already been taken to apply such techniques in the classroom through the analysis of audio tapes and video tapes which allow teachers and clinicians to observe themselves in action. Such observation is combined with a theoretical structure which enables them to analyze their own performance and systematically choose alternative methods to more adequately insure their reaching instructional goals. Thus, the teacher can institute question asking which is more conducive to student inquiry, even as the football tackle sees that placing his feet parallel preparatory to the charge will give him greater balance.

These new methods and instructional devices are in a crude developmental stage now but represent the promise of the future for instructional improvement, not only for teachers in their traditional preservice training but also for teachers on the job. There exists the real promise for a continuous training program for teachers in the field. If such systematic observation and feedback can be made into a continuous training program, then the term inservice training can be rescued from its current inglorious meanings.

Unthinkable Thought Number 4.
Dissemination of Ideas and Actions

Do the professor and the library represent the best ways of translating new ideas into educational action? The entire area of idea and action transmission has undergone drastic revision within the last decade. The university professor has been the sole transmitter of knowledge, and it does not speak ill of him that such transmission, particularly of methods, was not often carried into the classroom. Now, additional organized attempts are being made to spread knowledge more effectively.

One of these is the educational retrieval system ERIC, sponsored by the Bureau of Research in the US Office of Education. Of the almost twenty centers in the country being developed to store and transmit up to date information on all types of research and development activities, one is devoted solely to handling information on exceptional children. This center, at The Council for Exceptional Children in Washington, D. C., will eventually be able to feed back stored information to local schools so that if a person wishes to have up to date knowledge on the effectiveness of various reading programs for educable retarded children, he could get a listing of work done on that problem, and copies of those works that he wished to examine at first hand.

Another example of a new mechanism for dispensing educational information is the development of Regional Education Laboratories whose major job is dissemination of new and proven ideas into action in the field. Unhappily for special education, only one or two of the twenty labs have staff or programs geared to the needs or interests of special education. Unless we pay close attention to the developments in this area, we may find that special education has been bypassed.

It is the unthinkable thoughts that we need always to contemplate as we view the rapidly changing future of education. There is a price that we must pay for getting involved in all of this innovation, change, and modification. Each generation and each group has to decide for itself whether or not it is willing to pay that price. When we involve ourselves in innovation, we must realize that if our days are filled with anxiety, it's because new ideas are rarely soothing. If the comfortable past and familiar things seem far away, it is because the future beckons. The cost of intellectual adventure always involves some ulcers on the psyche.

Let us look on the situation this way. Suppose fifteen years ago I had approached the brightest and most ambitious college and high school students and told them that if they sought adventure and opportunity, why not try education? Today, we can look them squarely in the eye and say this. If we maintain our attitude of purpose and adventure, special education will continue to get the best of this crop of fresh talent now entering education and nothing more optimistic can be said about our organization and its future.

JAMES J. GALLAGHER is Associate Director, Institute for Research on Exceptional Children, University of Illinois, Urbana, and Visiting Adjunct Professor, Education Improvement Program, Duke University, Durham, North Carolina.

JAMES J. GALLAGHER

Unfinished Educational Tasks
(Thoughts on Leaving Government Service)

The many problems that plague effective government action in education center mainly upon *how* important decisions are made. I wish to state some of these problems and possible solutions as a final statement upon leaving Government service.

In Washington, we still play the game of hero and villain, as the press testifies daily. However, villains in Washington are far fewer than most people believe. Many of the problems are imbedded, rather, in failure within the organization and system of government itself. These flaws extend beyond particular individuals in temporary leadership positions. Before major improvements can be made in the construction and implementation of sound educational policy, the Washington decision making system must be corrected in a fundamental manner.

"Four problems have been major frustrations . . ." Four of these organizational problems have been major frustrations in our work and none of them seem to be getting much better:

Erosion of Authority of US Office of Education I believe that the US Office of Education should be the major center for the development of national policy on education and the principal educational spokesman of the Federal government, once the broad outlines of White House interests have been stated. At the present time, however, virtually all major educational policy decisions and statements are being made at other

Exceptional Children, Summer, 1970, Vol.36, No.10, pp. 709-716.

228

governmental levels with only perfunctory recognition of the existence or the role of the Office of Education. The Office has had only limited participation in the plans for desegregation of education, higher education, educational research and development, and other areas.

One of the consequences of that limited participation was the negative tone in the White House Messages on Education which appear more critical than constructive in their approach to education. Various administrative spokesmen, from the White House down, seem willing to make education and educators the scapegoat for a multitude of societal problems not of their making, but at the same time are not willing to provide the high priority and necessary resources to get needed educational tasks accomplished.

Uncertain Commitment to Research and Development One of the new thrusts of the new administration which persuaded me to become the Deputy Assistant Secretary for Planning, Research, and Evaluation was a major concern for meaningful advances in research and development as a means of improving American education. We started with high hopes. However, the treatment of the initial 1971 budget requests by the Bureau of the Budget in cutting existing research programs by over $15 million, while allowing modest starts for new efforts, was a distinct shock. It was the first, but not the last, indication that fiscal considerations and budget technicians often determine major educational policy decisions, no matter the rhetoric of the visible spokesmen for the administration.

I am naturally pleased that the new program of Experimental Schools—designed to carefully test major new innovations—and the proposed National Institute of Education—designed to provide a major visible center of planning and action for educational research—are receiving favorable comment. Having worked hard to develop these new and promising concepts, I am gratified that they are receiving careful consideration. But these new programs alone do not make a total research program. Rather, the major efforts that began in 1966 under Title IV of the Elementary and Secondary Education Act should be the base upon which future educational research and development should be built.

If effective programs in existing Research and Development Centers, Educational Laboratories, and other past innovative efforts are starved in order to feed new programs, American education will not profit. The 1972 budget is, of course, crucial and there will be strong temptation for those solely concerned with fiscal considerations to transfer or cut the more established programs, and transfer funds from those programs into new efforts by the National Institute of Education. Such a move could be accompanied by lofty statements of "exciting new advances in research," when, in fact, the total educational research money available may show little or no increase. Many concerned individuals and organizations will be watching the 1972 budget carefully to see if there is a genuine increase in research funds, or merely a transfer of funds from old to new programs.

The concept of the National Institute of Education, as a visible indication of our commitment to systematic improvement of educational programs, affords much promise in leading us into a new era for research and for the educational consumer. The National Institute can attract first rate researchers from many disciplines such as psychology, economics, and anthropology, et cetera, as well as talented educators. It could create a greatly improved environment for research administration and planning. It would be tragic if this promising agent for educational improvement became immersed in political or budgetary legerdemain. In this spirit, there is a strong need to keep the staffing patterns of the proposed National Institute as free from political influence as possible. The country deserves, and the educational community requires, the best from a National Institute, and the political affiliations of top staff are an irrelevancy.

Can the Government Keep Its Promises?

The credibility of the Federal government is under serious and justified attack because of its failure to follow through on programs once they have begun. Title III of the Elementary and Secondary Education Act and the educational laboratories are only two of many programs that began with great expectations. In the second or third year of their efforts—their political glamour worn off—their favored place was taken in the Administration by new, bright, and shiny programs that are polished by hope and unsullied by experience.

The odds now seem to be against the realistic use of long range educational planning for the foreseeable future at the Federal level. Although most everyone admits to the importance of planning in the abstract, the existing governmental organization or system is designed to inevitably frustrate it. There are simply too many persons, some at quite low levels in the hierarchy, who have the power to change the signals on previous commitments and long range programs. The plans designed in past years become the victims of persons who have no sense of history or respect for programs begun before their entry upon the scene but who are eager to push their own pet projects to "make their own mark" in Washington.

"Too many persons . . . have the power to change the signals on previous commitments and long range programs."

Outside the Office of Education, at the present time, there are at least five or six major sources of policy review identifiable within the Executive Branch itself. Reviews by the Secretary's Office of Program Planning, by Evaluation, by the Department's budgetary analysts, by the staff of the HEW Secretary, by the Bureau of the Budget, by various parts of the White House staff, et cetera, lead to many amendments and modifications. The number of these people and their participation in policy decision making appears to be increasing daily. Moreover, they do not hesitate to exercise veto power over these programs. The multiplication of people who have authority to change programs but who leave others to face the often negative consequences of their actions is one of the most severe morale problems in government. Even after programs run this gauntlet, they must be reviewed again by the Congress where another variety of special interests are brought to bear on the programs.

Government officials have often been accused of being inconsistent in their policy statements and program decisions. Often such inconsistency is the result of the swirl of shifting alliances of power groups within government that throw up new policies like corks on the waves, and just as easily submerge those not in current favor. It would be a miracle if consistent planning for priorities could survive such a chaotic operation—and miracles are currently out of style.

It seems to me that until fundamental changes are made in the unlimited power of myriads of people to change or manipulate programs, budgets, and priorities of the Office of Education every few months, it will be impossible to carry out a program with long range goals and objectives. As we start new programs again, and paint our bright portrait of what those new programs will accomplish, is there any reason to believe that the same cycle of excitement-frustration-despair will not be repeated by the way in which we make our future decisions? I think not, unless we adopt specific changes in procedure, such as those detailed below.

National Neglect and the Handicapped Student

"... There remains a glaring gap between need and national action for handicapped children of school and preschool ages."

My interest in joining the Office of Education three years ago was to direct the then new Bureau of Education for the Handicapped. Although some substantial progress has been made during this time, there remains a glaring gap between need and national action for handicapped children of school and preschool ages. Over half of the estimated 7,000,000 handicapped children in our nation are still not receiving needed special education services in our schools. The United States stands in unfavorable comparison to most of the countries of the civilized world in our educational and health provisions for handicapped children. To rank below the top ten nations in the prevention of infant mortality is one of the many sad statistics for a proud nation.

What is needed is not just small percentage annual increments in a $100 million program (currently representing an average investment of less than $20 per student), but a dramatic increase, representing a doubling or trebling of effort in a program that has proven itself to be effective, and has demonstrated its ability to encourage states to increase their own efforts. This program is small enough to profit materially and visibly from a major influx of funds, whereas the same amount might disappear without a trace in larger programs.

The program for handicapped children always seems to be too small, on a fiscal basis, to ever merit a major priority role in the Office of Education's budget plans, even though Congress has been quite favorably disposed to programs for the handicapped. The notion that we might double or triple the Federal effort for the handicapped may seem dramatic, but actually

*"I cannot think of a single
important reason why these
three unlikely companions (health,
education, and welfare) share
the same Department."*

represents much less money than has been regularly moved back and forth in the budget checker game with larger programs. I would not mention these problems if I did not think there were ways to solve them. There are some constructive steps that can be taken.

No other major country in the Western world tries to combine the immense fields of health, education, and welfare into a single cabinet level department. After three years in the Department of Health, Education, and Welfare, it is easy to see why few other nations have been tempted to follow this example. Table 1 shows that the budget of the Office of Education already exceeds that of five cabinet departments (Interior, Post Office, Commerce, Justice, and State). We actually have within Health, Education, and Welfare three separate operating departments bound together only by a burgeoning bureaucracy at the Secretarial level. Over 2,000 persons now operate out of the Office of the Secretary, originally conceived as merely a coordination service between the operating agencies of Health, Education, and Welfare.

Education's share in the budget of the Department of Health, Education, and Welfare has dropped from approximately 33

TABLE 1

1970 Budget Authority and Number of Permanent Personnel Employed at the End of 1970 for Cabinet Level Departments and the Office of Education

Departments and Agencies	FY 70 Budget Authority (in billions of $)	Rank	Number of Permanent Personnel at end of 1970	Rank
Defense	74.5	1	1,196,600[a]	1
Treasury	19.1	2	86,700	3
Agriculture	8.7	3	83,000	4
Transportation	7.9	4	63,600	5
Labor	4.9	5	10,300	11
Housing and Urban Development	4.6	6	14,900	10
OFFICE OF EDUCATION	3.8	7	3,030	12
Interior	1.8	8	59,300	6
Post Office	1.4	9	567,000	2
Commerce	1.0	10	25,600	8
Justice	.8	11	37,600	7
State	.4	12	23,900	9

[a] Includes 30,700 civilian and 1,165,900 military personnel.

Source: Office of Program Planning and Evaluation in the Office of Education.

232

percent to 18 percent in the time I have been in Washington. In real dollars, the 1971 budget level is below the budget back in 1966. There is the further fact that the proportion of Federal contribution to the total educational costs has fallen from 8 percent to 5.5 percent in the last three years despite the major financial crises felt at the local and state levels.

This is not to say that the money given to health and welfare is not appropriate. It merely points up the difficulty that education has in competing within a single HEW budget. The tasks of the Office of Education are becoming more and more complicated by the additional layers of bureaucracy that must be negotiated to achieve effective programs. I cannot think of a single important reason why these three unlikely companions (health, education, and welfare) share the same Department. Moreover, there are many other educational efforts being mounted in a large number of agencies with little or no coordination with the Office of Education or HEW.

The earlier HEW goal to have all of the basic three elements of the Department work together to deliver total service to the individual was found to be not viable, and was essentially abandoned some time ago. With different regulations, different local and state agencies, different guidelines, it does not seem likely that we can work toward a coordination objective within the total HEW Department any better than if each element (health, education, and welfare) were in a separate department. A cabinet level Department of Education would allow for the effective bringing together of the many Federal efforts in the education domain.

Helping the Government Keep Its Promises

There is little hope of saving the bright priorities of last year's programs unless some type of protective environment is established for long range educational programs of high priority. This means that both the Executive Branch and Congress would need to give tacit approval to the concept that perhaps 20 percent of the budget be set aside annually for long range goals, and not be thrown each year into the same gladiatorial arena that the rest of the programs face.

Such a formula would earn the special blessing of those constituents in the nation's school systems, universities, and educational industries who would have the chance to accomplish something effective with some consistency of Federal support over a period of time. These constituents now have to face constant uncertainty, anxiety, changed signals, and radical budget adjustments.

This protection of priority programs would not be a request for a free ride for these programs. On the contrary, the most stringent criteria would be applied before putting a program into this protective category, and a careful review could be made at a given point in time before any long term renewal. It does mean that we wouldn't be yanking up the fragile educational plant every six months just to see how the roots were growing.

As a general rule, we should continue to strive to give maximum flexibility to local school administrators to use Federal funds. Education is too complicated a field to think that any one neat solution such as revenue sharing will meet all of the existing tough problems.

There are many valid reasons why we should provide some system of general support funds to the beleaguered educational agencies that would improve the general delivery of educational services to all students. In addition, a special Federal role seems clearly indicated in strengthening those components of the total educational system that lie beyond local resources such as research, training, and educational communication.

"My experience . . . has convinced me that a major Federal initiative is an absolute must."

Not every school system can develop its own mathematics curriculum or develop the specialized tests to measure its effectiveness in improving student attitude. My experience with research and its specialized requirements and broad applications has convinced me that a major Federal initiative is an absolute must. State and local educational administrators have shown their inability to support such items in the face of the immediate and overriding pressures to provide needed educational services.

". . . Federal assistance is required to insure that no child with handicaps suffers because of an accident of residence and geographical location."

Not every community nor every state can provide entirely for the specialized needs of blind, deaf, cerebral palsied, or multiply handicapped children. The evidence is clear that special Federal assistance is required to insure that no child with these handicaps suffers because of an accident of residence or geographical location. The handicapped have always represented a kind of proving ground for the development of new approaches in education such as individualized instruction, clear establishment of behavioral objectives, the creative use of media, and preschool education. Providing Federal initiatives in this program is more than a moral issue—it is sound national educational policy.

A legitimate debate could be held about whether education's major barrier is lack of imagination or poor transportation of ideas. We have many examples of excellent practices and programs, but few examples of the technique of how to move them from one place to another. A clear responsibility of the Federal government is to invest heavily in dissemination of better ideas and practices. The means by which we can transport new ideas and new practices in education are complex and still somewhat obscure. We have some minor starts in small information systems, but there is a clear Federal responsibility to insure that good ideas and superior practices get from Portland to Austin and from Long Beach to Utica. Programs of educational communication are not currently receiving more than token support—perhaps $10-15 million in all.

"There is . . . Federal responsibility to insure that good ideas and superior practices get from Portland to Austin and from Long Beach to Utica."

I have occasionally felt that we in the government are actors in a badly written or badly produced play by a long forgotten author. Good actors can disguise the flaws in the play for a time, while bad actors make them immediately apparent, but the flaws remain and merely changing the cast of characters doesn't help that much. We need to do something about the play, or in this instance the way in which decision making occurs on educational matters in government. There will be few meaningful accomplishments in Federal education policy without this reform.

The President in his White House Message on Elementary and Secondary Education has called for educational reform, and well he might. A scattered and financially impoverished set of autonomous 20,000 local school districts was built for a bygone era, with simpler goals. We need to, as a nation, pull our educational system vigorously into the last half of the twentieth century. But we need educational reform at the Federal government level as well.

Unless we can organize ourselves at the Federal level to keep our educational promises, to identify one clear spokesman for Federal education policy, to support and give leadership to special programs directly related to educational improvement (i.e., research, training, educational communication) then the Federal government may well be crying out for educational reform on the outside, when the needs for reform may be greatest on the inside of the Federal establishment.

"We need to . . . pull our educational system vigorously into the last half of the twentieth century."

MAYNARD C. REYNOLDS

A Crisis in Evaluation

Abstract: Recent federal support programs for education in the United States have emphasized innovation and evaluation. Little attention has been given to the evaluation problem. Special education bears a special responsibility because it has been a favored area in recent federal legislation. Despite many difficult technical and psychological problems, efforts must be made to meet the rising problem of evaluation.

About three-quarters of a billion dollars were appropriated for this year by the United States Congress to support new school programs for "educationally deprived" children. Next year the appropriation is expected to be higher. The legislative reference is to Title I of Public Law 89-10, which is the single most significant enactment within a broad pattern of legislation which has created a large and, in many ways, new federal partner in educational affairs of the United States at elementary and secondary school levels.

I wish to underline two things about this legislation and the programs it supports. The first is the emphasis upon innovation. A community which offers preschool classes, speech correction, psychological services, or other specialized programs will usually qualify for federal support if *and only if* the service is new. As a result, thousands of school districts are taking on new functions this year. The political leaders and the new administrators in the expanding federal educational bureaucracy are saying, in effect:

> The school programs of the past have been held too closely to the mainstream; there has been too little change; by their very organization and emphases, schools have compounded the problems of neglected children. Create more streams. Broaden the options. So serious is the problem that we hereby allocate most of the federal educational resource to the support of new programs.

The second point of emphasis is the insistence upon program evaluation. Every project under Title I of PL 89-10 requires a report of evaluation. Many of us have not yet begun to realize the wide implications of this requirement. It certainly proposes a radical change in the habits of educators. Miles (1964, p. 657) reports that "educational innovations are almost never evaluated on a systematic basis." This conclusion is supported by recent reviews made in our two most populous states (Johnson, 1964; Brickell, 1961). The evaluation problem created as part of the new federal support program is now rising and rolling toward us and will soon reach shock wave intensity. Of course, we've always had an evaluation problem, but until now it has usually been relegated to some dark place for hiding.

A unique and rigorous test is being placed upon the schools of the United States this year. After years of talk, federal support became a reality. Planning and discussion were perfectly open for all to see for a long time, and even the time interval from authorization to appropriation on PL 89-10 was long enough to give fair warning to those who wished to hear and to plan ahead. But how well were the schools organized for change? How effectively is the shift from talk to action taking place?

I see some failure and some clear success, but mostly a barely passing performance this

Exceptional Children, 1966, Vol. 32, No. 9, pp. 585-592.

first year. Many problems of long standing have become visible just in trying to design and launch new services—problems such as inadequate staffing of state education offices, inadequate school district size, personnel shortages, and general inflexibility in meeting new problems. These early difficulties should stir us to help mobilize the forces necessary for improvement.

My guess is that even surpassing the present difficulties in organizing new programs will be the problems of evaluation. Little preparation has been made for this phase of present developments, and again some fundamental and longstanding problems are likely to come to surface. Failures and successes here may not be highly visible in the short range, but they can be of crucial significance in longer range.

The Purpose of Evaluation

We sometimes think of evaluation in very threatening terms. Especially if funds for a project come by special grant from an external source do we fall easily into thinking about evaluation as a kind of final positive plea made just before the verdict on project renewal is reached. This puts evaluation into a kind of good-bad, general accounting framework.

Reflection quickly suggests the futility and even the danger of such an orientation. The most important requirement of an evaluation is that it reveal as objectively and as fully as possible what is happening as a result of the project. It should show the specific abilities or other attributes that are developing among pupils, the extent of such developments, and the interactions among pupil characteristics and other variables as the project proceeds. Out of this kind of knowledge, programs can be improved! The purpose of evaluation in education is simply to contribute to improvements in instruction—certainly not to justify projects.

A Special Responsibility

The field of special education has a particular responsibility in this context, partly because it has been favored as an area of emphasis in recent legislation. Many of the new programs under Title I of PL 89-10, for example, are de-

signed to serve handicapped and gifted children. But other forces also serve to bring a spotlight to special education at this time. Our field is ripe for innovation because of a new and more open attitude. We're less sure today than we were even a few years ago about the potentialities of the children in our classrooms. Perhaps we have less to be defensive about than some other fields, just because we are of a mood to admit that old base rates for educational progress aren't very stable or very impressive.

This changing outlook undoubtedly has roots in many social and economic conditions and forces. Organized parent groups, insisting that their handicapped children can and should be helped, have been a goading external force of great influence. But there has also been much ferment in the community of those who think mainly of research and theory.

Besides "Batman" reruns, we're seeing frequent reruns these days on the nature-nurture studies of the 1930's and later. Recent reviews suggest that although many of the early studies were faulty in details, the total weight of all evidence suggesting the importance of environmental determinants of functional intelligence cannot be neglected (Hunt, 1961). A few recent practical demonstrations, such as Kirk's (1958) preschool study of the influence of school programs and the price of educational neglect on the intellectual development of children, have added force to a shift in views. The view which is emerging does not ignore genetic factors, but it does encourage a more optimistic outlook concerning the extent to which the achievements of children can be influenced by particular kinds of efforts. Many of the interesting new programs in special education grow out of this optimistic framework.

A growing and more radical general influence is a resurgence of the psychology of the empty organism—the view that behavior can be understood in surface or peripheral terms. The central procedure of the behavior modifiers a la Skinner is operant conditioning, which simply involves rewarding desired behavior (or approximations of it), thereby shaping the behavior and influencing the probability of its reoccurrence. Those who are committed to this highly environmentalistic outlook have generated a great deal of openness and optimism. McClelland (1965) has classed them with religious missionaries in the sense that they believe so strongly that almost any human behavior can be changed if only one approaches the task with conviction, appropriate techniques, and patience. Scholars of this persuasion have great appeal to teachers, because they accept a very practical test for their ideas. That test is simply: does it work? Many new projects may be observed in special education which grow out of the specific ideas of Skinner (1953) and his associates.

The intellectual ferment also includes elements quite opposite to those of the operant conditioners—an emphasis upon central structure and processes, especially cognitive structure and processes. Those of this persuasion insist that much more is involved in understanding complex behavior than knowing about environmental contacts and reinforcement histories. Between sensory input and responses are mediational processes of varying degrees of complexity. A great many new programs are being launched in special education which have their theoretical base in theories relating to cognitive development and intellective processes.

However different and conflicting the theories may be, there appear to be a few common themes, including a more open view concerning human potentialities and a special emphasis upon the early years of life as the period of greatest modifiability. I cite these somewhat theoretical notions not because they are uniquely relevant to special education, but simply because special educators, more than other educators, have been paying attention to the theoreticians and vice versa, with the result that thinking and innovative developments in our field have been influenced markedly by theory.

Much impetus and specific form for innovation grow from this surge of ideas. There is some danger that theorists will recruit teachers to their views prematurely and that we will get a kind of "choosing of sides" among educators. The desirable course for teachers is to proceed with the innovative developments proposed by theory, but to maintain a rigid objectivity in testing outcomes.

The Values in Evaluation

Imbedded not very deeply in the word evaluation, yet often repressed, is the base word "value." This suggests a pause to think carefully about what it is we are trying to accomplish in our programs—what it is we value. It is not enough simply to measure what we're doing to test whether present programs are effective, nor do statistical tests of differences tell us whether differences are really important. The question is: what *ought* we to be doing in the schools for exceptional children? This is by no means entirely a technical question.

A bit of history shows how fickle we have been about the values represented in special education curricula for the handicapped. At various times and places we have seemed to slant our values toward vocational training, development of personality and motivation, academic skills, simple relief to parents, social adjustment, sheer happiness, or use of leisure time. We seem all too ready to let new curricula or technology sway our objectives. Today there seems to be a strong surge of interest in what has been called a kind of intellectual plainsmanship. "Find the child's weaknesses or disabilities and remedy them" is a common theme.

Let me illustrate the problem further by citing a few specific concerns about what it is we ought to accomplish. Some observers note that in present programs, retarded children tend to become outer directed or greatly sensitive to cues from other people, rather than inner directed, self-reliant, and forthright in their behavior. Do we think this is desirable for them, perhaps as a precondition to the greater degree of supervision they may require from others? Or do we regard this as a specific problem to be avoided by teaching them in ways which make them more self-reliant or inner directed? I believe we can and do influence children on this variable. What's your choice?

Should everyone learn to read, even if it involves agonizing difficulties and great sacrifices in other kinds of learning? How much time and attention should be given to teaching directly for intellectual development of the retarded? How successful do we need to be in such efforts to justify neglect of other dimensions of learning in which modifiability may be greater? Under what circumstances is it justifiable to teach children a communications system (such as manual methods for the deaf) which is usable only in special and very small social systems? How much time can we justify spending on teaching severely crippled children to walk?

These are difficult questions which must be answered in specifics, not glossed over in highly abstract terms. When we have been clear about what it is we want to accomplish, we can then proceed to teach and to put yardsticks on the operation to gauge success and to plan improvements.

The Measurement Problem

It would be a happy circumstance, of course, if all the needed technical background for this next step—measuring program variables—were well established, but unfortunately that is not the case. Indeed, we have only a dawning awareness of some problems in this sphere.

One of the difficult problems is concerned with measuring change or growth. To assess the effects of a treatment, we are often interested in changes that take place in children during a specific interval of time. Commonly we give pretests and posttests and look at the differences which individuals show during the interval as growth or change. It all seems simple, but appearance is deceiving. An indication of the problem is that on variables of interest in education we so often get negative correlations between measures of change and measures of beginning status. What is becoming clear is that instruments which are useful in measuring current status may not be useful for measuring change. The measurement of change presents its own distinct problems of reliability and validity (Harris, 1962).

The problem of measuring change can be seen most clearly at the level of evaluating individual progress. If we have repeated measures of individual children, we're likely to find that those of high achievement tend not to be changing much, and those of lowest achievement show highest gains—whether judged in raw score or grade score terms. Such observations may result simply from technical problems of measurement. Unfortunately, there are no neat solutions to this problem as it concerns individual pupils. I mention it here because there are so many misinterpretations of measurements on this point.

A closely related and equally fundamental difficulty concerns the ability of most of our present tests to differentiate among groups receiving different treatments. Almost all of the tests commonly used in the schools have been constructed by techniques which serve to accentuate differences among individuals. Thus, in the typical experimental paradigm of pretest-treat-posttest, we get wide variations among individuals on both the pretest and the posttest. For purposes of comparing one method against another, however, it would be better to have near zero mean scores and zero variability at the beginning of the experiment, with posttest results showing substantial means and variances. Tests to serve in this way would be exceedingly difficult to construct. They would need to be developed by techniques which are specific to the problem of differentiating treatment differences, rather than individual differences (Glaser, 1963).

A third closely related technical problem, one which is particularly bothersome in special education, relates to regression effect. When we select children for special programs on the basis of very high or very low performance on some measuring device, it is almost inevitable that they will tend to be less deviant on a retest, even if given the next day. Those who score low initially will go up and those who score high initially will tend, in relative terms, to score lower on the retest.

Many reports of special education research appear to show most striking treatment effects in the initial part of the study. It is difficult in such cases to justify arguing for treatment effects against the simpler hypothesis of mere regression effects. A similar observation may be made when several measures are taken on individual children. Even if tested the next day, children will tend to show improvements on their lowest scores and decrements on the variables where they initially scored high. These circumstances frequently lead to misleading interpretations of the effects of remedial programs. Fortunately, definite corrective actions can be taken to avoid such misinterpretations through use of control groups for comparison purposes.

There are, of course, many other measurement problems. For example, Guilford (1959) is undoubtedly correct in his view that present school measuring devices tend to emphasize mere awareness, retention, and single answer problem solving. We badly need to develop procedures for assessment of evaluative abilities and productive thinking of more diverse forms. If we wish to teach for abilities in this expanded domain, then we must somehow begin to assess individual and group pupil progress over a similarly expanded domain. Deep issues and problems exist which are concerned with norming, range restriction, and format of scales specially created for exceptional groups.

Psychological Barriers to Evaluation

An equally serious problem is a tendency to avoid careful evaluation of creations for which we feel special responsibility. This problem is certainly not unique to special education. Kendall (1964) has said:

> . . . creators of experimental programs often impress one as being men of conviction who have little question about the efficacy of the changes they have introduced. They know that the courses they have developed are the best possible under existing conditions; and in the light of this assumed fact, systematic evaluation seems superfluous (p. 344).

Brickell's (1964) study of innovation in schools of New York state led him to this somewhat similar comment:

> . . . design, evaluation and dissemination are three distinctly different, irreconcilable processes. The circumstances which are right for one are essentially wrong for the others. Furthermore, most people prefer to work in one place, and find working in the others uncomfortable if not distasteful. People preferring different places often have an abrasive effect on each other when brought into close contact (pp. 497-498).

A further comment from Brickell (1964) is insightful: "Almost every research specialist the writer met in a local school system seemed somehow misplaced. His desire to hold a new program steady in order to evaluate it ran headlong into the teachers' urge to change it as soon as they sensed something wrong" (p. 498).

The three phases of innovation as outlined by Brickell—design, evaluation, dissemination—make a proper sequence, but the clear fact is that almost always we have skipped the middle step. Perhaps this is because it is so difficult, expensive, and intrinsically threatening to subject our programs to test. If Brickell is correct (as I think he is) in saying that different people will often be involved in design and evaluation, then evaluative efforts may also involve personal confrontations that are threatening.

The major thesis of my remarks is that despite all the difficulties, we must proceed in all seriousness to evaluate programs. Design and evaluation must be seen not as competing activities (the latter only delaying and denying needed services), but rather as necessary parts of a sequence and broader cycles of activities designed to build programs that are dependable and worthy of our high responsibility.

Some Possible Guidelines

I do not have solutions, much less tidy ones, to all of the above problems; but I would like to reflect a bit on a few possible approaches to solutions. Above all other suggestions, perhaps, is the simple one that we turn more attention, talent, and time—and the sooner the better—to problems of evaluation. But let us proceed to a few somewhat more specific considerations.

The Questions We Ask. There has been a tendency in the recent past to over emphasize large questions when we think about evaluation. In the past decade, for example, there have been a number of studies concerned with comparing the efficacy of regular classes and special classes for retarded children. I agree with the Robinsons (1965), who say that few of these studies deserve serious review. The main difficulty with most of these studies is that they started with a group of children already in special classes and then proceeded to compare them with control groups recruited in very different ways. It is very difficult to be sure what a special class or a regular class is, yet there have been some incautious generalizations from the recent studies.

We need more patient work, biting away at processes of learning and teaching, trying to specify the variables about which we should be sensitive in teaching exceptional children. And in a gradual way, hopefully, we will re-shape programs toward workable total systems. It is to be hoped that as evaluations of the new programs now being launched go forward, we will not always feel obliged to make total, summary judgments. Of course, there are occasions for the big scale comparative studies, but we will be better off with only an occasional and carefully planned big horse race.

Experimental Design. Many of the evaluative efforts we undertake will necessarily fall short of the ideal designs which statisticians create. Sometimes the truly important problems involve people and situations which don't bend to fit the design model. The answer here is to compromise the design of studies as little as possible and to be aware of what we're doing. One particularly important requirement in studies is that we run control groups for comparison with experimental groups and that we do this with utmost care. Many of the problems which we otherwise encounter are curtailed if we do a conscientious job of setting up controls.

A serious deficiency encountered repeatedly in reports of evaluations is failure to describe in sufficient detail what the experimental variable was. To make results useful in any broad way, it is necessary to clearly and operationally define treatments; and it is helpful if description of control conditions is also given.

Development of Measurement Techniques. In earlier portions of these remarks I've stressed the very great technical difficulties we face in attempting to measure educational outcomes. There are no quick and easy solutions here. This problem should alert us so as not to be misled into evaluation schemes biased simply by availability of particular tests. I prefer the judgments of disinterested colleagues—a kind of *Consumers Report*—to studies overly refined in design, but weak at the point of measurement.

Strong efforts should be made to develop techniques and instruments of measurement which are useful in special education. This exceedingly important activity comes up too often, just as an ad hoc effort within a broader study. Instrumentation deserves to be a well supported activity apart from specific experiments. The successful development of instruments then becomes a springboard for later application in evaluative studies.

A New Team. The evaluation problems stressed here are those of the classroom, school, and clinic—the practical marketplace of education. Not many specialists in evaluation reside there. There are too few specialists of the kind we need anywhere. Some are in colleges and universities.

If designers and evaluators work far apart, can we expect effective collaborative work? Freeman and Sherwood (1965) suggest that the evaluator, if at a distance, can set his evaluative techniques after simple guessing about overall goals and later be told he was wrong; or "he can insist that program persons provide them (goals) in which case he should bring lots of novels to the office to read while he waits, or he can participate or even take a major responsibility for the development of the action framework." Their conclusion is that "if the researcher is going to act responsibly as an agent of social change through his evaluation research, it is probably mandatory for him to engage himself in program development" (p. 17).

In the future the schools will themselves more frequently employ evaluation specialists in addition to the use of part time consultants from universities or other agencies. All of us must anticipate new team relationships and join in constructively, defining new roles in the expanding enterprise of evaluation.

Borrowing from Friends. Many more guidelines and problems might be explored. If time were available, I would especially stress the importance of more adequate training in evaluation for all special educators and of training more specialists in the area of evaluation. The fact is that most special educators are not very sophisticated about evaluation procedures, and we will need to do all we can to upgrade ourselves and to utilize talents from neighboring fields as well. I would also stress the importance of looking to other specialties, such as agriculture, for guidance in ways of dividing up jobs of design, evaluation, and dissemination. We will probably need a few very large centers and some regional experimental centers to carry out major tasks in evaluation.

Each community needs to decide for itself

when its local circumstances alter the applicability of evaluative findings from other communities and when values generally held for specific programs are not acceptable. Every school district has its evaluation problems, but individual school systems will rarely be able to do large scale systematic research. Indeed, it would be wasteful for every school district to undertake systematic studies of every new program. Thus we need to plan and build, probably in concert with developments relating to other aspects of education, a variety of kinds and levels of research centers.

An Antidote for Unlimited Openness. As commented earlier, there is a great deal of openness of views in special education these days with respect to possible achievements of exceptional children. It is to be counted a gain that views are more open and positive, but there are dangers inherent in such a situation as well. The indefiniteness of the situation invites attempts at closure by the untutored and by those who would play the charlatan's role. Some will be seduced by simple charismatic appeal.

All of us must clarify for ourselves an attitude in this matter. Somehow we must be open in our views, yet realize that it is no kindness to be unrealistically optimistic in instances of specific children. It is necessary to make predictions, at least of short range, concerning particular children in order to plan for them, and sometimes what we honestly foresee is not very encouraging. How do we achieve the needed balance between openness and realism?

The key is simple honesty. In dealing with individual children, predictions and decisions must be made on the basis of present knowledge and programs. It is not relevant to the immediate problem that we and others may think that much more promising programs are "just around the corner." At the same time, we can maintain a general openness and strive to design and evaluate programs which will create the more favorable prognosis in the future.

Summary

The schools of the United States are engaged in a very rapid expansion of specialized school programs. The leaders who have allocated re-

sources to support the programs have also insisted upon systematic program evaluation. The implications of this have not really registered with us in a broad, practical way, and there is some danger that we will let evaluation procedures slip to perfunctory levels. This great challenge comes with heavy force in the field of special education, because programs for exceptional children have been favored in recent federal legislation. All of this arises at a time of great intellectual ferment relating to our work.

All of us must be concerned about the response which is given in this situation. Almost one hundred years ago, there was much eager school building for the handicapped. Theories of that time and some practical demonstrations were encouraging, but views changed and expectations of some of the leading program advocates proved to be unrealistic. Professionals deserted the field for half a century. Only very recently has there been a return to the task of educating all children, including those we serve in special ways. Much depends upon careful evaluation of the programs we are now building and upon our ability to reshape programs in accordance with the hard facts of results.

If we proceed incautiously, there is risk of coming up with seriously wrong answers. We must not put special education at risk in that way. If we proceed carefully, exceptional children will be better served. We are about to be called for an accounting. Let us do the difficult job and do it well!

References

Brickell, H. N. The American educational system as a setting for innovation. In M. B. Miles (Editor), *Innovations in education*. New York: Bureau of Publications, Teachers College, Columbia University, 1964. Pp. 493-531.

Brickell, H. N. *Organizing New York state for educational change*. Albany: State Education Department, 1961.

Freeman, H. E., and Sherwood, C. C. Research in large-scale intervention programs. *Social Issues*, 1965, 21, 11-28.

Glaser, R. Instructional technology and the measurement of learning outcomes. *American Psychologist*, 1963, 18, 519-521.

Guilford, J. P. Three faces of intellect. *American Psychologist*, 1959, 14, 469-479.

Harris, C. W. *Problems in measuring change.* Madison: University of Wisconsin Press, 1962.

Hunt, J. McV. *Intelligence and experience.* New York: Ronald Press, 1961.

Johnson, D. W. Title III and the dynamics of educational change in California schools. In M. B. Miles (Editor), *Innovations in education.* New York: Bureau of Publications, Teachers College, Columbia University, 1964. Pp. 157-182.

Kendall, P. Evaluating an experimental program in medical education. In M. B. Miles (Editor), *Innovations in education.* New York: Bureau of Publications, Teachers College, Columbia University, 1964. Pp. 343-360.

Kirk, S. A. *Early education of the mentally retarded.* Urbana: University of Illinois, 1958.

McClelland, D. L. Toward a theory of motive acquisition. *American Psychologist,* 1965, 20, 321-333.

Miles, M. B. *Innovations in education.* New York: Bureau of Publications, Teachers College, Columbia University, 1964.

Robinson, H. B., and Robinson, Nancy M. *The mentally retarded child: a psychological approach.* New York: McGraw-Hill, 1965.

Skinner, B. F. *Science and human behavior.* New York: Macmillan Company, 1953.

MAYNARD C. REYNOLDS *is President, The Council for Exceptional Children, and Director, Department of Special Education, University of Minnesota, Minneapolis. This paper was presented at the 44th Annual CEC Convention, Toronto, April, 1966.*

243